TAKING THE CURTAIN CALL

THE LIFE AND LETTERS
OF
HENRY ARTHUR JONES

THE MACMILLAN COMPANY
NEW YORK · BOSTON · CHICAGO · DALLAS
ATLANTA · SAN FRANCISCO

MACMILLAN & CO., Limited
LONDON · BOMBAY · CALCUTTA
MELBOURNE

**THE MACMILLAN COMPANY
OF CANADA,** Limited
TORONTO

HENRY ARTHUR JONES AT 74

(By courtesy of Messrs. Lafayette Ltd.)

TAKING THE CURTAIN CALL

THE LIFE AND LETTERS
OF
HENRY ARTHUR JONES

BY

DORIS ARTHUR JONES

"Endurance, not enjoyment, is man's
pass-key through this world."
Cutler in *The Divine Gift* by
Henry Arthur Jones

NEW YORK
THE MACMILLAN COMPANY
1930

TO THE DEAR MEMORY OF MY PARENTS,
IN LOVE AND ADMIRATION

A LETTER

My dear Doris Thorne,

All good wishes to you in your task of writing the Life. I gather that you want to be judicial as well as filial. Assuredly that is what Henry Arthur would have liked you to be. In fact, without being judicial you can't be filial. A presentment of faultlessness is very lovely; but it has two drawbacks: it annoys, and it doesn't convince. Let Henry Arthur's faults be duly stressed, for his own sake and for ours. But—what were they? Off hand, I really couldn't say. I seem not to have noticed them, though I knew their possessor for almost forty years! I will continue this letter in the hope of finding them.

At the age of eighteen one is very observant, especially of a celebrated man whom one sees for the first time. Did I observe no faults in Mr. Jones on that morning in the autumn of 1890 when he sat in the drawing-room of The Grange, at Hampstead, reading to my brother, Herbert Tree, the crisp typescript of *The Dancing Girl?* He had ridden up from London, and his cord riding-breeches and lustrous riding-boots and spurs were certainly faultless, making the chintz armchair he sat on look very unworthy of his horsemanhood. Nor did Rotten Row occur to me as the right place for him. He should have been charging and caracoling around his native county, Bucks. He was of rural aspect. His fresh pink complexion and very clear blue eyes, and the thrustfulness of his russet beard, were suggestive of nothing anywhere near the four-mile radius. Is great vitality, is an air of eager concentration, a fault? Then let it be granted that Henry Arthur was all wrong. Young though I was, I had heard two or three other plays read by their authors—read in a rather diffident, apologetic, faintly hopeful tone.   There was none of that nonsense about Henry Arthur.   He forged boldly and resonantly ahead.   With much force of shoulders and elbows and beard, and with full use of a strong and well-managed voice, he ground his way through his work joyously.   Is self-confidence a fault?   Not, I thought, in Henry Arthur, whom I liked much already at first sight.

I was about to become an undergraduate.   I was not cast for a small part in *The Dancing Girl*.   Had I been so, my liking for the author would not, I fancy, have waned; but it would have been mingled with much fear.   Is quickness of temper a fault?   It might have seemed so to me. I have seen Henry Arthur at rehearsals of several plays. These would have passed more calmly if he had at some early stage in his career been himself an actor.   In virtue of that past he might have been able to get, among actors and actresses, his own way without friction.   Or, again, all might have been well if he had started in the Diplomatic Service.   The lot of a playwright is hard, and unlike that of other artists.   His work when he has finished it has not yet begun.   He has to watch it beginning in the hands of others—others who are anxious, but (not being he) not always able, to please him, to fit exactly his impassioned and clear preconception.   To get his way, he should seem to be more easy-going than he is.   Henry Arthur (faultily?) could not compass that deceitfulness.   Nor was his mind of a quality amenable enough for him to conceive that his preconception was not at all points attainable and might not at some points even be surpassable.   The War Office allows—or used to allow—soldiers to act as supers. It was a pity for the peace of Henry Arthur's very positive mind that Heaven did not lend angels for the principal parts.   But even then, I think, he would have pined for automata.   I suppose such idealism *is* rather reprehensible.

I don't think he ever was a member of the Garrick Club, was he? I can't imagine that he would have been welcomed with very wide-open arms in those quiet halls of good-nature and good-fellowship; and I fancy that the arms of such dramatic critics as were members would have been even less outspread than those of the actors. The Press, I daresay, treated him quite well and fairly in his early days. But in my own early days it had ceased to do so. It praised him grudgingly, it blamed him with zest. He had got its back up by constantly writing in Reviews and lecturing upon platforms about the state of the British Drama. Dramatic critics in those days were, with but three or four exceptions, very simple souls, very slightly educated, and not imaginative; and the state of the British Drama was quite good enough for *them*. Yet here was this Henry Arthur Jones fussing around and trying to teach them what to think (as though it was their business to think), and quoting Matthew Arnold (the man who had been confoundedly rude to the *Daily Telegraph*), and— well, the simple souls loved Henry Arthur not. In 1898 I became one of them, the *Saturday Review's* one, in succession to that complex soul, G. B. S. From him Henry Arthur had always received full justice; and I trod in his footsteps, and on my colleagues' corns, for many years. Nor, as I look back, do I feel that I was wrong in admiring your father's plays—his comedies and "drawing-room dramas"—more, on the whole, than any other English dramatic work in that time. No playwright was more essentially "of the theatre" than he: none had a keener sense of what the theatre is for and isn't for—of the effects that can be made there and not elsewhere, and of the effects that can be made much better elsewhere than there. None had in greater measure the gift for easy, quick, pointed dialogue. None had humour so robust and genial. And none, I think, knew nearly so much about the hearts and minds of human beings.

I hope, for the sake of past readers, that I was able to find and demonstrate many serious faults in those many plays of his; and (priding myself on acumen) I have no doubt that I was. But what about serious faults in *him?* Did I like him so much that my acumen was always in abeyance as soon as he came into the room? No; I protest that his entire naturalness, his directness, his lack of any kind of pretence, were quite appalling. What is civilisation if not artificial? And what was Henry Arthur if not free from frills? And what is London if not a place to be rather jaded in? Surely it is not a place for the yeomen of Bucks to revel in, to rejoice in and expand in, to draw deep breaths into their lungs in? Or is it? Perhaps it is! Your father, at any rate, behaved as though it were. And this was one of the reasons why he was so dear to me. Such a full, fresh, spacious man! Ill-health and suffering tried his courage in vain. Or, at least, I never saw any sign of their success, hard though they tried. Did he, in whom I saw no guile, ever pretend, for pride's sake, to be happier than he was? I hope not.

I remember that when I was dining with him *tête-à tête* one evening many years ago, I vaguely mooted the old academic problem as to how much in a man's life depends on his character, and how much on mere chance. "Exactly half-and-half," said Henry Arthur instantly, with a beaming smile. One could not have had a wiser answer; and it was very typical of him and of his way.

In his own case, character had certainly done well. Chance seemed to have been very propitious, too, on the whole; and I like to think that your book will confirm my impression that his life was a truly happy one.

Yours affectionately,
MAX BEERBOHM.

VILLINO CHIARO,
  RAPALLO.

INTRODUCTION

My father charged me to write his life. He knew that I did not propose to make a critical study of his work. So many critics and men of letters, especially in America, have written books and pamphlets about his plays and books, and they are far better qualified than I am. It is difficult, if not impossible, for a daughter to be an impartial critic, but I do not believe any member of his family or any of his friends knew and understood my father better than I did. I have told the truth, and I have endeavoured to avoid stating my own opinions, or to offer any criticisms except when they spring from deep conviction. I want to show my father as the man he was—courageous, persevering, and industrious. These outstanding traits in his character were indissolubly linked with a supreme, deep, and abiding love for and devotion to his art. He was a most dutiful son, a highly appreciative husband, and, although he was not a model father, he was always a devoted and indulgent parent and grandparent.

Although I never told him, when I knew I was to write his life, I made a habit, especially when his old friends came to see him, of sitting behind his big armchair to take down in his own words what he felt and thought about the many interesting people and events he had known during his life. I christened this little book "H. A. J.'s Table Talk," and the quotations I have made from it throughout the book give a most valuable insight into his character.

In writing my father's life I have borne in mind the following passage from his book, as yet unpublished, *The Shadow of Henry Irving:*

"Who would wish after death to be decorated with

xi

the cheapest trinket, the smallest grace that did not rightly belong to him?

"Great Searcher of all hearts, from whom no secrets are hid, when I have passed, avert the fiercest of Thy lightnings from that which has been and that which remains of me; or let them play so mercifully upon these rags, these stains, these follies, these sins that my fellows may not shrink from remembering me with something of Thine own pity and loving kindness. Yet let me be known to all men as I am known to Thee, every spot, every blemish of me apparent in the broad daylight—rather than be found strutting about after death in stolen glories and painted virtues."

* * * * * * * * *

I wish to express my very grateful thanks to the following correspondents of my father for permission to quote their interesting letters:

Dr. Alington, Sir James Barrie, the Hon. James Beck, Mr. Max Beerbohm, to whom I am most particularly indebted for the prefatory letter to this book, Major John Hay Beith, President Nicholas Murray Butler, Sir Hall Caine, Mrs. Patrick Campbell, Dr. David (the Bishop of Liverpool), Sir Arthur Conan Doyle, Mr. St. John Ervine, Sir Johnston Forbes-Robertson, Mr. John Galsworthy, Mr. R. B. Cunninghame Graham, Mr. H. Gwynne, Mr. Clayton Hamilton, Mr. Monckton Hoffe, Mr. Baliol Holloway, Professor L. P. Jacks, Sir Arthur Keith, Mr. Rudyard Kipling, Sir Sidney Low, Sir John Martin-Harvey, Professor Gilbert Murray, Dr. Norwood, Sir Gilbert Parker, Sir Arthur Pinero, Sir Nigel Playfair, Mr. H. F. Rubinstein, Mr. George Bernard Shaw, Mr. Harold Terry, and Mr. H. G. Wells.

And also my indebtedness to the respective executors for the kind permission granted to me to quote letters from the late:

Sir George Alexander (Lady Alexander), William Archer (Mrs. Archer), Matthew Arnold (Lady Sandhurst), Wilson Barrett (Miss Wilson Barrett), Joseph Conrad (Mrs. Conrad and Mr. James B. Pinker), Sir W. S. Gilbert (Lady Gilbert), Sir Edmund Gosse (the Hon. Evan Charteris and Dr. Philip Gosse), W. Hale-White, "Mark Rutherford" (Mrs. Hale-White), Thomas Hardy (Mrs. Hardy and Mr. Sydney Cockerell), W. D. Howells (Miss Mildred Howells and Doubleday, Doran & Co.), Sir Henry Irving (Mrs. H. B. Irving), William Morris (Miss May Morris), T. P. O'Connor, Lord Roberts (Countess Roberts), Robert Louis Stevenson (Mr. Lloyd Osbourne), Dame Ellen Terry (Miss Edith Craig), Theodore Watts-Dunton (Mrs. Watts-Dunton), E. S. Willard (Mr. Alfred W. Stowe, Mr. Willard, and Mrs. Willard), Sir Charles Wyndham (Lady Wyndham), and Israel Zangwill (Mrs. Zangwill).

I here express my deep appreciation and gratitude to my father's old friends, Mr. M. H. Spielmann, Mr. Max Beerbohm, Mr. H. C. Shelley, and Mr. Clayton Hamilton, for the invaluable help and information they have given me, as also my sincere thanks for the kindly helpfulness of many of my father's friends in America—in particular President Nicholas Murray Butler, the Hon. James Beck, Mr. Montrose J. Moses, Mr. Robert Gould Shaw, Curator of the Theatre Collection, Harvard College Library, Mr. Roger Howson, the Librarian of Columbia University, Mr. H. M. Lydenberg of the New York Public Library, Mr. Edwards, and Mr. Barrett H. Clark of Messrs. Samuel French & Sons.

Doris Arthur Jones.

CONTENTS

PART I, *Early Life*, 1851–1882.

Chapter

⬚I, *Success*, 1882–1902.

xv

---

self thought, ⬚ had worked all his life ⬚ writing to the high standards ⬚ lish literature.

These disclosures are to be found ⬚ the biography, *Taking the Curtain Call*, which Doris Arthur Jones has built up out of her father's life and letters. (Macmillan.) Henry Arthur Jones was an important force in the theater of thirty years ago. He opened the stage to the interpretation of many new ideas and episodes. He was a pioneer in New York City no less than in London. But as it happened he was ahead of his day by but a few years. The age of liberation caught up with him. He threw down the barriers, hoping to give freedom to a fine and dignified phalanx of English playwrights, and a horde of irresponsible craftsmen broke into the pasture. Toward the end of his life he could not have entered a theater without fearing apoplexy. The liberty which he had worked for had become license.

* * *

Doris Arthur Jones, most naturally, thinks that her father "fought hard and fearlessly for years to establish the right of English dramatists to depict life as it is, and not as an emasculated, trumpery pageant suitable only for young ladies of a past generation." By the nineties the theater was so stuffy that somebody had to bring it back to reality. Henry Arthur Jones did so within the limitations of his carpentry. He constructed plays according to a preconceived formula.

CONTENTS

PART III, *Later Years*, 1902–1929.

CONTENTS

LIST OF ILLUSTRATIONS

xix

PART I

EARLY LIFE

1851–1882

CHAPTER I

My father came from a Welsh family who settled near Winslow, in Buckinghamshire, at the end of the eighteenth century. His grandfather, William Jones, was born at Marsh Gibbon about 1791, and some years after his marriage, in 1814, to Sarah Hazzard, an Englishwoman, he came to live at Winslow. He was a prosperous farmer, innkeeper, and baker, the proprietor of the Three Pigeons Inn at Winslow.

William's son Silvanus, Henry Arthur's father, was born in 1827 at the little village of Grandborough, three miles from Winslow. Though he was born in England, Silvanus was Welsh in character and feeling, and throughout his life he remained an ardent Welshman. He was a hard-working, capable, energetic man of a most independent character. He was not at all lovable, in spite of a great sense of humour, but humour tinged very often with a streak of malice. A few months before my father died, speaking of his father, he said to his nurse, "I never met a man with more natural humour. That is where I got it all from, you know, Nanny."

My grandfather married Elizabeth Stevens, the daughter of a farmer, in January 1851. They were neither of them very ordinary folk, and, in reading their many letters to my father, I am struck with the ease and fluency with which they expressed their sentiments; both seemed to me unusually well educated for people belonging to the farming class.

Silvanus was a hard, unsympathetic man, and he was not kind to his wife. She sometimes complained to her

3

son; in 1880 she wrote: "I look at Papa and feel so sorry, as I don't think he has anyone to really love him. As he has treated me so lately, I do not love him as I used— I can't."

Though their father was deeply interested in, and concerned for, the welfare of his children, it was their mother whom the boys adored. She was the object of their deepest love and devotion. She was an extraordinarily sensitive, highly strung woman; to-day we should call her neurotic. She lived on her nerves, and my father, whenever I asked him what she died of, always replied, "Nerves; she was worn out." Henry Arthur, in an article he wrote for *Cassell's and T.P.'s Weekly*, under the title "The Days of My Youth," said that his father "from the age of ten till thirty worked on an average fifteen hours a day. Till he was sixty he generally worked not many hours less." He expected the same energy from his wife, but she was not physically strong, and most of her life she suffered from an internal complaint for which she took large doses of laudanum. My father told me that when she was a young girl she once took an overdose by mistake, and her parents had a terrible time walking her about the room all night. She died when she was sixty-one, as my father said, worn out.

The informing motive of her whole life was an unusually deep religious belief. H. A. J. once said to me, "Now, my dear mother was the nearest to a Christian I have ever met;" and to my brother Lucien, "My mother was one of the best women I've ever known. My mother wasn't as good a woman as your mother, not so sensible or so kind. She was a professing Christian and your mother wasn't." In all the many letters she wrote to her son there is not one in which she did not speak simply and naturally of God's love and mercy. When she was dying, she said to my father, "Oh, Harry, you'll want it when you come to lie where I am." When telling me this, H. A. J. said that she worried because he was not a believer, and added, "My mother was a real Christian woman; she believed in the Puritan ideal." In referring to her belief, he told me of some dispute she had with the curate over the milk she sold, and that my grandmother summed up with, "Let it be, bigoted Churchman." My father said, "She couldn't get it out of her head that anything could be right except that particular brand of Baptist religion she'd been brought up in." He gave her Thomas à Kempis's *Imitation of Christ*. Her remark after reading it was, "A very nice book with some queer Catholic ideas in it."

The Church of England at that time was not too kindly disposed towards Dissenters. When my father went to school, the little boys whose parents were Dissenters had to sit on a bench away from the Orthodox Church of England lads. H. A. J. often told me how intensely proud his father was when, at the age of ten, he captured the prize for Scripture knowledge from all the other lads, many of them older than himself and most of them Orthodox. He was very proud of this prize, a Bible in which he marked certain passages, and he used it all his life. It now belongs to the Players' Club, New York.

My father was born at Grandborough, Bucks, in September 1851, in a house which was pulled down many years ago. A new one, now known as Ley Farm, was erected on the same spot. When he was a few years old, his father moved to a house in Horn Street, Winslow, where he lived until he died in 1914. Henry Arthur was the eldest of five sons. His brothers were Charles, a farmer; William, my father's favourite, who became a well-known theatrical manager under the name of Silvanus Dauncey, and was for some years associated with Sir Herbert Beerbohm Tree as well as with many of my father's theatrical enterprises; Owen, who died of consumption when he was nearly seven; and Davey, who died of the same disease at twenty-two.

My father was always his mother's favourite, and long before he became famous he was the darling of her heart. To the end of his life he remained what we should call Early Victorian in many of his ideas and feelings; in reality they were Puritan. I believe it was his mother's teaching and example which left this imprint on his character. Castigation was the rule and not the exception in those days, but I gathered that if H. A. J. was ever whipped, it was very seldom, for he was a good and happy little boy, and unusually intelligent. He told me, "I knew my letters when I was twelve months old. I used to say 'R for the Rooshians.'" He often told me how vividly he remembered the peace celebrations after the Crimean War. From a very early age he lived in a world of his own imagination. He said to me, "I was always acting from the time I was three years old. When I went for a walk to my uncle's farm, I was carrying on battle, slashing the stinging nettles"; and he loved to go into the big backyard and play and act to himself. I think he was an independent little boy. When he was four or five, a band came down the street, and he went up to the man with the big drum and asked permission to beat it, and was allowed to do so. Many children would be seized with that childish desire, but not very many would have had the courage at so early an age to ask permission.

In "The Days of My Youth," he wrote, "When I was four years old, my father bought me a pony, and before I was six I was an accomplished horseman. In my Christmas holidays, from my eighth year, I had many a good run with the Bicester and Whaddon Chase." His father was also a follower of the Whaddon Chase, which often hunted over his land; but on one occasion "Old Syl," as he was called in Winslow, warned off the whole of Baron Rothschild's staghounds. The stag took refuge in one of Mr. Jones's barns, so he shut and locked the door, and, facing the angry hunt, cursed them all roundly and said they had no business on his land and he would see them all damned before he would release the stag; nor did he do so until the next day.

All his life, until his serious operation in 1913, my father was fonder of riding than of any other exercise or relaxation. In September 1928 he said to me, "I wonder I haven't been bitten with horse-racing; I was always devoted to horses and a great rider." He was also a great walker; up to 1924 he went for a several miles' walk nearly every day.

He first went to school when he was five years old—a small girls' school—and from there in 1859 he went to Mr. John Grace's Commercial Academy, which he attended regularly until he left school for ever at the age of twelve. It was a very hard life for a child. In "The Days of My Youth" he wrote, "When I was ten years old, my daily routine in the summer months was to go to the excellent town school at six a.m., and to have lessons till seven. I then went home to breakfast. Breakfast over, I was sent round the town with a large milk-can to sell our surplus supply of milk at a penny a pint. I had to be back in school at a quarter to nine. I went home to midday dinner, and had to be in school again at a quarter to two. Afternoon school finished at four, and I went home to tea, with as much of the finest butter and the richest cream as I could tuck in. Then came the rush hour, for I had again to divert myself from learning to my alternative occupation of selling milk, and after that to be in my place punctually at evening school, while the old full-toned bells from the church tower were chiming 'St. David's,' and drowsily admonishing the town folk not to hurry through life. Evening school finished at seven, and I was then free till six o'clock next morning."

CHAPTER II

AT twelve years old, Henry Arthur began to earn his living. At the end of his life it was his proud boast that he had never borrowed a farthing from any man.

His father had often talked of sending Henry to Oxford, as he showed so much ability in his school work; but, instead, "when I was twelve and a quarter, he packed me off to his brother, the deacon of a Baptist chapel, who kept a shop at Ramsgate. I never had a day's schooling afterwards, and I consider this to have been a great advantage. I was able to educate myself in my own way and at my own expense, by keeping up a constant and loving acquaintance with the English classics, and with some of the French and German masterpieces; by a close study of social and political economy; and by extensive foragings among the sciences."

When he first left home, his father said that if he liked to be a teetotaler for three years, he'd give him five pounds at the end of that time. H. A. J., in recounting this, added, "That was a good thing for me. He was a fine man in spite of his faults."

His uncle kept a draper's shop in Harbour Street, Ramsgate. Henry Arthur loathed and hated the work, and loathed and hated his uncle. I do not think he minded very much working fourteen hours a day, seventeen on Saturdays, for a salary of £20 a year, but he could not bear the drab monotony of his life. He longed to get away from it. It was while he was at Ramsgate that he started writing odd snatches of poems and stories in the very few leisure hours he had to himself—I imagine mostly on Sunday afternoons.

After three and a half years at Ramsgate, H. A. J. went to a draper's shop in Gravesend, run by a man called Bryant, who afterwards became Mayor of the town. He told me how very proud he was when a lady customer complimented him upon his handwriting, which she noticed when he was making out her bill. The earliest example I have of my father's writing is in a letter he wrote to my mother shortly before his marriage in 1875. The writing is small, energetic, and beautifully clear, and throughout his life it changed very little, if at all.

It was at Gravesend that H. A. J. began his constant and life-long reading of Milton, his favourite poet. A few years ago he said to me, "Shakespeare's line is fluent, human, colloquial almost—Milton's line is much stronger, and often after writing a play I've indulged myself by reading a book or two of *Paradise Lost*. De Quincey said that Mrs. Siddons could read Shakespeare, but she couldn't read Milton." My father and I read all through *Paradise Lost* in the winter we spent at Nice in 1903. We used to climb up to the pine woods above Mont Boron; I loved to hear him roll out the majestic lines. Writing to his son Oliver in 1916, he said, "I can't tell you how pleased I am you have taken to Milton—read him constantly and get to know *Paradise Lost* by heart. Charles Lamb said he could repeat it from end to end, but perhaps while remembering *Paradise Lost* he forgot to tell the truth. But, anyway, Milton makes a splendid foundation block for anyone who intends to write English." In another letter to Oliver, written in July 1918, he said, "Do what I will, my brain comes to a full-stop sometimes. Milton never wrote *Paradise Lost* in the summer. I should find it difficult and will abstain from trying." In his Notes he said, "Music? Wagner? Handel? Beethoven? Mozart? The greatest musician is Milton in *Paradise Lost*. A brother Puritan of mine, too." Speaking of Milton a few months before he died he said, "For real pleasure and meat I like *Samson Ago-nistes* or a book of *Paradise Lost*. Read those strong Miltonic lines and the easy, fluent lines of Shakespeare will come easily afterwards." I often got him to read me the end of *Paradise Lost*. He could never do so without tears in his eyes.

His love for "a brother Puritan" nearly cost him his job in the draper's shop. One day, deeply engrossed in *Paradise Lost,* he was very annoyed when an extremely fussy woman came in to buy some ribbon; he showed her one or two boxes, but she wasn't satisfied; so he cleared the counter, got down solemnly every box and tray of ribbon in the shop, spread them all out, and said, "Make your choice, madam," and returned to Milton.

Henry Arthur came to live in London when he was eighteen years old. It was not his first visit, as he had come up with his mother in 1857, when she took him to Vauxhall Gardens and he was so tired that she carried him in her arms all the way back. He was for some time in a warehouse in Friday Street, and, along with the other young men, slept in, but he managed to get to the theatre constantly. He wrote in "The Days of My Youth," "Although I wrote a play at sixteen, I never went to a theatre till I was eighteen. At that age I came to live in London. I went to the old Haymarket, where that fine actress, Miss Bateman, was playing Leah, 'supported' as they quaintly say on the programmes, by W. H. Kendal. Most of the members of the incomparable old Haymarket company appeared during the evening. We began at seven with *Blue Devils;* we then had five acts of melodrama in *Leah;* and we finished with two more acts of farce in *His First Champagne.* We were well through this varied orgy at five minutes past midnight." This first visit to the theatre made a tremendous impression. H. A. J. said, "I left off writing a novel I was engaged upon, and gave most of my leisure to seeing plays and reading Herbert Spencer.

HENRY ARTHUR JONES AT 23

I used to hurry from the City almost every evening at six to see the same successful play for perhaps a dozen times, till I could take its mechanism to pieces." One of the plays H. A. J. went to was Tom Robertson's *War*, on its first night in 1871. The hero was supposed to be missing, and Lionel Brough, as the uncle of the heroine, attempted to break the good news of his return, but, as this would have brought the play to a conclusion, his efforts were continually interrupted. At last a man in the gallery, as bored as my father, yelled out, "Oh, tell her, Brough!"

One day, when he was seventy-six, he started to sing Eccles's song from Mr. Robertson's play *Caste*, and breaking off, he said to me, "Oh, how well I remember how I loved that play the first time I saw it."

Henry Arthur told me that even in those days there were theatre queues, but if he could arrive by four o'clock he always managed to get in front. "I generally fell in love with the leading lady who was acting in it. The most enduring object of my youthful passion was that splendid Shakespearian actress, Adelaide Neilson (oh, what a glorious Rosalind!) whom I adored with 'the desire of the moth for the star!' Six evenings in one week did I watch her in a play of Westland Marston's from the gallery of the Lyceum, and when I had done clapping and shouting for her at the fall of the curtain, I used to hurry to the stage-door and patiently wait to see her enter her four-wheeled cab. I struck up an acquaintance with her cab-man, and offering him no greater inducement than a pint of beer, I learned from him that she lived at 68, Margaret Street, Cavendish Square. I declare that I obtained this information with no sinister motive, but only that I might stand for an hour or two in the street outside and watch her window." This passage reveals characteristics that formed a mainspring of my father's work: undaunted energy and great enthusiasm. They remained with him, growing stronger and broader throughout his life.

The memorable first visit to the Haymarket decided the medium in which he was to express his genius. He wrote several one-act plays during the first year he was in London, but those he sent to managers were always returned. He wrote, "I grew disheartened and went back to prose fiction. After giving two years of my leisure to writing a novel that I thought was a masterpiece, I took it to Kegan Paul, the publishers. It was declined with this comment: 'It is not a good first-rate novel; I cannot honestly say that it is a good second-rate novel, but I think it may be classed as a good third-rate novel.' " He also tried his hand at adapting *The Mill on the Floss,* and started to dramatise *Jane Eyre.* Many years later Henry Arthur was to write a successful play, *Hearts of Oak,* in the room where George Eliot wrote *Middlemarch.* Wilson Barrett lent him her house, The Priory, in St. John's Wood, when H. A. J. left Chalfont and was moving into Townshend House.

Disheartened at the rejection of his "masterpiece," H. A. J. said he "gave up writing novels, and must enter a firm protest against a very generous estimate of George Moore, who in an American interview said that if I had given myself entirely to fiction, I should have written better novels than Thomas Hardy."

Mr. Littlewood, in an article, "Henry Arthur Jones's Country," quotes an old schoolfellow of the name of Dickens who said, "I can see him now as a little lad standing in the dough-trough in his father's bakery, and saying that what he meant to do when he was grown up was to make clocks all the week and preach the gospel on Sunday morning." An old lady who also remembered my father said, "Strange that he should have took to play-writing—I always looked to see him in the pulpit."

It was shortly after he first came to London that my father met a young man six months older than himself, named Emery Walker, who was working in the same warehouse. They had a discussion about logarithms. This discussion was the beginning of a remarkable lifelong friendship, which, starting in early manhood, grew stronger with the passing years and definitely enriched and influenced for good all my father's life. He had "a genius for friendship" and was deeply attached to a great many people throughout his long life; but the hold Sir Emery Walker had on his affections was unique. It was through him that H. A. J. knew William Morris and his friends; and Morris and Walker guided and influenced him in his love for, and his purchase of, many beautiful things.

During those early years in London Henry Arthur's love of the theatre led him to take part in some amateur theatricals. His first appearance on the stage was as the Second Grave Digger in *Hamlet* during the winter of 1871, and the following year he acted in some theatricals given by the Grove House Amateur Theatrical Society at the old St. George's Hall. He played Bylis in H. T. Craven's *Miriam's Crime,* and Cousin Joe, Buckstone's part, in *A Rough Diamond,* and so keen was he on these performances that he paid George Barrett the enormous sum, for him, of 7*s.* 6*d.* a lesson to coach him in the parts. In telling me about his appearance he said, "In that performance I was secretary, treasurer, bill-poster, and low comedian," and he added, "I remember after that performance your dear mother was kind enough to give me her first kiss." I can picture the two young people chatting happily about the evening's entertainment, and my mother's excitement and pride in her young man overcoming her reserve. I like to think that my father's enthusiasm and hard work received so sweet a reward. He told me also, "I had such a good notice in the *Era;* by George, I was proud! The notice said, 'The first piece was the little comedy of *A Rough Diamond,* in which Mr. Arthur Jones exerted himself to good purpose as Cousin Joe, being rewarded with peals of laughter whenever he appeared. If we could not quite endorse the flattering verdict of his friends, we are bound to say Mr. Jones displayed considerable talent, and in one thing he was very successful indeed. He had a capital laugh, and anybody who can laugh well on the stage is certain to carry the audience with them.' "

Several years later my father's business as a commercial traveller took him to Weymouth, where a company was appearing in his play, *Hearts of Oak*. The actor who was playing Ned Devenish left the cast, and Henry Arthur took his part. He told me, "I played the leading young man's part, and by Jove how bad I was; the girl was a capital actress and played the love scenes so well that I couldn't act, I was busy watching her."

About a year after he first came to London, Henry Arthur had occasion to call at a warehouse for making artificial flowers, which was owned and managed by a Mrs. Seely. One of her young daughters, Jane Eliza, aged seventeen, was working in her mother's shop, and she met my father. The young people were mutually attracted, and before they had seen each other many times they fell deeply in love, and became engaged. Marriage seemed a remote possibility, as my father's salary was a small one, nor were my mother's parents greatly taken with the young man. The first time my mother introduced Henry Arthur to her mother, who was an original, indomitable old lady, she looked him up and down and said, "What a nincompoop!"

Soon after he became engaged, H. A. J. obtained a job in a warehouse at Bradford, where he was for over a year. Whilst living there, he read through Samuel French's catalogue of plays, paying them a penny for every play he read. He told me that it was during the time he lived in Bradford in 1869 that he wrote his first long play, called *The Golden Calf*. He had seen Lord Lytton's play *Money*, and based his story on it.

The salary at Bradford was not much larger than the one he received in London, and my father realised that he must find a better job if he was ever to get married, so he applied to the firm of Rennie Tetley, textile manufacturers, for the post of commercial traveller for their west of England branch. He was much too young for the job, but when they asked him his age he said, "Well, I'm not yet twenty-seven." In reality he was a bare twenty-one. His salary was £150 a year up to £8,000 worth of orders, and 2½ per cent. over that. The first year he obtained over £10,000 worth of orders for his firm, and in three years he worked so hard that his ground, from being the worst covered by that firm, had grown into the most important. Moreover, on his small salary he managed to save quite a considerable amount; the only time in his life he ever put money by. Though the life was a very hard one, my father found it a welcome change after the stuffy atmosphere in a warehouse.

To indulge his love of the theatre he underwent a certain amount of privation, often and often going without his meals to have the price of a theatre ticket, and doing without little necessaries to buy books, Herbert Spencer among others, which he read during the long railway journeys. He believed that it was during these years, through scanty and insufficient meals, that he laid the foundations of the ill-health from which he suffered so long. During the time that he was a traveller for Rennie Tetley, he wrote to Emery Walker nearly every week, and in many of his letters he asks him to send him books. The following passages from his letters show how wide and varied was his reading:

"19th February, 1878.

. . . "I am still reading hard; all my spare time in the day and sometimes half the night. I am now approaching the end of Herbert Spencer's system of philosophy.

It has been a hard nut to crack, but I wanted first of all to get a good groundwork of the latest science to build upon. And Herbert Spencer must not merely be read; he must be learned.

"Keats, Shelley, and Wordsworth occupy my lighter hours. Shelley I have studied through and through and have taken possession of him. For airiness, for all the loveliness that is in the sky and the sunlight and the mist he is unequalled. He is no more of the earth earthy than a rainbow is. I wish you would read him. Keats is like honey, but he is less ethereal than Shelley, less full of intense purpose and devotedness to human kind . . ."

"7th Oct., 1878.

"At present I am nourishing my dry and atrophied wits with huge draughts of Rabelais. This is about the choicest, richest, fruitiest stuff I have ever imbibed. I have been trying two or three of Browning's also, but he is a dreadful heavy dumpling, the toughest and hardest-baked I ever stuck my jaws into. But then I have had a bad training for the study of his books, never having essayed anything more deep and philosophical and abstract than such mere child's primers as Herbert Spencer's *Psychology* and Lewes's *Problems of Life and Mind. . . ."*

Though my father was reading the great English classics all his life, he was intensely interested in scientific subjects, especially natural science and the science of mankind in all its branches. He read Darwin and Huxley, and in later years he delighted in reading and re-reading many of Sir Edwin Ray Lankester's books. At one period of his life he saw a great deal of Sir Edwin, and during the last few years he often said, "I wonder how Ray Lankester is" and expressed a wish to see him again. I remember that one evening at Mont Boron in 1903, the winter we spent in the South of France, Sir Edwin dined with us. During dinner I said, "Have fish got teeth?" I shall never forget Sir Edwin's shocked expression as, laying down his knife and fork, he exclaimed, "Good God, Jones, how have you brought up your daughters!"

The latest developments in cancer research fascinated him, and he had many talks on the subject with Dr. William Seaman Bainbridge, the American authority. He kept abreast of a great deal of research work in medicine, and the attraction scientific subjects held for my father gave him the enjoyment and occupied the place of a hobby in his life.

During these early years he devoted a very large proportion of his time to reading the great English early dramatists, as witness the following typical passages from his letters to Emery Walker:

"The following dramatists will be useful to me, if you will kindly look out copies of any or all of them—Marlowe, Webster, Ford, Ben Jonson, Chapman, Tourneur, Dekker, Rowley, Middleton, Shirley, Greene, Peele, Kyd, Beaumont and Fletcher, and perhaps two or three others whom I do not now call to mind. Congreve, Wycherley, Farquhar, and perhaps the two Colmans. . . . If you are quite sure you do not want that *Tristram Shandy*, I should like it, but as I have already one copy of it, I am not greedy for it." . . . "I want a complete edition of De Quincey and Landor, and I want your advice about a lot of books that I am looking for. The Elizabethan dramatists are my next essay.—Can you tell me what editions are best for Marlowe, Ford, Webster, Dekker, Tourneur, Beaumont and Fletcher, and Massinger?" . . . "Ben Jonson. If you think Barry Cornwall's edition is better than Chatto's and also as complete, I will have that, i.e. B. Cornwall's, but if not, I am afraid I must content myself with Chatto's as I have been spending no end of money lately."

CHAPTER III

DURING his long engagement to my mother my father was away travelling a good deal, and, though he wrote to her constantly, I have only one letter, written on 2nd July, 1872.

"JENNY DEAREST," he wrote, "Many thanks for yours received this morning; it was something like a letter. I had been out travelling and it was there waiting for me when I got back at dinner time. . . . The majestic dome of St. Paul's is clearly cut against the evening sky; there are one or two stars. Those stars vibrate light to each other across the firmament, but I who am only distant from you a few score miles cannot reach you. Can I? Yes, for when I think of what we said to each other in the afternoon, I bring you to me. I clasp you again, I hold you close to me, I cover 'the face of my own wife dear' with kisses. Now I am at home (if I can call this home) and as I go upstairs I think of the verse,

> *The light of the Sabbath eve*
> *Is fading fast away—*
> *What record does it leave*
> *To crown the closing day?*

Oh Jenny, I have not spent my Sunday well! . . . I shall come down to Ramsgate on Saturday . . . four more days to wait!

"Fly! Fly! Fly! Days and hours haste! Haste! Minutes and seconds! Run! Run! Thou hobbling, laggard old Father Time. Rattle thy hour-glass till every

18

sand 'twixt this and Saturday is run out. Then for Joshua's power to bid the sun to stand still, and to say to the moment when I clasp Jenny again, 'Stay; thou art so fair; be thou my eternity.' "

My mother was not beautiful; her features were not particularly good or regular, but she had great beauty of expression, which increased as she grew older, and when she was quite an old woman she often looked really lovely, especially when she smiled. Her chief attraction was magnificent thick brown hair which, even at the end of her life, reached down to her knees. H. A. J. told me that, when he was engaged, her lovely hair fascinated him: one day he begged her to let it down, and, with charming grace and modesty, she complied with a somewhat unusual request for those far-off Victorian days.

At the time of his engagement my father was clean-shaven, but shortly after his marriage he grew a beard, which he wore for the rest of his life. His hair was very thick and curly, of a distinctly reddish tinge, and, when it grew darker as he grew older, his beard remained a bright yellowish red. He had a large head, with a very fine broad forehead, which, even when he was an old man, showed scarcely perceptible wrinkles. His eyes were his most remarkable feature—not large, but a very bright clear blue. They were the most expressive eyes I have ever seen. At times they were alight with fun and mischief; he had such a roguish twinkle. Frequently when he was telling what appeared to be a perfectly serious story I could detect the merest shadow of a twinkle, imperceptible to ordinary observers, and he never once deceived me. Sometimes I have interrupted him half-way through a statement to tell him I knew a joke was coming. He had a beautifully tender, loving look when he spoke to us or to a dear friend, but in contrast, when he was annoyed, his eyes had a hard, cruel expression, and if he was very angry his look was diabolical—once or twice I have

seen it quite murderous. When he was suffering from
nervous exhaustion, the look in his eyes was pitiable; day
after day, month after month, they were the eyes of a
frightened child. It hurt me to see this scarcely chang-
ing expression—it lifted so rarely and for such short
periods.

His hands were notable: square, workmanlike, with
short, square-tipped fingers. They were very vigorous,
and he used them in talking a little more than is usual
in an Englishman. He had one very characteristic gesture; when he wished to emphasise a point or points he
would tick them off one by one on the fingers and thumb
of his left hand. Another frequent gesture was to push
his hat back and run his hand all over his face with a
wiping movement. When he was depressed, he would
sit for long periods with his head in both hands, but when
he was working and thinking deeply he would support
his head with one hand only. In all the Max Beerbohm
caricatures of my father he is in the same attitude, with
one hand outstretched. Soon after he died I asked Max
one day, "What is it you see in Daddy which has made you
portray him with his hand out: is he appealing?" Max
stood still for a moment thinking, moved his hands slightly,
and then, assuming the pose of his caricatures, replied with
his delightful smile, "No, just being eager."

His voice was unremarkable, neither pleasant nor unpleasant, but it was very flexible, and he was a good
mimic. In making speeches or lecturing he was audible,
and he hesitated rarely. In conversation he was quick
and eager, and more often than not he would leave a word
or a sentence unfinished to hurry on, but his talk was so
vivid that it was nearly always easy for his listeners to in-
fer the word or words he left unsaid. He did not often
laugh outright or very heartily, but he had a delicious
fruity little chuckle, which was most attractive, though
occasionally, if he was gloating over getting the better

PERSONAL REMARKS.
By *Max Beerbohm.*
HENRY ARTHUR JONES.

(By courtesy of Mr. Max Beerbohm)

of anybody in conversation, it had a horrid jeering note in it. His smile was very winning, and when he smiled his whole face lit up.

He had a ruddy complexion, and often joked with us and with his grandchildren about "my nice red nose." When my sister Gertrude was a little girl, he took her in a bus one day. She was chatting to the conductor when a man started to run after the bus. The conductor said, "Look, there's your father." She said at once, "Oh, no, it isn't; my Daddy's got a nice red nose."

He was below middle height, of slight build, and never at any time of his life fat. He was quick and energetic in his movements, and until the last three years he always bounded up and down stairs two stairs at a time. He never fidgeted.

He was not at all a vain man or in any way a dandy. The only point in his personal appearance about which he was fussy was the care of his beard. In the last few years, when he was too ill to go down to the hairdresser, a little Spanish barber came up regularly every week to trim it. After a visit to the barber he never failed to ask his wife or one of his children, "Have they done my beard nicely?" He was kindly, very simple and unaffected in his manner, and he was always completely free from self-consciousness.

In 1875 H. A. J. was making enough money to get married. The marriage took place at St. Andrews, Holborn, on the morning of 2nd September, 1875. Emery Walker acted as best man. They went to Dover and then on to Boulogne for the honeymoon—the first time either of them had been out of England. My father's work as a commercial traveller was still in the west of England, so he took a house, The Hermitage, Exwick, Exeter, where they lived for six years until 1881. The Hermitage consisted of four cottages which had been converted into one house, and after conversion the four front doors were left. One day a man selling samples called at the house. He knocked on each door in turn, and each time H. A. J. opened the door to him; the last time, quite bewildered, he asked, "Do you live in all these houses?" "No," replied my father, "I'm only a tourist." The exterior of The Hermitage was reproduced in Act II of *The Crusaders*.

Though he started writing when he was twelve, Henry Arthur had to wait sixteen years before his first play was produced. From the beginning right up to the end of his life he was to remain undaunted by failure, to find resources within his own nature of courage, patience, and endurance, which gave him strength at the commencement of his career to conquer and overcome sixteen years of barren work, and, when he had won recognition, to ignore and triumph over defeat by renewed effort. He felt his failures keenly, but he would not allow them to dishearten him.

All his life my father was a voluminous letter-writer, not only to his friends, but, when he became famous, to the papers; frequently on those subjects dear to his heart —the drama, literature, religion, and in later years the Great War and its manifold political consequences. It was as a letter-writer that he was to make his first appearance in print in 1874—as also his last, in a letter to the *Stratford-on-Avon Herald,* published on 4th December, 1925. The 1874 letter was a criticism of a sermon by the Dean of Exeter, and appeared in the *Exeter and Plymouth Gazette, Daily Telegrams*. In it there are early signs of the fine, vigorous, and often noble prose which distinguished so many of his articles, pamphlets, and books, and the prefaces to his plays, and which reached great heights of beauty in the later years of his life, notably in some passages in "Patriotism and Popular Education," "My Dear Wells," the *Daily Express* article, "My Religion," and his as yet unpublished book, *The Shadow of Henry Irving*.

As a child H. A. J. attended chapel regularly—a small

Baptist chapel dating from 1625, tucked away at the end of a cobble lane; but once he left Ramsgate he did not go to church very often. He went sometimes when he was at Winslow, or when he was travelling after he started to earn his living and during his early married life, and later on occasionally to hear a famous preacher. He would often imitate for us the manner in which an old bricklayer announced the hymns at this little chapel, and he always declared that his accent and pronunciation were relics of the old Puritan nasal twang.

Henry Arthur went to hear Spurgeon several times; in speaking of him to me one day, he said, "Spurgeon had a good deal of the low comedian about him. He had a beautiful voice. I heard a wonderful emotional effect he obtained one day (quoting): 'Brethren, some people talk of the faith you can have to-day and lose to-morrow—Brethren,' (his voice rising) 'my advice to you is LOSE it.' " In this connection H. A. J. remarked, "Religion sits upon people just according to their own temperament." He also liked to hear the Rev. H. R. Haweis preach, and often went to his house. The first time my father heard one of Mr. Haweis's sermons, he wrote to him as follows:

"I must send you a line to say that your service and sermon last night gave me the rarest pleasure. I have done without churchgoing for a long while past—being unable to accept the dogmas of orthodox theology, I have a little flattered myself that it was my duty to stay away as a sort of protest, an excuse that very well suited with my lazy irregular habits. But it seems that I have been merely cheating myself of a high emotional and spiritual delight, and setting a bad example to my neighbours. I was glad to find that the whole service had a wonderful attraction for me, and I shall cease to wonder (as I confess I have sometimes been in the habit of doing) at the continued hold the church has upon the affections of the people."

Mr. Haweis once asked H. A. J. to read the lessons at a service. He replied:

"It would have given me great pleasure to read the lessons for you, but the plain truth is that I am afraid scoffers might say my own private life is not strict enough to warrant my putting on a surplice. And if you say, 'Then why not mend your ways?' I am left without any reply. I know it is rather weak and cowardly of me to refuse to help one who is doing so much for the theatre as you are doing, and if at any time I can be of use to you on a week-night, and without donning a surplice, I shall only be too glad to make some attempt to show the gratitude of our profession for your kindness and broadness of view towards us."

My father was not a man of rigid principles, but he always faced the big issues of life squarely and there is an admirable honesty and simplicity in these letters. He met General Booth, the founder of the Salvation Army, at the Haweis's one day, and, in speaking to me of sincerity in clergymen, he said, "I came to the conclusion that even if he was sincere he was damned stupid." The preacher he most admired was the late Bishop of Ripon, Dr. Boyd-Carpenter, who told H. A. J. that the essence of a good sermon was co-ordination.

Shortly after he went to Exeter, Henry Arthur met a very remarkable clergyman, the late T. W. Chignall. More than twenty years after his death a friend, also a Unitarian clergyman, wrote to H. A. J. of Mr. Chignall as "that spiritual genius." My father, in his article "My Religion," said, "I may gratefuly dwell on the memory of my close friend, the Rev. T. W. Chignall, the Unitarian minister at Exeter, a cousin of Mark Rutherford. Although he had thrown away all dogma, his was one of the most religious minds I have held in communion. Together we found great religious support in Matthew Arnold."

After Sir Emery Walker, Mr. Chignall was my father's closest and dearest friend, and I think influenced him very deeply. Chignall was one of the greatest living authorities on the works of Spinoza and Goethe, and I am sure H. A. J.'s knowledge and love of Goethe was directly due to his friend's influence.

CHAPTER IV

My aunt told me that my parents' marriage was "a real love match," and, though H. A. J.'s work took him constantly away, the young couple settled down very happily at The Hermitage, my mother's sister Amy staying with her frequently to keep her company.

My father had a deep desire to have children, and when he was travelling, the letters he exchanged with his wife referred continually to his hopes, but it was not until October 1877 that their first child, a lovely boy, was stillborn. Chloroform was not used in those days, and I believe the tragic disappointment of their hopes left a deeper mark on my mother than on my father.

But a greater sorrow came when in 1879 their second child, a boy, Philip Arthur Exwick, was born, an invalid from birth. To his mother, until he died in 1896, he was by far the dearest of all her children. The unremitting care and tenderness she lavished on him called forth the deepest wells of love and devotion in her nature; but to my father, perhaps almost unconsciously, he was not only a disappointment, but almost a source of reproach. He was kind to Philip always, but he did not bear easily the frustration of being unable to take any pride in his eldest son.

Their third child, a daughter, Winifred Amy, was also born at The Hermitage in 1880; Ethelwyn Sylvia and Gertrude Mary were born in 1883 and 1884 at Lothian Lodge, New Hampton; the writer of this book, Jenny Doris, in 1888 at Townshend House, where Lucien David Silvanus was born in 1893, and Oliver Stacy Arthur in 1899.

26

From the earliest days of their marriage, for nearly fifty years, until she died in 1924, my mother was the most devoted, unselfish, loving, and tender helpmate and wife. She had a remarkably fine character; in her nature were inexhaustible wells of love and sympathy, so that her husband and her children never made any demand on her to which she did not more than respond. My father and his children always said that it was worth while being ill to be nursed by her. Her presence, her reassuring smile, the grip of her hand inspired courage and hope. She had an unshakable sense of duty, was upright and just in all her business dealings, and an excellent housewife. She had a nice sense of humour and a tender understanding for the failings and mistakes of others. She was a very generous woman. My father sometimes said, "I don't know what I should have done without your mother." After her death he missed her constantly and intensely, and he was always saying, "How I wish your dear mother were back," and "She was a wonderful woman—bless her, I wish I had been kinder to her." Of all those to whom he was united by the closest ties of love and kinship his wife, and in a lesser degree his mother, were the two people the character of whose love and devotion he really did understand and appreciate. One evening some while after the death of his wife in 1924, an incident, I forget what, reminded him very vividly of her dear presence, and the old man sat in his chair, with his hand over his eyes, crying quietly, helplessly, hopelessly for her.

As soon as they were married, my mother always sat with my father while he was working, often and often till one or two in the morning. He read to her every scene directly he had finished it, eager for her approval and suggestions. She copied out many of his scenes for him, and he said to me once, "I wrote a long novel after I married your mother and made her copy it out, poor girl." It was all about a clergyman who committed a murder; and

H. A. J. added, "It came in afterwards. I had that fine tap of remorse all ready to turn on for *The Silver King.*" Even after the children were born, and in spite of the cares of a small family, my mother still gave hours of her time to sitting with my father, and no household duty, though all were well performed, ever interfered with the time and attention she gave to his work. All the information in the earliest volumes of his Press cuttings is in her handwriting. She continued to give this daily attention and criticism to his work until increasing deafness rendered her immediate counsel impracticable. But after she became deaf, he would always run down to her from his study to give her each new scene to read as he finished it.

In the first years of their married life Henry Arthur wrote several one-act plays, but it was not until 1878 that he succeeded in placing one of them. In "The Days of My Youth," referring to the non-acceptance of his novel by Kegan Paul, he wrote, "I went back to the drama. Within a few months I gained my first production, a one-act play called *It's Only Round the Corner,* afterwards re-christened *Harmony.* Rousby, a fine 'legitimate' actor, who had been having a disastrous Shakespearian season at the old Theatre Royal, Exeter, read the piece and was willing to play the leading part if I would take half the dress circle, the highest priced seats in those days. The bargain was struck on the spot. There are times when the drama needs to be subsidised. Thus I became an acted dramatist. I quickly advanced to other subsidised productions—*Hearts of Oak* at Exeter, and *Elopement* at the old ramshackle theatre at Oxford."

It's Only Round the Corner was produced on 11th December, 1878, and also by Wilson Barrett in August of the following year at the Grand Theatre, Leeds, under the title of *Harmony Restored.* *Hearts of Oak* was produced at the Theatre Royal, Exeter, in June 1879. H. A. J. was overjoyed when two London newspapers, the *Illus-*

trated Sporting and Dramatic and the *Era,* noticed the play favourably.

Elopement, a two-act comedy, was produced in August 1879, at the Theatre Royal, Oxford. The notices were fairly good, though the *Oxford Times* said, "The title is not nice!" H. A. J. wrote to Sir Emery Walker the following amusing letter about this play:

"18th March, 1879.

"MY DEAR WALKER,

"I wouldn't trouble you for the world, but I wish if you can anyway scrape a spare moment you will let me have some news of yourself.—I went down to Northampton on Saturday week and read my new comedy *Elopement* to Duck's Company. The stage-manager liked it immensely, but Satan got astride Duck's imagination and reduced him to think it was improper. So to suit the hyper-queasy stomach of that abominable prude the British matron, I have got to castrate my hero. Talking about castration, a funny idea has just entered my head—for the life of me I can't help telling it you—it is this—how much those actors have felt who had to impersonate eunuchs in the old tragedies—upon my soul it's the last character in the world that I would desire to play —I suppose a conscientious actor would hardly think it necessary to undergo an operation before the performance —some people might call such a sacrifice an unparalleled devotion to art, I should call it consummate tomfoolery —the case of the man who blacked himself all over to play Othello would hardly be worth speaking about after an instance of this sort. God save us all. Let me know about my paper, my Ben Jonson, and my admission to the D. A. S.

"Thine,

"JONES."

E. S. Willard played in *Elopement* a year later at the Theatre Royal, Belfast—the beginning of a long and successful association with my father's plays. In the same year Wilson Barrett gave H. A. J. his first chance in London with *A Clerical Error*. My father was immensely excited at the prospect of a London production, as he felt that it might be the chance for which he longed—the opportunity to give up his commercial work and devote himself entirely to play-writing. The play was produced at the Court Theatre on 16th October, 1879, with Winifred Emery as the heroine. The notices were extremely good. H. A. J. did not "take a call," but, as the audience were loud in their demands for the author, Wilson Barrett pointed him out in his box. This piece was played at the Theatre Royal, Belfast, in August 1880.

An example of Wilson Barrett's friendly interest in, and unfailing kindness to, the young author is shown by the following letter, written just after he agreed to produce the play:

"MY DEAR SIR,—Please send me the detailed acceptance of my offer for *A Clerical Error,* and that will stand until there is time to draw up a more legal, though not less binding agreement. You had better keep the other copies of the piece by you, call in those out, if possible.

"Are you aware that by printing your plays and publishing them, you forfeit your American rights? A play kept in MS. or printed in slip as MS. for use of actors only is to a certain extent protected in the United States. This is of great importance to dramatic authors. I could write more freely if I knew more of you.

"Will you send me your card, if you have one, and if you can believe that I am asking not from mere idle curiosity, and tell me your profession or position?

"With compliments,
"Faithfully yours,
"WILSON BARRETT."

I have not got my father's reply to this letter, but I am quite sure he told Mr. Barrett he was a commercial traveller. He never at any time showed even the faintest trace of snobbishness as regards his birth or early commercial life. He often boasted that he was the son of a farmer.

Wilson Barrett was convinced that Henry Arthur would write finer plays than *A Clerical Error*. He wrote:

". . . The public are pining for a pure English comedy, with a pure story, in which the characters shall be English, with English ideas, and English feelings, honest, true men, and tender, loving women, and from which plague, pestilence, adultery, fornication, battle, murder, and sudden death shall be banished.

"The author who can do in three acts what you have done in one in *A Clerical Error* will take as strong a stand now as Tom Robertson took years ago.

"The characters must not preach virtue, let them act it, not spout self-denial but show it. The public taste is depraved no doubt, the more depraved the greater certainty of success for the man who will try to raise it. This seems paradoxical, but do not the most abandoned women, *in their hearts,* admire virtue most, the greatest cowards worship bravery? . . ."

Wilson Barrett was so pleased with the success of *A Clerical Error* that he chose a one-act play of H. A. J.'s, *An Old Master,* for the opening of the Princess's Theatre on 6th November, 1880, as a curtain-raiser to *Hamlet* with Edwin Booth. The notices were not very good, though on revival at the Vaudeville in July 1883, they were more favourable. *An Old Master* was running in London at the same time as *A Clerical Error*—very unusual occurrence in those days.

My father told me, "My first big play was *His Wife,* produced by Miss Bateman at Sadlers Wells on 16th April, 1881, an adaptation of a novel—a very sad ending." *His Wife* was followed by *A Bed of Roses,* a one-act comedy

produced at the Globe on 26th January, 1882.   Both plays
were received very favourably.   Thus in four years, with
the production of seven successful plays, Henry Arthur
attained a secure foothold on the stage.   In speaking to
me of these early plays he told me, "When I began to
write plays, all the plays were sent in in manuscript; I had
mine printed and sent one in to Barrett, so of course he
took it."   All his life H. A. J. insisted that he was the first
dramatist who printed his plays, and, though there was
an interval of some years between the printing of these
early plays and the publication by Macmillan's of *Saints
and Sinners* in 1891, as also those plays privately printed
by the Chiswick Press, commencing with *The Masqueraders,* his claim is a just one.   Except for one or two
critics in America, notably Professor William Lyon Phelps
of Yale University, his position as a pioneer dramatist in
this matter has been almost entirely overlooked.   H. A. J.
asserted constantly that the ultimate test of a play was
whether it could be read and appreciated in the library.

Early in 1879 my father had taken the momentous
decision of giving up his work as a commercial traveller to
devote himself entirely to writing plays.   That Wilson
Barrett urged him to take this step is shown by the following passage in a letter to Emery Walker: "I hardly know
how long I shall be with Wilson Barrett.   He has behaved
most kindly to me and written me the most encouraging
letters.   He is considering the question of whether I shall
give up bagmanship—I am almost safe to do it—indeed
I have quite made up my mind to take the plunge if he
will buy either of my other pieces.   You cannot imagine
what a wretched state of ferment I am in."   He met with
the strongest opposition from his own and his wife's
family.   Both his father and his father-in-law protested
against his imprudence and foretold disaster.

During these early years my father made several unsuccessful attempts to place his plays.   In 1880 he sub-

mitted a printed copy of a three-act play, *A Perfect Woman* (renamed *A Garden Party*) to the *Era* with a request for a verdict on its merits. On 22nd August it received an unfavourable review, which said, among other things, "*A Perfect Woman* is, we may say at once, a very imperfect play." Long before Matthew Arnold's memorable appearance at the first night of *The Silver King* my father wrote to him and sent him a copy of *A Garden Party*. Matthew Arnold replied:

"Pains Hill Cottage,
"Cobham, Surrey.
"*14th October, 1879.*

"MY DEAR SIR,

"Many thanks for your two pieces, and for your letter with its most kind expressions. I produce but little effect upon the general public, but I have some excellent readers nevertheless; I may count you as one of them. *The Garden Party* is extremely interesting; I hope it will appear in some magazine as you purpose. *The Clerical Error* I must try to see, which is far better than reading, some night when I am in town. I am afraid we are still a long way off from the attainment of a satisfactory theatre and a satisfactory drama, but they will come in time.

"Believe me, my dear sir,
"Sincerely yours,
"MATTHEW ARNOLD."

One of the plays of this early period was *Welcome, Little Stranger*. The opening scene of this play was a corridor —a nurse crossed the stage, a servant opened a door for a doctor carrying a bag, one or two other characters came on, and, after a certain amount of *va et vient*, the nurse entered and said, "It is a fine boy." Because of this preliminary scene the Censor refused to license the play. I believe it was when my father and I went to see *Spring Cleaning* that he told me with considerable amusement about this early piece. In later years Henry Arthur's vigorous and trenchant attacks on the censorship were influential in paving the way for the production of plays such as *Spring Cleaning* and *The Vortex*.

For most of these early plays my father received £2 2s. 0d. a performance; but after he had attained a leading position on the London stage he rarely received less than 10 per cent., rising to 15 per cent. or more. The earliest of his account-books I have shows that he made in fees in 1881, £527 15s.; and in 1882, £514 15s. 6d., but to the end of 1883, the year which included the fees from *The Silver King*, he made £3,398 6s. 9d. An item on the debit side of this book is, "By friendship—£50." He was always an extremely generous man, not only to his family, but to his friends.

PART II

SUCCESS

1882–1902

CHAPTER V

In 1881 my father moved from The Hermitage to
Lothian Lodge, Hampton Wick. The year 1882 was to
be the most memorable year of his life; with the production of *The Silver King,* on 16th November, he leapt into
the front rank of British dramatists, a position he was to
hold unchallenged for the rest of his life. Impressed with
the success of *His Wife,* Wilson Barrett asked Henry Arthur to write him a strong play, and suggested the late
Henry Herman as a collaborator. H. A. J. said, "I should
never have written melodrama but for the fact that Wilson Barrett was the only manager who would look at my
work in those days."

The play received great praise from all the critics. I
have read through the forty-five volumes of my father's
Press cuttings, and I consider the notices the most enthusiastic he received for any of his plays. Among the
criticisms, *Truth* was the only paper which drew attention
to the world-famous line "O God! put back Thy universe
and give me yesterday." Henry Arthur said, "No one
has ever said that line, or ever would say it, but every one
has felt it"; and he went on to tell me that Barrett was a
very religious man and objected to the line, he said, "I
mustn't say that." A few years ago a friend of mine was
on a sea voyage, and a fellow-passenger lost a bet of several
pounds because he was convinced the line was in the Bible.

A memorable event in connection with the first performance was the presence of Matthew Arnold, after an
absence from the theatre of nearly twenty years. The
praise and encouragement H. A. J. had already received

from the great man induced him to press Matthew Arnold to come to the first night. He wrote to my father:

"The Athenæum.
"*2nd November, 1882.*

"MY DEAR SIR,

"I will certainly come and see your play, but do you care particularly about my coming to the first representation? I am living in the country at present, but I shall be up in town for a week in the early part of December, and again for two months in the early part of next year; and at either of those two times I should be better situated for going to the theatre than I am now. If, however, you care much about my coming to the first representation, let me know the date, and unless I am actually engaged I will come....

"One line to Cobham, Surrey, and believe me most truly yours,

"MATTHEW ARNOLD."

An extract from Arnold's notice in the *Pall Mall Gazette* reads as follows: "The critics are right, therefore, in thinking that in this work they have something new and highly praiseworthy, though it is not exactly what they suppose. They have a sensational drama in which the diction and sentiments do not overstep the modesty of nature. In general, in drama of this kind, the diction and sentiments, like the incidents, are extravagant, impossible, transpontine; here they are not. This is a very great merit, a very great advantage. The imagination can lend itself to almost any incidents, however violent; but good taste will always revolt against transpontine diction and sentiments. Instead of giving to their audience transpontine diction and sentiments, Messrs. Jones and Herman give them literature. Faults there are in *The Silver King;* Denver's drunkenness is made too much of, his dream is superfluous, the peasantry are a little tiresome, Denver's triumphant

WILSON BARRETT AS "THE SILVER KING," 1882

exit from Black Brake Wharf puzzles us.   But in general throughout the piece the diction and sentiments are natural, they have sobriety and propriety, they are literature. It is an excellent and hopeful sign to find playwrights capable of writing in this style, actors capable of rendering it, a public capable of enjoying it."

My father delighted naturally and easily in his many friendships with famous people, but he always spoke with intense pride, though very humbly, of his acquaintance with Matthew Arnold.   About a year after the first performance he met Mr. Arnold out walking, and the latter enquired very kindly about the amazing success of the young dramatist.   H. A. J. happened to mention that he had made over £3,000 in fees, and he told me that the merest shade, not of envy, but of a feeling tinged with something less shallow than envy, passed across Arnold's fine countenance, adding, "And all England could do for her greatest scholar and poet was to give him an inspectorship of schools at a paltry £800 a year."

Among those who went to see *The Silver King* was Henry Irving.   My father told me, "Irving went to see *The Silver King,* and you know Irving's love for dark scenes, mysterious and gloomy scenes.   Barrett got out of the train in quite a light scene, and, when Irving went round after to see him, he said, 'Wasn't that scene a little light, my boy?' 'Well, you see, it's eleven in the morning.'   Irving: 'I should have had an eclipse.' "   H. A. J. added, "And he would."

We often talked of *The Silver King,* but, in spite of its enormous success and enduring popularity, it was not by any means my father's favourite play, though he liked to tell his friends that it was always being played somewhere in the English-speaking world.   During the last few years of his life he grew fonder of the old play.   It is a curious fact that of all his plays *The Silver King* is the only one which was produced in France, though *Michael and His Lost Angel, The Lifted Veil,* and *The Liars* have all been translated into French—the last by the great French critic Augustin Filon. Several of his finest comedies are more suitable to the French stage than this melodrama.

Henry Arthur often said the only incident from real life he ever used in a play was that of the tipsy passenger at the railway station. He saw this scene at Waterloo one night. An American once said to him, "I saw your play *The Silver King* in New York; the leading part of the tipsy passenger was very well done." My father laughed at this, but it was the only occasion when he was amused by over-acting or additions to his script throwing his play out of balance. It was his proud boast that, starting with the printing of *The Masqueraders,* he could take any of his plays to a manager and insist upon their production without the alteration of a single line.

Though *The Silver King* was not among the first half-dozen of my father's favourite plays, he suffered acute anxiety before the production; so much was at stake. He said to me, "I had a wife and two children, and about £300 between me and the workhouse, and night after night I used to think 'Good God! Will it come off?'" And on another occasion, "No one recognised me till I was over thirty. The morning after *The Silver King* what I felt was, 'This is going to make things easy for me!'" When his nurse asked him, in the year before he died, which was the greatest day of his life, he replied almost immediately, "The first night of *The Silver King.*"

No one but the members of his family knew of the restless suffering which possessed my father before his first nights. If the dress rehearsal had gone well he would get some broken sleep the night before a production, but if it had gone badly he scarcely slept at all. In the morning there would be endless small details to attend to, messages to be answered. He would go himself to choose a bouquet for the leading lady. He would peck at a little lunch, and then make a fruitless effort to get a short nap; but all day long he was padding about the house from one room to another—sometimes he would come in and go out without a word, often he would ask an irrelevant question without waiting for a reply. He would hardly touch the more than usually well ordered dinner, which was always a hurried affair. The cab or taxi would be called long before it was time to start, and once in the theatre he went as quickly as possible to his box, where, secluded behind the curtains, he would watch as far as possible the audience coming in, occasionally going round behind. I am afraid he very often harried the manager and artists unnecessarily. If the play was a success, tension was relaxed and we came home to chat, happily and at ease, over all the incidents; but if the play was a failure, or appeared to be, I think we suffered as much as he did. He was so gallant under defeat, so full of fight and courage, that our efforts to cheer or bolster him up were painful to us and affected him very little.

On the first night of *The Silver King* all these feelings and emotions were increased a thousandfold. It was the turning-point of his career. During the whole of the play, as if unable to credit the evidence of his eyes and ears, he kept up an incessant feverish whispering to his sister-in-law Amy, "How's it going, how's it going?" My mother being then too deaf to hear his lowered voice, Amy replied, "How's it going, Henry? I've split a new pair of white kid gloves applauding—what more do you want?"

He told me that for many years after the first production of *The Silver King,* every few months he had the most vivid nightmares, in which he dreamed that he had committed a murder. He attributed these dreams to the intense emotional strain he had been under while he was writing the play and during the rehearsals.

It is now more than forty years since the production of

The Silver King, and by the great mass of the English public my father is looked upon as the author of this famous melodrama, while Herman's name is almost forgotten. The verdict of the public is a just one. My father often said, "Herman gave me the end of the second act, but he never wrote a line of it." Mr. M. H. Spielmann, a very dear friend of my father, in writing to me about his life, said, "I knew Herman well at the Savage Club in the 80's and early 90's; we have talked of *The Silver King* and never to me did he claim more than a fractional share of the production."

Before there was any controversy as to the authorship of the play most people regarded my father as the virtual author. An article by him was published in 1883 in the September number of the *Nineteenth Century,* and on the cover was the announcement, "By Henry Arthur Jones (joint author of *The Silver King*)." In reference to this article Theodore Watts-Dunton, in a letter to H. A. J., said, "I have just been reading your article 'The Theatre and the Mob.' I had hurriedly glanced at it before. It is very good; but why do you call yourself *Joint* Author?" But shortly after the production Herman, envious of the praise and recognition accorded to his collaborator, went about claiming the lion's share of the authorship. My father was incensed by these discussions, both private and public, and he wrote a letter to the editor of the *Era* which was published on 12th September, 1885:

"Sir,

"Will you kindly allow me a little space to correct certain misstatements which have appeared during the week respecting the authorship of *The Silver King* and other plays in which my name has been associated with that of Mr. Herman? . . . Mr. Herman and I started to put together the framework of a drama which we hoped would be accepted by Mr. Barrett. . . . Some time in the spring we hit upon the idea of bringing a man up from a state of utter degradation and self-contempt to affluence, respectability, and self-esteem. For a long while the plot was in a very crude state, and when I read the first act to Mr. Barrett, it was in five scenes (Mr. Herman's construction), and the whole thing was so loose and unsatisfactory that Mr. Barrett rejected it. However, on my reading the second act, Mr. Barrett thought the strong domestic interest showed that the play contained possibilities, and he then and there gave us a new construction of the first act, which we adopted, and from that time forwards, through the writing of the three later acts, Mr. Barrett assisted in the building up of the entire scheme. . . . When Mr. Herman says that the story and whole scheme of *The Silver King* were his, the working out of its details and the construction of the play were his, it requires the greatest self-restraint on my part to summon up sufficient parliamentary courtesy to assure him that he is mistaken. . . . The idea of the man believing himself guilty of murder, being innocent, was suggested to me by a short tale in *Good Words,* called 'Dead in the Desert,' which had powerfully impressed me in my childhood. . . . Some few months after starting on *The Silver King* I had written a novel, in which I had traced the history of the feelings of a man who, through fierce stress of circumstances, had committed a murder against all the dictates of his moral nature. I had, therefore, ready to my hand all the terrible feelings of remorse which my former hero had endured, and I simply transferred it to Wilfred Denver. Many of the same expressions which are in the MS. of my novel are now nightly uttered in different parts of the world by various Wilfred Denvers. . . . The part of Jaikes was entirely suggested and designed by me and was put into the plot at first against Mr. Herman's wishes. . . . For my own part, I would not move a finger to lay claim to any portion of any plot, or to any situation in any play that was ever written,

of so little value do I consider plot or situation, apart from
the life-compelling power of the author that makes his
characters live and move in the situation. . . . So far as
my share in the construction and plot of *The Silver King*
goes, he may take it. But I am bound, in justice to Mr.
Barrett, to acknowledge that *The Silver King* would have
stood for a very curious and slipshod bit of stagecraft, and
its authors might have been ridiculed for their constructive
powers, if he had not come in and pulled it together. . . .

"To come to the actual writing of *The Silver King*. It
would be giving a truthful impression if I said that Mr.
Herman did not write a line of it. But there were a few
lines which he suggested upon my reading the different
scenes to him—I think not forty lines in all; to be quite
sure that I am well within the mark, I will again allow
him a hundred. As for the dream speech, Mr. Herman did
not write a single line of it or dictate a single line of it; and
I can only again assure him that in this instance his memory has been playing its old tricks upon him. . . ."

Several years after the first production Wilson Barrett
privately and in public talked and wrote of the play as if
he had been part author. It became necessary to refute
his claim, and an arbitration was held in January 1905
with Sir Squire Bancroft, Sir Charles Wyndham, and Mr.
Ben Greet as arbitrators. The award refuted in the clear-
est terms Mr. Barrett's claim to authorship. A year before
the arbitration my father wrote to him as follows:

"MY DEAR WILSON BARRETT,

"A recent interview with you in the *Sydney Morning
Herald* relative to the authorship of *The Silver King* has
been forwarded to me. If I re-open the old controversy
for the moment, it is neither to add to, nor to retract from,
my former statement on that subject. That statement
was written in your room at the Princess's Theatre, at your
incessant instigation and suggestion, and after repeated

refusals on my part to open my lips.   I have never to this day read a word of what was written in reply, and I have never ceased to regret that I was betrayed into doing what I knew to be a foolish thing, an ungenerous thing, a thing I can truly say I should never have dreamed of doing except at your urgent prompting, and from a motive of wishing to oblige you, who in giving me my first London opening had done so much for me.   The whole matter was so distasteful to me, that, as I say, I did not so much as glance at what was written in reply, but hurried to America without calling for the manuscript of *The Silver King*.   I had no safe or strong-room in my house at the time, and for the sake of security the manuscript had always been kept by Herman in his safe.   I afterwards heard that Herman had produced some sheets of manuscript in his handwriting. I remember his copying a sheet or two for me one Sunday from very rough MS., but the rough MS. of the scene in my handwriting still remained in his possession.   And as the whole of the manuscript was in his possession, it may be presumed that he produced all that was in his handwriting.   If not, why did he not do so, when every page would have helped to support his case?

"Let that pass.   My object in writing this letter is not to put in a claim that I relinquished thirteen years ago,[1] but to assure you that it will be quite safe for you to claim the leading part in the authorship of *The Silver King*. Herman is dead, I have no proofs, and I imagine the manuscript of *The Silver King* is destroyed.   Therefore, my dear Wilson Barrett, I am sure it will give you great satisfaction to know that you will be quite safe in posing as the author of *The Silver King*.   I see by the interview in the *Sydney Morning Herald*, that you have already done so by hint and suggestion and innuendo.   What is it that hinders you from doing so boldly and openly?   Nothing, my dear Bar-

---

[1] For some time H. A. J.'s name did not appear on the programmes as author.

rett, but that overweening modesty of yours which has ever
been the fatal defect of your character.   I invite you to the
contemplation of this stupendous modesty of yours, if indeed you have not often stood before it in rapt amazement and admiration.   Take, for instance, the first display
of it that comes to hand—a playbill of a joint production
of yours.   In it your name only occurs four times and never
larger than six times the size of your brother actors.
Think, my dear Barrett, what you have lost by your inability to take yourself at your proper value.   Why not
have your name eight or ten times on every programme,
and fifty times the size of everybody else?   For then will
not Fame herself take your name and blow it broadcast to
all the world, if not from the trumpet she holds to her
mouth, at least from the trumpet she holds in an opposite
position?

"Now in the matter of the authorship of *The Silver King*,
take my advice, conquer this fatal modesty of yours, and
brazen out the whole affair.   Don't hint and suggest and
whisper that you are the virtual author, but say it outright and stick to it.

"No critic of standing is likely to weigh the internal
evidence.   I have given a few trifles to the English stage,
but nothing that I should venture to compare with *The
Sign of the Cross*.   But if any critic is so wasteful of his
leisure as to compare *The Sign of the Cross* with *The Silver
King*, will he not discover in both plays a rich flow of pious
bathos, a tendency to holy-mouth diarrhœa, which he may
safely ascribe, in the one case to your pen, and in the other
to your influence?

"And so, my dear Barrett, as you wish to pose as the
author of *The Silver King*, let me assure you that the road
is straight before you.   Consider how great an ally you
have in the kindly affable carelessness of the playgoing
public, who only see what is placed before them, and have
always and everywhere seen your name announced in the

very largest capital letters in all the advertisements and programmes of *The Silver King*. Have you ever noticed how the public grow to associate a play, not with the man whose brain has produced it, but with the man who can manage to get his name plastered in the largest letters in connection with it? Believe me, my dear Barrett, having prompted me to write the former letter, you will now be a very foolish man if you do not from this time forth claim the virtual authorship of the piece. Rely upon my doing nothing to stop you. It will be rather awkward if by any chance the MS. of *The Silver King* should turn up. But that is in the last degree unlikely.

"Commending you,

"HENRY ARTHUR JONES."

"PS.—I hope you will excuse my saying a word upon your interpretation of the character of the Silver King. At the end of the first act you will remember that Wilfred Denver babbles the words 'I didn't do it!' over the dead body of Geoffrey Ware. Permit me to explain to you that these words are the involuntary jabbering protest of a stupefied, half drunken man, self-startled at the commission of a terrible crime, repugnant to his whole nature. They should be spoken in a horrified, involuntary whisper, and so spoken by an actor capable of realising the situation, I believe they would have immense effect. But you shout them at the top of your voice so that all Hatton Garden could hear, and the intelligent spectator asks 'Why?' The passage is not only robbed of its effect, but of its meaning. So much so, that I once heard two ladies talking of the scene as soon as the curtain had descended, and their comment was 'What ranting!' Alas, my dear Barrett, I could not contradict them! I hope you will take this suggestion in a kindly spirit, as showing that I am anxious that you should secure an intelligent interpretation of the part—a care I never took for myself when I was the reputed

author of the play.   There are several other passages in
the play which may be treated so as to convey that they
are serious, well-studied drama, or that they are mere
transpontine melodrama.   But in pointing them out to
you I fear I should be usurping the position of an author.
I beg you will excuse me."

From the earliest days of his friendship with Max Beerbohm, Henry Arthur had a high regard for his opinion.
He sent Max a copy of this letter to Wilson Barrett, and
received the following reply:

"Savile Club, W.

"18th October, 1899.

"My dear Mr. Jones,

"Poor Wilson Barrett!   Your letter was indeed a masterpiece of cruelty, and how the worthy gentleman survived it I cannot imagine.   I hope you will let me keep
the copy you sent me, if you have another of your own.   I
will of course keep it discreetly, for my own private enjoyment, and as a model to be copied if ever I embroil myself
with a fellow-creature. . . .

"Sincerely yours,

"Max Beerbohm."

I found this letter to Wilson Barrett after my father's
death, and, though I have made enquiries, I cannot find
any trace of the statement he mentions having written in
Mr. Barrett's dressing-room.   I think it possible it was a
rough draft of the letter to the *Era,* as I have not quoted
from that letter several scathing references which H. A. J.
made to other plays written by Herman, or to Herman's
attempt to be described as part author of another play by
Henry Arthur, in which he had no share at all.

In speaking to me about the discussions as to the authorship, my father said, "It got me angry.   I suppose I was

a young man with a swollen head—I'd had sleepless nights about it," and he added, "Herman did the end of the second act." An amusing cartoon appeared showing H. A. J. and Herman quarrelling about a cow, while Wilson Barrett was quietly milking it. He also told me that, of all his plays, *The Silver King* gave him the most trouble to write, "as I didn't know so much then about writing plays."

In speaking of his connection with Barrett my father said, "Barrett was a good fellow, he was very generous to his company. Perhaps I didn't treat him very well; after the success of *The Dancing Girl* he wanted me to do another play, but it was always Barrett the manager, Barrett the actor, Barrett the author." Even before the great success of *The Dancing Girl*, Barrett was anxious to produce another play by H. A. J. I imagine my father told him he no longer wished to write melodrama, as Barrett wrote to him in 1889 the following letter:

"DEAR JONES,

"I did not say a melodrama—but a play. Do not be unjust to *The Silver King*, it will outlive many a better praised work and continue to draw when they are forgotten. Your letter is not quite clear. You gave me to understand the last time we spoke together that you wished me back in a theatre of my own, and to write a play for me. Have you changed your mind? If so, why?

"If we continue as we have begun, we shall take the largest amount of money ever drawn from a dramatic entertainment in one week at this theatre.

"The new theatre will not be too large, or too small, for any good play. Do you fear this?

"When can I see you?

"Yours always,

"WILSON BARRETT."

H. A. J. said about Herman, "He was a very good-hearted man, very vain and weak." When he died my father purchased a grave for him in Kensal Green Cemetery. Just after Herman's death in 1894, his widow wrote a letter, published in the October number of the *Stage,* in which she gave eloquent testimony to the kindness and sympathy shown to her by my father and Augustus Moore.

The Silver King, which ran for 289 nights, was revived by Wilson Barrett several times, produced at Wallack's Theatre in New York in 1883, chosen by His Majesty King George in May 1914 for the command performance in aid of King George's Pension Fund for actors, and revived at the Strand Theatre in the same year with H. B. Irving as the Silver King.

The play was turned into a novel by Wilson Barrett, and again, recently, as a serial. It has been filmed twice. The early original but incomplete manuscript, which was discovered after his death, now belongs to the Bodleian Library.

In reasoned and critical opinion *The Silver King* will live as the classic melodrama of the nineteenth century.

CHAPTER VI

THE immense success of *The Silver King* freed my father from financial anxiety, and although, whenever he was suffering from nervous exhaustion, worry about his pecuniary position was a prominent symptom, and although in the last twenty-five years of his life he was often overdrawn at the bank, he was never other than well off from 1882 to the day of his death.

The moment he was released from any real concern for his material prospects, Henry Arthur devoted an ever-increasing proportion of his working hours to a ceaseless campaign by letters, articles in the papers, pamphlets, lectures, and speeches, on behalf of the great art he revered with every fibre of his being and served whole-heartedly and faithfully to the day of his death. He contended that the Drama was the highest and most difficult form of literature, and in the first twenty years of his career as a playwright he hammered away unceasingly in his efforts to get the general public to realise that the Drama is a part of literature. As he grew famous and came into contact with famous writers and men of letters, he made every endeavour to draw such men to the Theatre or to interest them still further in the Drama. Among those who were numbered among his friends, and with whom he corresponded and talked about the Theatre, and some of whom were present at his first nights, were Matthew Arnold, Thomas Hardy (who went to the pit for the first performance of *The Triumph of the Philistines*), Frederic Harrison, William Sharp, Swinburne, Watts-Dunton, H. D. Traill, Stopford Brooke, Mark Rutherford, Sir Edmund

51

Gosse, Sir Sidney Lee, Dr. Furnivall, Richard Whiteing, William Morris, and Sir James Knowles. Sir James often assured him that the pages of the *Nineteenth Century* were always at his disposal whenever he wished to write on the subject dearest to his heart—an offer of which he availed himself on several occasions.

In March 1883 he wrote to the *Era* in reply to a letter from Mr. Herman Merivale, in which the latter said, "Playgoers of to-day do not care for literature on the stage." My father wrote, "Yet they perversely throng to the Lyceum and make believe to like it," and he went on to say, "Have we not had nearly enough of these complaints of the dulness and stupidity and ignorance of the British playgoer? Although the Drama is still in a bad enough plight, are not things gradually improving? Have we not made great advances during the last ten years in plays, in criticisms, and, above all, in audiences? The old type of burlesque has long ago dragged its ribald and putrid body to the spital, and there died of senile gangrene; farcical comedy, getting wilder and wilder, has at length dashed its brainless feather-head against one of the posts of its numberless hide-and-seek entrances; sensation, like some huge porpoise cast upon the shore, lies puffing, and bloated, and sprawling, with nothing left it but to bellow its bad luck, and flounder deeper and deeper into the mud; and, further, it is rumoured that at the end of the run of *Iolanthe* Mr. Gilbert will cease to persuade people to nourish their brains by standing on their heads. . . .

"The truth is that audiences want literature, they want poetry, but they do not want unactable, intractable imitations of Shakespeare's form, without his vitality. They want life, they want reality; they demand that the characters they see on the stage shall be, not the ghostly abstractions of the study, but living, breathing human beings, with good warm red blood in their veins."

His first article, "The Theatre and the Mob," appeared

in the same year in the September number of the *Nineteenth Century*. He wrote: "A clever and thoughtful dramatist has lately complained that playgoers of to-day will not accept literature and poetry from modern authors. The question thus raised is too wide and complex to be settled by a definite 'Yes' or 'No.' . . . The great majority of playgoers never have come to the theatre, and in no period of time that can be safely reckoned upon are they likely to come to the theatre, for literature or poetry, for any kind of moral, artistic, or intellectual pastime. They come jaded from the impure air of shops, factories, and offices, from the hard stress of business, professional, or domestic duties, and they are incapable or impatient of the intellectual exertion and prolonged attention necessary to judge a serious work of art. . . . Milton's noble wish, 'Fit audience let me find though few,' must always be held in scornful reprobation by theatrical managers and dramatic authors. . . ."

He went on to say that the standard of dramatic work had been lowered by the general desire to strike the fancy of the public immediately.

"Thus, on enquiring why we have no national drama at all worthy of the name, at all to be compared with the advances we have made in the sister arts of poetry, music, and painting, we are met first of all by the fact that the drama is not merely an art, but it is also a competitor of music halls, circuses, Madame Tussaud's, the Westminster Aquarium, and the Argyll Rooms. It is a hybrid, an unwieldy Siamese Twin, with two bodies, two heads, two minds, two dispositions, all of them, for the present, vitally connected. And one of these two bodies, dramatic art, is lean and pinched and starving, and has to drag about with it, wherever it goes, its fat, puffy, unwholesome, dropsical brother, popular amusement. And neither of them goes its own proper way in the world to its own proper end, but they twain waddle on in a path that leads nowhere in particular, the resultant of their several luggings and tuggings at each other." To the end of his life he always insisted upon this double aspect of the drama, as a fine art and as mere popular amusement.

"But the demand for truth, for reality, for thought, for poetry, for all kinds of noble and inspiring examples, difficult as it may be to rear at the first, is yet perennial, constant, assured, and eternally fruitful. Every position of honour, every position really worth coveting in the dramatic world to-day, whether of manager, or actor, or author, has been gained, not by the base idea of catering for every passing appetite of the multitude, but by unflagging appeals to the nobler instincts of the few, by coaxing, by watching, by alluring, by guiding, by resolutely refusing to pander to the public. . . .

"Then we have a great body of newspaper critics, cultured, devoted, alert, earnest, enthusiastic, generous, warmly appreciative of every new piece that shows the merest mustard-seed of promise. . . .

"Best, most hopeful, most cheering sign of all, we have on our first nights, interspersed with perhaps a few ticklish but easily quieted elements of mischief, that serried pack of bright, earnest, intelligent faces in the first row of the pit, lovers of the drama for the drama's sake, whose self-appointed duty it is to give a loud and unmistakable verdict of approval or condemnation. In reply to the charges of ill-conduct and rowdyism brought against this body it may be mentioned that though many bad plays have been rightly and necessarily condemned by them, yet so far as the memory of an old first-nighter may serve, no play within this generation has been damned on its first act, however bad."

From his earliest days as a member of the pit and gallery, Henry Arthur had always a warm affection for, and an understanding of, that most important section of the theatre-going public. In his later years he was keenly interested in the Gallery First Nighters' Club, and often enjoyed a chat with Leslie Bloom, who was President of the club for several years, and other enthusiastic members. It gave him great pleasure when the club held a dinner in his honour in January 1924.   He had a bad throat and was forbidden by his doctor to make a speech, but he indulged in one or two reminiscences.   Speaking of his great admiration for Adelaide Neilson, he said: "I remember sitting with a friend of mine in the front row of the pit for Adelaide Neilson's benefit in *As You Like It,* and how we both walked home afterwards in a state of ecstasy, my friend being so enthused that in his abstraction he descended the steps of London Bridge on his anatomy, bumping down every step.   Has any member of this club done as much for Shakespeare?"   He was not always in sympathy with the judgment of the pit and gallery; it is recorded of him that he was present at the first night of somebody else's play, and, when the pit booed it, H. A. J. turned round in his stall and booed and hissed the pittites.

I have quoted extensively from his article in the *Nineteenth Century,* because the sentiments expressed by my father in 1883 (notably the paragraph about the Siamese Twins and the one immediately following) were to remain unaltered, save in detail, throughout his life; though his views on the drama as a great art were to gather deeper conviction and purpose and to become stronger as he grew older and more experienced.   The article is interesting as an early example of his fine vigorous prose and as a definite advance in the quality of his writing.   It was reviewed very favourably in several papers.

In a long letter written in 1918 to his dear and valued friend Mr. M. H. Spielmann, he summed up his views on the Drama thus:

"24th January, 1918.

" . . . I must thank you again very warmly for the encouragement you have given me.   Actors often say that they can play much better if they know that one person in the audience is watching them with sympathy.   Your letters have had a like effect on me.   Apart from my plays, I know that I have shown in my essays and lectures the only way that leads to a development of a worthy national drama.

"(1) The modern drama must be recognised as a branch of English literature, and English men of letters must know and study and love it, not only in books but in the *theatre,* and must make their influence felt there.

"(2) The *drama* must be seen to be in many ways opposed to the *theatre,* and must no longer be considered by playgoers as a negligible appurtenance to the theatre.

"(3) Actors and actor-managers can never reform the *drama.*   It is not their business, nor is it their interest to do so.   But they can render the drama some useful service at times.   They can also do the drama an immense injury if they are allowed, as they have been during the last 15 years or so, to get the upper hand of the drama, and pursue their own aims.

"(4) The drama will only flourish when the author has authority and vogue with the great play-going public, and when he is in supreme command of his own work.

"(5) The drama must be recognised as something different from popular entertainment, although it must always supply popular entertainment. On the actual stage there will never be a clear line between them.   But it must be judged from a different standpoint from popular entertainment and with a different measure—it must be judged and criticised as a fine art.

"(6) The drama should be encouraged and supported by Government and the municipalities, but care must be taken to endow only very charily and with the utmost circumspection, and only according to the growing knowledge and taste of the general public.   It will, I think, be hopeless to endow a national theatre for many years to come.

"(7) Plays must be read by playgoers—a habit of play-reading must be cultivated, as in France.

"All these, and many other things, I have been saying to the English public for more than 35 years, not because I wanted to write essays and lectures, but because I found myself hampered in my play-writing at every step, by the conditions prevailing in the English Theatre, and by the general want of care and knowledge on the subject. And so I keep on writing, while our present civilisation is breaking up; visibly, rapidly breaking up. And much that I have written may be as foreign to the conditions of 1930 as the fierce discussion as to how many angels can dance on the point of a needle. But I do know that I have set forth a few great rules that are the foundations of any possible school of drama. . . .

"I couldn't give the time and patience to write a novel. I see all life in terms and forms of drama, and this I think would be evident in any novel I might write. After 40 years carefully training myself for drama I cannot adopt what would be new and irksome methods. Beside, the delight of play-writing lies in its difficulty compared with the novel. There is no craft so difficult as playwriting. There is scarcely any 'craft' in novel-writing. It takes no, or little, apprenticeship. Almost anybody, without practice, could write one good, or at least passable, novel. I once tried to persuade Thomas Hardy to write a play, for he is a potential dramatist. I should have been glad to give him any technical advice. 'Hardy,' I said, 'do write a play. Novel writing is *unskilled* labour.' And so it is. Play-writing is in itself a higher and finer art, because its limitations are so many, and so severe. . . ."

All his life Henry Arthur took as much pains over writing his articles, pamphlets, lectures, and speeches as he did over the writing of his plays; sometimes he gave more thought and care to an article than he did to a play, because in play-writing, he would say, the dialogue "wrote itself"—he frequently wrote at a white heat, especially the strong scenes; this was never the case with his essay-writing. There is the following illuminating paragraph in his books of Notes, "Sometimes the words come galloping and catch the wind, and make my sentence perfect sense and perfect music. Sometimes they won't come at all. That just exact word—why won't it come? I fidget, and I fidget, and I fidget, and it will not come. Is it in the dictionary? In the thesaurus? No. Is it in Shakespeare, in Milton? No. Can't I pick it up in the street? No. In American slang? No. Is there such a word? I don't believe there is. Then I must coin it. No, that would be bad philological manners. I should only encumber the English language with another barbarism. Am I quite sure that I know what I want to say? Let me dwell on that. Am I quite sure that it is worth saying? Let me dwell even more on that. Yes—I've got something to say. Will say it. Let me think of what I've got to say and not about myself. Ah, here come the words trippingly off my pen; and that very right word. Why, it was in my head all the time."

I have known my father give a whole morning to the writing of one sentence. He told me a very curious and interesting fact in connection with whatever he wrote, even if it was only a letter: as he wrote them down he always heard the words in his head as distinctly as if they were being spoken aloud.

In 1884 he contributed a short article on how he wrote his plays to one of the London newspapers.

He said: "A dramatist will never draw characters of vital force and lastingness except they belong to the actual life that he has known and studied and loved—his own village, his own city, his own country. Without this knowledge of life and men, however successful his play may be, his characters will never be more than bloodless phantoms of his fancy, or at best stage-puppets, reeking of the theatre. Thirdly, some knowledge of the best literature, not necessarily that of a profound scholar, but at least enough to give a literary touch and value to his work. Without this last acquirement his play will be a string of slipshod, commonplace dialogues, situations, and effects, a compilation neither literature nor art, that can never hope to

> . . . *ascend to fame's immortal house,*
> *Or banquet in bright honour's burnished hall.*

" . . . Art should teach as nature teaches—implicitly, silently, with unobvious, far-removed results. . . .

"The strong, passionate scenes I generally write off at a dash when I feel in the right mood, after perhaps some days of brooding. And except cutting them down I rarely alter them much. The comedy scenes I return to and polish and repolish many times. I try to avoid all delay in unfolding the story, especially at starting. An audience likes to see a play roll off instantly with self-sustaining action as soon as the curtain goes up. . . . I think the drift of every play should be towards the ascension of human nature, and not towards its declension. . . . Shakespeare, 'Sovereign master over wrack,' is our eternal model in this respect. While no human heart is by him left unsearched, no passion untouched, no vice unpainted or coloured to look like virtue, no abyss of evil left unsounded, what a final impression does his whole work leave of a sane, joyous, well-ordered world."

It gave him keen and lasting pleasure when he received the following letter from Robert Louis Stevenson, who had read his paper:

"Braillie Tower,
"Branksome Park,
"Bournemouth.
"30th December, 1884.

"DEAR SIR,

"I am so accustomed to hear nonsense spoken about all the arts, and the drama in particular, that I cannot refrain from saying thank you for your paper. In my answer to Mr. James, in the December *Longman*, you may see that I have merely touched, I think in a parenthesis, on the Drama; but I believe enough was said to indicate our agreement in essentials.

"Wishing you power and health to further enunciate and to act upon these principles, believe me, dear sir,

"Yours truly,

"ROBERT LOUIS STEVENSON."

In 1887 Mrs. Stevenson, who was in London, went to the first night of *Hard Hit* with my parents. Shortly after the production my father received the following delightful letters from R. L. S. and his wife, written on the same sheet of notepaper:

"Bournemouth.

"DEAR MR. JONES,

"Nothing but the beastly state of my health would have made me so much a laggard in thanking you for your kindness to Mrs. Stevenson. She enjoyed herself greatly. She tells me there is some hope of your coming down here. Please do; it will give me great pleasure. I know we have a thousand things to say; for though a duffer, I am an ardent theorist about the stage—and from what I learn from Mrs. Stevenson, I do not believe we shall quarrel.

"Yours very truly,

"ROBERT LOUIS STEVENSON.

"If I am illegible, please remember I write in bed."

"DEAR MR. JONES,

"I should have written before to thank you for your kindness to me, but not only did I find Mr. Stevenson very ill, but I have been not much better myself. If you could do no more than run down on a Saturday night to return on Monday morning it would be a great pleasure to us both. Please present my regards to Mrs. Jones and her sister (whose name escaped me) and say how sorry I was not to be able to call upon them before leaving London, but I had to be off on the first train next morning. It was very kind of them to let me join them in their box on a 'first night.' I hope all goes as well with the play as things promised. How fortunate you were to have two such actors as Mr. Tree and Mr. Willard; such a villain as Mr. Tree was almost too irresistible. I do not see how the most virtuous of heroines could withstand his charm and elegance.

"With many thanks, yours truly,

"F. DE V. STEVENSON."

For some little time after the success of *The Silver King* my father continued to work in collaboration with Herman and Wilson Barrett. He would not have objected to the term "hack-work" as applied to *Breaking a Butterfly*, a free adaption from Ibsen's *A Doll's House*, which he wrote in collaboration with Herman. It was produced at the Prince's Theatre on 3rd March, 1884, and received some very good notices. H. A. J. always became very indignant when anyone said he had been influenced by Ibsen. He knew very little of the great dramatist's plays till he was long past middle age, and he resented the imputation that his work had been guided or moulded in any way by Ibsen. In 1928, speaking of Ibsen, he said to me, "Every now and then he flashes out a bit of imagination, which is his only value to me."

In 1924 he wrote to Mr. James Waldo Fawcett repudiating a suggestion that Ibsen had influenced him when he was writing *Saints and Sinners.*   He said:

"*3rd September, 1924.*
"In reply to yours relating to the question of Ibsen's influence on *Saints and Sinners:*

"I cannot remember when I first read *Pillars of Society,* and I am not sure whether I saw the play when it was done for a matinée in 1880.   I am under the impression that I did see this single performance; but I think I may safely say that I was not indebted to Ibsen's *Pillars of Society* for the drift and bearing of *Saint and Sinners.*

"The setting in my play was mainly that of my own early life in a small English Dissenting community, and the view that I took of English middle-class life was that of Matthew Arnold.   If you read his prose writings, you will note their influence on *Saints and Sinners.*

"I should not in the least mind acknowledging my indebtedness to Ibsen, if I thought I owed anything to him; but, although it has often been supposed that Ibsen influenced me in my work, I think I should have written very much the same plays if he had not existed.   At the same time, I own to a great admiration for the imaginative side of Ibsen's work, and for his searching veracity."

In 1891, he made a public protest against "a school of modern realism which founded dramas on disease, ugliness, and vice," a direct reference to Ibsen's influence on the English Theatre.

Chatterton, a one-act drama, written by my father and H. A. Herman, was produced at the Princess's Theatre on the afternoon of 22nd May, 1884.   Wilson Barrett played the leading rôle, and received magnificent notices for his performance, while the criticisms of the play were, with few exceptions, very favourable.   My father told me,

"Herman and I made a present of *Chatterton* to Barrett in return for his kindness."

Although Matthew Arnold criticised the theme of the play, my father was delighted when he received the following letter:

> "Athenæum Club,
> "Pall Mall.
> "*29th May, 1884.*

"MY DEAR SIR,

"I have been travelling about, or I should have written before to thank you for the stalls, and to say that there was good writing in *Chatterton*, and good acting in Mr. Wilson Barrett's interpretation of the part, but the thing is too painful. I feel so strongly the defects of a situation where 'everything is to be endured, nothing to be done,' that I suppressed a dramatic sketch of my own on that account; and though I afterwards restored it at Mr. Browning's request, I restored it for reading only. I would never have restored it for representation.

> "Very truly yours,
> "MATTHEW ARNOLD."

Saints and Sinners, a five-act drama, was produced at the Vaudeville Theatre by Tom Thorne in September 1884. My father was the sole author. It is the story of an old Nonconformist minister, Jacob Fletcher. Rather than allow one of his parishioners, a widow, to be turned out of her home, he faces the scandal of his daughter's seduction being made public. In consequence of this exposure he is obliged to resign his living, but even in poverty and disgrace he shelters and protects his greatest enemy, who has been instrumental in forcing his resignation. The play received a very mixed reception, as some of the pit and other parts of the house objected to the scriptural quotations used by the characters, and the audience hissed and booed loudly.   The notices were favourable on the whole, the papers agreeing that the work was sincere, but nearly all the reviews commented unfavourably on the use of quotations from the Bible.   My father wrote the following letter to the dramatic critic of the *Daily News,* in which it appeared on 29th September, 1884:

"DEAR SIR,

"I am unwilling to write to the newspapers and defend myself against the charges of irreverence which have been so freely flung at me, but I should like it to be known that in *Saints and Sinners* I intended no offence to religious susceptibilities.   At the same time I can see no reason why large fields of modern life should be closed to treatment on the stage merely because the truthful portraiture of them is unpalatable to the *unco guid.*   Nor do I think the *unco guid* have any right to cry to the dramatist 'hands off us!' I will vouch for the absolute faithfulness of the types of character I have presented in 'Hoggard' and 'Prabble' and for their wide dispersion among the Dissenting classes. I can only urge in my defence a couplet from Burns:

> *There's none ever feared*
> *The truth should be heard*
> *But they whom the truth would indite . . .*

"Faithfully yours,
"HENRY ARTHUR JONES."

My father replied finally to the inordinate criticism of his use of Biblical quotations in an article entitled "Religion and the Stage," which appeared in the *Nineteenth Century* for January 1885.   In this article he says:

"But when a playwright is challenged by a part of a first-night audience as to his right to depict any section of the community, or rather as to his right to depict them truthfully, and make them use the language that is natural to them . . . in such a case he may perhaps be permitted a word of apology and explanation upon the ground that, small and unimportant as the individual case may be, and not in itself worth a moment's consideration, yet, seeing that the meanest matters may contain the widest issues, the entire question of the future development of the English Drama and its right to press on and possess itself of the whole of human life, is more or less raised when any veto is placed, or sought to be placed, upon the dramatist's perfect freedom of choice of subject, persons, place, and mode of treatment. . . . It is for those who would deny to the dramatists the right to depict religious life on the stage, to show either that religion has become a quite un-essential and useless portion of human life, and is effete and defunct and has no bearing upon character in England to-day, in which case the playwright can afford to treat it as the naturalist does an organ that has lapsed into a rudi-mentary state, or it is for them to show why religion should not occupy the same part in the dramatist's scheme and view of human life as it is supposed to do in the outer world around him—shall we say a seventh. . . .

"The mere mention of *Tartuffe* and its acknowledged position as one of the glories and masterpieces of universal dramatic literature, is a sufficient reply, one would think, to all who urge that it is not lawful to treat religion upon the stage. The play and Molière's preface to it remain as a triumphant assertion for all time of the sovereignty of the Drama in its own domain. And that domain is the whole of the nature, and heart, and passions, and conduct of men. . . . The quotation upon the stage by any char-acter of any portion of the noblest example of our noble literature, could never have sounded strange in modern ears until the debts of our language to those writings had been forgotten and annulled by those who would rather see our stately and beautiful mother-tongue turned into the roaring, gossiping, evil-speaking trollops of every vile resort, than employed as the mouthpiece and bearer of any intelligible message to mankind."

Referring to this article, Mark Rutherford wrote to my father:

"11th January, 1885.

"My dear Mr. Jones,

"I have read the article in the *Nineteenth Century* which you were kind enough to send me. I need hardly say that I agree with it, but nevertheless I doubt very much if people will practically believe it. It is a curious thing that, as religion becomes more unreal and divorced from daily life, people become more hypocritically sensitive to any admixture of the two. A man, who, like our ordinary Englishman, goes to his church once on Sunday and denies his God all through the week, casts up his eyes if a Biblical phrase is introduced into common conversation and calls it profane. If his Bible were part of himself it would enter into all his existence and give point even to his jests. I honour you for the enterprise upon which you are bound and hope you will prosper.

"I went to see Wilson Barrett's *Hamlet*. It was a careful, honest performance and as good as it could be within the limits of his powers. It was not a philosophic study, and he is unable to depict and make explicable by his acting that profound moody contemplativeness which flashes into such wild passion. The real tragedy of Hamlet is that, being born a meditative thinker, a duty is imposed upon him of exacting a bloody revenge. The conflict, the tumult, the madness thence arising are the whole secret. However, I am not going to expound to *you* of all men in the world a theory of Hamlet. No actor I often think can express *all* Hamlet—we must be satisfied if each one gives us a bit. . . .

"Faithfully yours,

"W. Hale-White

"(Mark Rutherford)."

This controversy as to religious manners and customs being depicted on the stage was revived by the church scene in *Michael and His Lost Angel*. Mr. Bernard Shaw proved a redoubtable champion of the dramatist's right to depict any form of religious life in his plays.

In 1920 my father and I went to the first night of **Mr. W. S. Maugham's** fine play, *The Unknown*. At the end of the second act, after Miss Haidée Wright's magnificent outburst, "Who will forgive God," H. A. J. and Dame Madge Kendal, who was near us, were in tears, and as he turned to me, whilst applauding heartily, he said, "And I was hissed on the first night of *Saints and Sinners* for a few scripture quotations." He told me that he drew the character of Hoggard from his Uncle Thomas, in whose shop he worked at Ramsgate; he said, "He didn't know I made use of him afterwards in *Saints and Sinners*." Matthew Arnold went to see the play in December, and wrote to my father as follows:

"The Athenæum,
"Pall Mall.
"*23rd December, 1884.*

"MY DEAR SIR,

"I went to see *Saints and Sinners,* and my interest was kept up throughout, as I expected. You have remarkably the art—so valuable in drama—of exciting interest and sustaining it. The piece is full of good and telling things, and one cannot watch the audience without seeing that by strokes of this kind faith in the middle-class fetish is weakened, however slowly, as it could be in no other way. I must add that I dislike seduction dramas (even in *Faust* the feeling tells with me), and that the marriage of the heroine with her farmer does not please me as a dénouement. Your representative middle-class man was well drawn and excellently acted.

"Very truly yours,
"MATTHEW ARNOLD."

In spite of the unfavourable reception and comments, *Saints and Sinners* ran for 182 nights.   It was produced in New York, at the Madison Square Theatre, in 1885, and revived by Tom Thorne at the Vaudeville Theatre in 1892. When rehearsals were in progress at this theatre, my father and Tom Thorne had some difficulty, if they pronounced the name correctly, in getting the cabmen to understand which theatre they wanted to go to; so they always said, "To the Vorderville."   One day, H. A. J., on calling this out, was somewhat taken aback when the cabby said, "Do you mean the Vaudeville, sir?"

Saints and Sinners was published by Macmillan's in 1891, and was the first of his plays to be made available for reading by the general public.   In printing it, Henry Arthur was the first English dramatist to take advantage of the passing of the American Copyright Law.   Hitherto, as has here been said, the publication of an English play had meant the forfeiture of the American stage rights. My father always agreed that the title was one of the best he ever found, but he was not particularly fond of the play. From the production of *Saints and Sinners* onwards, notices of my father's plays produced in London appeared in many American papers—a sure sign of the foothold he had gained in the drama of the English-speaking world.

In October 1884, Henry Arthur made his first public speech, an address on "The Modern Drama," which he delivered at the opening of the Playgoers' Club.   He said the two tests to be applied to any play were, "Does it truly paint character?" and "Is it literature?"   In the next few years he lectured several times on the Drama in London, Newcastle, and Manchester, in addition to writing various letters and articles on the same subject.   His central theme was always an insistence that the Drama should be regarded as a part of literature, and a clear and definite distinction made between the Drama and mere popular amusement.   In 1889 he responded for the toast of the

Drama at the Royal General Theatrical Fund Dinner. In his speech he quoted Swinburne, who said that, "The greatest glory of England is her literature, and the greatest glory of her literature is her Drama," and he went on to say that only ten years previously Matthew Arnold had said, "In England we have no drama at all."

In general my father received great praise for his fearless and incessant campaign on behalf of the elevation of the Drama, but there were also many writers who attacked and jibed at him, an occasional under-current of criticism which resented the dogmatism of his views and the position he had attained as a spokesman for the more thoughtful and intelligent section of theatre-goers. The English Drama and the English stage have made great progress and travelled so far since those early days, that few playgoers to-day, and not even all thoughtful critics, realise the appalling trash presented on the boards of most English theatres when my father started writing for the stage, and for a decade after his first appearance as a dramatist. His teaching and his work have an honourable share in the influence which has brought about the higher level of modern dramatic work, compared with that of the seventies and eighties of the last century.

Written in collaboration with Wilson Barrett, *Hoodman Blind* was produced at the Princess's Theatre on 18th August, 1885. The play ran for 172 nights and was revived by Wilson Barrett in 1892. In February 1886 *The Lord Harry*, by the same collaborators, was produced at the Princess's Theatre. It had some good notices, but its reception was not enthusiastic. My father stated his opinion very frankly about these plays in the following letter to Wilson Barrett:

"17th June, 1886.

"DEAR BARRETT,

"I cannot help feeling that *Hoodman Blind* and *The Lord Harry* are not good plays, that they are not nearly such good work as I could have done, and have done on my own account. And when other people see this and say it, how can I contradict them and defend the system that produced them? Frankly, I think that the year I spent in writing them was, so far as any artistic end is concerned, quite waste time. If I take up my pen at all in this matter, I shall be obliged to state my opinion of these plays and I am sure I shall only make matters worse. You know that I told you before *The Lord Harry* was begun, that there wasn't an idea in it. However, I am quite willing to accept the verdict and to let things alone. So far as your motives are concerned you must see that this is a matter upon which no one can defend you so well as yourself. I am quite determined I won't be dragged into another row if I can help it, but if I have to raise my voice in this controversy it must be on the side of perfect freedom for the dramatic author to work upon his own ideas, and not upon other people's.

"Always yours,
"HENRY ARTHUR JONES."

It had always irked him to write in collaboration, and three years earlier he had written to Barrett refusing to collaborate in another play with Herman. The deep love Henry Arthur always felt for the children of his brain is revealed in the following illuminating letter:

"*5th July, 1883.*

"MY DEAR BARRETT,

"I have just written 'curtain' to the 5th act—you must not think me perverse in this business, you must not indeed —if you knew how I loved the characters I have drawn, you would understand how impossible it is for me to let anybody else have the handling of them. I will gladly accept any suggestion from whatever quarter, and incorporate it in my work, but I cannot let anybody else touch the men and women I have created—I know I am jealous in this matter—I cannot help it. I would rather sweat my heart out than let anybody else come between me and my puppets. If I have read your aims aright, you are trying to make the Princess's Theatre the home of an English literary drama—if this were a Drury Lane piece there would be some reason in the manager, scene-shifter, and devil-knows-who claiming part-authorship, but in a drama that pretends to be a piece of literature how dare anybody pretend to have written it but the man who has put his heart and soul and brains into it? . . .

> "Always faithfully yours,
> "HENRY A. JONES."

With the production of *A Noble Vagabond* at the Princess's Theatre on 22nd December, 1886, Henry Arthur's long and extremely successful connection with Wilson Barrett came to an end. Dorothy Dene, who played the heroine in *A Noble Vagabond,* had been a model of Lord Leighton's. She was a charming as well as a beautiful woman, and my parents were delighted when she went to stay with them at Chalfont. Charles Warner, who played the Noble Vagabond, was a great friend of my father's, and stayed at Chalfont frequently. The notices were bad, and the play received a terrific slating from Clement Scott. William Archer, in the *Pall Mall Gazette,* wrote an almost equally strong criticism in defence of the play. My father often said to me, "A bad notice from Clement Scott would send more people to see a play than a good notice from many of the other critics," and on one occasion, "Clement had a real love of the theatre. We always used to say a bad notice from Clement, however damning, would send more people to the theatre than the best notice by Archer —he was a cold creature." In speaking of the failure of *A Noble Vagabond* in connection with his friendship and admiration for William Gillette, H. A. J. said to me,

"When Gillette came along with *Held By The Enemy* and I'd got the Princess's with *A Noble Vagabond,* oh! I was shivering for the little money I'd got, and then his play was a big success, so I owe him a great debt of gratitude." I believe that, in addition to receiving a good rental for the theatre, my father also received a share in the profits from Mr. Gillette's play.

CHAPTER VII

In 1884 my father removed to Hill House, Chalfont St. Peter, where he remained for the next three years. In the same year he paid his first visit to the South of France with Tom Thorne. The place and climate delighted him, and he went to the South nearly every succeeding year until 1914. He wrote many of his plays at Nice and Grasse.

In 1885 he went to America for the production of *Saints and Sinners*. It was the first of many trips. He stayed only five weeks, but the liking he felt for America and the Americans was to develop into a deep and lasting love and admiration for the country and her people.

He made many friends at the great Universities—Harvard, Yale, and Columbia; among those he knew well were President Nicholas Murray Butler of Columbia, President Lowell of Harvard, and President Hadley of Yale. He delighted to tell the following story about President Hadley, a very lovable personality, with a slight but most engaging stutter. I believe I am correct in saying that at Yale there is not a regular preacher and that preachers of all denominations are welcome; one Sunday it might be an Episcopalian, the next a Presbyterian or a Roman Catholic. An eminent divine who was noted for the wearisome length of his sermons was due to preach; he said to President Hadley just before the service, "May I enquire the length of time set aside for my discourse, because I have very weighty and important matters to deal with?" The reply was, "T-t-there is n-no set t-time for the sermon, b-bu-but we have a tradition souls aren't saved after t-t-twenty minutes."

Amongst his many friends in the American theatrical world, both men and women, I think he was fonder of Charles Frohman than of anyone else. He used to say, "a great little man," and he was always thankful to remember he was able to pay a last tribute of affection and respect to his friend's memory when he acted as a pall-bearer at his funeral.

He knew and entertained over here all the distinguished American ambassadors from John Hay onwards. He would remind me how John Hay used to tell him that when he was in Washington he would go to the White House and back to the room he used to occupy as Abraham Lincoln's secretary, and muse over the old days. In this connection my father said that he remembered very vividly hearing the news of Lincoln's assassination, and that, owing to the fact that the cable was not in working order, no one in Europe knew whether Lincoln had survived, until the next boat arrived ten days later—and with what increasing excitement all England waited for news!

On one of H. A. J.'s trips to America, just as the ship was picking up the pilot, an Englishman standing near him said that he had made only two previous trips to America; on the first occasion, as the ship steamed in, those on board received the news of President Garfield's assassination, and on the second the pilot announced the assassination of President McKinley. An American standing near said, "Guess it would pay our country to keep you out of America."

Hard Hit, produced on 17th January, 1887, at the Haymarket Theatre, was the first of many plays in which my father was associated with Beerbohm Tree at this famous playhouse. My father's position in the English Theatre at this time was summed up by *The Times*, which said, "We hear much of the dearth of dramatics. The complaint is one which is probably as old as the stage itself; but some colour would certainly seem to be lent to it by the fact that at the present moment the London theatres are largely dependent upon the literary efforts of Mr. H. A. Jones."

My father's mother died on 22nd April, 1887. She had been ailing for a long time, and the end was expected. Her son went down to see her a few days before she died, but she seemed in no immediate danger, and he returned to London. He felt his mother's death very keenly—more deeply, I think, than did any other member of her family. H. A. J. found it difficult to shake off his grief, and that summer of 1887 he went with his wife for a much needed holiday to Bude, a return to his beloved West Country. On the journey down the train pulled up for a few minutes; workmen on the line were singing the following ditty— he never forgot the words and tune, and we often made him sing them to us:

> *Then kiss me, oh, kiss me, dear mother,*
> *Oh, weep not, oh, weep not for me;*
> *There's a stormy cloud hangs o'er old England;*
> *Yes, fortune's across the blue sea.*

While he was still in bed after his severe operation in 1926, he sang this song to his granddaughter Jean, and added, "So perhaps they had labour troubles in those days." In speaking of this ditty he told us that W. S. Gilbert declared that he heard Cornish fishermen singing "I have a song to sing-o," and that he took the words and tune and made them into the famous song in *The Yeoman of the Guard.*

He would tell us, too, of another incident which occurred during this holiday. Returning from a very long walk one very hot August morning, he noticed a crowd near the canal bank, and, on enquiry, was informed that it was occasioned by a man who had been rescued from drowning and was still unconscious, though desperate efforts were being made to revive him. H. A. J. rushed off up the hill to his lodgings, and returned at full speed with a small flask of brandy, which he proffered to those attending to the unconscious man. His offer was refused for the moment, so he withdrew to the outskirts of the crowd. A man near him said, "Excuse me, sir, but I see you have a restorative, and all this commotion and the sight of the poor creature has upset me dreadfully. May I have a drink?" My father refused with great indignation, "Certainly not, I am surprised at your suggestion—why the poor man may need it at any moment." Within a minute or two he was overcome himself by the heat and excitement, and, slinking behind the nearest tree, he tossed off the contents of the flask.

On 22nd November, 1887, *Heart of Hearts* was produced at a matinée performance at the Vaudeville Theatre, with Tom Thorne in the leading part. The notices were very good, and the play was immediately put into the evening bill. The week after production Paul Merritt wrote a letter to the *Era* in which he claimed that my father had copied nearly all the incidents from a play by him called *The King of Diamonds,* produced at the Surrey Theatre in 1884. H. A. J. wrote to Mr. Merritt repudiating the suggestion in the strongest terms; he gave his word of honour that he had never seen the piece or heard any account of it. How many times have I heard my father say, "God sends me more plots than I know what to do with"; and after his collaboration with Herman and Wilson Barrett he refused emphatically to collaborate with anyone. Mr. George Moore wrote to him several times that he had the plot of a very fine play he wanted to write with Henry' Arthur. At last my father saw him and told him he did not wish to hear the story, as he had so many ideas of his own, but Mr. George Moore was very insistent and would not be denied. His story was that of a very rare and lovely creature married to a man who did not in the least understand her; she meets her soul-mate, also a rare and beautiful character, and after prolonged moral struggles they elope together. "Well?" said George Moore at the end of the recital of his plot. "Well," replied my father, "do you know I think it is a situation you could handle much better than I can."

In 1887, Henry Arthur moved to Townshend House, Regent's Park. He was to spend the fourteen happiest years of his life in this old house, years of almost unbroken success with *The Middleman, Judah, The Dancing Girl, The Masqueraders, The Case of Rebellious Susan, The Liars,* and *Mrs. Dane's Defence,* while his two greatest failures, *Michael and His Lost Angel* and *The Tempter,* were as memorable as any success.

H. A. J. and all his family were fonder of Townshend House than of any other house he lived in. It had been the home of Sir Laurence Alma-Tadema, R.A., who had painted several parts of the house; in my mother's boudoir was an inscription "Where friends meet hearts warm," and a magnificent painted ceiling in my father's study. An amusing incident occurred the first week after moving in. The bath was out of order and a plumber had been sent for. A tall, dark, good-looking foreign man called, and, when the maid opened the door, he held out his hand and said, "Seeven and siskpence." My mother was told, and she said, "It's absurd; the man must see the bath first; he can't know how much the repairs will cost until he has seen what is wrong; take him upstairs." The man, still muttering "Seeven and siskpence," was led protesting to the bathroom, and the door closed upon him. After an interval he re-appeared, and eventually disappeared, still begging for "Seeven and siskpence." We discovered later he was a model of Alma-Tadema's who had called for payment.

Wealth was produced at the Haymarket on 27th April, 1889. Matthew Ruddock, the principal character in *Wealth,* is a wealthy iron-master. He has no son, and is anxious that his daughter Edith should marry a favourite nephew, John Ruddock, who will inherit his business. Edith loves Paul Davoren, a rival iron-master, and despises John, who is a worthless character. Matthew gives a party to announce his daughter's betrothal to John, and there is a tremendous scene when John interrupts Matthew and tells the assembled guests of Edith's love for Paul. The old man turns his daughter out of the house. John obtains a hold on Ruddock, persuades him to speculate, and under the strain of the break with his daughter his mind gives way, and he imagines alternately that he is as rich as Crœsus and as poor as Job. Edith, happily married, returns to her dying father, who in a last short lucid interval blesses her and her husband, leaving them his property.

Most of the notices were luke-warm in their praise, though they spoke of the part of Matthew Ruddock as "a fine psychological study," admirably played by Beerbohm Tree. My father valued Watts-Dunton's opinion very highly, and after the bad notices given to the play he was much heartened when he received the following letter:

"The Pines,
"Putney Hill.

"MY DEAR JONES,

"Interesting as was the play to me, I fear the newspaper folk are right in saying the general public demand something more amusing or more romantic. I should much like to see it again one day next week. . . . Of course, there are scenes in it of immense power wonderfully rendered by Tree, scenes which, when a *New Way to Pay Old Debts* was produced, would have met with nothing but applause; but other times, other manners and tastes. It is a critical canon of mine that once make your characters interesting, and whatever afterwards shall happen to them will become interesting, and that no other source of vital interest is possible in art. Unromantic characters such as Ruddock do not, it seems, interest contemporary audiences, however firmly delineated. At least so I gather from the papers. Perhaps, however, the truth is otherwise after all and the piece really is taking with the public. I sincerely hope it is.

"With all best wishes, in which Swinburne joins,

"Yours ever,

"THEODORE WATTS."

Wealth was successfully produced in New York, and the play was translated after the production of *The Middle-man,* and produced in Holland, Belgium, Denmark, Austria, and Germany.

In February 1889, my father lectured at the New Islington Hall on behalf of the Ancoats Recreation Movement. He borrowed the title of his lecture, "White and Blue," from Rabelais, one of his favourite authors. Gargantua's colours were white and blue, the white signifying gladness, pleasure, delight, and rejoicing, and the blue, heavenly things. H. A. J. held that art should possess, first, gladness, delight, and rejoicing, and, secondly, mystery, exaltation, prophecy, and spirituality. He went on to plead with his audience not to indulge their desires in debased forms of amusement, or they would rob themselves of the power of enjoying healthy wit and humour. The lecture was widely reported, and the *Globe,* in commenting on H. A. J.'s opinions, said, "It is at least doubtful if the stage has any duty at all." My father replied to this article in a letter in which he said, "Nothing could be more curiously illustrative of the condition to which the modern stage has sunk than the question whether the calling once practised by the greatest Englishman who ever lived has any responsibilities at all, whether the man whose professed business it is to put on the modern stage some sort of a picture of human life has any need to trouble himself whether he does it truthfully or untruthfully, profoundly or superficially, carelessly or well. Because, if he has any responsibilities in these matters, surely they constitute the 'duty' of his profession in the strictest and every sense of the word. But, as you say, and unfortunately the present condition of the stage justifies you in saying it, 'It is doubtful whether the stage has any "duty" at all.' Alas! one would have liked to cherish the illusion that one has some small sense of responsibility towards one's work, were it only the illusion that one is the only serious *farceur* in a world of *farceurs!*" He spoke in the same strain at the Royal Theatrical Fund Dinner in 1890, at which he was chosen to respond to the toast of the Drama—an honour which greatly delighted him.

Throughout his life he regarded his duty as a dramatist with intense earnestness and sincerity. To him writing plays had become not primarily the way in which he earned his living—it was a mission which sprang from the noblest and most urgent feelings in his nature. He was a born fighter, and any criticism of the Drama which implied that it was not one of the greatest arts, or that it need not be taken seriously, acted as a personal challenge to which he must respond by lectures, speeches, pamphlets, letters to the papers. His pen was ruthless, and he made many enemies because he could not stop to consider small personal issues; he felt too deeply the far more important matter at stake—the attitude of the English people towards their Drama.

A few months after the Ancoats lecture my father was involved in a correspondence in the *Daily Telegraph* with Pinero and Justin Huntly McCarthy. H. A. J. was in favour of opening the music halls to stage plays. Pinero and Justin McCarthy were afraid that the serious intellectual drama would be swamped by a flood of empty frivolity. For several years my father continued to advocate the performance of stage plays in music halls, but it was not until January 1912 that the necessary license was given.

E. S. WILLARD AS "CYRUS BLENKARN" IN *The Middleman*, 1889

*(From the Souvenir Programme of the 101st Performance of "The Middleman"
December 16, 1889)*

The production of *The Middleman* at the Shaftesbury Theatre on 27th August, 1889, was the beginning of a long and successful association with E. S. Willard's management here and in America. *The Middleman* is the story of the struggles of Cyrus Blenkarn, a pottery-maker, to discover the secret of the old method of glazing. His daughter had been ruined by Julian Chandler, the son of Blenkarn's employer. Cyrus in his frantic efforts to succeed is reduced to the direst poverty, and, almost in despair, he breaks up his furniture and every piece of pottery he has, to feed the furnace. At the end of the third act, after repeated failures, in a state of almost unbearable emotion, he withdraws from the furnace a perfect specimen at last. The fourth act finds him rich and successful, living in Chandler's old home, with his daughter happily married to Julian.

The play was a great and immediate success; it ran for 182 nights at the Shaftesbury, was warmly received in New York, and was the first of several of H. A. J.'s plays to be produced on the Continent.

Henry Arthur wrote to his old friend Sir Arthur Pinero to ask his advice about the Continental production. He received the following answer:

"15th October, 1889.

"MY DEAR JONES,

"I intended to walk round to you this morning to answer your question in person, but letters and bothers kept me in till there was no time but for the necessary 'constitutional.' So I must reply to yours in this fashion, but hope to have a talk with you ere long.

"I am to have 45% of the fees paid for *The Profligate* in Germany, and something rather less for *Sweet Lavender,* which is supposed to need more 'adapting.' This adapting is a serious point and one—if the German market is to be regarded as a serious business—upon which an English author should be firm. They may adapt *Sweet Lavender* till it is sage and onions for all I care; but *The Profligate* I have stipulated shall be merely translated. Let me advise you to treat *The Middleman* in the same way. Don't let 'em adapt it! They may tell you that certain phases of our life and manners are not within the ken of the Germans, and that your Pottery should be a printing press, or a loom, or a mangle. But make them drink liquor from the pot of your own baking. (The real old Tatlow, in point of fact.) I think you'll agree with me it is far better to be associated with a good play that the Germans *can't* understand than with a bad one which they *can*.

"I may tell you that I have never yet soled my boot out of German fees. *Der Blau Grotte* (*The Magistrate*, adapted) is a popular play and is always being acted in cities with extravagant names. The fees, however, are less extravagant—possibly they too are adapted ere they reach,

"Yours very sincerely,

"Arthur W. Pinero."

H. A. J. often said that a dramatist should be able to give the outline of a plot in a few words. He was challenged on this point, and immediately wrote the plot of *The Middleman* within the circumference of a shilling piece! A reproduction was published in the *Strand Magazine*. He told me that he saw the title *The Middleman* in *Punch,* and thought what a good title it would make for a play, but that it was years before he could use it. He saw Willard in a bad play by Tom Taylor about an inventor, and that gave him the rough idea. The original manuscript of *The Middleman* now belongs to Yale University.

Willard produced *Judah* at the Shaftesbury Theatre on 21st May, 1890. Judah is a fanatical clergyman who falls deeply in love with a young girl, who, at her father's instigation, deceives people into believing she can cure them by fasting and faith-healing. When Judah discovers her trickery he protects her, but in the end he realises that their life together cannot be built up on a lie, and, determined to start life anew, he makes a public confession. Great as was the praise accorded to *The Middleman,* most of the critics acclaimed *Judah* as a notable and definite advance in my father's art. The construction of the play is defter and more compact than in any of his plays which preceded it. The story is more profoundly moving, and there is a lyrical quality in the writing absent from his earlier works. The love scenes in *Judah* are as beautiful as those in *Michael,* the motives actuating the characters more comprehensible to the majority of the public. All the criticisms spoke of the play as original and daring.

Among those present at the first performance in London were Lord Morley and Theodore Watts-Dunton, who wrote enthusiastic letters praising the play; Mark Rutherford and Thomas Huxley also wrote letters of high appreciation. Watts-Dunton said:

"The Pines,
"Putney Hill.
"*22nd May, 1890.*

"My dear Jones,

"It was impossible for me to get a word with you after such a triumph as that of yours last night. I will not trust myself to give full expression to my admiration of the play. To me, at this moment, it really seems the finest, the greatest play that has been acted in my time. Moreover, it belongs to literature. The same canons of criticism have to be applied to it as are applied to the plays of Browning and of Swinburne. And should it, as I hope it may, inaugurate a new day in the acted drama of our time, your literary position will be quite unique among your contemporaries.

"This is a play that you should certainly *publish* as soon as the commercial reasons for withholding it are gone.

"As to the acting, it was superb throughout.   Willard's beyond all praise.   Does Miss Brandon ever visit you at luncheon or dinner?   If so, I should take it as a kindness if you would invite me to meet her some day.

"Ever yours sincerely,

"THEODORE WATTS."

Mark Rutherford said:

"The Admiralty, S.W.

"15th August, 1890.

"MY DEAR JONES,

"We have seen *Judah*.   I so seldom go to the theatre that I am a most incompetent critic and what I think about plays would I am sure be mere schoolboy silliness to a well trained dramatic correspondent. . . .

"However I cannot resist a very inarticulate expression of delight.   About the 'moral' and 'aim' and all that I will say nothing because it goes without saying.   What I enjoyed was the artful contrast between the love-making of those two scientific people and that of Llewellyn and Vashti.   It was an admirable trick of yours, in the best sense of the word.   Then again, when the irreproachable female was going up the steps to lock up the reproachable lying Vashti, all my sympathies went out to the sinner to such a degree that I wished the jaileress would tumble into the moat.   Such is the attraction of love against the ten commandments.   It was as good as it could be too that the Welsh Calvinist should be taken with such a girl and venture to damn his soul for her.   The exhibition of such a passion as that is surely the noblest of 'morals.'   The curse of curses nowadays is not that we don't keep the Law, although we do not do much in that line, but that we don't know what Love means and touch one another with the tips of gloved fingers.

"Faithfully yours,

"W. HALE-WHITE."

When *Judah* was published in 1894, with a preface by Joseph Knight, Bernard Shaw wrote my father the following amusing letter:

"29 Fitzroy Square.
"*19th November, 1894.*

"MY DEAR SHAKESPEARE,

"Ben Jonson, as you say, is an excellent judge of a man; but on the whole I should prefer your autobiography to his biography.

"Far be it from me to rage against Jo; he and the rest have treated me devilishly well, all things considered; but the fact remains that Joseph's observations on *Judah* are supremely uninteresting. One wants to know what *you* have to say about it.

"*Judah* amused me. It consists of clever preliminaries; and when the real play begins with the matrimonial experiment of Judah and Vashti, down comes the curtain as usual. Come: I will write plays for the next ten years at £150 apiece, as the outside of my hopes for fees; and then the public will be ready to hear the solution of the problems you so fancifully pose it. You will find me making a terrible pace for you in a few years, if you don't run away from Townshend House and take to vegetarianism, sandals, and the pilgrim's bowl.

"G. B. S."

Though Henry Arthur regarded *Judah* as one of his finest plays, he did not speak of it often or with great affection. A few of his plays were like dearly loved children to him, and he was always ready to talk about them, and often re-read various scenes in them. It was his habit during the London run of any of his plays to drop in occasionally for half an hour and see how the piece was going. In this connection he delighted to tell the following story: One very hot Saturday afternoon he went to the pit to watch the second act of *Judah*.   He sat next to a workman who appeared to have had a comfortable midday meal with a pot or so of beer.   The man stared and stared open-mouthed at the play, blinking his eyes from time to time, and when the curtain came down he turned to H. A. J. and, jerking his thumb in the direction of the stage, said, "Rot! ain't it?"   The original manuscript of this play now belongs to Columbia University.

Less than a year after the production of *Judah*, my father had a far greater success with *The Dancing Girl*, produced at the Haymarket in January 1891.   Wilson Barrett in *The Silver King* and Willard in *The Middleman* and *Judah* gave memorable interpretations of H. A. J.'s characters, but with Tree as the Duke of Guisebury he found the ideal actor for the part.   He often said, "I can never say how much I owed to Tree in *The Dancing Girl*."   The Duke of Guisebury, lovable but self-indulgent, neglects his property and spends his money on Drusilla Ives, the daughter of one of his Quaker tenants, who has made a great reputation as a dancer, while her father supposes her to be earning her living as a governess.   For years the Duke has paid no attention to repeated warnings from his agent that a crash is inevitable.   Faced with ruin, he begs Drusilla to marry him and help him to make something of his life. When she refuses, the Duke determines to give one last reception, at which Drusilla will dance for his guests, and then commit suicide.   Drusilla's father discovers her mode of life, and, forcing his way into the house during the reception, he denounces and curses his unrepentant daughter. The guests all leave hurriedly.   Guisebury, supposing himself alone, is about to take poison, when Sybil Crake, the crippled daughter of his agent, creeps up to him and stays his hand.   In the last act he is back on his property in Cornwall, with Sybil and her father, working hard to redeem his oft broken promises to his tenants, whose love and respect he is gradually winning back.

JULIA NEILSON AS "THE DANCING GIRL," 1891

(By courtesy of Messrs. Elliott & Fry)

The notices, with one or two exceptions, were extremely favourable. The *Saturday Review* said, "A great play comes only about once in a generation; but Mr. H. A. Jones has nearly written one in *The Dancing Girl,*" though the writer added: "A feebler fourth act has rarely tested the patience of an audience."

The play ran for nearly a year—310 nights—and was revived by Tree at His Majesty's eighteen years later in 1909, though not very successfully. It was produced in New York in August of the same year as the London production, and was a success in spite of some very unfavourable and, in some cases, unjust criticisms.

Among the many letters of congratulation and praise received by my father, none gave him keener pleasure than a letter from Herbert Spencer asking him to go and see him. *The Times* criticism of the play referred to the lines where Sybil Crake, in speaking of Herbert Spencer, says, "I've found out." Guisebury, "What?" Sybil, "That he teaches exactly the same thing as Dante. Dante says, 'In His will is thy peace,' Spencer says, 'You must bring yourself into perfect agreement with your environment or get crushed!'" Herbert Spencer was very pleased at this quotation from his teaching, and H. A. J. derived the keenest pleasure from the talk he had with the great man. He told him how, as a boy not out of his teens, he had commenced reading all his works, and how deeply and lastingly he was indebted to their teaching for his intellectual development. My father said constantly, "Any clear thinking I've done I owe to Herbert Spencer."

Henry Arthur went to America for the production of *The Dancing Girl.* The visit was a short one, but it laid the foundations of his close and affectionate friendship of nearly forty years with Brander Matthews. Their feeling for each other developed into one which was brotherly in its love and intimacy. When my father was in New York, he nearly always spent his Sunday evenings at Mr. Matthew's house, and he often said that these parties, where he met and enjoyed the conversation of many of the finest men in America, were among the happiest memories of his life.   Among H. A. J.'s closest friends there were only three men he called by their Christian names—Brander Matthews, Oliver Herford, and Max Beerbohm.   There was a special quality of tenderness and devotion in his feeling for them.   My father was deeply distressed when he received the news of Mr. Matthew's last long illness, and, for over a year before he died, very few days passed when he did not refer to his friend's illness.   He was always saying, "I wonder how dear old Brander is getting on?"

When my father died, Clayton Hamilton, another very dear and valued American friend, wrote to me as follows:

"22nd February, 1929.

"My dear Doris Thorne,

"When the news came to us, at The Players, of the death of one of the most distinguished of our Honorary Members, we delegated our Vice-President, Mr. Otis Skinner, as the only proper person, to express our sentiments to you. . . .

"I had always been a great admirer of your father's work.   It was my happy privilege to dedicate one of my own books to him.   And it was my still happier privilege, in a summer of comparative leisure, to edit the Library Edition of his Representative Plays.   I did this as a labour of love; he appreciated my desire; and no other minor accomplishment in my career has given me so much enjoyment.

"It fell to me to break to Brander Matthews the news of the death of his beloved Henry Arthur Jones.   Dear old Brander, as you know, has long been clinging to life by a very slender thread, with his memory dimmed, his mind obfuscated, and his speech rendered incoherent by aphasia.

When I told him of the death of your dear father, he sat a long time silent. Then, struggling hard for utterance, he said, 'A great workman! a sweet soul! tell somebody—tell somebody—sweet soul—knew his job—our friend.'

"My dear Mrs. Thorne, I loved your father. On that account, if on no other, please try a little to remember me throughout the years that are to be.

"Ever yours faithfully,

"CLAYTON HAMILTON."

I am happy in the knowledge that, while they were both alive, Brander Matthews, in talking with my father, often expressed to him the sentiments contained in this last touching and pathetic tribute to his old friend's memory. My father valued Brander Matthews's opinion very highly, and praise from his old friend always gave him the keenest pleasure. There is a pathetic note at the end of a letter he wrote to Mr. Matthews in 1924:

"25th October, 1924.

" . . . I am pleased that my selected play will come into your hands for review. Looking back at what the drama was in 1884 (*Saints and Sinners* year), I think I helped to move things. But there was so much to sweep away. I've written in all about ninety plays, and have had great and world-wide successes. But only four or five times in my life have I been able to write the play I should have written if the conditions of the English Theatre had been as easy for the dramatist as they are to-day. However, I must not blame 'conditions' for the mistakes and failures that are due most likely to my own weakness and cowardice. . . .

"Did I tell you, a year or two ago, Anatole France sent me a tiny volume inscribed, 'A mon illustre confrère, Henry Arthur Jones, avec toute l'admiration de Anatole France'?"

When writing to each other, they continued their many discussions on literature.   There is a characteristic letter from Henry Arthur, written in 1912, in which he said:

> *"7th November, 1912.*
> "In reply to your 'Here's another of 'em,' I say, 'Let 'em all come!'   I've enjoyed 'The Gateways of Literature.' It has, like all your writing, the French ease and urbanity and clearness.   I liked the note on Anatole France and your just appreciation of his deliberate formlessness. Johnson you may belabour as you please.   But I shall say a good word for Ruskin and a better one for Carlyle.   I think you might have noticed his infinite tenderness in certain passages.   I love the old bear, and *I admire his style*—for him.
> "You'll be able to make out a good case against Dickens, but you won't win it. . . ."

During my father's long association with E. S. Willard their relations were very friendly, with the exception of a serious public controversy on the position of authors and actor-managers, which my father entered upon soon after the production of *The Dancing Girl*.   At that period of his career H. A. J. did not believe that the actor-manager system was the most beneficial for the English Theatre. He contended that actor-managers in the dual rôles of principal actor and manager occupied such an important position, and their authority was so great, that authors were often obliged to alter their plays to suit the leading actor, who would not produce them otherwise.   Moreover, the position of actor-managers was magnified by the habit of advertising their names on programmes, advertisements, etc., in very much larger letters than those used for the author's name, so that the mass of the public were led to attribute the success of a play almost solely to the actor-manager, and the position of the man who wrote it was a very secondary one.   My father's caustic letter to Wilson Barrett on the authorship of *The Silver King*, which I have quoted in Chapter V, expresses the bitterness he felt at the injustice of this custom.   Up to this date H. A. J. had enjoyed great success during his connection with Wilson Barrett, Willard, and Tree, and his attitude aroused considerable hostility.   Willard voiced the feeling of a great many people in the theatrical world when he attacked my father in the most vitriolic terms in the *Pall Mall Gazette* of 13th August, 1891.   Henry Arthur replied to his criticisms in the *Pall Mall* on the 15th.   The most serious charge my father brought against Willard was that, when he played *Wealth* in America, he altered the last act and gave it a conventionally happy ending, which exposed the play to the censure of the New York critics, and was strong proof of how dependent and helpless an author was in the hands of an actor-manager.   In spite of H. A. J.'s successes with various actor-managers, his experiences had not always been fortunate, and he had been obliged on several occasions to conform to their dictates.   It was not long before he and Willard were reconciled and shook hands warmly—a prelude to many future successful partnerships.

In the years to come my father's views on this important question underwent considerable modification, and he came to believe that, in England at any rate, the actor-manager system, though not an ideal one, was for the majority of theatres the most suitable, and in the long run the most successful.   He often said, "The public want their star, and if you don't give them one they'll make one for themselves."   During his fifty years as a dramatist and a writer on the drama, the actor-manager system was the only outstanding question about which my father modified his views.   In September 1927 he said to me, "A national theatre is the ideal system.   The actor-manager system is next best when you catch your actor-manager. I can't say how much I owe to Tree in *The Dancing Girl*."

Before the production of *The Dancing Girl*, Henry Arthur had decided to rent a London theatre in order to produce and manage his own play. He chose *The Crusaders* for this important venture. It is a satire on a band of people who are trying to reform London; the result of all their efforts is to add 2*d*. to the income-tax. He had great faith in the play, which had taken him a year to write, and he determined to spare no expense over the production and mounting. He gave William Morris *carte blanche* to design and make the furniture, and I think he was prouder of his William Morris room than of any other of his beautiful possessions: it was exhibited at the Ideal Homes Exhibition at Olympia in 1929. When he moved to Portland Place in 1902, he bought Morris's magnificent tapestry of Botticelli's Spring, and the tapestry and inlaid screen designed for *The Crusaders* were exhibited at the Louvre in 1914.

H. A. J. had a profound admiration for Morris's genius. In 1902 he gave me a copy of *Architecture, Industry, and Wealth,* with the following inscription:

"Xmas, 1902.

"MY DEAR DORIS,

"This was the greatest man I have met in my life.

"Your loving DADDY."

He always said that the three greatest men he had ever known were William Morris, Hiram Maxim, and Veniselos, and he never altered his opinion. My father introduced himself to Morris at Earl's Court station, soon after Emery Walker had pointed him out to H. A. J.; they travelled together in the same carriage as far as Hammersmith, discussing Socialism vigorously the whole way.

H. A. J. said to me once, "Morris was a fourteenth-century workman who fell into the nineteenth century by mistake," and he was never tired of quoting Morris's dictum, "Have nothing in your house you do not know to be useful or believe to be beautiful." Among many letters to my father there is one replying to an invitation to be present at the first night of *The Masqueraders*, in which Morris says:

"Kelmscott House,
"Upper Mall,
"Hammersmith.
"*23rd April, 1894.*

"DEAR MR. JONES,

"I am sorry but I cannot come out on a Saturday; though I am *not* an Israelite, it is a kind of sacred day to me. I wish you all manner of success for your new play.
"Yours very truly,
"WILLIAM MORRIS."

When my father had completed *The Crusaders,* he had great faith in the play, and he felt that it would not be presumptuous to ask Swinburne to write the words for the rose-song. He sounded Watts-Dunton on the matter; this was the reply:

"The Pines,
"Putney Hill.
"*3rd October, 1891.*

"MY DEAR JONES,

"I can answer your question right off the reel. Our friend *cannot* produce even a sentence of prose to order, much less a song. Impulse, *involuntary* impulse *alone,* can enable him to write at all. Here he is, I think, absolutely unique among poets. He has often been asked to do something like what you now ask, but has *never* even made the attempt.

"With all best wishes to you both,
"Yours ever sincerely,
"THEODORE WATTS."

A few months later he wrote as follows:

"The Pines,
"Putney Hill.
"Monday.

"MY DEAR JONES,

"For the new year a thousand good wishes from The Pines. Swinburne was much gratified to get your message anent the little poem.

"I shall be delighted to go with you to the Haymarket, and will meet you as you propose, if you will name the *exact* moment for this. When does the play begin? Neither Tree nor Irving nor Ellen Terry remembered The Pines when they were throwing out broadcast first-night invitations among the non-entities (*sic*) of the 'fashionable world' ('fashionable world,' ye Gods!) and the *flaneurs* of New Grub Street—so that the mere scholars and students were not allowed to *buy* seats. They manage these things better in France, where, on the revival of *Le Roi S'Amuse,* V. Hugo sent the *first* two tickets to Swinburne and me. But in France they know that, in the long run, it is not the *flaneur* nor the empty-headed 'fashionable' person who form opinion, but the very people whom the genteel English manager despises.

"When does your new play appear? I was talking to Morris about it the other day.

"Yours ever,
"THEODORE WATTS."

In addition to the beautiful scenery and furniture for *The Crusaders,* H. A. J. paid for a finely printed programme on hand-made paper, which was distributed free on the first night. This novel departure on my father's part involved him in a law-suit. He wrote a letter to the *Star* protesting against the enormous profits made from the sale of programmes. The *Star,* in commenting on this letter, stigmatised the system as a barefaced swindle; an action was brought against the paper by Arthur Payne, who owned the programme and refreshment monopolies. He was unsuccessful; but, when my father attempted to go on distributing free programmes outside the theatre, Mr. Payne sued him for breach of covenant and libel, and won his case, being awarded £20 for breach of covenant and £40 for libel. The libel was contained in a letter published in the *Daily Telegraph* on 23rd November, 1891, in which H. A. J. said, "Of all the greedy and ugly exhibitions of the 'middleman' or 'parasitic' spirit, the programme system seems to me one of the most outrageous and indefensible." The sympathies of the Press and public were with my father.

The play, which was produced on 2nd November, 1891, was a failure, and there was a rowdy reception with a good deal of booing on the first night, though the audience on the second night were enthusiastic and H. A. J. had to make a speech. All the papers praised the scenery and the mounting, but their criticisms of the play were in most cases severe.

My father's first venture into management cost him over £4,000, and he vowed it should be the last, but several times during his career he undertook partial responsibilities for the management of his plays, and each time he did so he incurred heavy financial losses. He was pursued by ill-luck in this respect, because he sometimes had an offer to take a share in a play which was a great success, and refused. Each time he lost money he vowed it should be the last, but he was often tempted to break his word.

CHAPTER VIII

In 1892, my father took a prominent part in the movement for the Sunday opening of museums. He said to me, "I remember speaking about it at the old St. James's Hall, and, oh, Lord, how nervous I was about it! I had to address 3,000 people." It is amazing now to read the various letters and articles of those who were violently opposed to the movement. H. A. J. found an ardent supporter in Henry Irving, who wrote him the following letter:

"Lyceum Theatre,
"11th March.

"My dear Jones,

"You are to my mind taking an excellent stand in your advocacy of opening Museums and Picture Galleries on Sundays, and I most heartily wish that the movement may be successful. The promoters—or rather the spokesmen of the movement (for the great mass and bulk of the workers of all kinds are the true promoters)—have and will still have much uphill work before them, many doubts to overcome—much prejudice to sweep away. I cannot myself imagine how anyone with a brain to think for others and a heart to feel for them can wish such a measure of public wisdom even postponed. . . . There need not be even a mechanical difficulty in the matter. In such places the attendants are few, and all that would be required would be an addition of one-sixth to the existing working staff in each case, so that each person employed would get his weekly holiday. I fear that want of due consideration of this aspect leads some persons to believe—and many more to pretend for other purposes that they believe—that if Museums and Picture Galleries were to be opened on Sundays, the next step would be to open the theatres. If anyone is so foolish as to believe or to argue any such point, you can easily show that there is no analogy whatever between Theatres and Museums, etc. A theatre is a workshop on a large scale—why in the Lyceum we employ daily some hundreds of people varying between 300 and 500 with the play. These people are all workers and six days work is quite enough for them—as it is for anyone. . . . Besides, the actors themselves would be the first to resent any encroachment on their day of rest, in fact six performances a week are quite enough for all, and where excessive work is attempted there is often a lamentable result. . . . If I had any power with those in high places, I would say, 'For God's sake let a little life and a little light into the dead and dark places of our cities—and give our toilers a chance of learning and enjoying something beyond and above the sordid routine of their lives!'

"Sincerely yours,
"HENRY IRVING."

Ellen Terry agreed warmly with Henry Irving in his objection to actors appearing on Sundays. Some years before the date of his letter she wrote to Henry Arthur:

"MY DEAR MR. JONES,
"Nothing could induce—tempt—compel me to act on Sundays. I have always looked forward to that day for many reasons as the happiest day in all the year—I'm sure all actors think the same.

"Yours most sincerely,
"ELLEN TERRY.
"I've seen The Middleman!—a masterly play."

Not long after the successful run of The Middleman, Ellen Terry wrote to my father:

"Lyceum Theatre.

"I am wondering whether or no Mr. H. A. Jones might chance to have a *wee* play by him—knocking about somewhere, perhaps only half done—something out of the common run—something *very bright,* perhaps rustic—perhaps a servant girl and a soldier—a sailor and a fisher girl—a gnome and a fairy—a Bobby and a fat Cook. . . .

"*Anything* but a 'young lady and gentleman' in a four-walled room. I know if I had something 'nice' in which the parts were equally good that Mr. Terriss and I could have some fun in it, and do it all by ourselves without troubling H.I. at all about it (same as I did *The Amber Heart*—I took tremendous pains with that, rehearsing it every day for a month, for hours and hours!). I've never played in anything of yours and yet there's *one* part, in a play you have written, I believe I could play better than anybody on the stage—(There's nothing like blowing one's own trumpet!)

"This very untidy scrawl is to ask you whether you have anything *by* you which wd. take about an hour to play— and if so whether you wd. let me read it?

"I hope you are well—you and yours—this jolly weather.

"I am very sincerely yours,
"ELLEN TERRY.

"*2nd April, '91.*

"*Robin Grey* is lovely, but it is so sad!"

My father's friendship with Ellen Terry had begun some years earlier, as witness the following delightful letter:

"*15th November, 1886.*

"MY DEAR MR. AND MRS. JONES,

"I know this (tardy!) note will find you in the deepest, crapiest mourning for the loss of that lovely tea-pot—to think that it is *mine*—and no-mistake-about-it, is a delightful thing, and I can't tell you how very kind I think you are to give it me. You know it is much too good for 'The Audrey Arms'—Uxbridge—and so I shall keep it up here at my town mansion!—and I'll promise you a really good cup o' tea from it if by chance you are in this neighbourhood and will come in about 4.

"I fear I shall not be down for the Meet on Tuesday, they are going to serve me up for supper to-night at the Lyceum—hot—from the Witches Kitchen!

"Thank you—thank you for that

"Tea-pot!

"Sincerely yours,

"Ellen Terry."

In 1893, Henry Arthur published his first political article, "Middleman and Parasites," which appeared in the June number of the *New Review*. He made a vigorous attack on the middleman system whereby thousands of men made a living through the ignorance, carelessness, and folly of their fellow-creatures. The whole tone of the article expressed sympathy with the lower classes; but his attitude as he grew older altered entirely, and at the end of his life it was only rarely that one could wring from him a grudging and superficial acknowledgment of the wrongs or disabilities of working-men.

He wrote: "I am a citizen of England, and an heir to all her greatness and renown. The health and happiness of my own body depend upon each muscle and nerve and drop of blood doing its work in its place. I will not fill any post or pursue any business where I can live upon my fellow-citizens without doing them useful service in return. For I plainly see that this must bring suffering and want to some of them. . . .

"A recent review article by John Burns, amidst much other manly good sense and clear thinking, proposed to establish a Department of Labour and the Fine Arts.

This seems to me worthy of immediate consideration by the Government. By all means let us have a Department and a Minister of Labour and the Fine Arts. And let Labour come first, because it is more necessary for us to have wholesome bread and well-built houses and good clothes than good pictures and plays. Yes, put Labour first."

As a young man, under the influence of Emery Walker and William Morris, my father flirted with Socialism, but from the Great War onwards he became an uncompromising Die-Hard. He often quoted Swinburne, who said to him, "When Topsy (Morris's nickname) was at Oxford, he was the bluest of blue Tories. You always know when a man talks one sort of nonsense when he's twenty, he'll be talking the other kind when he's forty." In his Notes he says, "He could work but he could not think. What a splendid worker was Morris! But he thought that he could think. That is the great evil of democracy. It teaches men to think that they can think. And upon this quite unproved hypothesis it entrusts them with votes."

Although he would never admit it, he had a great dislike for the lower middle-classes, from whom he sprang. This dislike had a basis of justification in the many examples of prejudice and narrow-mindedness from which he suffered as a lad and during his early manhood. It was reinforced by an active aversion to his father-in-law, who typified for him the lower middle-class qualities and failings which he hated. Moreover, his father-in-law was a very mean man, and H. A. J., an extremely generous one, despised him for this fault. He said to me once, "Now, your mother's father was the meanest man I ever met; when she came away on her wedding-day, I had to give her a few shillings." My mother, who adored her father, said it was his only failing.

Henry Arthur often told me of an incident at one of his first nights, when Mr. Seely, who was a common old man, came up and pressed himself on my father when he was talking to some influential people. To the end of his life H. A. J. dropped his aitches very occasionally—a legacy of his Buckinghamshire origin—but from 1882 onwards he mixed constantly with well-bred, cultured people. He acquired quickly and easily the outward marks of a man of the world, the small graces of good society which were a fitting, though minor, supplement to his inherent fineness of intellect. There was a marked contrast between his manner of speaking and that of most of the members of his own and his wife's family.

In his later years his hatred of the lower classes was strengthened by his depressed mental outlook. Whenever he had a nervous breakdown, one of the most prominent symptoms was a dread of losing what money he had saved. Democratic legislation increased this dread. He saw the mob laying greedy hands on his possessions. I shall never forget the concentrated vehemence with which he said to me one day a year or two before his death, "I *hate* the name of Labour— I *hate* the name of Labour." Although he hated the proletariat as a class, there was no trace of this feeling in his relations with individuals. He loved chatting with labouring men, and he was always kindly and accessible. All his servants liked him, in spite of the exigencies of his work, which interfered constantly with the regular performance of their duties. All my life I remember at irregular intervals the following plaint from my mother, "Henry, your study hasn't been turned out for weeks," and his invariable reply, "It doesn't matter, I can't have my work interrupted." In the last years of his life most of the tradespeople with whom he dealt knew him well, and when he went out for a walk he would drop in at various shops to have a talk.

In his Notes he says, "I cannot bother about money. There are so many things of much more importance. I *must* bother about money or the children whom I love will have a dreadful fight in this hard world." On going through his account-books after his death, I found that he had made over £150,000 in fees from his plays; he left £15,000. In reference to his inability to save, he was never tired of quoting his old father, who said, "As fast as I made money with one hand I hit it away with the other," and H. A. J. would strike his clenched fist on the palm of his other hand to emphasise this remark. He did blame himself continually for the reckless way he allowed money to slip through his hands, and I am sure that his frequent tirades against democracy served as an unconscious outlet and an alternative to self-reproach.

* * * * * * * * *

My father's long and greatly successful associations with Sir Charles Wyndham began with the production of *The Bauble Shop* in 1893. Just a year before he died he told me, "*The Bauble Shop* is the only play I've ever written to order for a manager."

I believe Henry Arthur had a profounder admiration for Wyndham's acting than for that of any other actor who created the leading parts in his plays. Willard, in a letter written to him in 1899, said, "Has any other actor for whom you have written come so near satisfying you in three such different characters as Cyrus, Judah, and Baily?" He agreed with this statement, and he always praised Willard's acting very warmly. He referred repeatedly to the great debt of gratitude he owed Tree for his magnificent performance in *The Dancing Girl*. But Wyndham's acting in all H. A. J.'s plays was on a higher level of excellence than that of any other leading actor. Moreover, Sir Charles always showed great respect for the author's conception of a part. Henry Arthur declared only a few months before he died, "All the years I knew

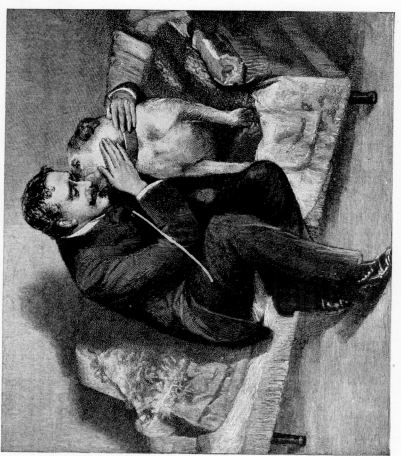

TREE AS THE DUKE OF GUISEBURY IN "THE DANCING GIRL,"
HAYMARKET THEATRE, 1891

From an Instantaneous Photograph taken by the Flash Light on the Stage

(By courtesy of "The Graphic")

Wyndham he never took the least liberty with the dialogue or business—he was a model for that."

I believe that another reason why my father had so high a regard for Wyndham was the admirable way in which Sir Charles managed him. He was, like a great many authors, difficult at rehearsals, and with most of the other managers with whom he was associated there were discussions, difficulties, and sometimes bitter quarrels; but during his long partnership with Sir Charles and Miss Mary Moore I believe I am correct in saying that no really unpleasant incident ever occurred at rehearsals. A great deal of credit is also due to Miss Mary Moore's unfailing tact and charm. In August of the year before he died we were speaking of Lady Wyndham, and he said with emphasis, "A very clever woman—and a very clever actress."

The Bauble Shop was produced at the Criterion Theatre on 26th January, 1893, and ran for 135 nights. Lord Clivebrook, the Prime Minister, has an implacable enemy, a Radical named Stoach. Just before Lord Clivebrook is to introduce a bill on Public Morality Stoach discovers that the Prime Minister has been visiting a young girl late at night. Though the visits are innocent, Stoach spreads the story in the House of Commons on the night of the debate on Lord Clivebrook's bill. The bill is thrown out, and Clivebrook is ruined. He marries Jessie, and the audience are left with the impression that he will make a fresh start. The notices of the play were good and the reception enthusiastic. William Archer, however, criticised the play very adversely in the *World,* and a great many critics found fault with the details of political life, especially with the act which takes place in the room of the Leader of the House of Commons. There was some correspondence in the papers, but I feel sure that in essential details my father was correct. He knew the late Lord Bessborough very well, and while he was writing the play he went to the

House of Commons with him, and frequently consulted him on various small points. (Lord Bessborough, then Viscount Duncannon, was secretary to Mr. Speaker Peel.) I believe no noteworthy tribute has ever been paid to a minor but excellent quality in all Henry Arthur's plays. He never made a mistake on technical matters. Before he wrote *The Lord Harry,* he read nothing but books on the Civil War and that period; again with *The Tempter,* he steeped himself in the atmosphere and literature of mediæval England; for two years before writing *Carnac Sahib* he read books on India; and when he was writing *The Heroic Stubbs,* for weeks I went round all the boot-shops in London making notes for him of the words and phrases used by the assistants. I do not think any doctor or barrister or other professional man who has seen a play by H. A. J. has ever been momentarily annoyed by a mistake on a technical matter. He made a very small mistake in *The Tempter* when he spoke of "fleur de lys" instead of "flower de luce"; when this slip was pointed out to him by Mr. M. H. Spielmann he wrote:

"16th February, 1918.

" . . . Of course, I ought to have called the inn 'The Flower de Luce.' I am ashamed to be convicted of such a mistake. I am glad you could say a kind word about *The Tempter.* H. D. Traill and Watts-Dunton were very lavish in their praise of it. Traill wrote me 19 sheets of approving criticism—which I have lost. But the newspaper critics were very cold. I feel that I succeeded in the character of the devil, that I made him live—but this was not the general opinion. . . ."

He was delighted with the following letter from Watts-Dunton, who was present on the first night of *The Bauble Shop:*

"The Pines,
"Putney Hill.
"*Saturday.*

"MY DEAR JONES,

"Amid the chorus of praise with which your most original and fascinating play has been received, I feel that *my* voice is very small.   Still, a word or two of thanks for all the pleasure you gave me the other night is demanded by a sense of common gratitude.   Not that I was quite satisfied by the doom awarded to Stoach (what a name that is: Swinburne declares that it is unmatched only by Balzac!). . . .

"I am genuinely rejoiced to think that you have scored still another success.

"Ever yours,
"THEODORE WATTS."

Lady Dorothy Nevill and her daughter Meresia were in my father's box on the first night of *The Bauble Shop.* She was very fond of Henry Arthur, and from that occasion onwards for thirteen years she never missed being in his box at all his first nights.

Though Henry Arthur had a great many very close friendships with men, there were very few women he cared for deeply.   All his long life there were not more than half a dozen women for whom he felt a strong attachment. Lady Dorothy Nevill was among the foremost of his friends.   When she was in town, he lunched with her almost regularly on Sundays.   I am sure he learnt a great deal from communion with her fine, bright intellect, and many of the characters and scenes in his comedies owe their life-like portrayal to his association with her wide circle of friends.   He often recounted to me a delicious story Lady Dolly told him about Disraeli and a very well-known peeress.   This lady was a great figure in society in those days, and was also famous for her amorous disposition.   One night Disraeli was at Lady Dolly's, and, as he had not got his carriage, Lady —— said she would give him a lift to the House of Commons. He said, "Very well, Lady ——, but if you pinch me I shall scream." She replied, "Oh, you naughty man, I won't take you," whereupon he answered in a confiding voice, "Very well, I won't scream."

When Lady Dolly's memoirs, *Under Five Reigns*, appeared, my father told me of an interesting personal link with the past: he knew Lord Llandaff, who had attended Madame Récamier's receptions. Lord Randolph Churchill was one of the many interesting personalities whom my father met at Lady Dolly's. He invited H. A. J. to the last dinner-party he gave before going round the world.

My father was also very fond of Lady St. Helier, Miss Violet Vanbrugh, and Lady Stanley, *née* Dorothy Tennant. During the last years of his life he often regretted that he had lost touch with Lady St. Helier, as he saw her constantly over a long period of years and often stayed with her and Lord St. Helier at Arlington Manor, Newbury. I have a delightful sketch which Kate Greenaway made for Henry Arthur, when they were both staying with the then Sir Francis and Lady Jeune. On another occasion when he was staying with them, Princess Christian was the guest of honour. My father told me how annoyed he was because, on the first night, he kept the party waiting several minutes for dinner. It was altogether a somewhat disastrous evening, as after dinner Lady St. Helier begged H. A. J. to read them the first act of the new comedy he was writing, *The Manœuvres of Jane*. Henry Arthur did not feel in the mood to do so, nor did he think that the audience was, on the whole, an ideal one; and, though usually he read his plays magnificently, he did not acquit himself well on this occasion—just after he had started reading, he glanced down and was much upset to discover that he had spilt soup all over his shirt-front.

He told me how amused he was when a parcel arrived,

and Princess Christian said, "Oh! don't cut the string; it would be a pity to cut such a nice piece."

For Violet Vanbrugh he had a specially tender regard and admiration. He always said, "What a dear, sweet woman." He was devoted also to Lady Stanley, and in the last years of his life, though he went out but rarely, I could always tempt him to take me to tea with her on a Thursday afternoon. We often talked about her gentle, gracious, and charming personality, which, allied with an unusually keen intelligence, made her a truly remarkable woman. H. A. J. told me that when she married Sir Henry Stanley in Westminster Abbey, as she returned from signing the register, she leant down and placed her bridal bouquet on Livingstone's tomb—a lovely act prompted by a lovely spirit.

It was during the nineties that my father formed one of the most outstanding and enduring of all his many friendships—that with Max Beerbohm. Henry Arthur grew to love Max dearly, and his admiration for his work was profound. He always said that his caricatures were supreme in their genius, and that they were not even approached by the work of other men. H. A. J. admired the grace and finish of Max's literary work, and the whimsical side of many of his writings made an immediate appeal to him. I like to think that there is a touch of Max in some of my father's essays; his "Christmas Meditations on Alcohol" and the essay "English Dukes and American Millionaires," which he wrote especially for the Queen's Doll's House Library. Max's feeling about his own work is revealed in the following letter to my father:

"48 Upper Berkeley Street, W.
"*Monday.*

"MY DEAR HENRY ARTHUR,

" . . . I was very much honoured by what you told me about your pleasure in my new book of essays. As to the

difference between my writings and my drawings, I myself have often been puzzled by it.   But I think that in the
past few years the two dissimilar 'sisters' of whom you
speak have really been growing a little more like to each
other.   My drawing has been growing a little more delicate and artful, and losing something of its pristine bold-
ness and savagery; whilst my writing, though it never will
be savage or bold, is easier in style, less ornate, than it used
to be.   At least I think so.

"Looking forward to the 26th.

"Yours sincerely,

"MAX BEERBOHM."

An article he sent to H. A. J. called forth the following
interesting letter:

"*24th June, 1898.*

"*Private.*

"MY DEAR MAX,

"This is very suggestive, but I don't think it's quite
right.   Experience has much to do with it.   I have often
found myself, at the most supreme and solemn moments,
at moments of intensest feeling, abdicating my position
and standing aside to watch myself.   At other times I have
recalled, during the next hour or the next day, how I felt
at the eventful moment.   You will find that the difference
between experience and observation is almost the difference between tragedy and comedy.   Observation of life
leads to comedy.   Experience of life leads to tragedy.   Of
course, you may call my momentary abdication of myself
'passionate observation,' but the artist uses both experience and observation.   He does not put his raw experience
on the stage or in a novel, but he uses it, at least I should
say he transforms it and then uses it.   The whole process I
should describe as 'imagery from memory.'   Your rule
would shut out the Brontes, wouldn't it? . . . I should

say the artist selects from *everywhere,* from his experience, from his observation, from books, from tales—takes his *biens* when he finds them, and if necessary grinds his bride into paint, and peeps and botanises on his mother's grave.

"Kindest regards.

"Always yours,

"HENRY ARTHUR JONES."

To which Max wrote an equally interesting reply:

"4, Holly Mount,
"Hampstead.
"*28th June, 1898.*

"MY DEAR MR. JONES,

"Many thanks for your very interesting letter.   I should much like to steal your theory of

Experience	Observation
Tragedy	Comedy

and to make a long article out of it.   But I see that your letter is marked 'Private,' and I have not yet been in dramatic criticism long enough to have lost all scruples. I admit that I overstated my case against 'experience,' which, as you say, is often of great value to the artist. What I meant to suggest is merely that fine works of art have sometimes been the result of the artist's impotence to realise in life the phase of life with which he is dealing. . . .

"The old story of the newspaper 'correspondent at Rome' who had never been to Rome and who—being sent there by his proprietor, as a treat, after twenty years of admirable work—wrote such poor stuff that he had to be dismissed, has always seemed to me rather a fine allegory. However, you are of course right in your general theory, as

I see now, though I do not regret that I propounded a fallacy, since your letter to me was the outcome of it.

"I am yours very sincerely,
"MAX BEERBOHM."

Henry Arthur always read all Max's articles, and he occasionally wrote to him about them. Here is one of many letters:

"I liked your article last week on Sutro's prose—he does really manage to get some sense of style into his dialogue without being unnatural or uncolloquial. Oscar was rarely colloquial, rarely natural, rarely differentiated his characters.

"Oh you happy literary gents, who can box the whole compass of the dictionary, who can embroider your columns with the most variegated verbiage, while no child monitor taps you on the shoulder and sternly reminds you, 'I say, old fellow, people don't talk like this you know.' See what a style I have abdicated, only to be chidden by Walkley for using a word in the exact copy of Jeremy Taylor."

I was much touched after my father's death when Mrs. Beerbohm told me that she never once remembered her husband speaking of him as "Henry Arthur," but always as "dear Henry Arthur."

Another very dear friendship my father formed, that with Bernard Shaw, began in the early nineties. Henry Arthur found G. B. S. a very delightful and stimulating companion. A funny little snapshot of them both, standing by their bicycles, which was taken soon after they first knew each other, is here reproduced. Their many talks gave Henry Arthur the keenest pleasure, and, when they were away from London, they continued their discussions in the many letters they exchanged. No great man has written more significant or self-revealing letters than G. B. S. All those he wrote to my father are interesting,

GEORGE BERNARD SHAW AND HENRY ARTHUR JONES
IN THE EARLY 'NINETIES

and many of them are amusing, but there are two which are of unusual interest; both were written in reply to letters from Henry Arthur. In the first G. B. S. said:

"West Cliff Hotel,
"Folkestone.
"*2nd December, 1894.*
"(*Beastly wet day.*)

"My dear H. A. J.,

"Here I am at the seaside between the finishing of one play and the beginning of another, just the time to send back the ball to you.

"All that you say is quite true statically. Dynamically, it is of no virtue whatever. Like you, I write plays because I like it, and because I cannot remember any period in my life when I could help inventing people and scenes. I am not a storyteller: things occur to me as scenes, with action and dialogue—as moments, developing themselves out of their own vitality. I believe you will see as I go on that the conception of me as a doctrinaire, or as a sort of theatrical Joyce (of *Scientific Dialogues* fame), is a wrong one. On the contrary, my quarrel with the conventional drama is that it is doctrinaire to the uttermost extreme of dogmatism—that the dramatist is so strait-jacketed in theories of conduct that he cannot even state his conventional solution clearly, but leaves it to be vaguely understood, and so for the life of him cannot write a decent last act. I find that when I present a drama of pure feeling, wittily expressed, the effect when read by me to a picked audience of people in a room is excellent. But in a theatre, the mass of the people, too stupid to relish the wit, and too convention-ridden to sympathise with real as distinct from theatrical feeling, simply cannot see any drama or fun there at all, whilst the clever people feel the discrepancy between the real and theatrical feeling only as a Gilbertian satire on the

latter, and, appreciating the wit well enough, are eager to
show their cleverness by proclaiming me as a monstrously
clever sparkler in the cynical line.   These clever people
predominate in a first night audience; and, accordingly,
in *Arms and the Man,* I had the curious experience of
witnessing an apparently insane success, with the actors
and actresses almost losing their heads with the intoxica-
tion of laugh after laugh, and of going before the curtain
to tremendous applause, the only person in the theatre who
knew that the whole affair was a ghastly failure.   The same
thing is occurring now in Boston, Philadelphia, etc.—there
is about as much of me in the affair as there is of Shakespeare in Garrick's *Katherine and Petruchio.*   Here and
there, of course, I come across a person who was *moved* by
the play, or by such portions of it as got played any better
than a pantomime opening; but for the general paying
public there needs a long fight, during which my plays will
have to be produced in spite of all economic considerations,
sometimes because the parts are too fascinating to be re-
sisted, sometimes because Pinero is not ready with his
commissioned play, sometimes because I am willing to
forgo an advance, sometimes because Nature will not
submit wholly to the box office.

"Now here you will at once detect an enormous assumption on my part that I am a man of genius.   But what can
I do—on what other assumption am I to proceed if I am to
write plays at all?   You will detect the further assumption
that the public, which will still be the public twenty years
hence, will nevertheless see feeling and reality where they
see nothing now but mere intellectual swordplay and satire.
But that is what always happens.   You must remember
my musical experience.   I remember well when even cultivated musicians could hear no melody in *Lohengrin,* not
to mention *Die Meistersinger,* and when they thought
Spohr's and Mendelssohn's oratorios, and Mozart's *12th
Mass,* the summit of musical sublimity and profundity.

The public is still as great an ass (to speak in that way) as it was then; but it now knows that Wagner's work is all melody and feeling, and that the other stuff is nine-tenths formality and twaddle. Consequently I am absolutely confident that *if my work is good* (the only assumption on which I can go on with it) all the miracles will happen, and it will be quite well worth my while to make £150 a play or even to make nothing and starve, or play Wagner to your Liszt in the sense of borrowing all your spare cash.

"And now as to the barrenness of politics. What conviction can you really have as to their barrenness unless you have fallen in love with them and found that no child came of their embraces?—or unless you have actually worked in the arena with politicians all through their apprenticeship. You have to swallow all the formulas if you are to know what they really taste like and what effect they have on the constitution.   Politics are just as much a part of life as gambling or poetry; and it is extremely instructive to see how impotent the political opinions which men *think* are to produce action, and how potent the political prejudices which men *feel* are to produce it. I am a politician because life only realises itself by functioning energetically in all directions; and I find on the platform and in council opportunities for functioning away like mad with faculties that would otherwise be atrophied from disuse. My passion, like that of all artists, is for efficiency, which means intensity of life and breadth and variety of experience; and already I find, as a dramatist, that I can go at one stroke to the centre of matters that reduce the purely literary man to colorless [*sic*] platitudes.

"Do you now begin to understand, O Henry Arthur Jones, that you have to deal with a man who habitually thinks of himself as one of the great geniuses of all time?— just as you necessarily do yourself. We may be deceiving ourselves; but why add to the heavy chances of that the absolute certainty of such a deception as would be involved in the notion that we thought ourselves common fellows with a bit of talent.

"Have you ever considered the case of Dickens carefully? Don't you think his last (and greatest) works would have been much greater if he had had something of the systematic, philosophical, historical, economic, and, above all, artistic training of Goethe? I grant you it is a difficult question; but surely so fine a spirit could have been rescued from the reproach of being a Philistine, a guzzler, and an ignorantly contemptuous reporter-politician?

"G. BERNARD SHAW."

I imagine that H. A. J., when writing to ask Mr. Shaw's advice about a copyright performance, went on to speak of Wagner; probably he said he liked to "swim about" in music without understanding it, as G. B. S. said:

"Blen-cathra, Hindhead,
"Haslemere, Surrey.
"8th January, 1899.

"Now Lord bless your innocence, popular dramatist that you are, people don't get up parts for copyrighting performances. The whole thing is the hollowest fiction. The performers take the parts in their hands and simply read through the play, just as they do at a first rehearsal, except that there is no bother about the business. So long as a bill is stuck outside to say that the performance is going on and that anyone can come in for a guinea if they like, and that somebody has actually come in and paid a guinea (a confederate of course), the thing is a legal performance just as much as a first night with all the honours at the Lyceum is. I should never have dreamt of suggesting that W. should learn the part without a book. Since she is no longer on tour, the notion falls through; and I will get Miss Farr to go through the usual farce some morning at Bayswater.

"Cleopatra, by the way, is nearly as good a part as Dolly in *You Never Can Tell*.

"It is all very well to swim about in Wagner, without bothering as to his meaning; but the best established truth in the world is that no man produces a work of art of the very first order except under the pressure of a strong conviction and definite meaning as to the constitution of the world.   Dante, Goethe, and Bunyan could not possibly have produced their masterpieces if they had been mere art-voluptuaries.   It may be that the artistic by-product is more valuable than the doctrine; but there is no other way of getting the by-product than by the effort and penetrating force that doctrine braces a man to.   Go straight to the by-product and you get Gounod instead of Wagner. Fricka is not Law; she is the dramatisation of a woman with a legal mind, proceeding on the fundamental legal error.   I have pointed out in the book that this is the only way in which an allegory can become a drama.

"It is odd that you do not find in your own experience the clue to Wagner's way of working.   What makes you the only considerable dramatist now in vogue in England is precisely because you are the only one who ever drives at any purpose with sufficient concern for extra-theatrical concerns to make his art a by-product.   In your plays you make the audience feel the world behind the scrap of it represented on the stage, just as Wagner does.   Only, you are vaguer; you get stopped in the realisation of your own drift by your amazing theology, which prevents you from seeing what Wagner saw: that is, the tragedy of God Almighty between Law on the one side and stupidity on the other.   And when I point the way out of the muddle, you beg not to be rescued from it, and plead for mere swimming in the music.   Well, swim away; but don't tell me that my 'theory' is all wrong.   It's not a theory; it's a translation into intellectual terms of something that has been expressed by its author only in dramatic terms.   Read the dramas through; and you will find that unless you accept my version of the scenes between Wotan and Brynhild, Fricka and Erda, you will be driven to the impossible conclusion that they are absolute nonsense, which by some accident has fallen into grammatical shape in the middle of an orchestral swimming bath.

"You say 'I can't grasp the technique of any art except play-writing—*if that has got a technique.*' Precisely. The secret of musical technique is that there is no technique in the mysterious sense of the amateur critics. Wagner was no more governed by rules in the choice of notes to express what he wanted than you are in the choice of words.   There is no difficulty except what lies on the surface.   You have to know what notes a trombone can utter, and what they sound like.   The same for a piccolo, a tenor, a soprano, or any other instrument, human or orchestral, you use.   And you have to know how to write down the sounds so that the musician, reading his part (like the actor reading *his* part), may, as far as he is capable, make the sounds as and when you want them.   What is there difficult to grasp in all that?   It is odd that sounds should produce that magical effect; but there is nothing in that except the flat fact that they do.

"I don't agree at all about the stage directions.   They may bother *you;* but they make to the ordinary reader all the difference between an intelligible and readable drama and a mere dialogue which by itself can only be made self-explanatory by the obsolete devices of the Elizabethans, whose plays were recited, and not acted with business in our sense.   Take the ordinary actor at a rehearsal.   How often does he divine without a hint from you which way your lines are to be spoken in scenes which are neither conventional nor otherwise obvious?   How many actors playing Shakespeare can catch intentions in the speeches which are plain enough to you?   I scrupulously avoid any direction that could not be conveyed by the actor or make-up of the actor, as otherwise the play would no longer be a play. But I defy anybody to convey a complete impression of an acted play by dialogue alone. It is an attempt to do so that produces the literary play.

"Excuse all this talky-talky. My accursed foot is discharging again; and I think I shall get another bit of the bone removed. The relapse is trifling; but it shows that there is still a scrap of bad bone there.

"G. Bernard Shaw."

In 1893, a few months after Wyndham's production of *The Bauble Shop,* Tree produced *The Tempter,* a blank-verse tragedy in four acts. Henry Arthur was very proud of this play, which took him nearly a year to write, and in January 1928, when his nurse said to him that she thought *The Lackey's Carnival* one of his best plays, he replied immediately, "No, my best plays are *The Tempter, The Divine Gift, Michael, The Liars,*" and, as an afterthought, "*The Case of Rebellious Susan.*" On another occasion, when I asked him which he considered his finest plays, he said he could have written all kinds of plays, but those he preferred were (in the following order), *The Tempter, Michael*—he added, "my favourite play"—*The Divine Gift* (second best), *Grace Mary,* and *The Goal.* He went on to say that if conditions had been different, and serious work had won the highest recognition, he would have done more serious plays of the above type. Speaking to my sister Winifred (Peggy) the year before he died, he said, "I could have written any kind of play except a musical comedy." He claimed that none of his contemporaries had covered such a wide range in playwriting as he had, and would go on to say, "blank verse, comedy, drama, tragicomedy, and farce." A month or two before he died he said, "If I were to have a volume of plays to go into eternity with, and if—supposing I go up that way—I see Peter, the ones I'd tell him I'd have would be *Michael and His Lost Angel, The Tempter, The Liars,* and *The Case of Rebellious Susan."* He told me that of all the hundreds of characters he had drawn he enjoyed most writing the characters of Michael and the Devil.

Edward German composed all the incidental music for *The Tempter,* which was produced at the Haymarket Theatre on 20th September, 1893, my father's forty-second birthday. The notices were very mixed, but very few of them praised the verse. My father replied to the criticism of the *Saturday Review* in the following interesting letter to Mr. Moy Thomas:

"29th September, 1893.

"Dear Moy Thomas,

"The *Saturday Review,* in a very temperate notice of *The Tempter,* condemns me for the use of the words 'bedlam' and 'superior,' and censures them as anachronisms. Now, as the English spoken in Chaucer's day would be quite unintelligible to a modern audience, it follows that any play dealing with that age must be a frank anachronism from beginning to end. Indeed any play or any picture of a past age must always be crammed with anachronisms and anomalies. And it is precisely the masterpieces in each art that contain the boldest, the wildest, the most glaring anachronisms and anomalies. But I will not shelter myself behind the general law that denies life to any picture of the past which is not also impregnated with the very life-blood of the actual present. I will only claim, what surely will not be denied me by any student of English literature, that in writing a verse tragedy to-day it is permissible for fools to tread where angels have rushed in, and that we shall be secure from censure if we follow the usage and diction of Elizabethan literature. Now, both these words 'bedlam' and 'superior' were in constant employment by the Elizabethans. 'Bedlam,' as surely everybody but the *Saturday Review* must remember, was a favourite word of Shakespeare's. It is used 3 times in *Lear,* in dealing with ages long before Chaucer; it occurs in *John,* in *Henry V,* and in the 2nd part of *Henry VI.* 'Superior,' again, was in constant use amongst the Elizabethans. It is not used by Shakespeare, but it occurs in Chapman, in Sidney, in Tyndall, and in Sir Thomas More. It is surely the merest quibbling to censure such words as anachronisms when they are consecrated by such usage.

"I would not have troubled you at such length, but amongst much generous appreciation that *The Tempter* has received, so many criticisms start by denying the only conditions on which it is possible to write a drama of the past. Of course one can smile at many of the eccentricities of journals that do not pretend to have any care for literature, or any knowledge of it, but it is strange that a paper of the standing of the *Saturday Review* should base its censure on the grounds I have laid before you.

"Faithfully yours,

"HENRY ARTHUR JONES."

My father was greatly amused by a letter which appeared in *Morning* shortly after the production of *The Tempter.* It was written by a lady who protested vehemently against the indecent plays then running in London; she cited *The Tempter* and *The Second Mrs. Tanqueray;* and she wished to know why ladies should be compelled to witness in the theatre scenes or subjects they would not even venture to discuss among themselves. She said she would not dream of going to *The Tempter* with a gentleman, and she would like to know why, if the public wanted to see fine plays, they did not confine themselves to going to see productions such as *Little Lord Fauntleroy.* The letter was signed "Not a Prude." Though the play ran over 70 nights, it was a financial failure, as the scenery and dresses were very costly. Tree spared no pains on the mounting, and it was unfortunate that on the first night the shipwreck scene was a fiasco, as the gauzes caught fire and the ship refused to sink.

The play was published by Macmillan's in November 1898, with a preface by my father. It was mainly an attack on William Archer; Henry Arthur said, "I know of no critic who can be safely trusted to arrive at a wrong effect with so much precision and honest, painstaking effort as Mr. William Archer." H. A. J. had received great praise from Archer for many of his plays, especially *The Crusaders,* and his attack was very ungenerous. That he regretted it is shown by the following letter, written in 1899:

"26th June, 1899.

"My dear Archer,

"Your postcard announcing your change of address prompts me to send you a line. A few days ago I happened to look over the preface to *The Tempter;* it struck me as very ill-natured and egotistical. When I was preparing my plays for the press last autumn, I returned to your original notice. I had nothing upon my hands at the time, and *The Tempter,* in revenge for your scurvy treatment of him, prompted me to reply. I sat down and answered your attack in a tone that I thought was more polite and urbane than your own. But on taking up the preface now, it reads quite otherwise than I supposed, and I am sorry I wrote it. I shall withdraw it in any further edition. I do not suppose you are very sensitive about such matters, and I am sure you will readily believe me that I wrote more in mischief than in anger. Let me assure you that there has never been a time when I would not have readily taken your hand. . . .

"My wife joins in kind regards to you and Mrs. Archer.

"Faithfully yours,

"Henry Arthur Jones.

"As a further sign of grace I may mention I was reading *Peer Gynt* with great delight this morning."

Archer replied to this letter as follows:

"I am glad to have your letter, but I assure you it was quite unnecessary. We give each other little raps from time to time, indeed I am afraid you will find a little jibe at your combative qualities in the next *Fortnightly,* but I hope we are neither of us foolish enough to convert a little literary rapier-play into a personal quarrel."

G. B. S. also wrote to him after reading the play, and H. A. J. was gratified and interested by the following criticism:

> "Blen-cathra, Hindhead,
> "Haslemere, Surrey.
> "*2nd December, 1898.*

"DEAR H. A. J.,

"Just a provisional line to prevent your thinking me dead. I cannot go to Hayling Island; for it now appears that the one all important condition for the foot is disuse—rest brought to the verge of killing the patient with inaction. I went to my specialist last week, and demanded the immediate amputation of the bone and the attacked toe. He happens to understand the exact relation between science and good sense wonderfully well for a surgeon, and he observed that if it was his toe, he would stick to it. He declares that my health is improving visibly; that I am pulling up from a breakdown; and that if I hold on a while, possessing my soul with patience, I shall either escape an operation and heal up by Christian Science, so to speak, or at least reduce the disease to a small and perfectly defined spot which can be removed without any great loss to my foot. So I am waiting; but I regret to say that I have used up my recuperative energies this week in a most tremendous fourth act of *Cæsar and Cleopatra*.

Since I cannot come to Hayling Island, H. I. had better come to me. If you drop in on us from that end of the line, get out at Liphook, which is very little further off than Haslemere, the road being beyond all comparison better and less steep. Our gate is on the main Portsmouth-London Road, about 100 yards from the 40th milestone from London.

"My mother, whose opinion is as incorruptible as that of Molière's cook, and who never knows or cares who a play is by, writes that *Jane* at the Haymarket is very good and she would quite cheerfully see it again, whereas *The Three Musketeers* bored her extremely.

"Later on, if I don't see you in the meantime, I must write a screed about *The Tempter*, which is a most amazing freak of yours. The blank verse is a model of speakability; and it's curious how its compliance with this condition forces it into relationship with Elizabethan blank verse, though you, Heaven be praised, are no Elizabethan. Altogether a rum business, which I would applaud as a *tour-de-force* and a lesson to the accursed literary amateur, if it were not that you say you gave a year and a half to it— which was a most prodigal sin. More of this anon.

"This place beats Pitfold all to fits. I am a new man since I came here; the air would make a dramatist of— who shall I say?

"By the way, you forgot in that preface that Archer's special pet as a dramatist is Pinero. Or did you? It would have spoiled the joke to make an exception, perhaps; and nobody will remember the point.

"I cannot express myself clearly after dinner; come and talk. The missus thinks you vastly inferior to me as a dramatist (Shakespeare also); but she appreciates you as a man.

"Yours ever,
"G, BERNARD SHAW."

He was delighted when he received an enthusiastic letter of praise from Sir Hall Caine, who wrote:

"Peel,
"Isle of Man.
"*6th May, 1893.*

"MY DEAR JONES,

"I have just read *The Tempter*. It is a great play. Not so great in scheme as in execution. If it had been that it would have been by very long odds the greatest play of the century. The mischief is hardly enough; it seems too accidental; not grounded deep enough in the inevitable; not the tragic of fate, of human love, but of the secondary thing, human blundering. It is true that so mighty a work as *Othello* is partly chargeable with the same fault—if I dare say so. True, too, that the complications based on love may be partly accidental and yet tragic.

"But this is ungracious cavilling. The outlook on the government of the world is broad and from a real height of thought and feeling. Some of the passages ring with most noble power.

"As verse the play astounds me. There are lines in it finer, it seems to me, than any living man has written. Such strength, variety, and density of diction I had not expected to meet with anywhere nowadays. . . .

"I look forward to seeing the play acted, God sparing me. We go up to London, by present arrangement, the first week in January and stay three months, all well. Before that I hope to finish or nearly finish my new book. It is the strongest and most human thing I've ever done, and my friends are very sure that a play ought to be made of it.

"I cannot congratulate you—that is too poor a compliment. You have enriched the literature of the drama; we are all the richer for a work like this, and the stage is ennobled by it.

"With kindest greetings,
"HALL CAINE."

H. A. J. felt no lasting bitterness over the failure of *The Tempter*, but I believe he thought that the play might have been a success if Tree had been more suited to the part; he always said, "He couldn't play *The Tempter*—he was a weak-kneed devil."

Early in 1894 my father had a great success with *The Masqueraders*, which was produced at the St. James's Theatre on 28th April. It was his first association with Sir George Alexander, and, in spite of many difficulties with Mrs. Patrick Campbell, who played Dulcie Larondie, it was a very pleasant and memorable partnership.

H. A. J. often told us that "Alec" would never allow him to read a play, because he said he would then be certain to think the play a good one, as H. A. J. read all his plays magnificently. He always said, "Alec was the best judge of a play of any man in London." On receiving the manuscript of the play, Sir George wrote:

"8th December.

"MY DEAR H. A. J.,

"Day brought me the manuscript last night. I read it to my wife before going to bed. She was as delighted as I am with it. She feels there is only one Dulcie, and that is Ellen Terry. Whether Mrs. P. C. will be able to show the requisite amount of fun, and still more the necessary refinement, is a moot point.

"Yours very sincerely,

"GEORGE ALEXANDER."

Henry Arthur told me that he sent Ellen Terry a copy of *The Masqueraders* on the day of production, and that, although she was acting at the Lyceum, she rushed round to see him just before going to the theatre to say how she loved the play; that she had been lying on her bed in the afternoon reading the play and acting the part of Dulcie. She wrote him the following adorable letter about the part:

MR. HERBERT WARING   MRS. PATRICK CAMPBELL   MR. GEORGE ALEXANDER

THE CARD SCENE IN "THE MASQUERADERS," ST. JAMES'S THEATRE, 1894

(*By courtesy of "The Sphere"*)

"22, Barkston Gardens,
          "Earl's Court, S.W.
                    "*Sunday.*

"Oh, but you're a happy man to-day I know—to *do* a thing WELL!   Sumptuous delight of feeling.

"To *try*—and then *do it* BADLY—ah, WITHERING.   I know it all (allowed, that *sounds* VAIN!)   That brilliant play!   How good of you to send it me.   Thank you. That girl!!   Dulcie—she *lives*—her heartbreak is so true— her DEVILMENT so entrancing—enchanting—she's a Woman and a Fairy.   She's a Witch—she's a Devil—an Angel—no, a Woman—and you're a *magic man* and with all my heart (in a hurry—as usual!) I congratulate you, not on your 'success,' but upon *your work.*

               "Yours affectionately,
                         "E. T."

In speaking of her enthusiasm, H. A. J. said, "She'd have been magnificent, as she would in *Michael;* different from Mrs. Pat of course, but very fine."

Henry Arthur also sent a copy of the play to G. B. S., who wrote:

               "29, Fitzroy Square, W.
                    "*11th June, 1894.*

"MY DEAR JONES,

"This is about as near return of post as I can get to acknowledge the copy of *The Masqueraders* you sent me. I am rather curious to see it on the boards, as there is a certain fanciful quality in it that attracts me; and I want to see how much of it they succeed in getting across the footlights.   I like the fairy-tale in the bar of a country hotel, the fantastic woman, the star-gazer, and the vaporous brother.   The comedy is of course first rate: you have never appreciated yourself fully in that department, or you would have given us more in the way of unmixed thorough-paced comedy. The rest I forgive you for, though I believe you faked up that atrocious nurse for the express purpose of infuriating me. And there is such a lot to be done on the stage with the real hospital nurse. My real soldier in *Arms and the Man* would not have been in it if you had risen to the occasion. Every one of that woman's allusions to duty elicited a howl of rage from me. She morally outrages my tenderest sensibilities.

"I have just had a visit from Sigmund Lautenburg of the New Theatre, Berlin. He has come to London under the impression that the two great successes of the year in England are *Arms and the Man* and *The Lady Slavey,* now being played in Nottingham. I explained to him that Nottingham is not a district of West Central London, and that *Arms and the Man,* with its splendid advertisements and its applicants for stalls turned away nightly, has only twice drawn as much as half the cost of sending up the curtain, and has on two other less happy occasions in Whit week and the cab strike gone down to £14. Having thus placed him on his guard against the wiles of London, I got the paper and told him where to go to see the really successful pieces, and who were the leading authors. As he wrote to me a few weeks ago I have made enquiries about him and found that he is *the* man to do Berlin business with; so if he calls on you or otherwise opens negotiations about *The Masqueraders,* be good to him for my sake, as I am greatly touched by his illusions on the subject of my eminence, and on his complimenting me on my strong resemblance to Jesus Christ. He is at De Keyser's Royal Hotel, Blackfriars Bridge, in case you should know him already.

"We put Wyndham into a delicate situation the other day. When you arrived I was in the act of reading to him an extremely advanced farcical comedy of mine called *The Philanderer,* he having shown a very proper sense of

my gifts after witnessing the Avenue show. As I know
that you are doing a play for him, I felt disposed to wink
at you through the crack of the door. For Heaven's sake
don't write him anything that will run long.

"Your advice in business matters has been invaluable
to me. I enclose a duplicate of the draft agreement for
America, from which you will see that I did exactly what
you told me. For the provinces I have arranged for ten
per cent. in the half-dozen big cities, seven and a half in
the thirty next in order of importance, and five per cent.
in the rest. I have no faith in its success in the provinces,
especially as it has failed here so signally with the pit and
gallery; but since the provincial success of *A Woman of No
Importance* the notion has got about that there is business
in 'advanced' plays on the road; and I have found a man
willing to risk it.

"I shall have a brilliant article in next month's *New
Review* on *Arms and the Man,* giving all my authorities for
the military realism (there is not an original notion in the
whole affair from beginning to end) and stating my position as regards cynicism and all that sort of rubbish.

"By the way, talking of that, how frightfully pessimistic
your play is! Hang it all, Regent's Park, with all its drawbacks, is better than Andromeda. Why don't you chuck
up these idiotic moral systems according to which human
nature comes out base and filthy? It's the systems that
are wrong and not we. I believe in the good old Molière-
Labiche-Sheridan line; they would have been very well
contented with myself and Walker and Morris and the
rest of us, and not have sighed for any Andromeda.

"Yours sincerely,

"G. Bernard Shaw."

The reference to advice on business matters is explained
by the following letter:

"29, Fitzroy Square, W.

"*24th April, 1894.*

"MY DEAR JONES,

"I got your telegram with great pleasure on the first night of *Arms and the Man*. With signal ingratitude I am now going to give you some further trouble at a moment when my own recent experience teaches me that no man of the feeblest altruism would take up a moment of your time.

"The trouble is, American rights. Overton wants to buy them for Palmer. His offer is £100 down; play to be produced within a year; Palmer to have U. S. and Canadian rights for five years; my royalties to be 5% on $4,000 a week, 10% on to the next $2,000, and 15% on anything over. He is evidently very keen on the bargain and pressed the £100 cheque repeatedly on me to-day. But I declined and said I would draft the agreement for him myself.

"Now I have no doubt that I could get £150 down if I stood out for it; but about that I do not care, as I can perfectly well afford to wait. What staggers me is the application of the sliding scale. At the Avenue I get 5% when the receipts do not exceed £100 a night (a rather common circumstance so far), 7½ when they do not exceed £150, and 10% after that. This is quite a different thing from 5% on £100 of the receipts, 7½ on the excess up to £150, and 10 on the balance, which is the system proposed by Overton for his 5, 10, and 15. I should prefer 10% all round. At the Avenue, too, I have only given a license for the bare run of the theatre and nothing more, whereas Palmer ties me up for 5 years. Overton, however, assures me that these are the usual terms; and I have allowed him to assume that I will close with him on that understanding.

"Can I do better? Am I being had? I have to ask you because you are the only person I know whose business faculty inspires me with the smallest confidence. To enable you to answer with Yes, No, or a figure, I enclose a sheet of questions, as if you were a parliamentary candidate. It will save time: No use in wishing you success, when asking you a favour. Besides, *you're* safe.

"Yrs sincerely,

"G. BERNARD SHAW."

Undoubtedly George Alexander was the ideal choice for the part of that romantic dreamer, David Remon. *The Masqueraders* is a struggle between two men, Sir Bryce Skene, a dissolute, drunken waster, and David Remon, a high-minded, hopelessly unworldly astronomer, for the possession of Dulcie Larondie, an attractive, wayward girl who has never had a decent chance. Dulcie marries Sir Bryce, but he treats her shamefully, and she only remains with him for the sake of her child. Remon unexpectedly inherits a large fortune, and in a tremendous scene between the two men he offers to give up his money to Sir Bryce if he will relinquish his wife and child. They agree to cut the cards and leave the decision to Fate. Remon wins, and in the last act, after installing Dulcie and her sister in his home, he leaves them to go on an astronomical expedition to Africa.

The audience at the first night was one of the most brilliant ever present at any of my father's plays. The Prince and Princess of Wales were there, with the Duke and Duchess of Teck, Baroness Burdett-Coutts, the Dowager Duchess of Rutland, Lord Balfour, Lord Randolph Churchill, Professor Dewar, Marcus Stone, Mrs. Perugini, Lord and Lady Londonderry, Sir Norman Lockyer, Sir Hall Caine, H. D. Traill, Lord and Lady St. Helier, while Lady Dorothy Nevill and her daughter were in H. A. J.'s box. King Edward and Queen Alexandra went to see the play about a fortnight after the production.

The Masqueraders was successfully produced in New York at the Empire Theatre, in December 1894, and it ran

for 139 nights in London.   It was taken off during the
summer, when Sir George Alexander went on tour, but the
run was resumed on 11th November, with Evelyn Millard
in Mrs. Pat Campbell's part.   I believe the choice of Miss
Millard was partly due to the many difficulties Sir George
had with Mrs. Pat during the original run.   There is a story
which has become almost a classic in the theatrical world.
It is said that Sir George was not on speaking terms with
his leading lady, so he wrote to her as follows, "Mr. George
Alexander presents his compliments to Mrs. Pat Campbell and he will be much obliged if she will refrain from
laughing at him during the last act."   I have been told
that her reply was, "Mrs. Patrick Campbell presents her
compliments to Mr. George Alexander.   He is mistaken,
she does not laugh at him during the last act.   She waits
until she gets home."

One of my proudest possessions is a beautifully bound
copy of *The Second Mrs. Tanqueray*.   Within is the inscription:

Mrs. Tanqueray sends the best of good wishes to
The Masqueraders.

Arthur Pinero
to
Henry Arthur Jones.
April 28th, 1894.

And on the opposite page my father wrote:

"MY DARLING DORIS,

"I value very highly this gift from my friend Pinero,
which came to me when his fine play of *Mrs. Tanqueray*
gave way to *The Masqueraders*.   Accept it in recognition
of your loving and constant care, especially on my 76th
birthday.

"Your loving father,
"HENRY ARTHUR JONES.

"September 23/27."

When *The Second Mrs. Tanqueray* was revived in 1922, H. A. J. wrote to Sir Arthur Pinero:

"5th June, 1922.

"My dear Pinero,

"I am delighted at the success of the revival of *Mrs. Tanqueray*.   When a dramatist has drawn a vital character, it is astonishing how many varied and even opposing personalities will fit it.   Look at *Hamlet*.

"Always cordially yours,

"Henry Arthur Jones."

CHAPTER IX

My father fought hard and fearlessly for years to establish the right of English dramatists to depict life as it is, and not as an emasculated, trumpery pageant suitable only for young ladies of a past generation. That is why, in spite of Sir Charles Wyndham's urgent and repeated pleadings, he refused to alter *The Case of Rebellious Susan,* his next important play after *The Masqueraders.* H. A. J. told Wyndham the plot soon after he started to write the play, and read him the various acts as they were finished.

The theme of *Rebellious Susan* is "what is sauce for the goose is sauce for the gander," but poor Susan suffers considerably in her efforts to prove that a wife is entitled to the same amount of licence as her husband.

Both Sir Charles and Miss Moore liked the play, but they were extremely anxious that the question of Susan's infidelity should be left indefinite. Sir Charles wrote to H. A. J. very strongly urging his point of view:

"After reading the third act to Miss Moore and myself you promised to consider the excision of a line or two, so as to leave an opportunity to the audience of guessing what conclusions they most affected as to Sue's guilt or innocence. You will remember on reading the second act you expatiated on the advantages of this uncertainty as giving rise to discussion. Personally I adhere to my opinion rigidly—that Sue should be innocent—and I am strengthened in that belief by the enclosed letter from Jeune.

"However, you think differently, so—to my regret—let it be. I want you, however, to expunge the line, P. 34.

132

MARY MOORE   CHARLES WYNDHAM   C. P. LITTLE

IN "THE CASE OF REBELLIOUS SUSAN," CRITERION THEATRE, 1894

Sir Richard: And if there is any little natural disinclination to make each other's acquaintance, let me give you a formal introduction.

" 'I should kill myself if anyone knew.'
and
" ' . . . never boasted . . .'
leaving the line
" 'You have never spoken of me to any of your men friends?'

"These do not in any way interfere with your plans, but they afford one an opportunity of overcoming the strong repulsion to the whole idea which must be as evident to you as it is painful to me, and will allow me to go into the part with good will.   Failing this I am beginning to feel that my participation in the piece will not only be useless but positively dangerous."

Shortly afterwards he wrote again:

"Hotel Petersburg,
"St. Moritz.
"*23rd August.*

"MY DEAR OLD MAN,

"Nothing in the world will give me greater pleasure than to have your sympathetic society up here.   The place is lovely, and if you are willing for a walk, we will on leaving here have 3 or 4 days' tramp in these regions before descending into the depths of commonplace Europe.

"As, however, you will come with the special purpose of reading and discussing the play, it will be wise to remember our utterly irreconcilable views as to the treatment of your subject before deciding to come.   You are so earnest and love your work so much that I fear lest in our discussions some of that pleasant intercourse may be damaged. If you can put your parental feeling on one side, there will be no danger—or if you are prepared to content yourself with reading your third act and then religiously determine to make no further reference to it till we return to London, —your visit will be most enjoyable both to yourself and to me.   If on the other hand you are going to talk about it and discuss it, taking so much to heart my necessarily harsh strictures on the present condition of the piece as far as I know it, the result I fear will be regrettable.

"You wrote to me some time ago to put into writing my impressions, so that in the hour of success you may be able to laugh at me—but you coupled with the request, another —that I should not fetter your hands whilst you were writing the third act. . . .   Well.   I record first my belief that my part, so far as I know it, does not afford any particular opportunity for acting—that it is a good part to any uninitiated observer, but that to the actor it does not appeal to any of these attributes, with which I am credited— possessing neither buoyant humour, nor tenderness, nor passion, nor in fact any demonstrative emotion of any kind which is calculated to further an actor's reputation.   The part is a sound one, but in no way a profitable one.   I mention this, not in the spirit of discontent, because being a manager and, I hope, a sensible one, I have not that supreme contempt for pounds, shillings, and pence that dominates the æsthetic soul of Beerbohm Tree.   I mention it only to guard you against disappointment. . . .

"It is, however, of the spirit of the play that I, in obedience to your wishes, record my impressions.

"I stand as bewildered to-day as ever at finding an author, a clean living, clear-minded man, hoping to extract laughter from an audience on the score of a woman's impurity.   I can realise the picture of a bad woman and her natural and desirable end being portrayed, but that amusement pure and simple should be expected from the sacrifice of that one indispensable quality in respect for womanhood astounds me.

"I am equally astounded at a practical long-experienced dramatic author believing that he will induce married men to bring their wives to a theatre to learn the lesson that their wives can descend to such nastiness, as giving themselves up for one evening of adulterous pleasure and then return safely to their husband's arms, provided they are clever enough, low enough, and dishonest enough to avoid being found out.

"Finally I am puzzled to wonderment as to the source from which he expects to draw his audience, since it is evident to me that married men will not bring their wives and mothers will not bring their daughters. . . .

"With the weakness in view, inherent to all humanity, of shifting responsibilities from one's own shoulders, I have hitherto refrained from pointing out to you that this, to me, most repulsive episode was not in any way fore-shadowed in your scenario that Sunday morning we talked together. I was then given to understand that Susan returned to England, having, it is true, fallen in love with a young man, which under the circumstances was natural enough, but no hint was given to me that this romance was vulgarised down to a commonplace and unworthy tem-porary intrigue. I thought the piece was going to show that Susan's threat to find romance was most inconvenient—to the verge of impossibility. I did not anticipate that the romance would be killed out of all sight. The first act as read to me that day bore out this idea—for the text of your sermon, if it had a text at all, was that 'there is no gander sauce'—but I will permit myself to doubt whether, ad-vancing in the first act that there is no such sauce, you are consistent in construction in abandoning the task of proving the truth of your assertion. . . .

"To my mind the piece is neither more nor less amusing where this episode is absolutely eliminated; where it appears that the woman's mind has strayed, but not her soul—that she herself in the second act realises that there is no gander sauce, and that nothing remains of her Cairo romance but a sentimentality, which of itself dies out in the third act under the awakening process she is submitted to. *Then,* her equivocation—her troubles are likely to be amusing—but never so where she has forfeited her woman-hood.   No man, to my mind, who has daughters of his own can advance such a theory as you wish in this piece—that a weak woman often goes to these extremes and then when there is no other refuge left, sneaks back to her husband's bed.   I am not speaking as a moralist, I am simply voicing the public instinct.

*   *   *   *   *   *   *   *   *

"Finally—I want to warn you.   Whether the Box Office supports or contradicts my views, *you will not laugh.*   You have achieved an enviable position, and people will wonder why instead of taking pains to construct a piece, you should rely on a gross and unnecessary piece of impropriety to give strength to a comedy which, coming from the hands of so successful a man, ought to have been above any such necessity.

"I have sent orders as you desired to make the announcement at once.   It is an odd coincidence that Grundy should have struck upon a similar theme.   If, however, the *Referee* is right—his New Woman is going to be a good woman, not a Lady Susan.   That—*per se*—will be a great advantage over you.   The tendency of the drama should always, if possible, be elevating.   If we depart from this ever, as in the case of *Mrs. Tanqueray,* and such like, the subject has to be grappled with seriously.

"I do hope, old man, that you will take all I have said in the same kind friendly spirit in which it is written. . . . If after this long and very unpleasant letter you care to come, do, and the sooner the better.   It is most charming, the weather promises to settle and the scenery is grand, whilst you will receive the warmest of welcomes from

"Yours sincerely,

"CHARLES WYNDHAM."

This letter is striking proof of the prudish and restricted atmosphere of the English theatre; of the falsifying of life demanded from playwrights in order to pander to Victorian squeamishness. I am glad that Henry Arthur refused to alter his play, though I understand Wyndham's attitude, which was the outcome of a definite and successful policy of management at the Criterion Theatre.

The play was produced on 3rd October, 1894. The Press notices were not at all enthusiastic, but, in spite of the critics, *The Case of Rebellious Susan* was a great success and ran for 164 nights. It was revived at Wyndham's Theatre in 1901, and again at the Criterion in June 1910 and in September of the same year. The New York production at the Lyceum Theatre in December 1894 was also very successful, and the American notices were favourable.

My father sent a ticket for the opening night to Israel Zangwill, who wrote:

"24, Oxford Road,
"Kilburn, N.W.

"MY DEAR JONES,

"Thank you very much for the ticket for *Rebellious Susan*. I could not resist reading the play at Antwerp the other night, and I have come back to England mainly to see it. The reading left a curious mixed impression as of a theme confusedly handled. From the theatrical point of view I saw a splendid part for Mr. Wyndham and I saw Fred Kerr as Pybus without knowing he was in the cast. Viewed purely as literature, the play seems to me to sin in your usual manner by combining comedy (which is almost drama) with farce. The quarrel between Pybus and Elaine seemed especially trivial, though the conception of the couple is exquisitely droll. Again the comic relief is extrinsic to the play proper. There are other details of construction I should cavil at, but of course as an outsider,

not as a working dramatist.   I like the first act very much
and agree with the vision of average human nature which
underlies the main conception.   But I mustn't bore you
with a long criticism here.   The play will cause talk; this
much of success it must certainly reap; and you cannot
write without humour and wisdom.   Whether the central
grip is strong enough to hold audiences I shall discover on
Wednesday night; meanwhile the airy critic wishes the
practical dramatist every success.

"Yours sincerely,
"I. ZANGWILL."

"PS.—That is a great saying: "Our real modern tragedy
—that we laugh at the tragedy of our own lives."

It has often been said that Henry Arthur wrote plays for
Wyndham and other managers.   Apart from *The Silver
King* and one or two early plays and *The Bauble Shop,*
H. A. J. never wrote a play to order.   When a plot had
taken shape in his brain and he had started to write, he
often felt that the principal part would suit a leading actor
or actress, but apart from that I am convinced that he
never added to or wrote up any one character in a play in
the hope of making it more acceptable to any particular
manager.   In the case of *Chance the Idol* my father refused to alter the part of Douce Kennett from a young girl
into that of a young widow or to add to the part so that
Miss Moore could play the character, and Wyndham did
not act in the play because of Henry Arthur's refusal.

The Triumph of the Philistines, produced by George
Alexander at the St. James's Theatre on 11th May, 1895,
raised a storm of adverse criticism, and the reception on
the first night was very hostile.   The theme of the play is
based on the never-ending antagonism between British
prudery and Bohemianism.   The *Daily News* voiced the
feelings of a great many of the critics and a large section of

the public when it spoke of "this wholesale disparagement of his fellow-countrymen." But there did not lack appreciative notices in the Press; the *Saturday Review* said, "The attack is not the usual sham attack of the stage moralist: it is courageous, uncompromising, made with sharp weapons, and left without the slightest attempt to run away at the end. . . . The acting is hardly as good as the play"; while William Archer's verdict in *The New Budget* was, "A profoundly melancholy, infinitely suggestive drama, filling us with an awe-stricken sense of the mystery that enwraps the moral government of the universe."

In spite of the London failure (the play ran for forty-four nights only, when the gross receipts were £4,500 for the run), George Alexander took the play on tour with some success in the autumn of that year, and it was also produced in the provinces by Mr. Fred Latham. Shortly before the first night H. A. J. sent Alexander a copy of the play with an inscription. Writing to thank him, Sir George said:

"MY DEAR H. A. J.

"Your dedication makes me feel rather small. I've been a little 'snappy' to-day I fear, but I always get into a state of nerves a few days before a production. You are always patient and everything that a good fellow should be during rehearsals, and I really must give you a 'rocking-chair' before long.

"Yours,

"ALEC."

I think this must be the only tribute to Henry Arthur's behaviour at rehearsals which he ever received from a manager, and I feel sure that Sir George's tact and charm and the way he managed H. A. J. were largely responsible for my father's unaccustomed docility.

The Triumph of the Philistines was published by Macmillan's in 1899, and, on receiving a copy, Mr. Bernard Shaw wrote my father the following postcard:

"Blen-cathra,
"Hindhead,
"Haslemere, Surrey.
"17th April, 1899.

"I forgot to acknowledge *The Triumph of the Philistines.* My wife is much delighted with it—thinks it no end of a play.   I am inclined to agree with her.   You should have got me to write the preface: I'd have said why it came to nothing at the St. James's straight enough.   Jimmy Welch, who was here on Sunday, knows the reason too—thinks Anson, in his best days, would have saved the situation.

"What is *Carnac Sahib* like—is it a disgraceful old potboiler, or another victim of the incompetence of the profession, or a success?

"I am laid up again in anguish—sprained the bad foot badly again (third time) on Monday, fooling with a bicycle.

"G. B. S."

In speaking to me of the play in 1927, Henry Arthur said, "I never got that play right, there wasn't enough stuff in it."   And he told me with pleasure that Thomas Hardy was in the pit on the first night of the play.   He would also refer with pride to the following letter from Mr. Hardy, asking for my father's advice:

"Max Gate,
"Dorchester,
"15th March, 1897.

"DEAR HENRY ARTHUR JONES,

"Can you tell me if the following are good or bad terms for a play?   I am in a hopeless fog on the matter.

"In a London theatre, average size:

Houses under £100	..	.. nothing.
From £100 to £130	..	.. 5 per cent.
From £130 to £170	..	.. 7½ per cent.
Over £170	..	.. 10 per cent.

"Probably produce play within a year.

"Ever sincerely yours,

"THOMAS HARDY."

Henry Arthur's first book, *The Renascence of the English Drama,* a collection of his lectures, articles, and pamphlets, was published early in 1895. It was very well received. In his preface he said, "The four chief qualities that any work of art can possess, be it play, picture, poem, or statue, are beauty, mystery, passion, imagination." Augustin Filon, the great French critic, paid my father a justly deserved tribute in 1895 in the September number of the *Revue des Deux Mondes:* "He is the most English of living dramatic writers," he said, "he who most faithfully and brilliantly expresses the soul of his race and generation." Nearly twenty years later Max Beerbohm, in his criticism of *Dolly Reforming Herself*, expressed much the same opinion.

Michael and His Lost Angel, as I have already implied, was the greatest failure Henry Arthur ever had; it ran for only ten days in London and for eleven nights in New York, but it was always his favourite play.

Michael and His Lost Angel is an epic of the age-long struggle between a man's allegiance to his religion and his love for a woman. Michael, though a stern ascetic, is swept off his feet by an overwhelming passion for Audrie Lesden, and, through a trick of fate, for a brief moment he yields to his passion. Michael insists upon their separation, and he eventually finds peace in the Roman Catholic

Church. Audrie, unrepentant and always most lovable, dies in his arms in the last act.

Henry Arthur was very anxious that Irving and Ellen Terry should take the play, but I believe that Irving did not like the part. In Sir Johnston Forbes-Robertson and Mrs. Patrick Campbell he had the ideal actor and actress for Michael and Audrie. From the first rehearsal there were difficulties with Mrs. Pat. She rehearsed for seven weeks, but she always hated the church scene, and objected to Audrie's lines, "I must just titivate a cherub's nose, or hang a garland on an apostle's toe." She thought the words were profane, and said so at rehearsal: a member of the cast told me how well he remembers H. A. J.'s voice ringing out in angry tones from the stalls, "It is not profanity at all, it is in the part." My father expressed the just resentment he felt at the difficulties made by Mrs. Patrick Campbell in the following letter to Forbes-Robertson:

"16th December, 1895.

"My dear Forbes-Robertson,

"If Mrs. Campbell is to play the part, she must play it exactly as it is written and upon the lines that I have laid down. But I feel it will be impossible to go through rehearsals without such constant scenes that it will be far better to engage Marion Terry. I am sure you will be wise not to risk it. Please understand I will not have the text altered. I must ask you to at once send me notice of any rehearsal that may be called, as I shall insist upon the right of being present, and if I find the least attempt is being made to alter the text or to play the piece in any way prejudicial to its success, I shall take the utmost means to enforce my undoubted rights.

"Faithfully yours,
"Henry Arthur Jones."

"DO YOU THINK YOU WOULD HAVE DONE BETTER WITH IT, FORBES, IF I HAD BEEN YOUR LOST ANGEL?"

"MICHAEL AND HIS LOST ANGEL"

ENTR'ACTE CARTOON OF

MRS. PATRICK CAMPBELL AND FORBES—ROBERTSON, 1896

When Mrs. Pat threw up the part a few days before the first night, a great many of the papers said that it was because she objected to several of the lines, and that Miss Marion Terry, who took her place, refused to say them, and the offending passages were omitted. That is not so; Miss Terry did not object, and she said the lines. H. A. J. did not quite hit it off with Forbes-Robertson, either, and at one rehearsal he did not like the way Sir Johnston was speaking his words, and interrupted him. Sir Johnston said very good-temperedly, "Well, you just come up here and do it yourself, my boy." H. A. J. went up there, but failed to show how he wanted the lines rendered. He could read his plays splendidly, but he was never very successful if he tried to show actors or actresses how to do their parts. Apart from the endless difficulties at rehearsals, Forbes-Robertson disliked the title of the play, and wrote to my father twice begging him to alter it. He said:

" . . . Now to a very important matter. I am perfectly convinced in my own mind that the title is wrong. A 'lost angel' has been a term for a lady of pleasure for many years. I think your title anticipates too much, and, if she is lost, he most certainly is too. *'Michael and Audrie'* would, I think, be simple and dignified, and would in a measure prepare them for the duologue nature of the play. Pray think seriously of this, for I am quite convinced it could not stand as it is, seeing that 'lost angel' is such a well-known term for a class to which 'Audrie' certainly does not belong."

And again:

"I have not cast any important parts without consulting you. . . . I shall be only too thankful if you will read the play to the company. It is my earnest wish you should do so. . . . I have never been so anxious about any part I have ever played as I am about 'Michael.' Had you seen your way to change the title I should have been very glad, and I think it would have saved the trouble we have so sadly got into. There are one or two small cuts that I hope you will allow me to make in the second act; and I still hope you will permit me to omit the 'image' speech in the fourth act. I cannot expect you to share my awful anxieties, I can only say that no money is being spared, and that we are doing all in our power to produce the play to your liking. . . . There is no unfriendly feeling on my part towards you. Pray put that out of your mind. All I wish to do is to act for the best for all concerned."

Before the production several papers commented unfavourably on the title; they said it was in bad taste, and some suggested it was profane. *Truth* said, "The title was as silly as it was objectionable."

When Mrs. Pat resigned her part, she wrote to my father:

"1st January, 1896.
"DEAR MR. JONES,

"I am most sorry that I could not enter right heartily into the part of Audrie, and that I felt obliged, in duty to my own feelings and to you as the author, to resign it. I thank you for your kindness in wishing me to play the part.

"With good wishes for success and all happiness in the New Year.

"Yours sincerely,
"BEATRICE STELLA CAMPBELL."

Forbes-Robertson went to him and said he was sure if H. A. J. asked her very nicely she would reconsider her decision; he replied, "I'll see her damned first." Miss Terry was very charming, but she was ineffectual and unsuited to the part.

The play was produced at the Lyceum on 15th January, 1896, and at the Empire Theatre, New York, on the same day. Nearly all the notices were very scathing or very enthusiastic, but most of the leading critics condemned the play, a notable exception being Bernard Shaw's criticism in the *Saturday Review*. G. B. S. said, "One of the greatest comforts of criticising the work of Mr. Henry Arthur Jones is that the critic can go straight to the subject-matter without troubling about the dramatic construction. In the born writer the style is the man; and with the born dramatist, the play is the subject. Mr. Jones's plays grow; they are not cut out of bits of paper and stuck together. . . . Mr. Jones's technical skill is taken as a matter of course. . . . When I respond to the appeal of Mr. Jones's art by throwing myself sympathetically into his characteristic attitude of mind, I am conscious of no shortcoming in *Michael and His Lost Angel*. It then seems to me to be a genuinely sincere and moving play, feelingly imagined, written with knowledge as to the man and insight as to the woman by an author equipped not only with the experience of an adept playwright, and a kindly and humorous observer's sense of contemporary manners, but with that knowledge of spiritual history in which Mr. Jones's nearest competitors seem so stupendously deficient. Its art is in vital contact with the most passionate religious movement of its century, as fully quickened art always has been. . . . I unhesitatingly class Mr. Jones as first, and eminently first, among the surviving fittest of his own generation of playwrights. . . . The last act is only saved from being a sorry business by the man's plucking a sort of courage out of abandonment, and by a humorous piteousness in the dying woman, who, whilst submitting, out of sheer feebleness of character, to Michael's attitude, is apologetically conscious of having no sincere conviction of sin. . . . The performance at the Lyceum has taken all the heart out of my hopes of gaining general assent to my high estimate of *Michael and His Lost Angel*. The public see the play as it is acted, not as it ought to be acted. The sooner Mr. Jones publishes it, the better for its reputation. . . . The melancholy truth of the matter is that the English stage got a good play, and was completely and ignominiously beaten by it."

The play aroused a storm of criticism and discussion, and it is possible, in spite of Miss Terry's unsuitability for the part of Audrie, that it might have been a financial success. However, my father told me that Forbes-Robertson took it off without informing him of his intention to do so. Henry Arthur always declared that in his view the receipts did not justify Sir Johnston's action. When *Michael* was produced, my elder brother Philip was desperately ill with pleurisy and double pneumonia, and he died during the run of the piece. His illness kept my father away from the theatre, and he did not know what was going on. On 7th February he wrote the following letter to Forbes-Robertson and Frederick Harrison; he also sent it to certain papers, and, although it was not published, a great many paragraphs appeared giving the substance of the letter:

"Dear Forbes-Robertson and Frederick Harrison,

"I was surprised to find that you took off *Michael and His Lost Angel* without giving me any notice. The sudden announcement in the papers of the last three nights was the first intimation I received of its withdrawal. As you know, I was kept away from the theatre by other matters, and was unable to take any interest in what was going on. You did not send me any returns, and I supposed, like everybody else, that the piece was a disastrous failure. When at length you do send me the returns, I find to my astonishment that, so far from the business being bad, the houses were very considerable and gave every appearance that the piece would be a financial success. Of course after

the very unfavourable Press notices it was only likely that
the first Monday and Tuesday houses would show some
weakness, but this apparently would have been only temporary.   You leave me no option but to publish this letter
with the exact returns, which I append herewith.   They
are considerably higher than the corresponding returns for
The Middleman, which proved an enormous financial success in England and America.

		£	s.	d.
15th January	. . . .	209	7	6
16th "	. . . .	128	9	3
17th "	. . . .	123	12	3
18th "	. . . .	203	5	5
20th "	. . . .	99	9	4
21st "	. . . .	99	9	11
22nd "	. . . .	114	14	4
23rd "	. . . .	121	18	0
24th "	. . . .	146	12	7
25th "	. . . .	231	7	0

"I may safely affirm that no piece has ever been taken
off with returns amounting to over £231 on the tenth night.
Further than this, no piece of mine has made such a deep
impression on those who did see it, if I may judge by the
large number of sympathetic letters that I have received
from strangers who were touched and excited by it. . . .

"I shall publish the play at once and leave it to speak
for itself.   But I must, in no ill-will to you, correct the
public opinion that the piece was a great pecuniary failure.
The above returns show that it was on the high road to be
a financial success.   And I must express my great astonishment at your pursuing so unusual a course towards
myself.

"Yours faithfully,

"HENRY ARTHUR JONES."

In reply to this letter Forbes-Robertson said:

"MY DEAR HENRY ARTHUR JONES,

"Your play was withdrawn because the business was *exceedingly bad,* but the notice in the papers of the last few nights brought some money in. It could not have held, as there was no booking whatever. I am sorry to hear the returns were not sent in the regular way, but I am not in the habit of sending returns. Mr. Harrison was frightfully pressed in consequence of the failure of *Michael,* or no doubt you would have got them before. Heaven knows I am sorry enough at having had to withdraw the play, it has been a great loss to me. It is too late now to look back, or place the blame. We all did our best.

"Yours,

"J. FORBES-ROBERTSON."

G. B. S., in the *Saturday Review,* said that the figures did not justify the piece having been withdrawn, and continued: "As to the real reason I do not know it; and I am so afraid that, with my romantic imagination, I shall begin guessing at it in spite of myself if I do not immediately break off, that . . ."

H. A. J. told me that on the Thursday evening after the first night Mrs. Pat danced into Miss Terry's dressing-room and said, "He's done it, he's done it, he's done it"; and when Miss Terry said, "What?" she replied, "He's taking it off on Saturday."

Pinero wrote him a charming letter, in which he said:

"I do not trouble you with any expressions of sympathy over the poor luck at the Lyceum. You will have accepted the matter philosophically, I feel sure—recognising that the theatres are in for a silly period. But, of all fashions, theatrical fashions are the least durable—a condition of things which operates both for and against the earnest writer; at the present moment he must console himself with the reflection that the next change of public taste is likely to be to his advantage."

Henry Arthur was so anxious that the play should be a success in New York that he spoke all the parts and stage directions into a phonograph at a sitting which lasted over seven hours. The cylinders were sent to America, and reproduced on another phonograph for the benefit of the New York company. But the play was a great failure in New York also, where it ran for only eleven nights. The notices were nearly all very hostile, though Henry Miller and Viola Allen received great praise in the leading parts.

Michael and His Lost Angel was like a very dearly-loved child to my father; it was always his favourite play, the darling of his heart. In October 1926, he said, "I was reading part of *Michael and His Lost Angel* this afternoon. By Jove, what a lovely play it is." And again, a year before he died, he said to me, "*Michael* has done more for my reputation than any success I've ever had." I believe his estimate to be very nearly correct. It has an enduring greatness widely recognised, not only by great literary critics and men of letters, and by the theatrical profession, but by an enormous number of the general public. Within a very few months of Henry Arthur's death we had requests from two managers to be allowed to produce the play. He spoke more constantly of *Michael* than of any other of his plays.

Although my father wished me to write his life, he was never very helpful in giving me information. In the last few years his health was very bad and he suffered from great nervous depression. When I asked him a direct question as to when or where he wrote a play, more often than not he would answer, "I can't remember," though his memory was remarkable, and in several instances which I shall quote, truly amazing. But he charged me solemnly more than once to write in full the account of the production and withdrawal of *Michael and His Lost Angel*.

CHAPTER X

On 21st April, 1896, just four months after the failure of *Michael,* Willard produced *The Rogue's Comedy* at the Garrick Theatre. This play is the story of a tremendous struggle between father and son. The son, ignorant of his parentage, succeeds in unmasking and ruining his old rogue of a father, who has had an amazingly successful career of crime and trickery. In spite of the boy's action, the old man is instrumental in helping him to win the girl he loves, without disclosing to him his parentage. Most of the notices were very good, though G. B. S., in the *Saturday Review,* was rather tepid, and certain of the critics said that the play showed signs of having been written in a hurry. In over half a century as a dramatic author Henry Arthur only wrote one play in a hurry—the last two acts of *Lydia Gilmore,* which was produced in New York in 1912, with Margaret Anglin in the leading part. The time he took over writing his plays varied enormously; he spent nearly a year on *The Tempter; The Liars* he wrote in three months, and *Dolly Reforming Herself* in six weeks. Whatever faults there are in *The Rogue's Comedy* are not due to hurried workmanship. Whatever the reason, the play was a failure, though Willard produced it with great success in America and played it there for several seasons.

My father felt the hostile reception of this play very keenly. He often said, "They booed me steadily for twenty-five minutes after *The Rogue's Comedy,* and I swore I would never again take a call." He kept this vow for over twenty years, when he took a call for *The Pacifists;* and as an old man of seventy-two he again faced a first-night audience after the production of *The Lie,* to be accorded one of the most memorable and wildly enthusiastic receptions of his whole career.

The Physician, his next play, is the story of a famous doctor who makes unavailing efforts to cure the dipsomaniacal fiancé of the girl he falls in love with. It was produced by Wyndham at the Criterion Theatre on 25th March, 1897. Both author and manager had high hopes of it, but it was only a very moderate success.

The following is one of the many delightful letters about his plays which my father received from Ellen Terry:

> "2, Barkston Gardens,
> "Earl's Court, S.W.
> "*Sunday.*

(*Printed*)

" 'Although Mr. Jones's new play *The Physician* is not published, it is printed, and copies were placed in the hands of a favoured few after the performance on Thursday.'

"Now don't be *horrid,* Mr. H. A. J.—and leave me out in the cold without a copy of your latest beautiful play, but *please* send me one this minute! I hope everybody in that theatre enjoyed it all as much as I did. It was *all* LOVELY! My love to Mrs. Jones and say I was absolutely *amazed* to see that youngest child of hers so big!

"Oh, Stars and Moons! How time gallops! Do you know your children came to see me when I was ill at Margate? *How* VERY *attractive* the grown-up girl is.

"*Please* don't forget to send me a *Physician* or I'll die.

> "Yours,
> "E. T."

All her letters breathe her radiant and enchanting personality.

In the autumn of 1897 Wyndham produced Henry Arthur's greatest play, *The Liars*. *The Liars* centres round the efforts of Lady Jessica Nepean's friends to rescue her from the consequences of a harmless escapade. Lady Jessica's jealous husband refuses to believe the cock-and-bull story told him by her friends, and Falkner, who loves Lady Jessica deeply, turns on Nepean at the end of the third act and tells him the truth. They decide to elope, but Sir Christopher Dering, in a tremendous speech, dissuades them and effects a reconciliation between husband and wife. On looking back, it seems almost incredible that many of the newspapers said that the title was not in good taste. Moreover, it was the smaller, less widely-read papers—the *Athenæum*, the *Sun*, the *Echo*, the *Lady*, and the *Weekly Times*—which acclaimed the play as Henry Arthur's masterpiece. *The Times* said, "It is excellent farce with a strain of melodrama running through it," and the *Daily Mail* spoke of the play as "a trifling, unreal, but not unamusing effort." *Punch* recognised that *The Liars* was the "best comedy that has been seen for some time on the English stage."

G. B. S. praised the play, though he said it was "one of his lighter works, written with due indulgence to the Criterion company and the playgoing public." He went on to say, "In *The Liars*, the 'smart' group which carries on the action of the piece is hit off to the life, with the result that the originals will probably feel brutally misrepresented.

"And now comes in the oddity of the situation. Mr. Jones, with a wide and clear vision of society, is content with theories of it that have really no relation to his observation. The comedic sentiment of *The Liars* is from beginning to end one of affectionate contempt for women and friendly contempt for men, applied to their affairs with shrewd, worldly common sense and much mollifying humour; whilst its essentially pious theology and its absolute conceptions of duty belong to a passionate and anti-comedic conception of them as temples of the Holy Ghost. Its observations could only have been made to-day; its idealism might have been made a long time ago. Against this I am inclined to protest. It is surely immoral for an Englishman to keep two establishments, much more three.

"The incongruities arising from the different dates of Mr. Jones's brain compartments have, happily, the effect of keeping his sense of humour continually stirring. I am sure *The Liars* must be an extremely diverting play on the stage. But I have not seen it there. Mr. Wyndham's acting-manager wrote to ask whether I would come if I were invited. I said Yes. Accordingly I was *not* invited. The shock to my self-esteem was severe and unexpected. I desire it to be distinctly understood, however, that I forgive everybody."

On 12th October, he wrote to my father:

"12th October, 1897.

"My dear H. A. J.,

"My notice drew a stall for to-morrow like a cork. The omission was an accident; and the honest truth is that I took advantage of it purposely to escape the performance. I shall enjoy seeing Falkner and Lady Jessica turned into Thalberg and Mary Moore—just exactly as much as I should enjoy seeing you skinned alive. If you will write a comedy in which all the characters are merely our actors in disguise and then have the luck to find the originals disengaged for casting, I'll go out and see them eagerly. But not on any other terms. It will end in your having to do what I am doing—throwing the theatre to the devil, and trying to do with my pen what the actors can't do.

"Will you look at the enclosed letter from the Society of Authors? I see that you are chairman of the dramatic sub-committee; and it seems to me that we ought to try to work up some sort of an organization with a view to getting a *minimum* price established for plays, and putting a stop to the ridiculous jobbing of 'rights' that goes on at present through the silliness and ignorance of the authors. . . . The difficulty is, of course, to find time for Trade Union work; but one feels that it ought to be done. It is all very well for you or me to put our individual wit and strength against Irving and Wyndham and the rest; but the small fry are bound to crumple up without an organization behind them. We also want to fight the system of forcing collaboration on authors, whereby some fool of an actor-manager spoils a man's play in order that he may collar half the percentage. . . .

"Mansfield has just proved to me by figures that he must lose $300 on every performance of *The Devil's Disciple* unless I reduce my percentage from 10 to 4. I have replied in terms sufficient to stand him on his head for a fortnight.

"Yours ever,

"G. Bernard Shaw."

I am glad Bernard Shaw drew attention to the veracity of Henry Arthur's portrayal of 'smart' society. During the nineties, and, in one or two American notices after his death, some of the critics contended that H. A. J. could not and did not know how to paint that *milieu*. His constant association over a long period of years with many men and women famous as leaders in London society enabled him to portray smart, well-bred people with the same faithful and striking accuracy as he had portrayed lower middle-class types in some of his earlier plays.

The Liars was produced at the Criterion on 6th October, 1896, and ran for 291 nights. It was revived for 100 nights at the same theatre in April 1907, and again during the war, in 1917, at the St. James's. I believe if my father had been asked which actor or actress most nearly approached

puts watch in pocket, faces Falk and Lady J very
resolutely) Now! I've nothing to say in the abstract
against running away with another man's wife. There may
be planets where it is not only the highest ideal morality,
but where it has the further advantage of being a
practical way of carrying on society. But it has this
one fatal defect in our country today — it won't
work! You know what we English are, we're not a bit
better than our neighbours ! but thank God, we do
pretend we are, and we do still make it hot for
anybody who disturbs that holy pretence.
And take my word for it, my dear Lady Jessica
my dear Ned, it won't work. You know the
has been tried — You know it's not an empirical experiment you're making.
It has been tried before. Have you ever known it to
be successful? Lady Jessica, think of the brave
pioneers who have gone before you in this
enterprise. They all perished, and their bones
whiten the artic matrimonial zone. Think of
them! George Nuncham and Charley Gray and Lady
Rideout, flitting shabbily about the continent at
cheap table-d'hôtes and gambling clubs, rubbing
shoulders with all the blackguards and demi-mondaines of Europe.
Poor old Fitz and his beauty, moping down at
Farnhurst, cut by the county, with no single
occupation except to nag and rag each other
to pieces from morning to night.
and Polly Atcheson That old idiot Sir Bonar Dancer —
paid five thousand pounds for two months
with the professional thing man's
wife George Nuncham and Mrs Sanders —
Jessica you remember Mrs Sandy George is
conducting a tramcar in New York and Mrs

the ideal portrayal of one of his characters, he would have replied, "Wyndham in *The Liars*," but I know he would have at once gone on to mention Willard in *The Middleman*, Tree in *The Dancing Girl*, Wyndham and Lena Ashwell in *Mrs. Dane's Defence*, Sybil Thorndike in *The Lie*, and Marie Tempest in *Mary Goes First*.

The Liars was produced at the Empire Theatre, New York, in September 1898, with John Drew and Isabelle Irving as Sir Christopher Dering and Lady Jessica Nepean. A month later it was produced at the Bijou Theatre, Melbourne, with Mr. and Mrs. Brough in the leading parts. Most of the American notices were favourable, but not enthusiastic, while several of the critics attacked what they termed the decadence of high society as pictured in *The Liars* and *The Case of Rebellious Susan*. Alan Dale, in the *New York Journal*, recognised the great and lasting merit of *The Liars* as "A delightful comedy, that almost induces you to say, 'Don't talk to me of *The School for Scandal* any more.' Here's something more modern and better. . . . Mr. Jones's lines are coruscations of sheer wit, and his lying characters resolve you into audacious chuckles." Since Alan Dale's notice, *The Liars* has often been compared with *The School for Scandal*, and in reasoned and critical opinion it will live as a classic comedy of manners of the nineteenth century.

In 1926, when a friend asked H. A. J. about the continued popularity of *The Liars*, he said, "Thirty years ago people were making love to other men's wives and telling lies— thirty years hence they will be doing the same thing." Freddie Tatton's famous line, "I may be an ass, but I'm not a *silly* ass," is still quoted to-day.

The summer before he died my father was very depressed and wretched, and I persuaded him one morning to drive down to the Athenæum Club. I suggested we should get some new packs of cards to play cribbage. He went out so very rarely that I thought even a slight change might help to lift the cloud of misery, if only for a little while. As we passed the Criterion, he said, "Oh! with what complacency I used to watch the crowds outside for *The Liars,* and think, 'I drew them all there.' "

My father was very much amused that at the time the play was produced it was rumoured that it had really been written by Oscar Wilde and that Henry Arthur Jones had put his name to it because of the scandal attaching to Wilde. A few years ago, when the piece was revived in California, a very eulogistic notice said, "It is well known that Mr. Henry Arthur Jones did not write *The Liars,* but only fathered it. After his seclusion, Oscar Wilde pulled himself together and wrote one supreme masterpiece, *The Liars.*" He was very fond of quoting Oscar Wilde's three rules for writing plays. "The first rule is not to write like Henry Arthur Jones, the second and third rules are the same!" But he never liked the man, and long before the scandal his family and many of his friends knew of his aversion to Oscar Wilde. He admired some of his work very much, and often said "The Ballad of Reading Gaol" was a great poem.

I have always thought it curious that, in spite of the great success of *The Liars* and the lasting fame it brought him, my father was not particularly fond of the play, nor did he talk about it very much, except in the last few years, when he said repeatedly he was sure that it would revive well. His attitude towards the play was such a contrast to his attitude towards *The Silver King,* which was affectionate, proud, but indulgent. His plays were like children to him; but it was not his most highly gifted child, *The Liars,* he cared for the most, but those over which he had taken the greatest trouble and which had been unfortunate— *The Tempter* and *Michael.*

Henry Arthur wrote *The Liars* partly at Townshend House, partly at Hindhead, and the last act at Ostend. This was unusual, as, when once he had started to write a play, he rarely left the place where he was writing, for fear of interrupting the thread of his work.   A great number of his plays were written at Hindhead or in the South of France.

One year he went out to the Mont Boron Hotel, just above Nice, before the season had commenced.   He was in a new wing of the hotel, where the electric light was not laid on.   When he was reading one night, as was his invariable custom, the mosquito-curtains caught fire.   H. A. J. jumped out of bed and immediately went over to his table, carefully collected all his manuscript on top of the table, in the drawers, etc., every odd sheet and various scattered scraps of paper with notes on, and put them all in his suit-case, and threw the case into the passage.   He then tried to extinguish the fire with a water-jug, but, being unsuccessful, he rang the bell violently, and eventually rushed out into the passage yelling, *"Au feu, au feu!"*   The head waiter came running up with a loaded revolver, in response to what he imagined were cries of *"Au voleur! au voleur!"*

* * * * * * * * *

Very soon after we came to live at Townshend House, my father found it difficult to write at home, with the inevitable noise and interruption caused by a growing family; the various discussions as to our behaviour, good or otherwise, our very presence at meals, interfered with the utter absorption which was a necessity to him when he was working.

My father was very fond of all his children, and often compared himself favourably with other well-known authors who were childless, but he never understood any of us half as well as my mother did.   He sometimes spoke of having so many children as if it were an unusual and praiseworthy feat; but on other occasions he would complain to people about his numerous family.   A remark he made to his old friend H. C. Shelley in 1928 is typical of his many gibes about us: "Providence has treated me very badly; I've had seven children and three operations, and not one of my brother dramatists has had one child or an operation." If ever we told him that such remarks were unkind, he was immediately contrite: "Oh, my darling, I'm so sorry; of course I didn't mean it."

When we were young, he alternately spoiled and neglected us. He was the most adoring and indulgent of fathers when he wanted our company, and the discipline of my mother and governesses was brushed aside if it in any way interfered with a passing desire to take us out or have us with him. We knew too well, and used too often, the trick of appealing successfully from one parent to another. In any case, my mother's deafness was a great handicap in dealing with a high-spirited and somewhat unruly family. Two or more children would often shout opposing versions of a dispute at her at the same time, and "Daddy says I may" nearly always overrode any rule she or our governess had laid down. I remember vividly an instance which shows how wanton was my father's disregard of any authority over us except that imposed by his varying moods and feelings. We had several times broken the springs of a very large double bed in our nursery, and my mother said the next time it happened we should all be whipped. Sentence had been passed, and we four girls were in the dining-room of Townshend House, gloomily awaiting execution, when my father came in and was told. I was so tiny that he had to kneel down for his face to be on a level with mine. He said that if I would give him a kiss and say I loved him better than I did Mother, he would give me sixpence and an assurance I should not be whipped. I refused, and, as virtue is so rarely rewarded, I am glad to say a closer inspection revealed that the springs of the old bed were all intact.

At that time, and until Lucien was born, I was the apple of his eye. Before I was three I remember sleeping with him in his room at the top of Townshend House and awaking screaming from a nightmare. He tried in vain to pacify me, but eventually had to carry me down to the ground floor, where my mother slept because of a weak heart, so that she could comfort and reassure me. In all our real troubles and sorrows we went to her first, because of a deeper, more genuine sympathy and understanding on her part, but also from a natural desire and from severe training that we must not worry or disturb my father at his work or do anything which might hinder and distract him. Countless times our childish play was stopped, as we must not make a noise because "Daddy is working!" When he was at work and during meal-times, if he was still busy thinking and jotting down notes, which was generally the case, we were non-existent to him, but when he wanted relaxation and amusement we must, regardless of lessons or suitable hours, be at his disposal.

He was an entrancing companion for his children, full of delightful jokes and interesting information. A joke he played on us in which he was undetected for years, was to stand on the steps leading down to the garden at Townshend House and flick ha'pennies, pennies, and often sixpences and shillings, into the air. We thought the heavens rained money unexpectedly, and as we rushed about seizing coins we'd sometimes call out, "Haven't you found any, Daddy?" It amused him enormously, but was not a good way of training children in the value of money. After we had found out the source of these windfalls, when we went for walks with him, he would amuse us by flicking up coins in front of any small urchins we might come across, and once or twice he was questioned, "Did you see where that come from, Mister?" I remember so well the delicious gravity of his replies and counter-questions.

We never tired of getting him to tell us about Georgie Eggleton, a great character in Winslow when my father was a boy. When a man was hanged for murder he said,

"That'll learn him not to do it again."   He used to give his children a penny to go to bed without their supper, and he would not give them their breakfast next morning until they had returned it.   H. A. J. would threaten us with the same treatment.   He told us that, when he was a little boy, the labourers on his father's farms would stop their work to watch a train go by, such was the novelty.

One of the keenest sources of pleasure in our company was when he took us riding with him in Rotten Row.   More than once all four of his daughters went for a morning ride with him.   But woe betide us if a button was off our gloves or any small detail of our kit awry.   We enjoyed these rides enormously, as we met so many interesting people.   My father often said that the little coterie we rode with was one of the most delightful clubs of which he was a member. H. A. J.'s old friends, with whom he rode constantly, in-cluded Sir Evelyn Wood, Seymour Trower, Mr. Cunning-hame Graham, Lord Wolseley, William Stone, Mr. Cyril Maude, Sir H. Beerbohm Tree, Sir George Alexander, and Sir Henry Fletcher.   One day H. A. J. was riding with old Sir John Tenniel, who was then about ninety years old, and my father asked him to what he ascribed his good health.   "Riding," was the reply.

We enjoyed most of all our constant talks on literature. He was a mine of information, and discussed his favourite authors and poets in the most entrancing manner.   He often said, "I was brought up on Shakespeare and the Bible."   After Milton, he loved Matthew Arnold better than any other poet.   In a copy of his poems which he gave to my daughter Dorinda he wrote:

"10th February, 1926.

"MY DARLING DORINDA,

"I hope you will read and study every word of this fine, high thinker, who has been a perpetual light to your Grandfather through all his weary days of seventy years and more.

"Your loving Grandy,
"HENRY ARTHUR JONES."

Our great delight was to try to catch him out on a quotation, and *vice versa*. We never succeeded, and he did nearly always. I can hear his tone now when he'd say, "But that can't be Shelley, it must be Wordsworth," or "That was written before the eighteenth century." This was the man who had not had a day's schooling after he was twelve. He allowed us to read any book we liked, even when we were small children, except cheap modern novels. He was quite furious sometimes if he found us doing that. Before I was twelve he promised me three guineas if I would read all Plutarch's Lives. I did not earn more than half that sum.

I think the keenest pleasure we had from our companionship with my father was his reading to us. He was a magnificent reader. All his family always say they have never seen any of his plays acted as well as he read them. He often regretted that he never gave readings from his plays and from Shakespeare. I believe he would have made a small fortune here and in America had he done so, but I do not think his health would have stood the strain.

We had special favourites which we could nearly always persuade him to read to us; the scene between Hotspur and Lady Percy in *Henry IV*, Tennyson's "Rizpah," Matthew Arnold's "Dover Beach" and "St. Brandon's Isle," Samuel Butler's "Oh, God! Oh, Montreal!" a chapter from the Bible, and, more rarely, Wordsworth's "The Leech-Gatherer." One day we were talking about Charles Matthews and Madame Vestris, and Henry Arthur said, "I could have seen him when he was playing in the West of England, but what I *do* regret is not going to Charles Dickens's readings."

Though we were allowed to read any of the classics, including Rabelais, my father was always most careful in his conversation in front of us. Even when we were grown-up and married I never heard him tell an unseemly story or make a loose remark. Often, when I was grown-up, he told me very witty stories which were improper, but all his life he was Victorian in his feeling about the kind of conversation which was permissible when women were present. I never once heard him swear—not even a mild "damn." I think "Confound it all" was the strongest expression he ever used. But my mother sometimes told the following story, and, though he always denied the truth of it, I feel sure from the manner of his denials that the episode really occurred. One day at lunch, before I was born, my mother suddenly exclaimed, "Damn the cabbage," which was not properly cooked. H. A. J. looked up horrified, and said, "Jenny, in front of the children!" Whereupon my mother said, "Now you know what it sounds like, Henry!"

He often said that Wordsworth at his very finest was finer than any other English poet. He knew Swinburne very well and loved the "music" of his poetry. He always promised to take me to tea with the poet. I never went, but one day he took my sister Gertrude. She was a schoolgirl, and asked Swinburne, "Please tell me, Mr. Swinburne, who is your favourite poet?" He replied simply, "Coleridge." We would often get Henry Arthur to talk about Swinburne. Swinburne told H. A. J. that he asked Jowett who was the greatest living writer of English, at a time when Carlyle, Ruskin, Meredith, and Hardy were all alive. Jowett hesitated a moment, and said, "I shouldn't hesitate a second if Dickens were alive."

One of my sisters did not get on well with him as a child. She had a strong will and was very independent, and he and she were so often at loggerheads that she was sent to boarding-school when she was eight. I remember the commotion which took place when my father found a diary of hers with the entry, "How much nicer Pip is than Father," Pip being our fox-terrier. H. A. J.'s sense of humour should have come to the rescue, but he always wanted to believe he cared as deeply and did as much for his children as he did for his work. This was never the case. In a letter to Professor William Lyon Phelps, written in 1912, he said:

"7th November, 1912.

"Many thanks for your kind gift of the little book on *Teaching in School and College.* I wish I could have read it twenty years ago—it would have given me some valuable hints in the management of my children—a business in which, like most fathers, I have notoriously failed.

"I never had the least taste for teaching, though I have a curious perverse itch for *preaching* on the drama, condemned to suffer from it

> *By the same fate that mocks*
> *The eunuch with hereditary pox.*
>
> (Swinburne, unpublished.)

"I am bringing out my new volume of essays and lectures in January. I will send you a copy."

From the time my brother Lucien was born until he was seventeen my father spoilt and indulged him immoderately. After the ill-health and death of his eldest son Philip, it was a source of the greatest pride and joy to him that Lucien was so bright, clever, and good-looking. The child could do no wrong in his eyes, and was very quick to find out that in any dispute his father would believe him rather than his sisters, though they were very much older. For years and years my mother made constant but unavailing efforts to counteract the ruinous effect of H. A. J.'s indulgence towards his eldest son; but she was unsuccessful.

It has always amazed me that my father's profound and unerring knowledge of psychology, of the motives and impulses of human nature, never seemed to enter into his dealings with his children. Years of the most varied intercourse with all sorts of people, of the keenest, most unremitting observation of his fellow-creatures, had given him the richest treasures of knowledge of the human heart, and yet he seemed incapable of drawing upon this storehouse of wisdom for the benefit of his children. He was always most generous over money matters with all his children. He did most sincerely wish to help any of us if we were in trouble; but, after a big crisis in our lives, more often than not we were left with the impression that we had seriously interrupted his work without having received any real help from him. He was distressed and anxious for us, but, except for financial aid, he was not always a truly wise or helpful counsellor.

CHAPTER XI

TOWARDS the end of 1897 my father wrote a one-act play, *The Goal*. He said he wrote the play for Henry Irving; meaning that as soon as the leading character, that of an old engineer who is dying of angina, took shape in his brain, he "saw" Irving in the part. He called it "A Dramatic Fragment," and he was very fond of this little play. After the war, he often quoted with great pride the old engineer's words, "There's a great world-tussle coming. Dan—I shan't live to see it—but it's coming and the engineer that ties England and America will do a good turn to both countries." H. A. J. would add, "I knew it was coming, even then." The first performance of *The Goal* was in New York in October 1914; it was not until 1919 that it was first played in London.

Another play belonging to this period was *Grace Mary*, a one-act tragedy in the Cornish dialect. It was never acted, but was thought worthy of inclusion in Clayton Hamilton's Library Edition of my father's plays. W. D. Howells, in an article on "The Plays of Henry Arthur Jones," published in the *North American Review* in 1907, referred to "that beautiful and touching little one-act play, *Grace Mary*. . . . The author reaches a height of poetry untouched elsewhere in his work. Next it, in a certain literary quality, is that mere scene which he calls *The Goal*, and which also is unalloyedly good."

In October 1928, I said to my father, *"Grace Mary's* a lovely little play," to which he replied, "Yes, it's a little beauty, isn't it?—there's real tragedy there too." Bernard Shaw thought very highly of the play, and after reading it he wrote to H. A. J. twice. Unfortunately his first letter was lost. In the second he said:

165

"20th May, 1898.

"One thing I quite forgot to say yesterday in writing about *Grace Mary*. Have you read Tolstoi's *What is Art?* It is beyond all comparison the best treatise on art that has been done by a literary man (I bar Wagner) in these times. His theory is right all through, his examples the silliest obsolete nonsense. Among other things, he is very strong on the Universality of good art, and the classiness of bad—that good art is as intelligible to a peasant as to a gentleman, etc. If there were any chance of his being able to wrestle with the Cornish lingo, I should send him *Grace Mary* as a striking specimen of the universal play.

"Miss Townsend is fascinated by it.

"By the way, would you advise me to get married?

"Yours ever,
"G. Bernard Shaw."

H. A. J.'s reply was:

"24th May, 1898.

"My dear G. B. S.,

"Yes, I would get married if I were you. But read the chapters in Rabelais and the advice that was given to Panurge on the subject. I hope you are getting on alright. I shall look in the first chance I get. I'm getting away on Thursday for a final tussle with my play.

"Always yours,
"H. A. J."

A few weeks later, H. A. J. received the following post-cards from G. B. S.:

"25th June, 1898.

"We are having such a honeymoon of it. A couple of days ago I fell downstairs and broke my left arm; so here I am disabled hand and foot, helpless as a baby, I am only

able to scrawl postcards.   The lady I talked to so much at
the Lyceum—the one on my left—was Mrs. Perugini—the
one on my right is now Mrs. Shaw, with her nice new
husband all broken and damaged.

"G. B. S."

"28th June, 1898.

"As we are both going to *Romeo and Juliet* for our sins,
why not lunch with us to-morrow (Monday) at 1.30?

"If you will come, ring up 14615 Central and say that
Mr. Henry Arthur Jones is coming to lunch; so that my
cook may do her morning's marketing with a carnivorous
guest in view.   Otherwise there will be nothing but plain
living and high thinking.

"G. B. S."

Many years later my father sent copies of *The Goal* and
Grace Mary to his old friend Sir Sidney Low, who in writing to acknowledge them said:

"13th January, 1920.

"I'm very glad indeed to have the *Theatre of Ideas* volume, which I have read with extreme delight and satisfaction, and shall often turn to again.   What a lovely Aristo-
phanic burlesque the prose piece would have made if you
had done it in that form!   And as for the one-act plays it
seems almost incredible that such fine and powerful little
dramas as *The Goal* and *Grace Mary* should not by this
time have been produced and re-produced over and over
again at our theatres!   In France—or Germany—they
would have become part of the stock repertory of the stage
and be played by capable actors to appreciative audiences
at several theatres every year.   *Grace Mary* is really a
most noble and moving tragedy, made all the more touching by the fine simplicity of the dialect.   I suppose it is
quite perfect Cornish, and it is at any rate entirely beauti-

ful—full of eloquence, music, and pathos. I wish you would write some more Cornish plays, so that even if they are not produced, I might have the pleasure of reading the dialogue, with its Biblical rhythm and memories. But what can one say of a public which has the chance of seeing this and goes for four years on end to *Chu-Chin-Chow?*"

In the summer of 1898 my father made a plea for the endowment of a National Theatre in a letter published in the *Daily News* of 28th June. "It might," he said, "for many reasons be argued that the director of a National Theatre has more right to public money than the director of a National Gallery. One reason is that the Drama is a swifter, more searching, more vivid, and more vital art than painting. . . ."

Although my father was always writing and lecturing on the Drama and the state of the Theatre, it was only occasionally that he wrote or spoke about the art of acting, except in conversation. But he did write a very interesting letter to Sir Edward Russell, after reading a lecture by Sir Edward on David Garrick:

"11th December, 1895.

"All that you say about the relations of acting to mimicry seems to me to be quite true. Mimicry is really an illegitimate half-brother of acting. It is a powerful aid to the actor in certain comedy and character parts; but for the great tragic parts, mimicry is as useless for building them up as wax for building up a statue. . . .

"I think I must challenge outright your claim that acting is the 'highest and finest art wherever it approaches perfection'—I scarcely think it is right to compare two different arts. There is really no equation or possibility of equation. But you would scarcely rate a perfect assumption of Hamlet as equal to the creation of the character by Shakespeare—I mean the creation of the one character, to say nothing of the highly complex art of fitting it into an involved story with infinitely involved relations to numerous other characters? And I should like to see a protest made against the word 'creation' as applied to the actor's work. Surely their work is embodiment, portrayal. . . . Creation, so far as we can attach a meaning to the word at all, signifies the making of something out of nothing. Now this does really approach the description of an author's work so far as it is original. But the actor embodies what is already 'created.' Who created Hamlet? . . . We get, say, forty differing Hamlets—surely the mere fact that one man happened to play him first ought not to give him a right to say that he 'created' the part. . . ."

Of all Henry Arthur's plays, *The Manœuvres of Jane*, produced at the Haymarket Theatre on 26th October, 1898, had the worst reception in the Press, yet it was one of his greatest successes both in London, where it ran for 281 nights, and in the provinces. It was also produced successfully in New York in 1899, and was revived there a year or two later. Jane Nangle is a high-spirited, unmanageable girl with a scheming young friend, Constantia Gage. Mr. Nangle, Jane's father, sends the girls to live with a Mrs. Beechinor in the hope of taming his daughter and breaking off her love-affair with George Lambert. After several adventures, Jane marries her young man and Constantia catches Lord Bapchild, Mrs. Beechinor's nephew. The critics were so scathing in their comments that it did not seem possible that the play could survive. Mr. A. B. Walkley, in the *Speaker*, condemned the play and labelled it a *coméedie rosse*; it was the first time he ever applied that expression to any work of Henry Arthur's. His abusive attacks on my father's plays and comedies closed the doors of the Garrick Theatre to him on the first night of *Whitewashing Julia*, produced several years later.

William Archer and Max Beerbohm were the only critics

who regarded the play favourably. "Max" declared that "Mr. Jones is always experimenting, learning, improving his art. . . . He has kept himself plastic and progressive. . . . I thought Mr. Jones's play an extremely good entertainment." And he went on to say that, apart from Oscar Wilde, "Mr. Jones has always seemed to me the only dramatist of any intellectual force, and the only dramatist with ideas."

My eldest sister had longed to go on the stage from the time she was quite a small child. My parents did not wish her to become an actress, but they eventually yielded to her entreaties, and my father sent her with my mother to Paris, where she studied under Coquelin *aîné* for several months. H. A. J. thought very highly of her work, and sent her, with her sister Ethelwyn, on tour in several of his plays. He was so delighted with her performance as Jane that he hired a special train and took an enormous party from London to Cambridge to see her act in the part. That his praise of both my sisters' acting was not due to parental feeling is borne out by the following letter from Bernard Shaw:

> "Ruan Minor,
> "Cornwall.
> *"23rd August, 1899.*

"DEAR H. A. J.,

"My health holds up; and I bathe twice a day with excellent effect on my muscles. Swimming is the only exercise I have ever taken for its own sake. I swim now for the most part under water, as my wife learns the art by using me as a life-preserver.

"You Never Can Tell is a whited sepulchre. It looks as if a play with that waiter and those twins *couldn't* fail; but that ten minutes at the end of the second act requires a double-first comedian; and where is he to be found? Mrs. Clandon too! who is to play her? Kate Terry, perhaps.

"Our next door neighbours saw your daughters Janing somewhere and declare that the performance was ever so much better than the Haymarket one. If they would like to try on *Y.N.C.T.* at any time for a lark, they are welcome; but a serious grapple with it is out of the question for various reasons, as (*a*) it wouldn't draw unless it came from London, (*b*) it would cost both money and trouble, (*c*) I have a dogged objection to spending either my own money or yours on the theatre, and (*d*) the actual production of my plays is a positive anguish to me; so much so that I cannot help noting the odd fact that though my quarrels with managers are always the managers' fault, yet somehow the editors do not quarrel with me half so much.

"You have evidently eaten meat enough for a lifetime. Try my grub for a while. You require spiritual food; both *Jane* and *Carnac* were abominably cynical.

"G. B. S."

Writing to my father a few months later, G. B. S. said:

"10, Adelphi Terrace, W.C.
"*14th November, 1899.*

"The circumstances seem to point to your escaping the infliction of a performance of *You Never Can Tell.* I heartily and sincerely envy you.

"If I had the management of the affair, we should have a performance all to ourselves, like Wagner and the King of Bavaria. Need I say that I am carefully avoiding any responsibility? They may arrange it how they please. I am up to my neck in vestrydom and in a book on Fabianism, miles aloof from the theatre.

"We spent Sunday on Hindhead: hence my absence from your side at the Argonauts. But as I never get anything to eat at a public dinner, and never go to one except for the express purpose of making a speech, perhaps it was just as well. I am on the cheeriest terms with C. W. [Charles Wyndham] privately, but publicly there would be a certain hollowness in our relations as manager and author.

"The *D's D* [*The Devil's Disciple*] must have been all wrong: they clearly made mere farce of the 3rd act. Burgoyne should have been grim and spartan—a ruined man playing it out to the end.

"Yrs. ever,

"G. Bernard Shaw."

G. B. S. also wrote and asked Winifred to take part in the copyright performance of *Cæsar and Cleopatra*.

Speaking to me about *Candida* in July 1928, my father said, "Shaw read me *Candida* before he had any great standing, and asked me whom I would recommend for the poet, and I recommended Esmond. He couldn't get him, so I suggested Granville Barker. I'd seen him play *Richard II*." G. B. S. wrote to Henry Arthur about his suggestion that Esmond should play the part.

"20th February, 1896.

"I am going to read *Candida* at Mrs. Ashton Jonson's (Dorothy Leighton's) on Sunday evening. Do you think Esmond could be persuaded to come? I believe Mrs. A. J. is going to invite him at a venture. If you happen to meet him in the meantime, tell him that the part of the poet is very considerably ahead of Little Billee."

Henry Arthur did not like the woman's character. He said to me once, talking about Nora in *The Doll's House*, "She was the first of the tiresome hussies—*Candida* was another." He always said that *The Doll's House* should have ended with the husband helping himself to a whisky-and-soda and saying, "Thank God, she's gone."

The Manœuvres of Jane was succeeded by a dismal fail-

WAITING FOR THE FIRST NIGHT OF "CARNAC SAHIB," HER MAJESTY'S THEATRE, 1899

ure, *Carnac Sahib*—the story of a minor rebellion in India
—produced by Beerbohm Tree at Her Majesty's on 12th
April, 1899.   The rehearsals were unusually stormy, even
for Tree and Henry Arthur.   There were constant disputes; and one day, after Tree had been trying for a long
time to say certain lines with a particular intonation demanded by H. A. J., he called out in exasperation, "Then
how do you want it done?"   My father got up, said, "Ask
Wyndham to show you how to do it," clapped his hat on,
and marched out of the theatre.   The next morning a friend
told me he found Henry Arthur walking up and down
outside Her Majesty's in a fearful temper because he had
been denied admittance to the rehearsals of his own play.

Eva Moore tells a delightful story of the production of
this play.   At the last dress rehearsal, which I believe
started early in the afternoon, the company were still in
the theatre at 2.30 the next morning.   Tree could not be
found anywhere, so the bored and discouraged actors and
actresses danced on the stage for about an hour.   Eventually Tree was discovered sound asleep in the Dome; he
came down, and took up his position on the stage for the
last scene, the Jewelled Palace at Fyzapore, with his head
in Eva Moore's lap, who was fanning him; the curtain did
not go up immediately, so Tree sat up and in plaintive
accents wailed, "Oh, God!   Oh, sweet God!   I am ready
to begin."

H. A. J. received considerable help over minor details
in the play from Sir Evelyn Wood, an old crony of his,
with whom he rode almost daily in the Row when they
were in London.   Sir Evelyn gave him information on
Indian names and military etiquette.   He was at several
of my father's first nights in the nineties, and wrote him
delightful letters of congratulation.

Though my father had so many rows with Tree at rehearsals, rows which led to their consulting their respective
solicitors on more than one occasion, H. A. J. was devoted

to him and had a very great admiration for his acting in certain parts. He often said, "Tree as Bottom had a blank stone wall of vanity—it was impassable—you couldn't get beyond it. He conveyed the absolute stolidity of the character. How well he managed to convey Bottom's enormous vanity." He thought him very fine in character parts, as Malvolio and Svengali. He often said, "Of all the actors I've known I would rather have spent a fortnight in Tree's company than with any of the others." His great personality and sense of humour appealed to Henry Arthur enormously. H. A. J. said he knew of only one occasion on which Tree's sense of humour failed him. A Japanese student, I think his name was Trebuski, came to London with an introduction to my father. They talked about the theatre in Japan and the production of Shakespeare in Japanese: Mr. Trebuski said that in Japan the Shakespearian plays were given in modern Japanese prose. H. A. J. suggested taking him over to see Tree, our leading Shakespearian actor, and on the way my father prepared a little joke, feeling sure Tree would see the point of it immediately. After some conversation in Tree's dressing-room my father said with a twinkle, "Mr. Trebuski tells me they do not speak Shakespeare's verse in Japan any more than they do in England." Tree replied rather pompously, "Well, we make a compromise."

In the last years of Henry Arthur's life one of his favourite walks was to go round by the Hampstead Churchyard, where Tree is buried. He always stopped for a few moments by his grave, took off his hat, and said some kind and gracious words about his old friend. I never heard him speak of Tree except with great affection.

Carnac Sahib was followed by another failure, *The Lackey's Carnival,* produced at the Duke of York's Theatre on 26th September, 1900. There were minor quarrels at rehearsals of this play also, and Evelyn Millard threw up her part as the heroine because she would not say the line, "I swear to you by my unborn child." She had just married, and she thought the public would consider the line indelicate. My father refused to alter the words, and Miss Wynne Matthison took up the part.

During the run of *The Lackey's Carnival,* two weeks after the first night, my father had one of his most memorable successes with the production of *Mrs. Dane's Defence* at Wyndham's Theatre on 9th October, 1900. The third act, which consists almost entirely of a conversation between Sir Daniel Carteret and Mrs. Dane and his cross-examination of her, is one of the greatest Henry Arthur ever wrote. As he wrote the play originally, the construction was faulty. As H. A. J. told me, "I made the mistake of allowing the judge to cross-examine and get the better of Fendick the detective, and when I came to the big scene —Sir Daniel knew already she was guilty, so there was no big scene."

My father knew he had not got the play right, and he went away to Switzerland. Suddenly one morning at Ragatz the correct construction flashed into his brain, and he wrote the whole of the third act in four hours at white heat. There was one small interruption; the funeral procession of the Burgomaster passed under my father's window, and he got up for a few moments to watch it pass by.

Even when the play was in rehearsal H. A. J. had not found a title for it, and it was Alfred Bishop who suggested *Mrs. Dane's Defence.* Mrs. Dane and Lionel Carteret, the adopted son of Sir Daniel Carteret, a famous judge, are madly in love, but little is known of Mrs. Dane's past, and when by mischance local gossips ferret out an unsavoury story, Sir Daniel insists that, before he can consent to Lionel's marriage, Mrs. Dane must clear her name. In the long cross-examination scene of the third act, Mrs. Dane breaks down and confesses her past. She is forced to realise the impossibility of uniting her broken life with a boy who is on the threshold of a brilliant career.

The play was well received, all the critics praising the third act very highly, but nearly all of them gave greater praise to the acting than to the play.   An exception was the enthusiastic review by "Max" in the *Saturday Review,* headed "This Inempedible Mr. Jones." "Max" said that, had Pinero written *Mrs. Dane's Defence,* the critics would have given the play much higher praise, "but then Mr. Pinero has never got himself disliked by the critics." H. A. J., he went on, "must expect no laurels from the critics as a class. But he may find consolation in the rare coincidence that he, whose plays have on the average longer runs and catch the public more surely than the plays of other men, is also the dramatist most admired by the few folk who take a serious interest in dramatic art."

The first night was one of the most memorable in Henry Arthur's career.   During the cross-examination scene the audience was tense with excitement; you could have heard a pin drop.   When the curtain fell on the third act, there was dead silence for a moment, and then an outburst of deafening applause. It was so overwhelming that Sir Charles Wyndham said, "You could lean up against it." The American, French, and German verdict was nearly as unmistakable.   The play ran for 209 nights, and was revived at Wyndham's Theatre on 5th June, 1902, at the New Theatre on 16th May, 1912, and again at the Lyric Theatre for two special matinées on 16th November in 1906, with Guy Standing in Wyndham's part.

When Sir Charles Wyndham was an old man, his memory for the words of a part sometimes failed him, so that one night during the revival at the New Theatre in 1912, in the famous cross-examination scene, when he should have questioned Mrs. Dane in the following words, "Her father was vicar of Tawhampton?" He said instead, "Let me see, your father was the vicar of Wakefield?"

My father always spoke with great admiration of Wynd-

Mr. Cyril Maude   Mr. Rudolph Birnbaum   Mr. Lewis Waller   Mr. Max O'Rell
    Mr. Henry Arthur Jones   Mr. Charles Wyndham   Mr. T. P. O'Connor

Mrs. Henry Arthur Jones   Mrs. Beerbohm Tree   Miss Mary Moore   Mrs. Cyril Maude   Mrs. Wyndham
    (Miss Winifred Emery)

A THEATRICAL DINNER-PARTY IN 1900

(By courtesy of Messrs. Langfier Ltd.)

ham's voice and articulation. "He'd only two notes in his voice," he said, "but he could do anything with them," and he would go on to instance the line in *Mrs. Dane's Defence*, "There was a child?" H. A. J. said it came from Wyndham in a piercing whisper as if it was one word only, and yet every syllable was clear. He told me that Wyndham said to Irving one day, "We haven't got much of a voice, you and I," and that Irving replied feelingly, "Thank God we haven't." My father regarded Sir Charles as the most capable manager he had ever known. He said to me a few months before he died, "Wyndham often used to say that a manager must be a cheese-parer."

In 1906 Lena Ashwell and Margaret Anglin gave two special matinées of *Mrs. Dane's Defence* at the Lyric Theatre, New York, alternating the parts of Mrs. Dane and Lady Eastney. H. A. J. said Miss Anglin gave a much better performance as Lady Eastney than Miss Ashwell did, but he said, "God made Lena Ashwell for Mrs. Dane, just as he made Mrs. Pat Campbell for Mrs. Tanqueray."

Early in 1902, Henry Arthur wrote a comedy, *James the Fogey*. It has never been produced. It is a charming play, but the story is slight, though it made a good film. In this play he drew one of his most lovable characters, Johnny Tatum, an old man with a stutter. Johnny is by way of being a philosopher who thinks "th-th-the world was b-born wrong."

The Princess's Nose was produced at the Duke of York's Theatre on 11th March, 1902. Although the play had a very cordial reception, the notices were cold, and it ran for only a few weeks. H. B. Irving and Irene Vanbrugh played beautifully as the Prince and Princess, but people did not like a wife resorting to the tricks of a mistress to try to regain her husband's affection. Bernard Shaw wrote to say that he would prefer to read the play before seeing it:

"20th February, 1902.

"Dear H. A. J.,

"If there is an occasion on which I loathe a theatre more than ever, it is on a first night.   And when the business in hand is the murder of one of your plays, I feel that my attendance is about as friendly an act as a seat in the front row at your execution.   If you love me, send me a copy of the book; and then, when I have had my first impression from you, I will slip in some night with my wife and see what they are doing with it.   Besides, you will be short enough of stalls to accommodate the regular first night crowd without shortening the supply still further for me.

"How do you get on with Granville Barker?   Do you realise that he is a great poet and dramatist who feels towards us as we feel towards Sheridan Knowles?   His *Marrying of Anne Leete* is really an exquisite play.   I truckle to G. B. in order to conciliate him when he is forty. He regards me as a vulgar old buffer who did my best in my day to play up for better things—his things, for example. In revenge I call him 'serious relief,' etc.   But he is always useful when a touch of poetry and refinement is needed: he lifts a whole cast when his part gives him a chance, even when he lets the part down and makes the author swear. He rebukes me feelingly for wanting my parts to be 'caricatured.'

"G. Bernard Shaw."

After reading the play he was horrified:

"22nd March, 1902.

"My dear H. A. J.,

"I have read *The Princess's Nose* and I am shocked— profoundly shocked.   I positively forbid any more La Turbie.   You will lose your public if you do not reform at once.   Fast, pray, forswear meat and alcohol, turn your back for ever on Monte Carlo, or you are lost.

"None of the criticisms I have read have really touched the black spot in this most turpitudinous play. I have often said, when Socialists talk Free Love, that Marriage is invincible as men are at present, because it is the most licentious of all human institutions; and I shall perhaps yet write a play to illustrate that fact. I quite admit that the proposition of your infamous old *raisonneur,* that a man's wife is simply his whore, and must compete with all the other whores if she is to retain her hold of him, is as a matter of fact true of a considerable number of marriages, especially those to be observed at Monte Carlo. But that you of all men should embrace this position and make comedy capital out of it, as if it were an entirely satisfactory and sensible one, and exhibit the old scoundrel, who deliberately preaches it to the young wife, as virtuously horsewhipping the infinitely less repulsive artistic ass who makes love to her, is utterly unendurable. That the author of the scene between Palsam and Rusper should descend to the horsewhipping of Eglinton Pyne (at odds of five to one) is evidence of the most frightful moral decay. I hoped to the last the Pyne would lick the Prince and draw the moral; but in vain. The dialogue writer is still there; but the dramatist's soul is gone; and the public is chilled and horrified without knowing why. These characters are the ghosts of old successes—I except from this the Prince, who is delicately done, and only needs to be placed in his proper moral bearings to be a fine piece of work. The Princess is interesting too, until she turns whore and does a seduction scene which puts her far below the other woman—flogged into theatrical activity by mere brutalities, poultices, and horsewhips and cantharidean *négligées* and so on. The Wyndham plays were immoral (as their climax in *The Princess's Nose* now shows); but they had character in them and humour; and they made money. But this thing will damage you more than a thousand murdered *Michaels;* it piles moral bankruptcy on top of pecuniary bankruptcy—adds Hell to Kentish Town, so to speak. By this I mean that you will have to live in Kentish Town and in Hell hereafter if you do not make your peace with outraged British morality. If you do it again, you are done for.

"All this is in the interest of the next play—the Lena Ashwell one, I suppose. If you are mad enough to write it at La Turbie, at least send me the MSS. and let me invest it with moral grandeur. But why not write it in Chiddingfold or wherever you wrote *The Crusaders?* I am now a respectable married man, and, as such, I positively decline to tolerate any more of these stalking horses for smart harlots. You can't really be morally dead; you talk all right and you look all right. You shall have one more chance; but if you miss that, I disown you for ever.

"Yours on the highest moral ground,

"G. BERNARD SHOCKED."

PART III

THE LATER YEARS

1902–1929

CHAPTER XII

IN the summer of 1902 we had to leave Townshend House which had become unsafe owing to the explosion on the Regent's Park Canal some years previously. The foundations of the house were badly shaken, and during the time we lived there the staircase shifted several inches.

Henry Arthur then took the lease of 38 Portland Place and had the whole of the house beautifully redecorated by William Morris's. He thought the many years of prosperity at Townshend House would continue, and, as his daughters were grown up, he wanted a fine house where he could entertain for us; but, as a matter of fact, he was away most of the time we lived there, or, when he was at home, he was so busy working that he rarely went out. I remember my mother's plaintive voice as she said one day, "Henry, that's the seventeenth dinner invitation you've made me refuse this season."

Just after the production of *Whitewashing Julia,* we gave a domino dance, preceded by a sketch we had written called *Blackmailing Jenny,* in which Leslie Faber, my sister Gertrude, and I acted. My father was away working, and we were all rather disappointed that he could not come up and see our little play. The evening was not a great success, for soon after the dancing started my sisters and I were very much upset and annoyed by one of the masked dancers, who followed us about pinching and kissing us on the sly. We were much distressed at the outrageous conduct of this unwelcome guest. We decided to consult our family doctor; one of us discovered "Dr. Teddy," and, taking him into a corner, we told him all the details. He advised us to wait until everyone unmasked just before supper. When we all did so, we discovered that the odious man who had pestered us was Henry Arthur, and that the man we imagined to be our family doctor was an entire stranger, a friend of Miss Ella Hepworth-Dixon. When all was revealed, we enjoyed my father's joke as much as he did.

My sisters and I all married during the first four years we lived at No. 38, and, as the house was too big, Henry Arthur sold the remainder of the lease at a loss of several thousand pounds. He often said, "I never had a success after leaving Townshend House," and he regretted bitterly not having bought the new house which was built on the site of that well-loved house. Yet he had three very great successes in the years to come—*The Hypocrites* and *Cock of the Walk* in America, *The Lie* here and in America, and minor successes with *Whitewashing Julia, Dolly Reforming Herself,* and *Mary Goes First;* but the last twenty wonderful years of increasing success and happiness were over, and during the remainder of his life he was constantly worried about money matters; his nervous breakdowns were more frequent, while his general health grew worse and worse.

Chance the Idol was produced at Wyndham's Theatre on 9th September, 1902, with H. V. Esmond and Lena Ashwell in the leading parts. It is the story of the desperate efforts of Ellen Farndon to recapture the love of Allen Leversage. In despair she gambles away a small fortune in the hope of making enough money to tempt her lover into marriage. Most of the Press notices were unfavourable, and the play was not a success. Henry Arthur was very anxious that Wyndham should play the part taken by Esmond, but Sir Charles refused the play because there was no character suitable for Miss Mary Moore. H. A. J. wanted his daughter Winifred to play the young girl, and, though he sometimes said he thought the play would have been a success with Wyndham and Mary Moore, he was glad he had not altered it to suit them, as my sister received great praise for her acting from all the professional writers.

My father wrote most of the play in the South of France. He had never been to a fortune-teller in his life, but, as he was anxious to draw a life-like character in Madame Esperanzo, he decided to consult one. He thought a little local colour might be of assistance, so he pulled his tie out, rumpled his hair and clothes, and rushed into the lady's sanctum screaming hoarsely, "J'ai beaucoup perdu; j'ai beaucoup perdu." The sibyl advised him to risk a very small amount the next day, and if he lost to come away; to try again the day after, again with a small stake; but, if he were unsuccessful, to stop altogether for some time. H. A. J. said it was the cheapest and wisest advice he ever received.

He said to me once, "As soon as I lose a hundred louis, I see the profound immorality of the whole business, and I always double up quickly on the even chances. I generally come out on the right side. I've been at Monte Carlo and gone into the rooms as soon as they opened, played till lunch, had my lunch, gone back until dinner-time, and again directly after dinner until the rooms closed." He often told me that on several occasions his trips to the south cost him nothing, as he won so much money in the rooms. He was not a gambler, but the excitement was a great relaxation and distraction after his work. In a letter to Sir Emery Walker he said:

"*April 1900.*

"Have been working splendidly and have commandeered £120 of the bank here, which just pays a fortnight's expenses. Awful disregard of morals and the value of cash sets in about twenty-four to thirty-six hours after arriving in this principality."

Henry Arthur was very hopeful about *Chance the Idol*, and greatly delighted, when he read it to Mr. and Mrs. Bernard Shaw, to find that they liked the play enormously and thought it would be a great success.

G. B. S. wrote to my father about it as follows:

> "Victoria Hotel,
> "Holkham,
> *"Norfolk.*
> *"31st August, 1902.*

"My dear H. A. J.,

"We are down here out of reach of the first night. Charlotte is much excited, and for two pins would go up on Tuesday; but I shall restrain her, as she would probably be disappointed after your reading. As for me, the theatre only exasperates me when I care about the play. I have almost come to the conclusion that actual performance is only advisable as the last resource of a thoroughly undramatic bungle. After all, one can't help planning the effect for people who know worse than if the author had written like a child for children.

"However, you are not so badly off as you might easily be elsewhere. Lena is a squawker; but she is a squawker of genius; and Esmond is never disagreeable; who is he playing, by the way? The *diable boiteux*, I assume.

"You should have got Cosmo Stuart for that husband of Lena's. You don't believe me; but I am right—oh, my eye! I am right. He would have been enormous.

"I wish you huge returns, the success being already, in my opinion, achieved.

"My next production—so I am told—is to be in Vienna.

"This isn't a bad place, cheap and simple, remote and slow, no annoyances and no conveniences of civilisation.

> "Yrs. ever,
> "G. Bernard Shaw."

After my father's death, Mrs. Shaw told me how well she remembered H. A. J. reading the play at Hindhead, and how kind and charming he was, and that she believed that visit to Hindhead was the first time she met my father. I turned to G. B. S. and asked, "Do you remember the first time you met Daddy?" He replied immediately, "I never remember the time when we weren't the best of friends," and he went on to say he supposed they first met at Emery Walker's. T. J. Wise told me a story of the first occasion on which H. A. J. set eyes on G. B. S. It was in 1885, at a meeting of the Shelley Society in the Botanical Theatre at University College, Gower Street. My father and Mr. Wise were sitting next to one another on the platform, and, after the official speeches had been made, members of the audience were invited to speak. A tall lank figure in grey flannels, with a flaming head and beard, shot up from the middle of the hall and said, "Ladies and gentlemen, I am an atheist (pause), a vegetarian (pause), and a Socialist (pause)"—Henry Arthur nudged Mr. Wise and said, "Three damned good reasons why he ought to be chucked out."

In 1902 my father was staying at the Hotel Metropole, where he wrote nearly the whole of *Whitewashing Julia,* his next production. Lord Rowton was staying there also, and he and my father lunched and dined together nearly every day. H. A. J. delighted to hear him talk about Disraeli. He assured my father that, when he first went to Disraeli as his private secretary, it was not then considered respectable to be seen walking down the street with him. Lord Rowton told Henry Arthur that when Disraeli lay dying, a crowd had gathered underneath his windows and were looking up curiously. He thought it would please the dying man to know the people were watching, but, when he was told, all he said was, "And a year ago they kicked me into a ditch"—referring, of course, to the General Election of 1880.

Whitewashing Julia was produced by Arthur Bourchier at the Garrick Theatre on 2nd March, 1903. Julia Wren, a fascinating widow, is the centre of gossip in the small town where she has come to live. Was she, or was she not, morganatically married to a Grand Duke? This question is left in doubt, but Julia marries Mr. Stillingfleet, who has proved her most redoubtable champion. The newspaper reception was mixed, but the play was a success and ran for 106 nights. It also had a fairly successful run in New York, where it was produced at the Garrick Theatre on 2nd December, 1903.

Bernard Shaw was to have been present on the first night; he explained his absence in the following amusing letter:

"*1st March, 1903.*

"MY DEAR H. A. J.,

"My disgraceful conduct about the seats is the fault of my marriage. I arranged with my wife that she should answer your telegram. This, I grieve to say, she stoutly denies, alleging that I carefully explained that I would wire on my way to the Borough Council. I scorn to argue with a woman. Let the blame rest on my innocent shoulders. Never shall it be said that I gave my wife away.

"Can you spare me a copy of the play? What is the use of going to a first night to see your work murdered, and to sit among the geniuses who remonstrated with you for the 'inconsistency' of the gentleman in *Chance the Idol?* I had much rather wait until I have reason to suppose that they are not making a hopeless mess of the play before I go to see it.

"Archer is taking lessons in Sandow's establishment with a view to perfecting his physical development.

"Vienna is in utter confusion in consequence of one of my plays having been produced there last Wednesday.

"Yrs. ever,

"G. BERNARD SHAW."

There was an enormous amount of criticism and discussion in the Press because A. B. Walkley, the dramatic critic of *The Times,* was excluded on the first night. A year before the production my father called on Mr. Moberly Bell and complained of the tone of A. B. W.'s notices of his plays for the last few years. He was assured that the matter would be "watched." Just before the first night Arthur Bourchier wrote to *The Times* to beg that another critic should review the play. When Mr. Walkley arrived on the first night, the manager politely requested him to leave. Mr. Bourchier agreed with H. A. J. that Walkley's notices were unfair, and they both wrote to the papers several letters in which they explained their attitude at length. Most of the comment in the London and provincial Press, and in the American and French newspapers, was good-natured, but one or two papers, notably the *Daily Telegraph,* resented H. A. J.'s action.

In all my father's quarrels and disputes with various people he never bore the slightest malice. He gave and received many hard knocks, but I do not think he knew the meaning of the word rancour.

Soon after I went to live in Cyprus I had a quarrel with a woman friend. Henry Arthur wrote to me:

"26th January, 1913.

"I hope you have quite made it up, and that you will contrive to get along with her and with everybody, else I shall think that I have vainly offered you a warning in my own life of the folly of having rows with people. Do remember how many times I have shown you by my own practice how useless it is to quarrel with people. It is true that I had the interests of the English Drama to think of, but even in so sacred a cause as that, I have often gone to unnecessary lengths in fighting people. So go easy. . . . "

But on another occasion he said to me, "I've a very choice collection of enemies, thank God. You ought to be as careful choosing your enemies as you are your friends."

He came to regret the quarrel, and he often said, "I was wrong to fight with Walkley," or, "I ought never to have had a row with Walkley." I am glad that not many years later they became friends; the Walkleys dined with my parents, who also went to their house several times, and, when Henry Arthur gave a dinner in honour of Walter Page at the Athenæum in May 1917, Mr. Walkley was one of the guests.

Joseph Entangled was produced at the Haymarket Theatre on 19th January, 1904. Through an unlucky mischance, Lady Verona Mayne is hopelessly compromised by an old friend, Sir Joseph Lacy. Mr. Mayne cannot believe that his wife is guiltless until, driven by jealousy, he deliberately listens to a conversation between his wife and Sir Joseph which establishes their innocence. The play was cordially received by the audience, but most of the critics were unfriendly, though "Max" wrote a very appreciative notice in the *Saturday Review:* "Others of Mr. Jones's comedies," he said, "have been more perfect in form, I think; but none has been more amusing, more alive. In the art of writing realistic comedy of manners he is far pre-eminent over our other playwrights. Not one of them can match him in that lightness of solidity which is the essential of the art. Not one of them can so quicken and vitalise a story. Vitality—that is Mr. Jones's chief point of excellence. Up goes the curtain, and with it our spirits, for not a moment is lost: we are already in the thick of the interest. . . . Mr. Jones never makes us conscious of his technique, and for that reason his technique is better than Mr. Pinero's. . . . In Mr. Jones's dialogue there is never a line that has not the true oral ring. To sound that note consistently should be the aim of every realistic playwright. Mr. Jones succeeds in doing it, and his plays have, therefore, a very real literary quality."

The first night was nearly a fiasco, as the scenery caught fire in the second act during a light comedy scene. First of all the footlights went out, and then from our box we saw the smoke billowing out on to the stage. Poor Cyril Maude, with the perspiration pouring down his face, and the rest of the cast, went on with their parts as best they could, but Henry Arthur stampeded to and fro from our box to the stage, utterly oblivious of the possible horrible outcome—it was just after the tragic fire in an American theatre, when hundreds of people were burnt to death—clasping his head, and muttering, "My God, my play's ruined!" Two of our maids were in the upper circle, with our butler, Hopkins, and one of them began to whimper and say she would go home or she would be killed. Hopkins said, "You certainly will, if you go off and start a panic, as Mr. Jones is sure to murder you when he gets home." Several of our friends in the audience told us afterwards they kept an eye on our box, having made up their minds, "If the Joneses make a move, we will also." It was a great tribute to British self-control that no panic occurred.

In the summer of 1904, Henry Arthur lectured at the Royal Institution on the "Foundations of a National Drama." I remember going to the lecture and how well he spoke. Shortly afterwards the *English Illustrated Magazine* published a symposium on the State of the Drama, to which my father, Bernard Shaw, Pinero, Jules Lemaître, Sir Gilbert Parker, "Carmen Sylva," Beerbohm Tree, and others contributed. H. A. J. summarised his recent lecture. "We must separate," he said, "the Drama from popular amusement—we must found a national or repertory theatre—insure that a dramatist shall be recognised and rewarded when he has sincerely painted life and character—bring our acted Drama into living relation with English literature—and ensure that plays shall be read and judged as literature. We must inform our Drama with a broad, sane, and profound morality, give our actors and actresses a sounder, better, and more thorough training, break down as far as possible the system of long runs, while establishing more repertory theatres in the country—and bring the Drama into relation with the other arts."

During the last fifteen years of his life he girded at repertory theatres, and often said how useless they were and how much money was lost on them. He disliked intensely the sort of plays which were constantly chosen; spoke of them as "the Pentonville omnibus school of drama" (in reference to Ruskin's remark that George Eliot's characters were like the sweepings out of a Pentonville omnibus). In his Notes he says, "I have great faith in myself. I believe that if I were to summon all my energies, I could write a play almost as dull as the masterpiece of the Pentonville omnibus school that they play in repertory theatres."

Arthur Bourchier produced *The Chevaleer* at the Garrick Theatre on 27th August, 1904. The Chevaleer is a travelling showman who, for his own ends, manages to hoodwink Lady Anne Kellond and her husband into believing that he is in possession of facts which would damage their reputation. Many of the notices were good, but William Archer's article in the *World* was hostile, and A. B. Walkley's in *The Times* was scathing: "*The Chevaleer* cannot with propriety be called a play, but is in fact a riot of noisy nonsense." Max and a great many other critics complained that the story, that of a married woman involved in some scandalous episode, was the same theme that Henry Arthur had used in too many of his plays— *The Lackey's Carnival, Joseph Entangled,* and *Whitewashing Julia.* I think this criticism was justified. H. A. J. said to me once, "*The Chevaleer* took me fifteen months to write, *Dolly Reforming Herself* only five weeks. I never got the plot of *The Chevaleer* right somehow." He did not think Bourchier was really good in the part,

ARTHUR BOURCHIER AS "THE CHEVALEER," GARRICK THEATRE, 1904

and said to me, "You know, Bourchier bouched it too
much." Two of the papers quoted as the mainspring of
the plot the Chevaleer's remark, "When I have committed
any delinquence, I have noticed that all the persons and
all the circumstances glare at me as if they knew." The
piece was a failure, and was withdrawn at the end of
October.

CHAPTER XIII

THE early part of 1905 was spent in writing *The Sword of Gideon*. It is a very strong play, with a fine part for an old man, but it needs a very fascinating actress for the leading woman. My father was fond of this play and believed it would be a success, if rightly cast, but it was never acted. After his death I found this note of his on the play: "Charles Frohman wanted this play for Miss Virginia Harned, but, on reading it, she said she liked it but could not possibly play it, as the man's was the leading part. I afterwards offered it to a leading actor; he said he liked it, but could not possibly play it, as the woman's was the leading part."

At the end of the year he was called to America on business, and he was there also in 1906, 1907, and 1908. He always enjoyed his visits enormously; he said that the New York air was like champagne, and that he never felt as well anywhere as he did over there. The noise and hustle never seemed to worry him, but he often felt the reaction on his return to England. These four trips to New York consolidated and strengthened many of his friendships and increased his enduring love and admiration for America and the American people. The vitality, gaiety, and energy in H. A. J.'s nature found immediate communion with a people who are pre-eminent in these qualities.

It was on the first of these visits that he met Mr. Clayton Hamilton and felt an immediate liking for the enthusiastic young man. Henry Arthur's friendship for Mr. Hamilton grew and deepened throughout the years, and at

194

the end of his life he counted him among the foremost of his friends.

He was an honorary member of the Players' Club, and whenever he was in New York he went to the Players' constantly. At a dinner given to him by the American dramatist, Charles Klein, in returning thanks he said, "The applause of an audience is honey; the praise of the Press is nectar, though sometimes it tastes suspiciously like vinegar, but then it has a medicinal effect. But the praise of one's brother craftsmen is honey, nectar, butter, and sugar-candy combined. . . . I'm afraid, gentlemen, I'm something of a monomaniac on the subject of the Drama. It is a very happy thing for a man when the business of his life is also his inveterate hobby. . . . I recently heard a story of a man who visited a lunatic asylum, and there saw a madman riding and furiously whipping a rocking-chair. The visitor said to him, 'That is a fine horse you have got there.' The lunatic scowled and said, 'This isn't a horse.' The visitor after a second or two asked, 'Then may I ask what it is?' The lunatic growled and replied, 'This is a hobby-horse.' 'What is the difference, between a horse and a hobby-horse?' asked the visitor. The lunatic replied: 'You can get off a horse, but you cannot get off a hobby-horse.' "

At another dinner in New York, in 1908, he said, "No public appreciation can be so sweet and so gratifying as the appreciation of one's comrades. . . . I have constantly affirmed that the Drama is in a livelier, lustier, more healthy state in America than in England. . . . It is better to have vitality than style. . . . I never found a keener interest and curiosity in the Drama than those I found at your leading American Universities. . . . I shall be deeply gratified if, in return for the generosity and kindness that Americans have shown me, I could think that any efforts of mine had served as a guide to the unrisen American dramatists. . . . I have been again immensely impressed and inspired by my visit to America, by the splendid relentless energy and youth of your nation." He went on to refer to two old friends who were unavoidably prevented from being present, Clyde Fitch and Augustus Thomas, and, in calling upon his dear old friend Bronson Howard to respond for the toast of the American Drama, he said, "Old friend, you and I are stepping westward, our eyes are towards the sunset." A few weeks afterwards Mr. Howard died, and in memory of his prophetic words at this dinner my father wrote the following beautiful sonnet:

Old friend, when many friends had gathered round,
Two years ago, to toast your country's stage,
I saw your fine keen features changed.   White age
Had touched and ripened you, and you were crowned
With sweetest, kindliest wisdom's wreath.   I found
Warmer your welcome; more serene, more sage,
My old-time comrade.   And from Wordsworth's page
I drew a greeting with a fateful sound.
'So we are stepping westward, you and I,'
Lightly I said, nor thought your swiftening feet
So soon would reach the sunset land.   Pass by!
Laden with love and admiration, greet
Your fellows there.   May 'stepping westward' be
To you 'a kind of heavenly destiny.'

Oliver Herford was one of the very dearest and closest of all H. A. J.'s friends, and whenever he was in New York he saw the Herfords several times a week. In speaking of the dangers of night life in that city, he often told me that when he dined with the Herfords, Oliver always insisted upon his taking a taxi back to his hotel, though it was only a few blocks away, as he did not think it safe for H. A. J. to return on foot. My father took a keen delight in Oliver Herford's delicate wit and poetry and his many charming and whimsical drawings. He was always very pleased when the American mail brought another token of remembrance from his friend in the shape of a signed picture, and he bought several copies of Oliver's books for the special purpose of giving them to various small children, and many of their elders, when they came to see him.

Henry Arthur returned from America just before Christmas 1905 to superintend the rehearsals of *The Heroic Stubbs,* which was produced by Mr. James Welch at the Strand Theatre on 24th January, 1906.

Stubbs is a bootmaker with a romantic but hopeless passion for Lady Hermione Candlish. He rescues her from a very compromising situation, content with the reward of having been of service to the object of his adoration. The notices were hostile and the play was a great failure; though Max in the *Saturday Review* praised Stubbs, which he said was a character peculiarly suited to Welch. He thought the first three acts were good, but that the fourth was an anti-climax and was unnecessary. It was Mr. Welch's first venture into management, and I think my father regretted the failure of the play more on that account than for personal reasons.

In 1906 he returned to America for the production of *The Hypocrites.* The play was produced under Charles Frohman's management on 30th August at the Hudson Theatre, New York, with Doris Keane, Leslie Faber, and Richard Bennett in the leading rôles.

The Hypocrites is one of the strongest of my father's plays; the story of a weak, but attractive boy, Leonard Wilmore, who seduces a girl, and the efforts of his family to hush up the scandal and buy the girl off. In spite of the fact that she is expecting a child, they want Leonard to make a *mariage de convenance.* Rachel, the girl, is willing to deny her relations with Leonard, though she is urged to tell the truth by the Rev. Edgar Linnell, who will not countenance the deception. In a tremendous scene in the third act Rachel confronts Leonard and his family and

retracts her story of their intimacy; as she turns to go out,
blinded with misery, she stumbles, and Leonard instinc-
tively puts out his arms to prevent her from falling.   The
touch of the girl he loves is too much for him, and he blurts
out the truth.   The family are forced to accept the situation, and there is every prospect that in time they will
approve of the marriage between Leonard and Rachel.

It was the greatest success my father ever had in America, and the first night was one of the most memorable of
his career.   My sister Peg, who was in his box, told us that
after the third act the audience were wildly enthusiastic,
standing up in their seats and, in spite of the great heat,
shouting and yelling with excitement.   Indeed their enthusiasm was so intense that Henry Arthur was compelled
to make a speech from his box.

One summer evening during this visit my father and
sister went with George Cohan, one of the directors of
Coney Island, and other kindred spirits, in two racing
motor-cars to Coney Island.   H. A. J. was exceedingly
fond of motoring, and the faster he went the better he
liked it.   (I well remember summer holidays at Ostend,
when he would stand on the front of a tram-car and, once
we were free of the town, bribe the driver to go as fast as
he dared.)   My sister said they all spent a most riotous
evening; H. A. J. insisted upon sampling the helter-skelter,
the scenic railways, the switchbacks—everything.   I recall how once, at Folkestone, when we were all children, he
and old George Grossmith, of whom he was very fond,
hired the switchback for the whole afternoon, and we had
a marvellous time.   My father was just like a schoolboy
on these occasions, full of high spirits and indulging in all
sorts of pranks, silly jokes, and quaint expressions.   It was
a tonic to be with him.   After the island was closed to the
public Mr. Cohan's party had supper, and he then asked
H. A. J. if he would like to see what would happen in case
of a fire.   The alarm was sounded, and in a few seconds the

whole place, which had been as deserted as Bond Street on a Sunday evening, was teeming with life, the showmen swarming out of their booths and little houses like ants.

On 31st October, 1906, Henry Arthur lectured at Harvard University on "The Corner Stones of Modern Drama." Professor George P. Baker was an old friend of his, and H. A. J. was always keenly interested in his work at Harvard on behalf of the modern Drama. He gave to the University his greatest treasure, William Morris's vellum bound Chaucer, and on the way over he wrote the following letter, which he sent with the book:

> "S.S. *Celtic.*
> "*26th October, 1906.*

"My dear Professor Baker,

"I have the great pleasure and honour of asking Harvard University to accept this volume as a tribute of my gratitude to you for making modern plays a part of the literary course of your students. It is the first recognition that literature and scholarship have given to the modern English Drama. I am sure that you must have met with considerable opposition and misunderstanding, but I hope that the wisdom and courage and foresight of your action will gradually become apparent to your contemporaries, as they cannot fail to be owned and honoured by your successors. . . .

"I may, perhaps, say a word about the book itself. It is the loving handwork of the greatest man whom I have known. It may be claimed for William Morris that his reputation would be a high and honourable one if it rested upon any one of his achievements; upon his poetry alone; his tales and essays alone; his dyeing alone; his weaving alone; his printing alone. In every one of these arts he accomplished the good and faithful work of an ordinary lifetime. He abides with us a living witness to the essential unity of art; he continually affirms that, like the other two great realities, like Religion, like Love, it is something that must be bought without money and without price. For this beautiful volume brought him no profit, and left him with no payment for all his labour and all his lovely designs. The main idea of his later years was a hatred of the base commercialism which has degraded the ordinary workman from an artist into a machine, and has cheapened and demoralised and disfigured the whole fabric of modern civilisation. But this hatred was not sullen or stagnant; it accompanied an active, ceaseless search for a social lever that could again raise the workman into an artist, and thereby bring taste and dignity and simplicity and beauty into ordinary everyday homes. With the hope that the spirit in which William Morris printed this volume may guide the nascent art of America, and with renewed assurances of gratitude and friendship towards yourself,

"I am, dear Professor Baker,
"Always faithfully yours,
"HENRY ARTHUR JONES."

The original manuscript of *The Dancing Girl* also belongs to Harvard University.

Five days after his Harvard address he lectured at Yale University, his subject being "Literature and the Modern Drama." The lecture was published in the December number of the *Atlantic Monthly,* and these two lectures, and also one he delivered at Columbia University in 1911, are reprinted in his book *The Foundations of a National Drama,* published in London and New York in 1913.

Although these addresses entailed a good deal of hard work and took up a certain amount of time when he was busy writing and rehearsing plays, he was delighted at the opportunity offered to him of speaking to young America on the subject dearest to his heart; but above all at the recognition shown to his work by the request that he should

MR. HENRY ARTHUR JONES, ENGLAND'S SCOURGE

(*Cartoon by Max Beerbohm*)

lecture to the students at these great American Universities.

From the time his work became widely known in America, H. A. J. received wider and more grateful recognition, praise, and admiration from the American people than he did from his fellow-countrymen. He was always more popular over there than in his own country. Many American men of letters, as well as students at the Universities, studied his work and wrote about it. Several students obtained their degrees by writing treatises on H. A. J.'s plays, and so, too, did one or two students in Germany. In speaking of his popularity in the United States and the great praise he had received there, he never appeared to regret that "a prophet is not without honour save in his own country"; but it was natural that he should feel a deep and lasting attachment for the people who always received him and his work with open arms.

It was one of the proudest moments of his life when, in June 1907, Harvard conferred on him an Honorary Degree. He said, and I believe he was correct in the assertion, that it was the first degree ever conferred by a University on a dramatist. From the way he spoke about it I think it was the recognition shown to the Drama as a great art, and not the personal distinction conferred upon himself, which gave him so much pleasure.

He took his degree with President Wilson, the Duke of the Abruzzi, Ambassador Jusserand, Lord Bryce, and Elihu Root. The degrees were conferred in the Sanders Theatre, and President Eliot, in conferring the degree upon my father, said, "In exercise of authority given me by the two governing boards, I now create Honorary Master of Arts, Henry Arthur Jones, dramatist, for twenty years a leader in the revival of the English Drama and its reunion with English literature."

One of the closest and most cordial of the friendships my father formed during these visits to America was with

Professor William Lyon Phelps of Yale University. There was always a quick understanding and sympathy between the two men, and they delighted in their many interesting talks on literature and the Drama. Each stimulated the other. Just after his return from America in 1906, H. A. J. wrote to Professor Phelps:

"9th December, 1906.

"My dear Professor Phelps,

"I think I will drop the Professor as I do with Baker and begin

"My dear Phelps,

" Your Jane Austen is in front of me, reproaching me with not admiring her. Well, the only reason I don't admire Jane Austen very much is, that I've never read her. When I say I've never read her, I mean I've never done anything more than take her up and drop her. The moment I begin to read a novel I throw all the onus on the author—I hold him responsible for my laziness, my preoccupation, my bad taste, my thousand deficiencies—I put myself in his hands, and thenceforth the affair is entirely his affair.

"Well, I've never finished a novel of Jane Austen's. But I do blush to say that—I blushed when I told you that I didn't admire her. But it was unkind of you to record the damnable fact. And now I've read your little book, *I do admire her.* So you are left recording an obsolete error of taste on the part of a Yale lecturer! I will go further and say that I not only admire her, but I will read her. I do know how fine an artist she is—one cannot dip into a page without tasting that. I think you are right in comparing her with Flaubert in *Madame Bovary;* there is the same resolute avoidance of fiction, of everything that the author has not himself verified in life. I question whether I will put her in front of Flaubert, but of course I can't say till I've read her. I re-read *Madame Bovary* lately; it is a very great novel.   Do you remember the fine passage describing the administration of extreme unction, almost at the end of the book? . . ."

"Always most cordially yours,
"HENRY ARTHUR JONES."

When Billy Phelps was in England in 1910, they met several times, and renewed and continued their discussions on literature.   Writing to him from Hindhead in February 1910, Henry Arthur said:

"I had a most pleasant two hours with you coming down in the train on Sunday, and another pleasant hour or so on Saturday.   I like the way you write; the shrewd humour and the telling right word on every page please me very much.   I find myself in very substantial agreement with your judgments.   I think you underrate *Tess* and *Jude the Obscure*.   In spite of its quite unnecessary faults, I think *Jude* a very great book, in some respects as great as anything Hardy has written.   But I only read it once when it came out, and a second reading of it, and a close comparison with the others, might cause me to shift my estimates.   I am glad you rate Hardy so highly—I think him incomparably greater an artist than Meredith—greater because he is so much simpler. . . ."

Just after my father received his degree at Harvard, he went to stay with W. D. Howells at Kittery Point.   He often referred, with keen pleasure, to this visit, and the delightful talks he had with his host on the subjects dear to the hearts of both.   My father corresponded with Mr. Howells fairly regularly, and, among the many delightful letters he received from him, he was very proud of the two here quoted:

"30th December, 1906.

"Your letter gave me the greatest pleasure; thirty, even twenty years ago, it would have given me courage; but at seventy one does not turn to a new trade. Still, in the impulse you have given me, I am going to take my little pieces to a dramatic agent here, and see what will happen. I sadly fancy, nothing—for one of the *comédiettes*—let us compromise in a foreign tongue—has been done by all that was starriest both in London and New York, without being asked to stay on the stage. Of course they have been done everywhere in private theatricals; and they have sold pleasingly enough. Mr. Douglas, of Edinburgh, is to publish a complete edition of them, counting twenty in all. He shall send them to you. . . .

"I have read your *Whitewashing Julia* aloud to my family, and if there had been no instruction outside of the dialogue, we should still have found it most satisfying and delightful. It brought vividly back to me the play as I saw it, with more time for its very artistic and amusing subtlety. I wish I knew where I could get all of your plays as far as printed.

"I am heartily glad you liked what I wrote about *The Hypocrites*. I should like to write of your whole drama—including your new play. You are now so well-known to the whole public that a paper about you would be widely interesting. . . ."

"10th March, 1907.

"I have received all the plays you sent me and have read them all but two or three; and I only wish there were more of them, and especially that *Judah* were among them. Out of them all I liked best that one about the rector and his lost angel (I never can recall the title). I have read them mostly at night when I woke up out of my first sleep and had an hour of wakefulness before me. They bore this test so well that I had to read something else before I could get to sleep again. They have been in every way most interesting to me, psychologically as well as artistically, for I kept putting myself in the place of the author, and although I felt that I 'rattled around in it,' as we say, still I felt that I realised something of his intentions and his consciousness in respect to the social and theatrical environment.

"The plays have taught me many things, and if I were thirty-five instead of seventy, I think their teachings would not be lost upon me. I should know how to leave more to the actors than I have ever been willing to do in my smaller attempts. I have seen a good half of the pieces played, and as I recall their fulness on the stage, I see how you have known and recognised the rights of the theatre, and have had the self-denial to leave a great part of the effect to the performers. At the same time you have written good literature; and something of this I shall wish to say when I come to write of the pieces in the long leisure of next summer at the seaside. . . . I wish, if you could, you would still send me *Judah*, which was the first play of yours I saw, and of which the impression still remains most vivid with my wife and myself. . . ."

The first London performance of *The Hypocrites* was under Charles Frohman's management at the Hicks Theatre (now the Globe) on 27th August, 1907, with Doris Keane and Leslie Faber in their original parts. The reception was enthusiastic, but the notices were mixed. Some were very good, but most of them condemned the play, and it was a failure. "Max's" notice in the *Saturday Review*, which was enthusiastic, was headed, "Re-enter Mr. Jones." He said that Englishmen took their national hypocrisy for granted, but "Mr. Henry Arthur Jones is exceptional in that he has never got used to the national feeling. Many things swim in and out of the ken of this student of life; but one thing, English hypocrisy has been the objective of his wrath." He went on to say that, "Mr. Jones's work is always notable for its vitality; and *The Hypocrites,* from the moment when the curtain rises, is as pungently and arrestingly alive as any play that he has written."

Keble Howard (in the *Daily Mail*) was damning; he set it down that H. A. J. had "truckled once again to the groundlings . . . gone back to the old melodramatic stockpot . . . knocked together a crude and wholly silly play. . . . Of course Mr. Jones is laughing up his sleeve and he does not mind being detected in that peculiar attitude. . . . Mr. Jones has packed his bag with some deliciously quaint old tricks." My father always said he could have sued the *Daily Mail* for libel on this notice, and he was convinced he would have received heavy damages. To the end of his life he never spoke of the notice without anger, and on one occasion when my sister was with Mr. Howard and she introduced him to H. A. J. he refused to shake hands. His resentment of this criticism was the only occasion throughout his career when he felt any lasting annoyance about a hostile criticism.

H. A. J. was delighted with the following letter from Sir Edmund Gosse, in spite of his adverse criticism of the fourth act:

"28th August, 1907."

"My dear Henry Arthur Jones,

"It was most kind of you to give us the pleasure and excitement of seeing *The Hypocrites* last night. I am confidently able to congratulate you on a great popular success. I am quite sure the piece will have a splendid run.

"The third act is amazingly powerful, and rises in temperature to the last moment magnificently. But why not leave it there? Why give us a fourth act which adds nothing to our knowledge? This is my old heresy at which you will once more indulgently smile. Yet, if we had all come away at the end of the third act, vibrating with emo-

tion, what a success you would have had over the nerves
of your audience!

"Yours very sincerely,
"EDMUND GOSSE."

Just before the production G. B. S. sent him a few lines:

"Hafody Bryn, Llanbedr,
"Merionethshire, R.S.O.
"*17th August, 1907.*

"Look at my address!

"Success to *The Hypocrites* as to *The Liars!*   Give your
next play an even more sensational title—I forget the exact
word—something like the Fabricators.

"G. B. S."

H. A. J. lost a good deal of money over *The Hypocrites,*
as he went into management with Charles Frohman for the
English production.

He delighted to tell the following story about Mr. Frohman; I believe the incident occurred during the rehearsals
of this play.   Mr. Frohman was always the busiest of
men; even when he was crossing the Atlantic he was rehearsing companies and reading plays on all his many
trips.   One day he got stuck in the lift behind the scenes,
and it was over half an hour before he was released.   In
fear and trembling the door was opened, as those present
expected to be cursed roundly for the mishap; but, as
Frohman stepped out, he said with his winning smile,
"That's the first holiday I've had for over twelve years."

Just after the production of *The Hypocrites* in England,
The Evangelist was produced in New York on 30th September, 1907, at the Knickerbocker Theatre.   The original
title was *The Galilean's Victory,* and the play was privately
printed with this title.   My father called it "A tragi-com-
edy of life in England."   When he read the play to Mr.

Klaw and Mr. Erlanger, the managers who produced it, one of them said, "My God, this'll raise unshirted hell"; but it was a very great failure, the greatest I believe in all my father's career, though Howard Kyle gave a superb performance as the Evangelist.

John Drew, another dear friend of my father's, used to tell an amusing story in connection with the failure of *The Evangelist*. They were both staying at the Hotel Gotham, and H. A. J.'s apartments were very high up. One day Mr. Drew went up to see him, and found him looking out of the window. "Drew," he said, "do you know why my play failed? It was because of the total lack of reverence among the New Yorkers." Drew demurred to this criticism, and said, "Everywhere you gaze you are looking down on church spires." "That's just it," replied Henry Arthur, "everywhere in this city you look down on churches, and that's why there isn't a damn bit of reverence in America."

So fine a judge as Gilbert Murray thought very highly of the play. He wrote:

"27th October.

"DEAR MR. JONES,

"I should have written to you before, but the beginning of term, together with the production of *Medea,* has left me scarcely a moment of leisure. I like *The Galilean's Victory* exceedingly. It is both a true and a most dramatic subject; and your skill in inter-weaving the scenes and situations seems to me, if you will excuse my saying so, really astonishing. You get four or five effects where an ordinary playwright would get one, and all of them naturally and without undue strain. It would be a terrible pity if such a play were to be smothered either by the Censor or by circumstances.

"I need hardly add that I agree most warmly with your position in 'The Corner Stones' and the other two lectures, and I am exceedingly glad to have the three little books by me.

"I find that Rebbings and Naomi are characters that live in my mind like real people.

"*The Hypocrites* I enjoyed also and cannot quite understand its not having more success. But I do not personally *like* it as much as *The Galilean*.

"I don't suppose much will come of this Censor campaign, tho' the Prime Minister seems to be generally sympathetic.

"Yours sincerely,
"GILBERT MURRAY."

I believe it was during this visit that Mrs. Patrick Campbell was in New York also, and staying at the same hotel as my father. Both of them had had great failures, and Henry Arthur told me that Mrs. Pat asked him to write her a play; she would say, "I'm quite manageable now—do write me a comedy." One night Mrs. Guinness gave a reception at which Mrs. Patrick Campbell and the Duc de Richelieu gave an amusing little Punch and Judy show, with only their heads showing above miniature bodies. It was received with great enthusiasm, and afterwards Mrs. Pat came dancing up to H. A. J. and said, "Now do, do write me a comedy; you see I am much better in comedy than I am in tragedy." My father said dryly, "Oh, yes, I liked you better to-night than I did as Lady Macbeth." Henry Arthur was not a malicious man, but I do not feel this comment was undeserved after Mrs. Pat's behaviour over *The Masqueraders* and *Michael*, and her published comments on those plays. He said to me once, "Mrs. Pat played Lady Macbeth and" (with a sweeping gesture of his hand) "let the part go by her." The last time my father met Mrs. Patrick Campbell was at a garden-party given by Eva Moore in the summer of 1928. His sight had been failing for some time, and, although he never knew it, he had cataract. Mrs. Pat came up to H. A. J. and said, "How do you do? You don't remember me; I'm the woman you hate." The old man said, "I don't hate anybody. Who are you?" He was greatly distressed by his failure to recognize Mrs. Pat, and he referred to the incident several times; he said he could not bear to think he had slighted, though unintentionally, so great an actress, who for some time had no big success, and who had been absent from the London stage for so long. After my father's death G. B. S. told me of an illuminating comment he made about Mrs. Pat: he said, "Mrs. Pat has remarkable sight for anything within six inches of her own nose."

In 1906 my father sold Portland Place, and before he moved to 37 Hornton Street, Kensington, in 1907, he took a furnished house at Brighton, and later stayed for some time at a London hotel. Just after moving to Hornton Street he took a house at Hindhead, where he stayed frequently during the next three years before he sold the lease.

My aunt told me that Henry Arthur suffered from his first nervous breakdown before his marriage, and that he was supposed to be going into a decline. All through his life he broke down at irregular intervals; during these attacks he suffered from acute mental depression, was very sleepless, and was quite incapable of doing any kind of work or of concentrating on any subject even for five minutes at a time. He paid the severe penalty of his temperament, which compelled him to live his life, not on an even plane, but in irregular periods of great intellectual activity, accompanied by intense nervous energy, excitement, and high spirits, to be followed by an appalling reaction of stagnation and misery, with very occasional intervals, which never lasted more than a few months, when he sailed along, so to speak, on an even keel.

Just before leaving Portland Place he was very sleepless, and went to the South of France for a change. On the journey to Nice he stuck his head out of the window for nearly half an hour, hoping that the force of the wind would blow away the cobwebs.   The result of this rash act was to bring on acute catarrh, and, though he had an operation on the antrum while he was at Hornton Street, he was never cured, and suffered severely from chronic catarrh for the rest of his life.   Whenever he had a breakdown, this chronic trouble became worse, and it was always a drain on his vitality.

His family dreaded his breakdowns almost as much as he did.   He could never forget himself for a single minute. Nothing that we tried to do seemed to help or distract him. He was absorbed in a cloud of misery.   Whatever subject was mentioned, if he joined in the conversation, within a few seconds he would refer to his own condition; for instance, if one of us said, "Things look rather black in Ireland," he would reply, "Not as black as I feel," or "How fresh the grass is after the rain"—"I only wish I thought I should ever feel fresh again," and so on and so on.   It was exhausting to be with him, as he absorbed all our vitality and energy and gave nothing in return.

I remember being with him in Hindhead in 1907 or 1908, when he was suffering from a very bad breakdown.   In these depressed conditions he was always haunted by the fear of madness, and I shall never forget the utter despair with which one day at Hindhead he put his hand on my lap and said, half crying and half moaning, "Oh, my darling, I'm going out of my mind!"   I had a special name for him when he was suffering from these depressed states—I called him "My old sick eagle," and he was quite fond of this appellation.   Although he was Early Victorian in many ways, he was very modern, or perhaps I should say indulgent, in the freedom with which he allowed his children, more especially myself and my daughter, to address him. Dorinda and I often called him "Henry Arthur," "Hank," and " H. A. J." to his face, and in speaking of him when he was present; more rarely still I sometimes called him, "Jonesy dear," and very occasionally I would twiddle his white hairs into a point on the top of his head and speak of him as "Joey."

When he was suffering from a nervous breakdown, he was always convinced that he was done for and that he would never be able to work again. We had to remind him, not once, but several times a day how often he had been in a similar condition before, and that when the bad time was over he always came back to his work "like a giant refreshed." He was never happy or at ease unless he was working, and in a letter to his son, Oliver, written in 1922, when he was suffering from a breakdown, he said, "I am at present taking a holiday in my usual way—that is moping about the house very depressed about everything. I've been working too hard, and have got to lie about and mope about till I come round. Meanwhile the general outlook seems very gloomy, although as a matter of fact there is nothing to mope about." About the same time he wrote to Mr. Spielmann:

". . . I've had a bad month in one of the lowest dungeons in Doubting Castle—a recurrent experience with good Christians like John Bunyan and myself. You lent me a lifting hand to pull me out of the horrible pit some years ago. However I am all right again, but going a little slowly. . . ."

I suppose our love and sympathy did help him a little; he certainly needed us all round him at these times. I am glad my mother's deafness spared her a great deal of suffering on his behalf, though he could not do without her, either, and her calm and steady cheerfulness was a refuge to him always.

CHAPTER XIV

In 1907 my father moved to 37 Hornton Street, Kensington, but he never liked the little house or the neighbourhood, and after two years he went to live in Hampstead at 6 Arkwright Road. Though he did not like this house either, he stayed there until 1916, when he bought another, 19 Kidderpore Avenue, just off the Finchley Road. He lived here until his death, and he often said the purchase of this house was the only good investment he had ever made. After Townshend House, we all liked No. 19 better than any other house where we had lived.

Early in 1908 my father finished a three-act farce called *Dick*. He had a contract with Charles Hawtrey to produce this play, and I do not know why it fell through. After his death I found a note on this play: "I was very ill and sleepless when I wrote it and was unequal to any great effort. With the right comedian in the leading part, it would stand the toss-up chance of hitting the public that all farces, even more than serious pieces, have to face, the stupidest of them proving the greatest success."

Several years previously, though I have no exact date, Henry Arthur wrote out in full the scenario for a farce, *The Mad Cook,* and only a few months before he died he referred to it, exclaiming, "Oh, good Lord! What a splendid idea for a farce—Willard would have done it well. I told him about it."

Henry Arthur had a very welcome success with *Dolly Reforming Herself,* which was produced at the Haymarket Theatre on 3rd November, 1908. He frequently chose a quotation which epitomised the theme of his play, and on

213

the privately printed editions of *Dolly Reforming Herself* is the following sentence from Voltaire, "Mennon conçut le projet un jour d'être parfaitement sage. Il n'y a guère d'homme à qui cette folie n'est pas quelquefois passée par la tête."   Voltaire was always one of his favourite authors, and he re-read *Candide* several times; putting his thumb and forefinger together and pointing it at his listener, he would declare his admiration for its irony, "so fine, biting, delicate, like a needle-point."

H. A. J. was singularly fortunate in having Miss Ethel Irving and Colonel Robert Loraine to play the leading parts in his comedy; both gave magnificent performances, to which he always referred when speaking of the play. There must have been one or two stormy scenes at rehearsals, for Bobby Loraine told me that he remembers one occasion when Henry Arthur was so exasperated that he gave vent to his feelings by taking a running leap from the back of the stage right over the orchestra into the stalls.

H. A. J. sent Shaw a copy of this play before the production.   I imagine that he asked his advice as to whether he should cut the play, as G. B S. wrote him as follows:

"8th October, 1908.

"My dear H. A. J.,

"The right title for the play—unless you can find a better—is *Turning Over a New Leaf*.

If you have Macaulay's *Essays* handy, look at the beginning of the one on Robert Montgomery, which quotes a fable of Pilpay.   Messrs. H. & H. are trying that game on your fourth act.   The scene with the Professor is a particularly good one.   The play, far from needing cutting, would bear another act (perhaps Harrison would like one of my nice long last acts; if so, anything to oblige a friend), and is quite the greatest piece of luck Harrison has had in the way of a new play since he parted company with Maude.

"Unless you are hard up for immediate royalties, I

should almost advise you to let Harrison give you back the play on paying twopence-halfpenny damages. If the cast is attractive enough, it is as likely as not to be another *Liars*.

"What ensanguined fools they are!

"G. B. S."

Most of the notices were very good. A. B. Walkley, in *The Times*, speaking of the third act, said: "The crescendo of quarrel has been most skilfully and drolly arranged—a scene, as we have said, on classic lines (boldly challenging and, what is more, sustaining comparison with Sheridan), but very modern too in its details, its rapid staccato talk and slang of the moment . . . a richly comic scene—as good a thing in its kind as Mr. Jones has ever done. . . . There could be no doubt about the delight of everyone in the theatre over the fine quarrel scene of the third act. We regard that as a specimen of English comedy at its very best." "Max," in the *Saturday Review*, devoted to *Dolly Reforming Herself* one of the finest notices my father ever received. "This new play of his," he said, "is surely as good a comedy as he has ever written. . . . I should say in evaluating Mr. Henry Arthur Jones that his greatest asset is his humour. The essence of humour is a tolerance for men and women as they are. We are grateful that Mr. Henry Arthur Jones has that comfortable gift which prevents him from dancing on us—that gift of humour whereby he is content to take us just as we are, and to laugh not less with us than at us. He sees that his duty lies in giving rein to the delight that he has in mere observation. No playwright is more joyously observant than Mr. Henry Arthur Jones, and none observes more accurately in the *milieu* he has chosen. Other playwrights may create more salient and memorable figures. But none of them creates figures so lifelike as Mr. Jones'. Nor is any one of them so fine a craftsman. We are not made conscious of it while the play is in progress. From the very outset we are aware merely of certain ladies and gentlemen behaving with apparent freedom and naturalness. It is only when the play is over that we notice the art of it." Henry Arthur was so delighted with this notice that he had it reprinted on the cover of *Mary Goes First,* when it was published in 1913.

Max Beerbohm's decision to live in Italy saddened my father very much. He missed him greatly, as also his dramatic criticisms in the *Saturday Review,* which he always enjoyed enormously, even when they were unfavourable to one of his plays. Soon after his marriage he wrote my father the following amusing letter:

> "The White Cottage,
> "Hythe.
> "*23rd May, 1910.*

"MY DEAR HENRY ARTHUR,

"Nothing, except the actual fact of my marriage, has given me greater delight than your kind and witty letter.

"I pray Hymen (as being just now the handiest of the gods) to deliver you safely from the dreaded affection of William Archer. But—Ibsen dead; Stephen Phillips *mal tourné;* H. V. Esmond sunken into silence; Shaw gone quite out of hand; none, in fact, of the old pets available! —it seems to me that your danger is a very real one. If I were you, I would write an encomium of Archer for one of the monthly reviews—'Lessing, Hazlitt, Archer—and After?'—or something of that kind. Then would W. A.'s dread of being corruptible compel him to depreciate you.

"My wife and I are just starting for Italy; and as soon as we come back I shall arrange for you and her what I know would be the great mutual pleasure of a meeting.

> "Yours ever,
> "MAX BEERBOHM."

And it was a year or two later that he sent him a letter enclosing the typically Maxian song:

"26 Oxford Terrace, W.

"*9th March.*

"MY DEAR HENRY ARTHUR,

"I do so wish I could come next Saturday, and renew the delightful time I recently had with you at the Athenæum.   But my wife and I have promised to go away that day to stay with friends in the country.   And there it is.

"Yours ever,

"MAX BEERBOHM.

"It might amuse you to have the enclosed ditty.   I send it on the chance."

DRINKING SONG

In days of yore the Drama throve within our storm-bound
　　　　coasts;
The Independent Theatre gave performances of Ghosts;
　　Death and disease, disaster
　　And darkness were our joy—
　　Ah, fun flew fast and faster
　　When Ibsen was our Master
And Grein was a bright Dutch boy, my boys!
(Chorus) *And Grein was a bright Dutch boy.*

Then, oh, just wasn't Sudermann a name to conjure with?
Echegarey to us was kin, and Bjornson Bjornson kith.
　　We said aloud, "The Stage is
　　The thing that shall employ
　　The faculties of Sages
　　And Heirs of all the Ages."
When Grein was a bright Dutch boy, my boys!
(Chorus) *When Grein was a bright Dutch boy.*

The future of the Drama was our theme, day in day out;
Pinero was most sanguine, Henry Arthur had no doubt.

'On, on,' cried William Archer,
And no man was less coy
Than Shaw (that spring-heeled marcher
In any new deparcher)
When Grein was a bright Dutch boy, my boys!
(Chorus) *When Grein was a bright Dutch boy.*

The movies moved not yet, my boys, Reviews were not in
     view—
The Present State of Things was unforeseen by me and
     you;
     We sailed o'er seas uncharted,
     Of Faith and Hope and Joy;
     None wailed, "Are we downhearted"
In those dear days departed,
When Grein was a bright Dutch boy, my boys!
(Chorus) *When Grein was a bright Dutch boy.*

My father lost a good deal of money when he sent a
company into the provinces to play *Dolly Reforming Herself* at "one night stands"; but in the following year he had
a notable success with a little one-act play, *The Knife,*
which was produced at the Palace Theatre on 20th December, 1909, with Violet Vanbrugh and Arthur Bourchier in
the leading parts. It was very well received all round.
"Max," in the *Saturday Review*, again praised Henry Arthur's method of coming immediately to the point; he
said that the play gripped the audience throughout, but
suggested that a finer ending would have been for the lover
to die under the surgeon's knife, and for the wife to realise,
when she looked into her husband's eyes, that he was no
murderer, but that his skill had proved unavailing. This
little play had the amazing run, for a one-act piece, of 150
nights. Henry Arthur re-wrote it as a complete film
scenario called *The Knife at the Heart,* and up to the pres-

ent time this play is the only one which has been made into a talking film.

Although my father was unable to give evidence before the Censorship Committee in October 1909, he took a very prominent part in the campaign to abolish the censorship, writing a 46-page pamphlet, *The Censorship Muddle and a Way Out*, which he addressed to Sir Herbert Samuel, the papers, various public bodies, and many of his friends. In forwarding a copy to Professor Phelps, he mentions that he put aside the play he was writing to devote his time and energies to work for the freedom of the Drama. It was not the first or the last time my father sacrificed his own work for the cause he had at heart. No one but a writer can understand what it means to break off when one is in full swing. He also sent a copy to Mr. Galsworthy, who wrote:

"27th October, 1909.

". . . I have seen a forecast of what the Committee will report in some of the papers.

"My feeling, assuming the correctness of this forecast, and I am told it *is* correct, is, that if we hold our tongues until the report becomes law, the game is in our hands and the Censorship dead. I think it vital that we should be very silent till the new Act passes. The effect of this law, if it passes, will be to band the managers together in an attempt to refuse all plays that are not submitted for license. We authors must in honour refuse to submit plays for license; the Managers will then surrender. All the influential authors are on our side. We will make those who have flannel knees stand straight out of sheer shame.

"But I feel we must be very careful not to let the skeleton of this situation appear before the House of Commons, or we may frighten them into refusing to pass the report into Law.

"We cannot, I think, quarrel with this optional Censorship; we have the substance, and we shall very soon have the shadow as well.   We started with a literary protest in 1907 headed by Meredith, Hardy, and Swinburne, etc."

In his pamphlet H. A. J. suggested that there should be an Inspector-General for all places of amusement, but that on no account should he be consulted or allowed to interfere before a production.   He pleaded again that plays should be performed on the music-hall stage.   He said that Zangwill had made an admirable division of dramatists into three classes—"pioneers," "plain men," and "pornographers."   Henry Arthur said that as regards the pioneers and poets the Censor was mischievous, that he was superfluous as regards the "plain men," and that he was impotent as regards the pornographers; as witness the sniggering indecencies and innuendos introduced nightly into hundreds of shows all over the country.   He said, "No modern serious English dramatist has claimed so great a freedom as is found in almost every book of the Bible, and every play of Shakespeare.   Why prosecute us petty offenders and let the arch-criminals Moses, Samuel, David, Solomon, Chaucer, Shakespeare, Fielding, and Sterne go uncensored, untried, and unhung?"   The case set up by this pamphlet was quoted and commented on very favourably in many English and some American papers.

On 21st October my father was a guest at the annual Oyster Feast at Colchester, where he and Mr. Sutro responded to the toast of the Drama, proposed by the Duke of Marlborough.   In his speech my father referred to the Censorship, and read out two letters he had received on the matter, one from Thomas Hardy and one from H. G. Wells. Hardy said:

"20th October, 1909.

"Dear Henry Arthur Jones,

"As you will have gathered from my telegram, I don't mind signing with others a protest against the retention of the Censor, and in a private capacity only (the society not being at all unanimous). The question really concerns me personally very little, as it does other mere book-authors, and I should not care to sign anywhere but low down, after the dramatic authors. They should certainly draw it up and come first—perhaps the chairman of the Dramatic Council, the Head (who is I believe yourself), and then the rest—Barrie, Shaw, Pinero, etc., authors of books, artists, etc., joining in the interest of representative art— as supporters.

"I have read a great part of your pamphlet, which is incisive, smart, and convincing, in my opinion.

"I hope you have had a rest this autumn previous to your (no doubt) winter theatrical campaign.

"With kind regards,
"Sincerely yours,
"THOMAS HARDY."

H. G. Wells said:

"MY DEAR JONES,

"I haven't written plays for a number of reasons, but one of the chief of these was the persuasion that my work might in the end be made abortive by the incalculable whim of the Censor. His recent obstinate campaign against Shaw does, I think, justify my discretion.

"Yours very sincerely,
"H. G. WELLS."

In his speech H. A. J. said that, had Hardy been born in France, he believed he would have given his time and talent to the stage.

And so Henry Arthur continued in the Press and on the platform his campaign against the Censorship and his plea for one licence for all places of entertainment. He delivered a lecture at the Alhambra Theatre on 27th February, 1910. Sir Herbert Tree took the chair for him, though H. A. J. had been very much annoyed because Tree was in favour of retaining the Censor. None of their differences of opinion, however public, made any breach in their cordial friendship.

Again, in November 1910, Henry Arthur wrote an open letter to Mr. Winston Churchill on the Censorship, in which he referred especially to the refusal of a licence for Mr. Laurence Housman's play, *Pains and Penalties: The Defence of Queen Caroline.* He said that it was estimated that 150,000 illegal performances of stage plays took place every year in England, and he hoped that, when Parliament met, legislation would be passed to end this absurd situation. The reader may be reminded that Mr. Housman's play was granted a licence fourteen years later, on condition that the word "adultery" was omitted.

The first stirring of that flaming patriotism which consumed my father during the last fifteen years of his life was marked by a little one-act recruiting play, *Fall in, Rookies,* produced at the Alhambra on 24th October, 1910. It is the only propaganda play he ever wrote. He was always in complete sympathy and agreement with Lord Roberts's noble work for his country, and he was delighted when Lord Roberts allowed him to read the play to him. H. A. J. did so in the little room off the hall of the Athenæum, and he told me that when, during the reading, he became very excited and raised his voice, "Bobs" hushed him down. Immediately after the reading, Lord Roberts took my father over to the United Service Club to introduce him to Lord Kitchener, and they had a very pleasant little chat. When Lord Kitchener was drowned in 1916, Henry Arthur wrote to his son Oliver: "It is a fine death. To die in harness is the best that can happen to any of us. I pray it may happen to me."

It was a constant prayer with my father that he might die in the full vigour of his powers, and during the last two years of his life, when he knew that he was done for, the knowledge that he was petering out like a guttering candle haunted him and redoubled his melancholy. In an interview in the *New York Tribune* in November 1920, when he was asked if he was going to write his recollections, he shook his head, and said, "Nor would I like to drag out an existence devoted entirely to the past. I wouldn't want to be like a rusty nail slowly being drawn out of a rotten plank. I should want to slip out quickly when my usefulness was over."

Lord Roberts was very much interested in H. A. J.'s little play, and before the production he wrote to him:

                              "*25th September, 1910.*
"DEAR MR. JONES,

"I should much like to see the little play you read to me a few weeks ago, and am disengaged both on the 17th and 24th October, but I cannot help telling you that I think the title is a mistake. It may be meant as a term of endearment, but the public will not take it as such, and I believe such a title will prejudice the reception of the play.

"Could you not, without in any way altering the play, change the name?

                              "Yours very truly,
                                   "ROBERTS."

I was in my father's box on the first night, and I shall never forget meeting the great little man and how impressive his personality was. Sir Hamilton Gould-Adams, who was afterwards High Commissioner in Cyprus, was in Lord Roberts's box, and when I went to live in Cyprus he told me that Lady Roberts, who was with her husband, had never before been to a music hall, and she was so nervous at the thought that the performance might shock her that she kept her car waiting the whole time in case she wished to leave at any moment.

In the next three years Henry Arthur had three failures
—*We Can't Be as Bad as All That*, in America in 1910,
The Ogre, in London in 1911, and *Lydia Gilmore*, in America in 1912.   My father's ill-health was increasing rapidly,
but, though not one of these plays is among his best work,
they all have considerable merits.   The dialogue in *We
Can't Be as Bad as All That* is very brilliant, especially in
the first act, and there is a strong, straightforward story.
H. A. J. went over for the production, which took place at
Nazimova's Theatre on 30th December, with Miss Katherine Kaelred and Mr. Nye Chart in the leading parts.   A
notable performance, to which my father referred very
often, was that of Miss Kate Phillips as Lady Katherine
Greenup; "Oh, how good she was!" he would say; "she
was magnificent!" Miss Phillips played the same part in
England when Miss Violet Vanbrugh took the play on
tour in 1916.   The notices both here and in America were
unfavourable, and the play ran for only a few weeks in
both countries.

I believe *The Ogre*, which Sir George Alexander produced at the St. James's Theatre on 11th September, 1911,
would have been a success with a different cast.   This
play is a modern version of *The Taming of the Shrew*, in
which the Ogre succeeds in taming, not only his wife, but
all his family.   Many of the notices were bad, and those
which were favourable were only lukewarm in their praise.

Henry Arthur was again in America for the production
of *Lydia Gilmore*, which took place at the Lyceum Theatre,
New York, on 1st February, 1912.   Miss Anglin was very
anxious to do the play, and wired to my father to ask if he
could possibly complete it by a certain date.   He replied
that it was impossible, but when she wired again he consented.   He wrote the last two acts rather hurriedly, and
finished the play on his way to New York on the *Olympic*.
In spite of his having worked under pressure, the third
act contains one of the strongest and most remarkable

GEORGE ALEXANDER IN "THE OGRE," ST. JAMES'S THEATRE, 1911

scenes he ever wrote, and, although he condemned the
play as melodramatic, all his family feel that among his
unacted plays in England it would stand the best chance of
a successful run.   The play was only a moderate success
in America, in spite of Miss Anglin's magnificent performance.

Whenever my father was away, and during the twelve
years I lived abroad, he always wrote to me once a week,
and very often more frequently than that.   I have hundreds of interesting letters from him, but the one I value
most highly is a short note written in 1919.   He kept every
letter I wrote to him; he had been going through them;
and in the letter to me he said, "I've been having a long
morning with these letters—glancing at passages here
and there—perhaps in days to come you will go through
them and remember all this tremendous time.   It has
been my greatest grief in life, I think, to be separated from
you the last 10 or 12 years."

The following is one of the many delightful letters I
received from him when he was in New York for the production of *Lydia Gilmore:*

"New York.
"*4th May, 1912.*

"MY DARLING DORIS,

"I got your letter from Nicosia and Billie's yesterday
evening.   I am glad *Her Tongue* went off so well.   I shall
have the programme framed with my other first-night
programmes.   You have been thinking so much of *Her
Tongue* that you have forgotten *The Divine Gift*.   Dear,
I've finished, finished at half-past one this morning, and
put 'Curtain.'   I was beginning to flag just a little—the
last morning or two I've felt inclined to dawdle—I had
really exhausted the possibilities.   This morning I did the
scene which joins to the final one.   I told you I had written the closing scenes—I had done them in pencil in my

notebooks these glorious afternoons by the Hudson. So I was sure of my final curtain. Every word was written. This morning I got up to the last scene and then had a delightful hour and a half writing in my best copperplate the last four sheets up to ninety-eight—Finis.

"Last night I went with Brander Matthews as his guest to the Round Table dinner at the Knickerbocker Club. I send you a card of the members present. It was a very interesting evening. I sat next to Choate, who is always delightful. He and Admiral Mahan got into a rather strong discussion about the Italian-Turkish war. Choate, as a lawyer, maintained that the Italians were thieves and that nothing could justify them. Mahan maintained that the Turkish rule was corrupt and effete, and in the interest of humanity the Italians were quite right in seizing Tripoli. I had a long talk with Mahan on religious matters: he is a devout Christian and believes that the world is governed by a Personal Deity who is a wise and benevolent Providence revealed to us in the Bible—thinks that the Apostles' Creed is literal fact and saving truth. Of course we never got alongside each other. He is a fine fellow. . . .

"I feel a little tired and brain fagged—but I'm in splendid form. I had my afternoon's sleep, and then went to see the suffrage parade. I waited nearly an hour, and got a good place on a builder's plank in Fifth Avenue. The procession was terribly depressing to me—the poor creatures walked so badly and looked so limp for the most part. I scanned all their faces—there wasn't one in twenty that wasn't mean or banal or blank or sheepish—what possible wise legislation is going to result from setting seven-sixteenths of them to vote against the other nine-sixteenths on questions about which they know nothing, except what they pick up from such papers as I am sending you every week. Though here and there there were a few fine intelligent faces. Oh, for God's sake, let them have a vote if they want it—children and all—two ineffably silly-looking girls about 10 and 12 carried a banner stretching across the road, 'My Ma wants to vote.' Oh, let her, let her vote! Thank God I'm not 'Pa.' The bands were the best part of it, and the men walked without looking sloppy and ridiculous. But how tired they will be to-morrow. However I suppose 'Ma' will get her vote both here and in England. The actresses made a poorish show, but there was a dear little fair-haired girl among the doctors whom I'd have given a vote to straight away— and if I can get her address I'll call her in next time I get a nervous breakdown.

"Love,
"Daddy.

"I know *nom de plume* is wrong, but why is *nom de guerre* right, and *nom de plume* wrong? What do you think of my *nom de plume?* I will use the phrase until I know why it is wrong—so tired."

In another letter written during this visit he said: ". . . looked in and saw Forbes-Robertson last evening; he is just finishing a tremendously successful tour in *The Third Floor Back*—has made £60,000 by asking American play-goers in his beautiful voice, 'Have you found Jesus?' . . ."

Just after I first went to live in Cyprus, Henry Arthur gave me permission to play the little one-act piece *Her Tongue,* which was written in 1912 and published in 1915 with his satire, *The Theatre of Ideas; The Goal* and *Grace Mary* were also included in this volume. *The Theatre of Ideas* is a satirical allegory. My father was very pleased with this piece of work and was always a little surprised it did not attract more attention.

It was his habit to give me the first copy which came into his hands of all his plays, books, pamphlets, etc., and in a copy of *The Theatre of Ideas* which he sent to me in Cyprus he wrote the following delightful inscription: "From the author of *Her Tongue* to its gifted and sufficiently loquacious first exponent,

"MY DEAR DORIS,
  "Let me render a tribute to your natural qualification for playing Patty.   How often out here I have wished that I could hear your tongue!

"Your loving father,
"HENRY ARTHUR JONES."

My father wrote nearly the whole of *The Divine Gift* during his stay in New York in 1912.   He was deeply absorbed in the piece, and he was very confident that it was one of the finest plays he had written.   He placed it next to *Michael,* not only in his affections, but in his judgment of its literary merit.   His feeling for the play and his opinion about it remained unshaken to the end of his life.   In a letter written to me on 5th April he said, "I know I have done a fine thing at last," and in another letter shortly afterwards he said:

"I have not placed a single piece, am not troubling very much, as I am so absorbed in *The Divine Gift,* or is it to be *Vox Humana?*   I am still confident that it is the best and highest thing I have done.   And Lora Delmar is the finest woman's character I have drawn—she beats Audrie in *Michael.*"

When he had finished the play, he wrote to me:

"New York.
"6th May, 1912.

"I feel very much relieved now that the play is done.   I think it is the biggest and sincerest work I've written, but, of course, I can't tell just now.   I'm too near it.   There is very little story, no surprises, no violent action, but the scenes are very strong and penetrating."

The play was published in 1913, with a long preface dedicated to Professor Gilbert Murray. When H. A. J. wrote to him to ask his permission to dedicate the book to him, he received the following delightful letter:

"5th March, 1913.

"DEAR MR. JONES,

"Thanks for your friendly letter. I shall feel it a great honour to have the play dedicated to me, and I am sure that I shall read the preface with lively interest, if it is at all like your other writings.

"As to the interview, I now remember it: I went for a walk with a young *Transcript* man in Boston, a very nice fellow and an enthusiastic Socialist, and we chatted casually about the Drama and other things. I do not remember at all what he made me say, but you will know from your own experience how apt interviewers are to put their own sentiments and phrases into the mouths of the interviewed. It is quite possible that I called you and Pinero old-fashioned writers, but if I did so, the epithet merely suggested itself as a natural contrast to the 'new-fashioned' Barker-Galsworthy set. As a matter of fact I vehemently agree with you that an epithet which applies to Æschylus and the Bible cannot be derogatory. Meantime I shall be delighted to see the play and the preface any time you care to send them, and still more so to have a visit from you yourself when you come back to England. . . .

"Yours sincerely,
"GILBERT MURRAY."

After reading the play he wrote again:

"11th March, 1913.

"DEAR MR. JONES,

". . . I have read the preface with great interest and amusement, and agree strongly with every sentence of it, except the statement that I was ever guilty of burying you alive. I never did such a thing either in deed or in thought. However, the whole tone of the preface is so good-natured and the accusation made in such an amusing way that I do not think it matters in the least; and I need hardly say that I feel it a great honour to have such a dedication from you and to be mentioned in such extremely good company. I hardly like to make any suggestion, but this has occurred to me. I see that the dedication page is at present left blank: you might perhaps put some such phrase as 'To G. M., who, I find on enquiry, did not bury me so deep as I had supposed,' or something or other of that kind. I send this note at once in case you should feel at all bothered about the preface. I will write later and at more leisure about the play, which I have only just begun.

"Yours very sincerely,
"GILBERT MURRAY."

"PS. After all I could not resist finishing the play right off. I think the subject is a really big one and extraordinarily interesting, and the contrast of the two women very striking. About Cutler, I cannot help wishing that he was not such a luxurious idler, that he had more of a suggestion of honest work about him somewhere. But perhaps this would have only landed one in a Dumas character like Thouvenin; and anyhow your judgment on this is worth very much more than mine. I will not say more, except that I enjoyed reading the play greatly.

"G. M."

Most of the English and American Press criticisms of *The Divine Gift* were favourable, though not enthusiastic.

Some of the critics praised the writing in the preface very highly and most of them thought the play interesting. One or two saw a resemblance between Cutler and Henry Arthur. Though my father never said anything that indicated that consciously or unconsciously he had written his own conception of himself into the part of Cutler, we all felt that he had done so; that he saw himself as the kindly philosopher and sage, the penetrating and illuminating chorus of the play. But his family always felt that if he resembled any character in one of his plays, it was Sir Robert Shale, the crusty old father in *The Lie*—except that my father was not a drunkard.

H. A. J. was convinced that *The Divine Gift* would not succeed on the stage unless it was ideally cast. I imagine Sir Johnston Forbes-Robertson agreed with him after reading a copy of the play which H. A. J. had sent him:

"*26th January, 1920.*

"DEAR ARTHUR JONES,

"I have read your strong and interesting play all through at a sitting. It has, if I may say so, the fearless truth of your finest work, *Michael and His Lost Angel.* Thank you for letting me read it. Later when we meet I will give you my reasons why I am not strongly in favour of its production.

"I am reading your *Patriotism and Popular Education,* and am at one with you in every word you say. I cannot, however, go with you in some of your remarks about the stage.

"Ever yours sincerely,
"J. FORBES-ROBERTSON."

Another letter which gave him great pleasure was from his old friend, Sir Gilbert Parker, who said:

"26th January, 1922.

"My dear Henry Arthur Jones,

"I have read your two books of plays—*The Theatre of Ideas* and *The Divine Gift.* Let me say quite frankly that *Grace Mary* is one of the best short plays I have ever read. It is living, real, and so convincing in its humanity and presentation of character. It enthralled me. You have indeed the great Gift. *The Goal* is a very remarkable one-act play and held me throughout. . . . Why these two plays have not been presented on the English stage is beyond me. It almost makes me despair. As for *The Divine Gift,* it is a play of great power and distinction and truth. It is too terribly true to be possible on the English stage or on any stage, I fear. It is beautifully and powerfully written, but it gets too near the core of life to be popular. But how amazingly well the characters are drawn, and how deep the knife of analysis goes! I shall remember Laura as long as I live. I have not yet read your introduction—or dedication—to Gilbert Murray, but I mean to read it to-morrow. I expect you put the core with discrimination and cogent reason.

"Thank you with all my heart for these two books. They will be 'prize-packets' for my study. As the author of *The Liars* and a dozen or more other plays, your place in the dramatic history of the world is secure.

"Yours ever sincerely,

"Gilbert Parker."

My father was fonder of Lora Delmar than of any other woman's character which he created, and to his last day he remained convinced that *The Divine Gift* was one of his finest plays. In a letter written to Mr. M. H. Spielmann in 1917 he said:

"8th December, 1917.

"Looking back, I have a general feeling that all my best work has been left undone—with the exception of

Michael, The Divine Gift, and *The Goal,* and a few other pieces.   Much as I have loved the drama, if I were thirty to-day, I would not write plays, but would give whatever powers I have to literature.   The English Theatre is the implacable and blind enemy of the English Drama.   And it will not be for a long, long time after the War that we shall have anything in our theatres that will be worthy to be called a National Drama.

"Always faithfully yours,
"HENRY ARTHUR JONES."

The reference to *The Divine Gift* in the following letter from Max Beerbohm pleased my father greatly:

"February 8th, 1914.

"MY DEAR HENRY ARTHUR,

"I haven't yet received *The Theatre of Ideas,* and I must bide my time for it until I get home from Rapallo. It is doubtless there.   My wife and I left our house in the care of an honest but rather helpless Italian woman; and soon after we arrived in England my wife had to write to her absolving her of the task of forwarding to us any parcels that might arrive.   One or two had arrived already and the woman in charge had utterly failed to get the postal authorities to send them on.   The postal authorities in Liguria (and I believe throughout Italy) revel in convolutions of red tape: a parcel of such-and-such a size must (or must not) be open at the ends—(must or mustn't) be registered if sent with sealing-wax from another country, in which case gum must be substituted for sealing-wax and cord for string, and—but no doubt your head is in a whirl.   So is mine when I want anything done in the local post-office.   My wife alone remains calm there and effectual.   But she could not at this distance train the caretaker.   And there the matter ends.   Meanwhile a thousand congratulations on *The Divine Gift,* which I have been reading in London: one of your finest plays, surely; and I hope it will soon be done. There ought surely to be no difficulty about the Censor?   The preface, too, is a lovely piece of work, over which I have immensely chuckled—mingling my chuckles with those of Matthew Arnold, to whom, in Elysium, your essay has made a peculiar appeal, with its urbanity and fun. . . .

> "Yours ever,
> "MAX BEERBOHM."

After his death I offered the British Museum the choice of all my father's bound and unbound manuscripts which belong to me, and it was *The Divine Gift* that was chosen.

Henry Arthur's visit to America in 1912 was unusually eventful and memorable. He was staying at the Marie Antoinette Hotel when the *Titanic* disaster occurred. The horrors of the Great War have almost wiped out the impression of that appalling disaster, but at the time the whole world was shaken by the tragedy. My father wrote me the following letter on the terrible subject:

> "New York.
> "*17th April, 1912.*

. . . "The *Titanic* disaster has thrown a gloom over the city. New York is more compact than London, more provincial, more like a large village. There is nothing else talked about, and the papers are full of it. I am sending you some of them; the portraits and petty details of gossip —about the millionaires and other personages supposed to be of some importance on the planet—Mr. Guggenheim for instance—would be amusing if they were not ghastly. All interest is centred in the arrival of the *Carpathia* tomorrow night. It will be such a scene as has rarely been witnessed—the whole city seems to be turning out. Since beginning this I have been talking on the 'phone with Percy Bullen, the correspondent of the *Daily Telegraph*. I

have arranged to go down with him on the Press boat and
meet the *Carpathia* and do a cable account for the *Daily
Telegraph*—I shall send you word of it in my next. . . .

My father met Sir Roger Casement in Washington in
January 1912.   They dined with Lord Bryce at the British
Embassy, and H. A. J. sat next to Sir Roger.   In 1927,
speaking about Casement, my father said to me, "He was
very interesting, fascinating, queer, which I put down to
his living in the tropics."

While he was in Washington, Henry Arthur was invited
to the White House.   He met President Taft two or three
times during his stay, and, though he found him interesting and genial, my father was not impressed as deeply
as by Roosevelt on the only occasion when he met him.
But H. A. J. always said that President Taft uttered one
of the best pieces of dramatic criticism he ever heard: they
were speaking about the Drama, and he said, with great
emphasis, "There is nothing so stupid as a stupid play."
When my father repeated this to me he added that he
heard another very good criticism from two pittites as they
were leaving a theatre; one said, "What did you think of
it?" and the other replied, "I thought it was just like a
play."

The invitation my father received for the reception at
the White House was addressed Sir Henry Arthur Jones.
It was a mistake made constantly, not only in America, but
by English people also, and it seemed to show how widespread was the feeling that his services to the Drama
should have been recognised by a knighthood.   As early
as the production of *The Middleman* in Vienna, an
Austrian paper described him as "Herr Sir Henry Arthur
Jones, Bart."   William Gillette always addressed him as
Sir Henry, and the letters he wrote to me were always
marked "C/o Sir Henry Arthur Jones."   In a delightful
letter to me he said that, though H. A. J. had not been

honoured by his own country, there was no reason why he (Mr. Gillette) should not bestow a perfectly good American title on him.

I am quite sure that during the last fifteen years of his life my father would not have accepted a knighthood had it been offered to him; he often said, "I am proud to be in the same category as William Shakespeare and Charles Dickens." But he had felt the omission keenly, especially after so many theatrical titles had been bestowed.

In a letter which Clayton Hamilton wrote to me after my father's death he told me the following rather touching little incident:

"New London, Conn.
"*31st July, 1929.*

"MY DEAR DORIS THORNE,

. . . "In 1910, in London, I dined as his guest one night at the Reform Club. The late newspapers had just published the news that the Order of Merit had been conferred that day on Thomas Hardy. After dinner, H. A. J. raised his coffee-cup and said to me rather wistfully, 'Do you suppose, if *Michael and His Lost Angel* had been written as a novel instead of as a play, I might possibly have been recognised as an author?'

"With a knighthood in his mind, he told me and Brander Matthews that he feared he was being held back by his plebeian name of 'Jones' and somewhat earnestly asked our advice about hyphenating his last name as 'Arthur-Jones'; and I can remember his disappointment when a knighthood did not follow the jubilee revival of *The Silver King*. I bring this point up because I always felt that he deserved a knighthood as much as Pinero, a baronetcy as much as Barrie, and the O.M. as much as Galsworthy. . . .

"Yours as ever,
"CLAYTON HAMILTON."

I feel certain that, before 1910, had my father ever hinted to any of his very many influential friends that a knighthood would give him pleasure, he would surely have received one; but I think after his public and aggressive attacks on the Censorship, and possibly after the production of *Mary Goes First,* the suggestion would not have been favourably received. For my own part, I believe that the omission to honour him in his own country is not creditable, and I know that my feeling is shared by many of my father's eminent friends. When he wrote to congratulate Sir W. S. Gilbert on his knighthood, Gilbert wrote to him as follows:

"10th July, 1907.

"MY DEAR JONES,

"I am sincerely obliged to you for your cordial congratulations. It is, I think, a good thing that the King should, at last, have turned his attention towards dramatic authorship as a profession worthy of recognition. The honour is conferred upon me by the melancholy virtue of my seniority—a kind of commuted old-age pension of an economical kind. Other dramatists may hope to receive it for reasons of a more complimentary description.

"Very truly yours,

"W. S. GILBERT."

About a year before his death the French Government offered my father the Legion of Honour, and the official papers were sent to the French Embassy in London. But there are Foreign Office regulations that services rendered to France by an Englishman during the War can no longer be taken into account, nor any other services, unless rendered within the last five years. I saw the head of the Treaty Department at the Foreign Office, but I was unable to persuade the authorities to relax their ruling, although I urged them to do so, as my father's case was not like that of a diplomatist or a civil servant. I think it very discreditable to those concerned that a man who for so many years had been a public figure held in esteem by his countrymen, and who had not very long to live, was not allowed to accept this mark of regard from a foreign country which he had always loved and admired. Henry Arthur was very proud to think that, although he had received no official recognition in England, America and France had honoured his work.

On my father's return from America he had one of the worst nervous breakdowns of his whole life, and he went for several weeks to a home near Redhill, where he was tortured by being kept in bed and stuffed with food. Just after leaving this nursing-home he received the following precious manifestation of Sir Arthur Pinero's friendship:

"*8th May, 1911.*

"My DEAR JONES,

"It grieved me to read in yesterday's paper that you have been ill and in a nursing-home. The statement may be untrue, but, as you were complaining when we last met of sleeplessness and of being generally run down, there appears to be some likelihood in it. At any rate, I hope you are now fully recovered. We have been fellow-workers for so many years—side by side, as it were—that any mishap to you comes to me with a sense of personal shock. Please, therefore, send me a line of good news of yourself, and believe me to be, with affectionate regard,

"Yours always,
"ARTHUR W. PINERO."

"I beg to be remembered kindly to Mrs. Jones."

It was my mother's prescience which was instrumental in discovering the reason of all those years of ill-health which had contributed to, if it had not caused, many of his breakdowns. The root trouble was cancer, and he had been suffering from auto-intoxication since early manhood. He owed his life to the genius of Lockhart Mummery, who in June 1912 performed a colotomy, one of the most formidable operations known to modern surgery—an operation which left the permanent and painful disability of a wound which required dressing several times daily. To a man of my father's temperament it was a daily martyrdom. But his physical courage was beyond all praise, and in the seventeen years of crippled life which remained to him none of his family ever heard a serious complaint pass his lips. He was not expected to survive the operation; and when he did so, we all supposed he had at the most a few months to live, and then perhaps a year or two. I believe his case is a record in medical history. I do not think he would have made such a marvellous recovery had he ever known that it was cancer, but we all lied successfully to him, and after a few years any doubts he may have had were dispelled when the trouble did not recur.

The first letter he wrote after the operation was to me, and, though it is in pencil, the writing is clear and vigorous. He said:

"Friday, 28th June.

"MY DARLING DORIS,

"I'm getting on splendidly—couldn't be doing better— am healing like a child—enjoying every meal and very hungry for it, but oh what a ghastly business—under the knife for about three hours—a very complicated double operation, and the pain and misery and helplessness since —I mustn't write—just a week since it was done, what an inferno since; but I'm getting round, hope all is well. Your mother will have written. Write about the play.

"My dearest love to you all,

"DADDY."

it aloud, because as I told you in my last letter, I have to be careful, and simmer down, and keep my mouth shut; then people form a moderately high opinion of me. So the doctor and I quaffed to Dorinda. We quaffed again, *Quelle noce!* We quaffed once more, and if you had been there, we should have quaffed and doffed. But as it was, we only quaffed. Then I showed them all the portrait in the *Bystander* of you, and Mummy, and me. They thought it was high art, especially the bow on the top of your head. They said that was the highest art of all.

"Then came the awful question. A lady who had a large nose, and couldn't help it, and a spot on the end of it, and couldn't help that either, made a digression into ethics—a very unnecessary thing to do at all times, and especially at Christmas dinner. She flummoxed me by asking, 'But is your little Dorinda a good girl?' She didn't look as if she had ever been a good girl herself, and she didn't look as if she could be good if she tried. And you can be good when you try—very hard—can't you? But I didn't ask her if she had ever been good herself. That would have been rude. And she might not have told me the truth about it. So I answered—'Potentially, and intentionally, and inferentially Dorinda is a very good girl. But as a matter of actual fact and practice, there are times when she hurls herself into the very abyss of cantankerous naughtiness.' 'Dear! Dear! Dear! Dear! Dear! Dear!' said the clergyman, and pulled such a long face that I was afraid he was going to say grace, though it was in the middle of dinner. And for your sake I thought it prudent to turn the conversation into other channels. But none of us said anything worth repeating, any more than they do in the newspapers, or in the House of Commons, or in the churches and chapels. And now it's time to go to bed. And I hope I shall spend next Christmas with my old pal.

"For I'm her jolly grand-daddy. Oh, I quite forgot.

You don't like me to sing to you, do you? Well, good night, old pal.

"Your loving

"GRAND-DADDY."

In January 1913, my father published his second book on the Drama, *The Foundations of a National Drama*, a collection of letters and articles he had written and delivered between 1904 and 1912. The book is dedicated to Professor Brander Matthews. Most of the English and American reviews were very favourable, though some of the writers thought my father unduly pessimistic. The *Daily News* drew attention to H. A. J.'s ceaseless campaigns on behalf of the Drama, declaring that, "Mr. Henry Arthur Jones is the only dramatist of the older school who has given to the world his opinions on art. . . . The author of *The Liars* has never been egotistical in his utterances, however; he has always dealt with the big, practical questions of the Drama as an art."

In the early months of 1913 my father was at Grasse writing *Mary Goes First*. In February he wrote to me:

". . . I am making capital progress with *Mary*—she is writing herself, and will I think be the best *light* comedy I have done—she will be more popular than *Dolly*, if I get her well placed. It is the kind of work that I do most easily. *Mary* gives me splendid chances of satire—titles; politics; lawyers; middle-class snobbery and pretensions. You will remember that I got the germ idea of the piece at Gibraltar on the night of Billie's dinner-party. I am getting towards the end of the first act and hope to finish it this week. The first act is always the most difficult and takes up the most time, as you have to lay the foundations of the whole play and be careful to provide all the explanations for the actions and motives of the characters."

Mary Goes First was produced on 18th September, 1913, at the Playhouse. Several of the leading papers—the

Morning Post, the *Observer,* the *Referee* and *Punch*—
spoke ill of the play; they said it was tedious and the
theme was slight.   On the other hand, the *Daily Telegraph*
was enthusiastic in its favour: "There was such ease and
certainty about all its scenes, such gaiety in the acting, and
such verbal wit, and above all such wit in the scheme of
things, that every moment was sparkling."   Every paper
praised Marie Tempest's superb performance in the leading part.   When the play was printed, Henry Arthur wrote
a charming dedication to Miss Tempest, in which he
said, "How wonderfully you have portrayed every moment
of Mary Whichello.   How right is every accent, how significant every glance, every look."

H. A. J. was rather proud of the following sentence,
which is printed inside the cover: "Thus it appears that
the Honours and Dignities adjudged by the State serve
often but to varnish the Stratagems and Pretences
whereby they have been obtained; and the Claim to Pre-
cedency is shown to be the Claim of those who have no
other Claim to our Admiration and Esteem.—Fettle-
worth's *Credentials of Merit* (1764), Chapter on 'Titles.' "
He told me more than once that it took him a whole morning to compose it, and he would defy any critic to challenge
its authenticity.

Soon after the production a Mr. George Whichelow
threatened to bring a law-suit against Henry Arthur for
using his name.   There was a considerable correspondence
with the infuriated gentleman, which on my father's part
was good-natured and chaffing, and the comments in the
papers were in favour of H. A. J.; so Mr. Whichelow came
to a wise decision and dropped the matter.

In the following year Miss Tempest opened her season
in New York with *Mary Goes First,* which was produced
at the Comedy Theatre on 2nd November, 1914.   My
father was in America at the time, and a characteristic
episode occurred in connection with the production.   He

MARIE TEMPEST IN "MARY GOES FIRST," THE PLAYHOUSE, 1913

(By courtesy of Messrs. Foulsham & Banfield)

went to one of the rehearsals, and afterwards told Graham Browne it was the worst company he had ever seen in his life; Miss Tempest wrote to me and said, "They had a real set to, and my husband told him he didn't know his job, which left him speechless, and he dashed out of the theatre.   After the first performance, with his customary great generosity, and the play being an enormous success, he came round afterwards and held out both his hands to my husband, and said, 'I apologise.' "

CHAPTER XV

I was in England staying with my father when war was declared. I shall never forget the intense excitement and distress which possessed him. Like the majority of the nation during the first few weeks, he did not think the struggle could last very long, but he was always inclined to lay stress on the gloomy side of any catastrophe, and, although he was anxious, it relieved his feelings a good deal to say, "I told you so"—"I knew it was coming"— "God knows where this will all end." No one could describe the effect the War had on him better than he did himself; he would say, "The War got hold of me." It had for him a personal meaning which, on the whole, prevented him from looking at it objectively. He would say, "I had both my sons and three sons-in-law at the Front," almost as if such an occurrence was unusual. He recognised and shared in the general suffering, but he demanded implicitly, if not openly, that his family and friends should acknowledge and sympathise with his own personal distress and anxiety. He often said, "If I'd been younger I should have gone; I'd have hated it, but I should have had to go. I'm a pacifist, you know."

There is an amusing story we often told of H. A. J. which is typical of one aspect of his attitude towards the War. He was playing bridge during an air-raid. When the players first heard the guns, they interrupted their play to listen for a few moments. The guns came nearer, and again the game was stopped. A few minutes later the noise seemed to be quite close to the house, and with one accord they all went to the front door and opened it;

246

when the sound of the guns became threateningly near, my father leant up against the door, and, with his hand to his head, said in a weary mutter, "I mean to say, I can't have it, I *can't* have it." He always denied this story, if we told it in front of him. The air-raids had a horrible fascination for him. He did not always take cover, and very often he exerted himself to try and get closer to them, but he invariably had a bad digestive upset after each raid.

He was anxious to do what he could to help in war-work, and in November 1914 he wrote to my mother: "I feel strongly that I ought to do something to relieve some of the distress caused by the War. I am offering the house at Winslow as a hospital, and will give £50, or £2 a week towards the expenses. This is a small thing considering what misery prevails. . . . It is our duty to do something and, if things go well here, I shall do more. . . ."

Directly the War started my elder brother, Lucien, went out as a war correspondent. He was the last Englishman to leave Antwerp. H. A. J. was immensely proud of the courage and resource he showed; as also of the brilliant work he did for some time after the War as Foreign Correspondent for the *Daily Express.*

Henry Arthur's father died in November 1914. For a year or two he had been in failing health. His son went down to see him in October before leaving for America. He was sitting over the fire very morose and depressed, and he complained bitterly of the little boys who were letting off fireworks. H. A. J. said to him, "Well, we always used to have fireworks for Guy Fawkes." To which the old man replied, "Ah! but they used not to begin so early."

Henry Arthur told us on several occasions that during the last years of our grandfather's life he had supported him. I am ashamed to say I could not bring myself quite to believe my father, though I felt sure he had helped my

grandfather.   But after H. A. J.'s death his solicitor at
Winslow, Mr. Wigley, wrote to me on the matter:

> "Winslow.
> *"24th January, 1911.*
>
> ". . . Whatever your Father must have spent on his
> Father I can hardly conceive, for he allowed him to collect
> rents and put them in his own pocket—he allowed him
> to occupy lands without any payment for rent, and
> finally, he bore all the expense of winding up his Father's
> affairs. . . .
>
> "Your Grandfather, of course, died whilst your Father
> was in America, and your Father gave me a Power of At-
> torney to deal with his properties in Buckinghamshire,
> with particular instructions to grant any reasonable re-
> quest of his Father so far as moneys and such-like mat-
> ters were concerned, and I am afraid that when he returned
> from America, I did not have a particularly bright report
> to give him. . . ."

I do not know why I ever doubted my father's word, as
he was a very truthful man, and his memory was remarkably accurate.   Many times he assured me that he had
written a hundred plays, of which about half had been
produced—and suggested that few other dramatists had
succeeded in achieving so high a percentage in so great
an output.   But, as I thought I had made a complete list
of them when I became his secretary, I always contradicted
him.   It was only after his death I found data about a
great many plays he had never mentioned to his family.

In October 1928 he was looking through my autograph-
book, and said, "Of all the people in that book I don't
know anybody I am prouder to have met than Foch."
Henry Arthur belonged to the society "The Friends of
France," founded, I believe, by his friend Mr. Victor
Fisher.   When Marshal Foch came over to England in
1925, H. A. J. was one of the deputation who went to meet

him at Victoria Station. My father felt the strongest emotion at this meeting, and, when he was presented to the great man, he bent over with the most charming gesture of homage and kissed his hand.

During the War my mother's prowess as a housekeeper was of the greatest benefit to her family. Her accomplishments with the body of a single hare, which was made to provide several appetising meals, would have made Mrs. Beeton green with envy. I remember her distress and indignation when she returned from a short holiday to find her husband and younger son sitting down to a luncheon which consisted of a single bloater. My father was always a difficult man to feed. He would say, "A little bit of anything will do for me," but very often "the little bit" was not on the table. He was inclined to eat the same dish for several weeks or months at a time, and in the last few years of his life this peculiarity became very marked; so that for a month or two on end he would eat nothing but sardines or castle pudding or Camembert cheese for luncheon and dinner. He ate literally nothing else but the one dish.

When the War started, my father said, "Thank God, Oliver won't be drawn into it." But he realised how deeply the results would affect the whole of his boy's life. In July 1915 he wrote to him from New York:

"I am sure you will take advantage of every moment now, as I am afraid you and every English boy are going to have a hard struggle for life. England will never be the same country after this war—every condition of life will be harder. It will be a very uphill fight for you, my boy, at the best. If the old country wins she will be exhausted and bled to death. If she goes down—God help us all. I do not think she will go down, but the outlook is very black. It is useless to talk about it, but I never get away from it for a moment."

Oliver obtained a commission in the Scots Guards.

During the whole of the time he was at the Front H. A. J. wrote to him every day without fail. He was immensely proud of the boy, though I think these daily letters were a belated effort to atone for the early years of Oliver's life, when he had taken very little interest in him. After the War he sometimes referred rather wistfully to all the letters he had written Oliver as a proof of how dearly he loved him. He was always greatly delighted when Oliver wrote to him, as the joint letters he wrote to his parents were always addressed to his mother. One morning, when Oliver was on the Gold Coast, H. A. J. was overjoyed when he came downstairs to discover a letter from Oliver addressed to him. Inside was a large sheet of paper with one word on it—"Beaver." My father immediately wrote underneath, " 'The eye that mocketh at his father, the ravens of the valley shall pluck it out and the young eagles shall eat it.' Proverbs, Chapter 30, verse 17. Why the ravens should reserve this dainty morsel for the young eagles Solomon doesn't say, but he had a correct notion of the respect due from boys to their fathers, and of the evil results to be apprehended from failure to pay it." Henry Arthur had a good chuckle over Oliver's letter, and his reply to it.

While Oliver was in London before he left for the Front, he and Henry Arthur went for many long walks together; a favourite one being along the Spaniards Road. Near the old inn there is a pump, and they invented an absurd little ceremony which they called "Saluting the Pump." The ceremony once started, nothing could have induced them to omit it when they passed by; and, when Oliver was at the Front, Henry Arthur went up several times a week, generally after dinner, to salute the pump, and on his return he would write to his boy and tell him how he kept alive the memory of their walks and talks together. Writing to Oliver in 1922, he said, "I've just returned from a salutation of the pump, performed in the presence of a few spectators and a stalwart policeman, to whom I explained the nature of the ceremony, and thus saved my reputation for sanity." Only a few months before he died, Nurse and I took him for a drive along the Spaniards Road; feeble as he was, he insisted upon getting out and tottering up to the pump, and solemnly went through the regulation salute, to the amazement of several on-lookers.

When my father went up to Hampstead Heath, he generally stopped to listen to the speakers who are in the habit of haranguing the crowds near the Pond. On one occasion, after H. A. J. had interrupted a Socialist orator several times, the exasperated man said, "What do you know about work?"—to which came the immediate reply, "What do I know about work—I'm over seventy and I've been working over thirteen hours a day since I was twelve years old." The man was nonplussed for a moment, and then he shouted back, "Oh! you 'ave, 'ave you—well, you ought to be bloody well ashamed of yerself—keeping a younger man out of a job."

He would say that I was the only one of his children who would always go for a walk with him. We had three seats near Kidderpore Avenue, two in Platts Lane and one on the Heath, which he always called "your seats." Before I left for abroad, we would go for a last walk and rest for a while on one or other of these seats. When writing to me he would often say, "I went for a short walk and sat on your seat for a while." His attachment to these links of affection with us was a very endearing trait in his character.

Soon after the outbreak of the War my father went to America for the production of *The Lie*. He had written the play at Grasse at the end of 1913 and the beginning of 1914. On January 6th, 1914, he wrote to me from Grasse:

. . . "By the time you get this I shall nearly, if not

quite, have finished the play. I shall finish the third act to-morrow, I think, and the fourth act, which has by far the strongest scene, will not be a long one. I've done 93 sheets of MSS., out of a probable 112 or thereabouts. I don't think I've ever written a play so easily. I started it at La Trayas six weeks last Friday. The weather here was cold and cheerless at the beginning of last week, but it changed to quite warm Riviera sunshine. I had a good spurt of work and made up my mind to stay on. I've been out under the olives lying on my rug and writing the play in a little note-book. The next morning I copy what I've written on to my MS. paper in ink, copy and revise and add and cut. When that is done I go out and write more under the olives. I have all the little pencil note-books in almost illegible handwriting. If the play is a success, I will give them to you. I put the MS. sheets in my writing-case as I do them every morning, and gloat over them as the bundle grows thicker. I've never once looked at them or read the play since I started. This is most unusual with me; it has never happened before. I generally read it over again and again as I go along and cut and alter and rewrite. But there it is, and I feel sure it's all right. Each scene has been right as I've done it, and I've never had occasion to look back. . . ."

The play was produced at the Harris Theatre, New York, on 24th December, 1914, with Miss Margaret Illington in the leading part. She gave a superb performance, and the play had a tremendous reception. The great success of the play was due chiefly to Margaret Illington's acting; and, when the play was published in 1915, Henry Arthur dedicated it to her. He said: . . . "In printing this play, I am giving those who witness your acting the chance of reading my words and comparing them with your impassioned utterance. They will then be able to judge how deeply indebted I am to you for your rendering of Elinor Shale."

Another of my father's plays, *The Goal,* was produced in New York in the autumn of 1914, with Holbrook Blinn in the part of the old engineer, while, soon after the production of *The Lie,* Grace George revived *The Liars* at the New York Playhouse. Both plays were very warmly received, and still further increased my father's reputation in the United States.

From New York my father went to Bermuda, as he felt it would be impossible for him to settle down to work in England. In addition to writing to me regularly, he found time to send my little daughter one or two charming whimsical letters. Just after her fifth birthday he wrote her a long letter in which he said:

"*17th February, 1915.*

"MY DARLING LITTLE DORINDA,

"I often wish you were over here in Bermuda so that I could take you over the island and show you all the beautiful and funny things there are in it. Of course you have funny things and people in Cyprus, but it can't be such a raree-show as Bermuda. . . . Oh, I do wish I could show you all these funny things—the Jabberwock, and the Anthropophagi, and the cockroaches, and the Wesleyan Methodist Church, and the messy stuff they call Cabinet Pudding at this hotel—well, as you aren't here I can't show them to you. So I must wait till you come to Arkwright Road, and then I must tell you all about them. Oh, I do wish this awful war was over, and that you and Mummy and Billy were all coming home this Summer to stay with

"YOUR OLD GRANDDADDY PAL."

He wrote the whole of *Cock of the Walk* during his stay in Bermuda. He was nearly always in love with the particular play he was engaged upon, but some of them took a deeper hold on him than others. He was particularly keen and excited while he was writing this play, as the following extracts from his letters show:

"Bermuda.
"*1st April, 1915.*

"What say you, my Doris, my diddle-diddle-dumpling, my youngest wren of five—what say you to this five-act comedy by Shakespeare and myself?   Doesn't it strike you as coming just at the right time—his tercentenary due next year, 23rd April, 1916—the War over, and everybody waiting to do him and me reverence—that is if we turn out the right play?   Of course his dialogue will be all right, and mine won't be far behind, as you may see by the sample I sent Dorinda—'with a rumpty-rorum didle-me-dorum-flappety-floppety-hi-ti.'   Of course you mustn't breathe a word or they'll be on to him.   At present you are the only one who knows anything about the collaboration.   So mum, even in your letters home.   I finished my third act this morning—our third act—of course he doesn't do his fair share, but he comes in every now and then with a corking bit of blank verse.   He has never been in better form.   Well, well, we shall see. . . .

"Bermuda.
"*13th April, 1915.*

. . . "Bill has left me to do nearly all the fourth act myself, and has only sent in a few scraps.   There is more work in it than I thought, and I shall scarcely get through it before I leave for New York on Saturday week.   But it will be a gorgeous act when I get it right—four bishops and four actor managers all titled.   Oh my, wot larks! ! . . ."

Cock of the Walk was produced on 12th October, 1915, at the New National Theatre, Washington, and in New York at the Cohan Theatre on December 27th, with Mr. Otis Skinner in the leading rôle.   The Washington notices were enthusiastic. The New York criticisms were not so favourable, though all the papers praised Otis Skinner's superb performance as Anthony Bellchamber. The play was a great success, and ran for fourteen months in America. This success was largely due to Otis Skinner's acting. Without his magnificent impersonation it is doubtful if a play so English in theme and characterisation would have had such a hold on American audiences.

My father always spoke with deep gratitude of Mr. Skinner's acting, and it gave him great pleasure during the last year of his life to renew his very pleasant friendship with the Skinners, who were over here on a visit.

Before my father went to America he offered through the Foreign Office to do anything he could during his visit to advocate the cause of the Allies. As he knew so many influential people, he was in a position to gauge the principal currents of feeling. He was asked to send in confidential reports on the attitude and opinions of many leaders of thought in America. He also invented a code which he sent in, and, as he would never tell us how it was constructed, I believe, and he did also, that it may have been used. He was severely shaken by the tragedy of the *Lusitania,* and he felt Charles Frohman's loss intensely. For a short time he was convinced that America would at once come in on our side. It was a bitter disappointment to him that she did not. He felt it just as much as if one of his own children had humiliated him. His son-in-law, Leslie Faber, had thrown up his career and a very big salary in New York to come over and join up. Shortly after he did so, an American manager, ignorant of his whereabouts, cabled to my father offering Leslie a fine part and an enormous salary in a forthcoming New York production. Henry Arthur's reply was terse and to the point: he said, "Faber busy avenging *Lusitania.*"

In 1917 my father wrote a very strong letter to *The Times,* in which he said, "The successive notes of President

Wilson have given to the Allies the impression that he is not merely neutral between the Allies and Germany (which is a necessity of his high position) but that he is neutral between right and wrong; between the foulest and bloodiest tyranny that ever tried to bestride the earth, and the hard-set people who are agonising to overthrow it." The day this letter was published H. A. J. knew he would meet Mr. Page at a Pilgrims Dinner. He felt a little anxious as to how his plain speaking would be regarded, so he thought he had better take the bull by the horns; he went up to the Ambassador as soon as he arrived and said, "I hope, sir, you didn't mind my letter in *The Times*." Page looked round with his bright, searching look, took my father's hand, and, shaking it warmly, he said, "Just what I wanted, just what I wanted." Of all the American Ambassadors whose friendship H. A. J. enjoyed, he was fondest of Page, and his admiration for this great man was profound.

In speaking of the War, he referred constantly to President Wilson's phrase, "Some nations are too proud to fight," and always with intense contempt and scorn. He would almost snort with rage as he said, "Was there ever such a man or such a sentiment?" When America joined the Allies, he wrote to Clayton Hamilton:

". . . I needn't tell you how glad I am that America has come into the war—and come in so magnanimously. She has done a splendid thing for us, and a splendid thing for civilisation, but she has done a still more splendid thing for herself. I am sure you feel as I do. We are giving a big dinner to Page on Thursday with Balfour as Chairman."

In 1916 Henry Arthur wrote a satire, *The Pacifists*. He was prompted to do so by the, to him, incomprehensible attitude of the Conscientious Objectors and the increasing number of people who sighed for peace at any price. Many years previously Sir Edmund Gosse had begged him to write a satire. In a delightful letter to H. A. J., written in March 1903, he said:

"3rd March, 1903.

"MY DEAR HENRY ARTHUR JONES,

"My wife and I were amused all through *The White-washing of Julia* and thank you for a most enjoyable evening. I hope it will be a very great success. It was very bold of you not to explain about the puff-box and the tortoise-shell comb, very bold and very right. Of course one could completely reconstruct what had happened. I wonder if it was not too delicate for the pit? The coarse magnitude of modern audiences is the greatest difficulty of the playwright, I think.

"I do wish you would now take up the idea which I have ventured to urge upon you more than once, and would write a direct satiric drama, attacking with laughter some pet vice of the age. I think that 'the woman with a past' might be put back into the box for a while. We have had all the fun out of her that there is to be got. But money—and greediness for excitement—and the freaks of professional vanity—and religion—and Whittaker Wright—and the speculative adventures—why the forms and types crowd upon you! Your difficulty is to choose one and stick to it through a strong and rather *hard* satiric play.

"I shall never cease to prod you till you shoot me for the sake of a little peace.

"Very sincerely yours,
"EDMUND GOSSE."

The play was produced at the St. James's Theatre on 3rd September, 1917, after a preliminary week at the Opera House, Southport. Its complete failure was a severe disappointment to Henry Arthur, but he never referred to it without giving the highest praise to Ellis

Jeffreys's performance as the wife, and he would add how good Sebastien Smith was.

Speaking to me about this play, he said: "The great general public don't understand satire—it is a good thing that they don't. They know that black is black and white is white. They don't want to be muddled about." On another occasion he said, "I have always said I had three ambitions—to have a week's leisure to read Hooker's *Ecclesiastical Polity*, to stop a night at the Cloche Hotel, Dijon, and to write a satire for the English stage."

He wrote to Clayton Hamilton:

"December 8th, 1917.

. . . "I had a great failure with *The Pacifists*—no other English dramatist except Shakespeare could have achieved so complete a failure. It was condemned as quite unworthy by the Press, and the public never got within miles of its meaning—or of the theatre. Yet it delighted a lot of cultivated men—such as Edmund Gosse and Henry Newbolt and Sidney Lee and a score of others on that level. I am sending you a copy and shall be glad to know what you think of it. I should have thrown the action into a more fantastic setting, where I could have dispensed with narrative and shown the events taking place, but I'm not sure whether that would have been more successful; and at the present moment, costly settings and large casts are forbidden by the necessity of saving all labour for the War —that is, forbidden to anyone who cares for the country." . . .

After his death I found a copy of *The Pacifists* on which he had made several disjointed notes, many of which are illegible. On the front page there is a list, presumably of people to whom he sent copies. Elsewhere he has scrawled, "Don't show any temper"—"Don't make too much of it" —"If it has failed as a play it is useless to defend it as an

allegory."—"To public—to critics—to company—if I
were to make any great claim for the P. I should make
myself ridiculous."—"Blind bastards begotten in the un-
timely old age of the Manchester bagman"—"Anatomy
of laughter"—"Then the anonymous correspondent—
defend himself against his suggestion—and preserve an
impartial demeanour"—"Apologise all round to the
company, to the critic for play as did in *Michael*"—"It
would be a very inconvenient and undignified attitude for
me to take—rows with critics of established reputations"
—"Vulcan—not that loud guffaw—bandbox—nor that
idiot roar at some veiled obscurity." All his life my father
was in the habit of making notes, such as these he wrote
on this copy of *The Pacifists*. He would jot down words or
phrases he intended to use. This copy of the play and the
original manuscript are now in the collection of Mr. T.
J. Wise.

Immediately after the failure of *The Pacifists*, *The Liars*
was revived at the St. James's Theatre. The air-raids at
night were then so frequent that the first performance took
place on a Saturday afternoon in the hope that the play
would not be interrupted. It was a wise decision, as on
Saturday night, five minutes before the end of the first act,
my sister Peg, who was playing Lady Rosamund, was told
that the signal had been given. She suggested that the act
should be finished before the audience was informed.
There is a glass roof over the stage at the St. James's, so
the whole company took refuge under the stage, where they
were joined by Henry Arthur and the Lord Mayor of
London, who was in his box. The audience would not go
home or even take refuge in the corridors, where there was
a greater measure of protection. My sister said the heat
was excessive, their hunger as time went on was great, and
their thirst even worse. A few brave souls, Bobbie Loraine
and Mr. Arnold of the box office, sallied forth from time to
time and brought back drinks, but at twelve o'clock the

manager went in front and suggested that the audience should go home, as it was impossible to finish the play that night.

In 1917 my father wrote a war play called *Finding Themselves*. His note on this play ran, "A play in four acts, its action taking place in London 1917. I had arranged with a leading London actor to play the chief part and we were looking for a manager and a theatre, when he was taken by the War Office for more important work. There being no other actor available, the play was necessarily put aside. The end of the War came, and England, theatre folk included, made haste to forget all about it and its lessons. The play, therefore, is out of date for the present. But in ten years time, according to the conditions then prevailing in our country, and the state of the theatre in that unimaginable future, this play, written at the time of the greatest stress in the War, may have some interest for playgoers as giving a picture of London life in those dark hours."

CHAPTER XVI

THE War called forth the strong pugnacious element in my father's character which was never dormant for very long, and, as he was too old to take up arms, it was inevitable that he should use his pen in the service of his country. Once he had completed *The Pacifists,* he devoted the greater part of the remaining years of his life to national and political propaganda. I do not believe that he would have given so much of his time and energy away from the Drama had he met with greater success during the fifteen years that preceded the end of the War; but the creative instinct was still strong in him. Balked and disappointed, it had to find an outlet. I am sure he would still have written a great deal on political matters; but I doubt if they would have had such a hold on him. He was a crusader; and had he never written a play, I believe he would have been famous as a pamphleteer. He wrote great English prose. In an undated letter, written about 1918, Conan Doyle said:

"MY DEAR JONES,

"I really think your prose, when you are stirred up, is the best prose now to be had in our tongue. I noted it before in your paper on France, and again now. It is splendid. May it rouse the strong feeling which has inspired it.

"Yours always,
"A. CONAN DOYLE."

H. A. J.'s pamphlet, *Shakespeare and Germany,* was written in 1916, during the battle of Verdun. It was a reply to an article in which the *Cologne Gazette* declared that the whole of Germany would contemplate with amusement and satisfaction our celebration of Shakespeare's Tercentenary. "To complete the festival," it said, "only one thing is lacking—that the dead Shakespeare should express his opinion of the living England." *Shakespeare and Germany* contains some of the most beautiful prose Henry Arthur ever wrote; in particular a long passage in praise of France.

"If Shakespeare lived to-day, how willingly would we lend him to thee—nay, share him with thee—to sing with thy own poets of thy victories and ours; from the far-spread scurrying Marne to stubborn, hardest, indomitable Verdun; and onwards to the gathering clash of great fierce battles to come; through supernal fervours and agonies to the sure final triumph; to the last great day of account when the righteous forfeit shall be called, and enforced to the uttermost farthing!

"How would Shakespeare swell his proudest notes to praise thee, and yet not praise thee enough! And turning from this havoc and ruin, how would he send his prophetic soul to dream of things to come; of the days when these bloodstains shall be washed from the face of Europe, and the earth shall be green again; when thy land shall be cleansed from abominable hoofs, and thy cities shall be redeemed and redressed in new arising loveliness; and thou, forgetting these long past harvests of corn and wine; handfast with roused, re-vitalised England; jocund and fecund with countless increase of innumerable sons, filling all the void places of their inalienable heritage to its utmost borders!

"O France, endure! England shall not fail thee! Many of our dearest, bravest dead are with thee; sacred morsels of thy soil; dust of thy dust; irrevocably thine; incorporate citizens of France, whose crumbling hands wave to us from the clods to uphold thee to the end, whose silenced lips do ceaselessly reiterate our lasting covenant with thee that England shall not fail thee. O France, endure, endure!"

In these days of disillusion we no longer feel like that; but such passages show how my father could write when he was deeply stirred, and how, in spite of all the rather savage criticisms of his country's Philistinism which had estranged her from him in the days of her purse-proud prosperity, he rallied to her friends with all his soul when the prosperity suddenly changed to deadly peril.

The pamphlet was translated into French, and forms part of the series, *Les Cahiers Britannique et Americains,* used in the French schools.   The original manuscript now belongs to the French nation; it is in the Bibliothèque et Musée de la Guerre.   In 1921 the Director of the Museum wrote to my father to say they would consider it an honour if he would give them a copy of *My Dear Wells,* and the writer went on to say, "Should you have other publications either on the War, or on subjects related to it, or on peace problems and reconstruction, I shall be grateful if you will include them."

Henry Arthur was convinced that the present system of educating the masses was fundamentally wrong; that, as eighty per cent. of the population had to earn their living by manual labour, it could only be disastrous to educate them away from their work instead of towards it; that popular education was one of the main causes of unrest in the working-classes.   He was never tired of quoting Carlyle's saying that of all ways of getting good government, counting heads was the worst.   He started to write an open letter to Mr. Fisher, the Minister of Education, on educational problems; but he found he could not express himself within the limits of a letter, and wrote a book, which was published in 1919 under the title *Patriotism and Popular Education.*

The book received much favourable notice, English and American, whilst several critics praised it very highly. My father was especially delighted with the following letter from Mr. Rudyard Kipling, for whose genius he had a hearty admiration:

"1st May, 1919.

"DEAR ARTHUR JONES,

"I have read and re-read your letter to the address of Mr. Fisher, but I don't suppose it will have the least effect on that authority. As you say, it is all in Jack Cade's mouth and Shakespeare knew it—as he knew everything else. We shall probably reacquire that knowledge by ways more dramatic than anything Shakespeare wrote, but it won't be a pretty fifth act. Meantime one has to carry on as best one can.

"Very sincerely,
"RUDYARD KIPLING."

The following letters from Cunninghame Graham and Professor L. P. Jacks also gave him great pleasure. Cunninghame Graham wrote:

"11th December, 1919.

"MY DEAR HENRY ARTHUR,

"A thousand thanks for your book.

"I was always one of your fervent admirers, but have seldom seen so vigorous and incisive a piece of prose from your pen. Your ideas are practically the same as those of poor old Morris, at whose feet I brought myself up, politically. Tell me, O social reformer, why do you say, 'feared to disturb your cherished principles'?

"If my principles are wrong, surely they want to be disturbed? Go to! I agree, I think, with almost every word of your book.

"When I was young, and after 20 years of a Ranchman's life . . . whereby (or wherefore) I gained this infamous handwriting, owing to a twist with a lazo, which was not improved by another I received three years ago in the

Argentine Republic, saddling a wild horse for one of our troopers to ride subsequently at the front . . . I became a Socialist . . . largely owing to Morris.

"I may say, before going further, that as I gained this writing by the 28 years of the frontiers, so did I achieve 'Rhinitis' by the 6 years I was at the Gas Works (House of Commons). It was my sole reward.

"I had hoped in Socialism to find a gradual demise of selfishness and the gradual establishment of a better feeling between man and man. You may remember that, then (28 years or more ago) the sweater was excessively aggressive, hours were long, and there was a brutal spirit of materialism about . . . deer-stalking and pheasant-shooting amongst the rich, and rabbit-coursing amongst the less rich. You will admit, I think, that my ambition was not a low ambition. That I was deceived, and that all the golden dreams of Morris have vanished in the nine bestial and inartistic years of the reign of King Edward, the War, and now in the increasing inartisticness of everything, the prostitution of the stage and literature, and now in the ever-increasing selfishness and lack of patriotism of the working classes, have not been my fault.

"The ambition (I think) remains all right. Poor, dear, old Morris! Take him for all in all . . . !

"Most of us see the dreams of youth become grey in age; but I do not despair, for as long as there exist men who as yourself are inspired with the highest ideals, and who can couch them in the finest and most inspiring language, the country is sound at heart.

"Yours very sincerely,
"R. B. CUNNINGHAME GRAHAM.

"PS.—The many long voyages in ships, in canoes, and on horseback; the long nights in the cold and wet and the constant struggling with fools in the past five years, have given me plenty of time to think. Often with seaboots on, or wet and miserable in a railway truck with the horses in the Argentine, or sweltering Colombia, or with the skipper on the bridge looking out for torpedoes, I have thought—where are the dreams of Morris? But on arriving at port, or at the camp, they have come back; they always do. Let us, I say, cherish them. . . . *Vale.*"

Professor Jacks wrote:

"13th April, 1919.

"DEAR MR. JONES,

"I have been reading your book, which I heartily thank you for sending me, and which seems to me full of *human* wisdom, the only kind that is wise among men. I find myself in essential sympathy with it. What you say about the League of Nations does not hurt me in the least—far otherwise. I have never believed in a political league, set up by political methods, and 'run' by political persons, and have said all along, though few have listened except with scorn, that the attempt to establish it in that form, as a system of international 'Government,' would wake up the sleeping dogs of three Continents—as it is doing even at this hour. There is, however, not the least reason to fear that such a thing will come into being; or if it did, infernal disruption would be its almost instant fate. The object of the league, the only kind which I support, is beyond all politics, at least the utterly degenerate thing which goes by that name. I should attach far more importance to our attempt to set up an international university, or to revive any of the arts, or to lift industrial civilisation out of the mud in any one of a number of ways that could be named. But the public are so completely obsessed by the 'political' idea—voting, elections, parliaments, law courts, policemen, and all the rest of the bobbery—that they can think of nothing else. Internationalism that takes that form is not worth a straw. But, as you seem to notice, there is another kind.

"Yours very sincerely,

"L. P. JACKS."

Here is a characteristic letter from Ellen Terry:

"It is a wonderful book your book *Patriotism and P. E.* (*Excuse* me for my eyes pain me greatly and are very dim.) You will surely be rewarded by success in your endeavour to *wake up* the Powers that be, and make them see the blessed Sun shines by day, by nt. for you are *simple* and the right people will read your words and *all* must *understand you.*—I have already sent a copy to my wonderful son—to Italy—for *his very* wonderful son and have ordered more copies from Smith.

"I thank you my dear friend for your gift. I am now at p. 179—and Mr. Wells—my eyes fail me for 'the moment,' and a matinee performance is calling for nurse. Farewell in every place, and blessings on you for the book.—'Excuse' my scribble and don't let other eyes see it *please*.

"Yours, yours,

"ELLEN TERRY."

Patriotism and Popular Education contains a direct and trenchant attack on H. G. Wells's political creed. From the publication of this book onwards Henry Arthur attacked H. G. Wells and Bernard Shaw unceasingly. He was persuaded that their political opinions would, if they were generally accepted, be the damnation of the British Empire. Before attacking H. G. Wells publicly, my father wrote to him announcing his intention of doing so:

"*10th March, 1919.*

"MY DEAR WELLS,

"In my forthcoming book, *Patriotism and Popular Education,* I have attacked what seem to me to be the most mischievous fallacies in some of your recent articles and

letters. You advocate principles and schemes which, so
far as they can be put into operation, tend to disintegrate
and shatter not only the British Empire, but all civilised
structure. Now as I wish the British Empire to be preserved and strengthened, you will not be surprised that I
have used the most effective means in my power to expose
what I consider to be the radical unsoundness of your political theories. I should not think myself a good citizen if
I neglected to fulfil this duty to my country to the best of
my ability—I will send you one of the earliest copies of
the book that comes to hand. I assure you that I have
written with the deepest sense of responsibility in this
matter. If my arguments are wrong, I shall think you are
doing me a service if you will refute them—that is if you
think it worth while to take any notice of them. I shall be
sorry if this action of mine loses me an old friend, and can
assure you that I shall always dwell with the kindliest remembrance on our long and pleasant associations. Indeed
I shall be glad to continue it on the understanding that we
can both speak our minds about each other with the utmost
frankness and sincerity, without ceasing to shake hands
when we meet.

"Always faithfully yours,
"HENRY ARTHUR JONES."

He received the following charming reply from Mr.
Wells:

"MY DEAR JONES,

"I am quite sure that nothing you can say about my
opinions is likely to alter the very kindly feelings I bear
you. I've no doubt you'll *go for* me with the utmost spirit
and violence and fairness. I think the British Empire in
its present form is a sham and a nuisance.

"Yours,
"H. G. WELLS."

Mr. Wells, as a matter of fact, never made any systematic reply to my father's attacks. He was busy with other work, and manifestly he did not want to be distracted and used up by the toil and passion of sustained controversy. There was no controversy. He addressed one by no means conciliatory open letter to my father in the *Evening Standard* at Christmas suggesting that he might now direct his attention to other offenders, and thereafter he left my father free to write and say what he liked about him. He allowed judgment to go by default. His only alternative was to specialise in the discussion as completely as my father had done.

Writing to one of his American friends, Mr. Klyce, on 24th February, 1922, my father laid emphasis on the fact that his attacks were not personal. He said: "It is a real encouragement to receive letters such as yours from all sorts of quarters, telling me of the way in which this book of mine has been welcomed and appreciated. . . . You have no doubt realised that my attack is not directed against Mr. Wells entirely, but that he is the peg upon which I have hung my denunciation of all the unpatriotic 'Haters of England.'"

H. A. J. had delighted for many years in his cordial friendship with Mr. Wells, and it was with reluctance that he attacked him. They had seen a great deal of each other in the years just preceding the War, and in a letter my father wrote me in 1912 he said:

"9th December, 1912.

" . . . Then called at H. G. Wells at about 9.45—he had few people there—Rothenstein the artist, Marillier (Mr. Fells), partners in Morris's—and a few others. We dressed up in curtains and draperies and danced and played the fool till midnight. I wish you could have looked in. I was draped in a green velvet curtain, with a poker in one hand and a toasting-fork in the other, conducting vigorously with both over Wells's head as he played the pianola. Wells was also draped and all the others in anything we could find. We played the fool to our hearts' content. . . ."

H. A. J. adored Wells's quaint humour and the many fascinating games he invented; each had the same delight in jokes and light-hearted fooling. He enjoyed many of his books, especially *Mr. Polly,* and *Tono Bungay.* He spoke of them constantly, and always with keen interest and pleasure. In a letter to Max Beerbohm he said: "Many thanks for the caricatures. How marvellously you have concentrated all the weakness and imbecility of the modern English Drama in my poor self! When I look at it, I feel I am a truly representative national figure. It is most kind of you to send me the H. G. Wells. I shall value it very much. Have you read his *New Worlds for Old?* It is a fine, clear, inspiring book—almost a great one."

My father's friendship with Shaw was one of the most delightful and cordial of all his many friendships. He had for Shaw a deep and strong attachment, and for more than twenty years G. B. S.'s companionship and their intercourse had been a constant pleasure and stimulation to him. He often referred to the times when G. B. S. was a journalist and used to stay with him. But soon after the War broke out Henry Arthur was amazed and disgusted at G. B. S.'s attitude. Writing to me from New York in 1914, he said: "Shaw continues his crazy attacks. I never felt more angry with any man. He is trying to keep up the strife between England and Ireland. I do not think I can meet him in the future." In 1915 he wrote: "No use talking or thinking about the War. It's awful, and Shaw is only anxious to get an advertisement out of it."

He felt that Wells and Shaw were the spokesmen of

the most dangerous and fallacious political creeds, and that it was his duty as a patriot to combat their influence with every means at his disposal. He was nourished and sustained in this conviction by the enormous body of approval and encouragement he received from all over the world. A great many prominent English men and women supported him in his campaign, and he received hundreds of letters from unknown correspondents, who thanked him for the public service he was rendering England.

Throughout the years which followed, whenever Wells or Shaw were mentioned, or in speaking of them, Henry Arthur always said, "I've no personal malice against Wells or Shaw."

Henry Arthur's open rupture with G. B. S. came in October 1915. Many of Shaw's fellow-dramatists bitterly resented his attitude on the War; and the secretary of the Dramatists' Club, which meets at a fortnightly lunch, wrote to him to say that several members had refrained from attending the meetings in order to avoid him, and asking if, in the circumstances, he would prefer not to continue receiving the Club notices. G. B. S., not knowing that my father had taken any part in the affair, sounded him and some of the other important members as to whether they approved, and soon convinced himself that he could expect little support. With a few others, he indignantly resigned, and has never since consented to bury the hatchet as far as the Club is concerned.

Ian Hay, one of the most prominent members, felt very strongly about G. B. S. Years after the War, in 1925, he wrote to my father thanking him for a copy of one of his books, and said, "I always enjoy your work, but I enjoy you most of all when you are putting it across Shaw."

Shaw sent the letter from the secretary of the Dramatists' Club to Henry Arthur, and wrote underneath it:

"29th October, 1915.

"My dear H. A. J.,

"I hope you are not one of the 'several members,' though in these raving mad times it is hard to know.

"Cheerful sort of Club, isn't it?

"Ever,

"G. Bernard Shaw."

My father replied:

"1st November, 1915.

"My dear Shaw,

"In reply to yours, I was present at last Wednesday's lunch, and I strongly supported the proposal that Paull should write to you in the terms of the letter you enclose.

"I believe that England's cause is a most righteous one. I am sure that England did not provoke this war. I am sure that Germany did. These are, to me, not matters of opinion, but clearly established facts.

"Your writings on the War have done great harm to our cause in America and neutral countries. Germany is everywhere making use of your utterances to justify her own actions and to befoul and slander England. Whether you know it or not, and whether you care or not, you are one of our country's worst enemies. And you are an enemy within our walls. One of the leading American papers, in commenting on your pamphlet, said that if you had written in Germany on behalf of her enemies, you would have been shot.

"I cannot think you are so shortsighted as not to have foreseen that you were furnishing Germany with a powerful weapon to attack England, that you were offering evidence that our cause was unjust, that we were to blame for this War.

"Even if what you said was true, it was yet a foolish, mad, and mischievous thing to say at that moment.

"But the evidence you offered on behalf of Germany is perversely false. If you allow that our cause is just, what can it be but a mischievous treason to give our enemies the chance of proclaiming that you are on their side and that you think our cause unjust? If you do not allow that our cause is just, do you wonder that every Englishman is against you? Do you wonder that you are regarded as a man who, for the sake of showing his agility, kicked and defamed his mother when she was on a sick-bed? You will say that England is not your mother—well then put it that Englishmen regard you as a man who kicked and defamed *their* mother when she was on a sick-bed.

"This is not intolerance; it is mere natural human feeling—always so hard for you to understand. But it is the primal instincts and emotions that govern men in days like these. And you should not be surprised that in the agony and bloody sweat of fighting for our life we have no patience with a man who tries to trip us up—and with us the mercies and humanities of European civilisation.

"Faithfully yours,

"HENRY ARTHUR JONES."

G. B. S.'s answer was:

"*2nd November, 1915.*

"Henry Arthur, Henry Arthur; what is your opinion of the war?

"If you think you are going to put ME off with a sheet of notepaper containing extracts from the *Daily Express* copied with your own fair hand, you have mistaken your man.

"Come! give me a solid Buckinghamshire opinion: I know the German-American-would-be-British-Patriotic opinion; what's yours?

"England's cause is righteous. Good; but what is its cause? Besides, it isn't fighting for its own cause, but for

Russia's. Are you a sound Russian patriot too? And a true blue Serbian? And do you fill the air with shouts of '*Banzai!*'? I take it for granted that you will shed the last drop of your blood for *Liberté, Egalité, Fraternité*. And we all love Italy. But what is the cause (since you mention it solemnly): WHAT is the cause? What IS the Cause? What is the CAUSE? Emphasise it how you will; but tell me what it is, since you won't hear my statement of what it is.

"Twelve months ago nobody had stated a case against Germany that was not the most obvious *postiche,* bound to be knocked into a cocked hat by the Germans in a month's time, as it actually was. My case has never even been scratched. It stands unshaken amid a storm of lies, of excuses, of recriminations, of Podsnapperies and Pecksnifferies and worse. Twelve months ago our statesmen were Solomons, our generals Napoleons, our diplomatists Bayards and Marcus Aureliuses. When I suggested that they were human beings, and by no means of superfine quality at that, there was a howl of execration. Read your patriotic papers *now*. They don't apologise to me; but read them, and then read me, and despise my timid moderation.

"Why should you blame the Germans for claiming that I am on their side? Whenever a German informs the patriots of Germany that they are talking nonsense, and mostly very caddish nonsense, instead of killing Englishmen, we claim that he is on our side. The Germans, in their first fury when I made them a present of the rubbish about 1839 and about our being unprepared for them, called me fearful names, of which the kindest was *Vaterlandslose Geselle;* but the moment it dawned upon them that I was being attacked in England by the brigade of self-righteous idiots whose short-sighted folly I had exposed, they cleverly turned round and told the world that Shaw the Poet, Shaw the Upright Man, was on their side. Natural enough, wasn't it? Now tell me, if you can, what service the idiots did, except to their own miserable wounded vanity, by confirming the Germans instead of contradicting them? I had said that to allow the Prussian military machine to conquer would be to shut the gates of mercy on mankind. The idiot brigade told the world I had said it would open them. And the Germans said: 'Hoch, the idiot brigade, our best friends!' And taught the Turks to say, 'There is no majesty and no might save in Shaw the glorious, the great!' It is a fact that I have actually had to write a prophetic call to the Moors not to revolt against the French in order to counteract the German appeals to my authority. A. E. W. Mason is taking it out. I offered England the most powerful literary weapon yet forged to employ against Germany. She let the Germans take it out of her hand and rap her knuckles with it. I convinced Sweden, sorely tempted to join Germany by her dread of Russia, that we loathed Russian tyranny far more deeply than the Germans did. I convinced thousands of people whom we were deafening with our own virtuous indignation over 'crimes' that we are steeped in (treaty-breaking and the like) and disgusting by our praises of ourselves and our ignoble interpretation of our enemies (the Crown Prince stealing spoons and so forth) that underneath all that clamour of cads there was a solid case and a still sound nation. What I said was printed and reprinted by the most pro-British daily in New York. I faced the public at meeting after meeting and challenged questions and criticism. I got applause galore and not a hostile word. On Tuesday last week I appeared again. Hundreds of people were turned away; and I was asked two questions, both about Jesus Christ. And you ask me do I wonder that every Englishman is against me! Oh, Henry Arthur, Henry Arthur, author of *Saints and Sinners*, *The Crusaders*, and *The Philistines*, do you believe that the editor of the *Daily Express* is England? Do you think you would rather lunch with Horatio Bottomley than with me?

"And you think England, your mother, is on a sick-bed. She never was stronger in her life, as you will find out if you annoy her too much by your shrieks of terror at the German menace.   Sick mother be damned, you recreant! Germany has not a dog's chance against her, and never had from the beginning.   You are like a prize-fighter who, with all the points in his favour, has to be shown his unbruised face in a mirror to encourage him to go on. Think of big Joffre, who told the world that there was no excuse for the retreat from Namur and that the French army had disgraced themselves.   You would have called him a pro-German and the 'worst enemy of his country.' Get out!

"When you pretend that you don't like me and kept away from the club on my account, I simply ask you, O degenerate doubter of your country's destiny, whither you expect to go when you die.   Such an AWFUL lie!

                                                                    "G. B. S."

On 2nd November, 1914, an interview with Shaw was published in the San Francisco *Bulletin*.   It was headed, " 'Shoot your Officers and Go Home,' says Shaw."   G. B. S. was reported as having said, "We prattle of British Courage, and for weeks sit around in a state of frightful funk, holding each other's hands and exclaiming, 'Be Strong!   Be Brave!   Business as usual!' " and that, "In both armies the soldiers should shoot their officers and go home."   The whole tone of the interview and its effect in America were lamentable.   This interview, Shaw assures me, was a fabrication; but it imposed on my father; and Shaw's authentic pamphlet, *Common Sense About the War,* which said in its author's most effective style a good deal that the American fabricator had expressed coarsely, infuriated my father still more.   He noted the following extracts—that we had "duped the Kaiser," that English people in August 1914 were "snivelling hypocritically about our love of peace, and our respect for treaties, and our solemn acceptance of a painful duty, and all the rest of the nauseous mixture of schoolmaster's cant and cinematograph melodrama with which we have been deluged"; and his reference to our "cant about the diabolical personal disposition of the Kaiser, and the wounded propriety of a peace-loving England, and all the rest of the slosh and tosh that has been making John Bull sick for months past." Fuel was added to the fire of his wrath by the fact that Shaw's statement, made to an American Senator, that the putting forward of the violation of Belgium's neutrality as the motive of England's entry into the War was mere eyewash and was sure to be exposed as such when the Germans reached Brussels, was used by the Germans in their attempt to stir up the Moors in Algeria and Tunisia to revolt against the French and force them to draw off troops from the Western Front to Africa. When this was brought to Shaw's notice, he immediately wrote a counterblast for distribution by our Mediterranean Intelligence Department describing with Oriental rhetoric the ruin that had overtaken Belgium for allowing herself to be drawn into a quarrel between two great Powers wielding terrible means of destruction, and warning the Moors that the same fate would overtake them, if they moved hand or foot in the matter.

Then Henry Arthur was deeply shocked by G. B. S.'s one-act skit on England in war-time, *Augustus Does His Bit,* produced by the Stage Society, and he agreed heartily with William Archer's criticism when he said, "One listens to it with regret. Serious well-aimed satire may be useful, but not mere promiscuous persiflage, which makes a comic catchword of 'our brave fellows lying in the trenches.'" The skit was, however, highly relished by the Foreign Office, which was embarrassed and exasperated by the

maladroit officiousness of our Augustuses; and this indulgence towards Shaw, which my father did not understand, culminated in sending him to the front in 1917 to
write a series of descriptive articles which were published
in New York and London simultaneously. No wonder my
father became more and more persuaded that Shaw was
an extremely dangerous man.

I have no desire to revive an old controversy, throughout
which Shaw displayed the utmost good temper and generosity—a fine magnanimity towards the man who attacked him; but in justice to my father's memory I am
compelled to republish some of the things G. B. S. said
about the War, so that impartial readers can judge how
far my father was justified in his efforts to combat the
sentiments expressed.

* * * * * * * * *

In 1921 Henry Arthur published *My Dear Wells, A
Manual for the Haters of England.* The book was a series
of letters addressed to Mr. Wells, which had already been
published in the *New York Sunday Times,* and in England
in the *Evening Standard.* A delicious cartoon by Oliver
Herford representing H. A. J. and G. B. S. is here reproduced. It represents also what Oliver Herford and several
of my father's friends felt about his repeated attacks on
Shaw. St. John Ervine wrote to my father the following
kindly letter:

"21st November, 1921.

"It was very kind of you to send me the book, most of
which I had already read in various papers. I like you all
three—Shaw, Wells, and you—so much that I hate to see
you scrapping with each other, particularly as I see that
each of you is right and each of you is wrong. Wells comes
out of the scrap unhappily for his manners, but then H. G.
never was good at keeping his temper. There you score

CARTOON BY OLIVER HERFORD

(By courtesy of Mr. Oliver Herford)

over him.   But, Lord, what a hammering you give Shaw—and how good-temperedly he replied to you in the *Sunday Chronicle* to-day. . . ."

My Dear Wells contains the longest sentence in the English language—a terrific indictment of G. B. S. in Chapter XIX, consisting of 602 words.   In his indictment Henry Arthur said, "The Nag Sedition was your mother, and Perversity begot you; Mischief was your midwife, and Misrule your nurse, and Unreason brought you up at her feet—no other ancestry and rearing had you."   After my father's death, in speaking to me about him, G. B. S. referred to this sentence with a laughing, good-tempered remark.   They were alike in a large-hearted generosity which precluded them from bearing rancour.

The criticism which gave my father the most intense pleasure was an article by Professor Paul Shorey, the eminent American classical scholar, published in the *Trend*. Professor Shorey wrote: "And quite apart from the thought of *Patriotism and Popular Education* and the wit of *My Dear Wells,* the two books contain 15 or 20 pages of as eloquent prose as has been written in the past 50 years. . . .

"No wonder Shaw said, 'It was a shocking book that ought never to have been written.'   But in all this we forget the main point—that this intemperate language, if you choose to call it so, is a statement of plain truth, or at any rate comes as the climax of clean-cut indictment of forty or fifty charges based on Bernard Shaw's published works and public acts, every count of which is true.   The London *Times* reviewer and Shaw and the friends of Shaw forgot to mention that.   But I, who have kept my own private note-book on the man, know the charges to be true.

"He did say that Belgium could not be neutral because geographically it lay on the road between Germany and France.

"He did say that Belgium's refusal to violate her own pledged neutrality by letting the Germans through was an act of war.

"His writings were and are used for German and Bolshevik and anti-English propaganda.

"He did, writing to American newspapers, try to undermine England in American opinion.

"He did and does, under the pretext of the free play of the critical intellect, make a mock of Christianity, marriage, education, the science of medicine, governments, property, courts of law and justice, Shakespeare—all the principles, all the traditions, all the ideals by which civilisation subsists—without contributing anything to replace them in the constructive thought of the minds which he thus unsettles.

"And the only answer to Mr. Jones's indictment is that Shaw is so witty, and we must be tolerant . . .

"In short and to conclude, Mr. Jones's two books contain—in addition to a few pages of eloquent and beautiful English prose—much wit and rollicking humour, some permissible buffoonery by way of comic relief—much serious argument on vital problems of to-day—many pertinent questions to be answered by Utopists and impossibilists and their dupes—and above all, valuable lessons for young writers in clear thinking, vigorous expression, and the art of passionate, intense, witty, strenuous, yet at bottom still fair, because rational, controversy."

Henry Arthur was overwhelmed with congratulations. Lord Sydenham was delighted with his attack on Wells, and thanked him for "exposing the dangerous rubbish which this clever impostor has scattered about." Sir James Crichton-Browne wrote: "You are doing a public service in deflating section by section a multilocular balloon that has been too long allowed to float unassailed." These and many other encouraging letters received by my father show how widespread was the distrust of Shaw's and Wells's political creed, and how grateful many people were that such a redoubtable champion should have appeared to refute them.

Many of Henry Arthur's eminent friends in America supported him. Professor Nicholas Murray Butler wrote to him: "That last letter of yours to '*My Dear Wells*,' printed in the *Morning Post* of 4th August, which you kindly sent me, is a gem. You will have that man's blood on your head before long, for I am sure the poor creature will commit suicide if you keep on writing to him. Please don't stop on that account."

None of G. B. S.'s public utterances during and after the War aroused my father to such a pitch of indignation as his three terrible articles, published here in the *Nation* and in America in the Hearst papers, on the Washington Limitation of Arms Conference, in which he said, "When Mr. Lloyd George replied to President Harding's demand for a Conference by saying that Britain's policy was Security First, I said that security means war, thereby throwing my old friend Henry Arthur Jones into convulsions." And again, "Now that Washington is the theme of our journalists, they are seething in the milk of human kindness, and backing up, for all they are worth, Mr. Henry Arthur Jones's pledge that it would take two thousand years of mischief-making to induce any Englishman to shed the blood of an American. But let us not deceive ourselves. All that reckless and brainless emotional self-indulgence, amiable as it may be, does not justify the faintest presumption that the British and American fleets may not be trying to sink one another, with Henry Arthur and the rest frantically cheering their own side, within three weeks or less." After that, as may be imagined, the fat was in the fire about peace as merrily as it had been about war.

After the publication of *My Dear Wells*, Henry Arthur directed his attacks solely against Shaw. During the next three years he was engaged in writing *Bernard Shaw as a Thinker;* but he was interrupted constantly, and never completed this work. The first six chapters were published in the *English Review* in 1923, and in 1925 he published in book form three chapters under the title *What is Capital?* The book was received very favourably, except by the Labour Press. Against that exception I may cite Shaw himself, who praised the pages on the impossibility of a nation living on its capital as sound Shavian doctrine.

Again my father received dozens of congratulatory letters. He was especially delighted with those from Mr. Rudyard Kipling, Sir Arthur Keith, and Dr. Alington. Mr. Kipling said:

> "Bateman's,
> "Burwash, Sussex.
> "*13th February, 1925.*

"MY DEAR ARTHUR JONES,

"Very many thanks for your last little book. It seemed to me a perfectly clear and reasonable exposition of a law that has governed the world since the first man did not finish all his day's rations in one day. That is, of course, the reason why you will be firmly corrected by those who know better than you (or I) how to make a new world with laws to match.

> "Ever sincerely,
> "RUDYARD KIPLING."

Sir Arthur Keith said:

> "Royal College of Surgeons of England,
> "*5th October, 1925.*

"MY DEAR H. A. J.,

"When you have done with Shaw there will be only feathers and blood left—I enjoy the way you set about him.

> "Yours sincerely,
> "ARTHUR KEITH."

Dr. Alington wrote:

> "Eton College.
> "*7th March, 1925.*

"MY DEAR MR. JONES,

"I am very grateful to you for sending me your book, which I shall read with great interest and shall also show to some of my more intelligent pupils. Like yourself, I have no personal feeling against Shaw, but I am always glad when anyone is courageous enough to challenge some of his more glaring paradoxes.

> "With many thanks once more,
> "Yours sincerely,
> "C. A. ALINGTON."

Henry Arthur had always found the columns of the *Morning Post* open to him, and he was very pleased when Mr. Gwynne, the editor, wrote to him, "I like your denunciation of Shaw immensely, and although it was certainly personal, I think he deserves everything you said of him." In another letter Mr. Gwynne wrote:

> "*1st September, 1925.*

"Please do not remain under the impression that I dislike the tone which you take over Wells and Shaw. On the contrary, I think you're doing a public service in showing up these two. If . . . at times I think that the method of direct address to both these authors is not perhaps the best way to deal with them, that is merely a question of taste about which, we are told by the Latin tag, we should not discuss."

My father's final attack on Bernard Shaw is contained in an unpublished book, *Mr. Mayor of Shakespeare's Town.* It was inspired by G. B. S.'s own statement about Shakespeare. He had said, "With the single exception of Homer, there is no eminent writer, not even Sir Walter Scott, whom I can despise so utterly as I despise Shakespeare when I measure my mind against his.   The intensity of my impatience with him occasionally reaches such a pitch, that it would positively be a relief to me to dig him up and throw stones at him."   On 23rd April, 1925, Shaw was invited to propose the health of Shakespeare at the Annual Festival. My father regarded the invitation as a monstrous insult to the memory of Shakespeare.   This book contains some of the most beautiful prose he ever wrote, especially the Introduction, and, at the end of the book, the invocation to Shakespeare.

Henry Arthur had a contract with Nash's to publish the book, with the usual clause that the author warranted it was not libellous.   Though Mr. Eveleigh Nash was in favour of the publication, his fellow-directors decided that they could not undertake it, as did also several other well-known publishers whom my father approached here and in America.   Shaw was asked, without my father's knowledge, to promise that he would take no action against the printer or publisher; but he refused, declaring that he would do everything in his power to force my father to stop wasting his genius on useless political invective and to return to play-writing.   The effect of this attitude of Shaw's was that a local printer who had been persuaded to set up the book became alarmed and broke up the type after six copies had been struck off.   H. A. J. sent one copy to the British Museum, and one to his old and very valued friend, M. H. Spielmann.   He gave one (now in T. J. Wise's collection) to my brother.   I have two.   In the copy he gave me he said:

"This first proof of *Mr. Mayor of Shakespeare's Town* has just come into my hands.   It is due to you for all your loving care of me.   Pray that this little book may go home to the hearts—and the brains of our English people."

The remaining copy he sent to his friend James Beck, then Solicitor-General, United States, to whom he wished to dedicate the book. For some years my father had delighted in his friendship with Mr. James Beck. He admired him greatly and valued his opinion very highly. Henry Arthur always declared that Mr. Beck was the finest orator he had ever heard. He said to me once, "Oratory ought to be oratory; the other thing's a side-show." He referred constantly to Mr. Beck's speech at the Pilgrims' Luncheon a fortnight after the Armistice. Speaking to William Gillette in 1925, he said, "It was a great occasion and he rose to it nobly. Beck is the finest orator I've ever heard." Mr. Beck wrote to Henry Arthur, after reading the book:

"Washington,
"*26th October, 1925.*

"I read with great interest both the little book and also your newspaper article. Both profoundly moved me, and each was very impressive in its own way. I think your *Mr. Mayor of Shakespeare's Town* is one of the most destructive pieces of invective that has appeared since the *Letters of Junius*. It is very powerful, and if you are solid in your facts, it admits of no answer. (I see that George Bernard Shaw has not attempted to answer it, slippery as he is as a controversialist.) Is it possible that Shaw ever said what you quote him as saying about Shakespeare? ... It seems almost incredible to me that he could have been so venomous about a man who has been dead for three centuries, and whose very shoe-latchets he is not worthy to unloose. I am sure that you could not be mistaken about the quotation, and I am curious to know where it appears in Shaw's writings, and what the context was.

"Do send me anything you write, for it is always an immense pleasure to read it."

A few other privileged friends were allowed to read the book, among them Baliol Holloway, whom my father regarded as our finest living Shakespearian actor. In writing to thank him, Mr. Holloway said:

'17th December, 1925.

". . . Have I thanked you for all the most interesting enclosures you have sent me from time to time? May I say how passionately I admire your championing of the *things that matter?* Shakespeare and Patriotism. (The two are synonymous.) How much this vulgarised, selfish age stands in need of you! And how lucky it is to have you!"

At the time my father thought the book would be published, several extracts from it were printed in the *Daily Mail* on 20th October, 1925. Among the dozens of letters from unknown correspondents praising his denunciations of Wells and Shaw there is only one criticising him. I reproduce this solitary protest:

"7th November, 1925.

"DEAR SIR,

"You are manifesting such concern to obtain publicity for your 'indictment' of Bernard Shaw, that you can hardly complain if an obscure member of the public is moved to address you in return.

"We are all equal in the sight of God and the postal authorities. You must permit me, therefore, as 'man to man' to inform you that, in my judgment, you are as incapable of understanding the mind of Bernard Shaw as was Judas (an honest man, it is currently believed) of understanding the mind of Christ. Shaw, like Christ, expresses himself largely through the medium of epigrams and paradoxes that are liable to misconstruction, whether wilful or in good faith, by the uninitiated.

"I must, however, question your good faith in reminding you that Shaw is—and is recognised as—(among other things) the greatest playwright of his generation, and that you are a playwright of his generation, whom he has perforce—certainly not by design—'put in the shade.'

"Do I insinuate that your motive in resenting the tribute of Stratford-on-Avon is common jealousy? Your motive, like all our motives, is a complex one. That it is based on—shall we say, wounded vanity, you yourself, sir, in your heart of hearts must know to be the case.

"That is presumably what makes the spectacle 'rather painful' to as magnanimous a man as the world of letters has produced. That, at any rate, makes it painful to one who owes to Shaw's genius—among other more spiritual benefits than he can number—the 'discovery' of a beautiful play called *Michael and His Lost Angel;* who accordingly has no hesitation in subscribing himself

"Yours sincerely,
"H. F. RUBINSTEIN.

"I have not the honour of his friendship."

I insert Mr. Rubinstein's letter to show that my father knew quite well that he was facing this misunderstanding, the fear of which might have silenced a smaller man. Shaw's own comment was, "What! Jones jealous of me as a dramatist! Nonsense! You don't suppose he considers me a dramatist, do you? To him I am only a critic who has mistaken his profession." This must of course be taken with a grain of salt; but it may make it easier for those who did not know my father to believe that professional rivalry had absolutely nothing to do with the quarrel.

There is another aspect of my father's patriotic labours which should be remembered. Not only was it true that the time he devoted to combating Shaw and Wells might have been given to profitable play-writing, but that such a book as *Patriotism and Popular Education* involved him in a personal expenditure of some hundreds of pounds. The explanation is that, in order to bring the book within the purchasing-power of the many, it was published at a price much below actual cost.

For several years my father had been suffering from increasing ill-health. It culminated in two severe operations in 1926, and his campaign against Shaw imposed a terrific strain on his vitality. It was never out of his mind; during these years, even at meal-times, Wells's and Shaw's misdeeds formed the major, and very often the only, topic of conversation. How often I have wished that he had confined his criticism of G. B. S.'s political activities to a remark he once made to me: "Shaw's economics are exactly those of Jack Cade in Shakespeare." He was always in a state of intense nervous excitement; and, when his repeated attempts to get *Mr. Mayor* published proved abortive, he broke down. His doctor implored him to put the book aside for the moment, but against his advice he sent for a local printer and had a long and exhausting interview. That night he had his first attack of angina pectoris; but, with almost foolhardy pluck and courage, he insisted upon another interview in the same week, which brought on another attack.

Several times before he died he made me promise him solemnly that I would use every effort to get this book published after his death. I gave him my promise, though I knew that it was unlikely I should ever be in a position to indemnify any printer or publisher against the possibility of a law-suit for libel. But, since my father's death, I have consulted Mr. M. H. Spielmann, whose discernment and opinion on such matters I believe he valued more highly than those of any other of his friends, and, after deep and anxious reflection, as to the moral, as well as the personal, aspect of the case, I do not feel that it would enhance Henry Arthur's reputation if *Mr. Mayor* were published.

From the very beginning of my father's friendship with Mr. Spielmann, he was in the habit of writing to him very fully about his work and of seeking his advice, which he often found most helpful. The following extract from a letter he wrote to Mr. Spielmann in 1919 is one of many testimonies of the profound regard he had for his friend's judgment:

"6th March, 1919.
"My DEAR SPIELMANN,

"Many thanks. You are right about the last sentence in the preface, and I will change it as you suggest. Or, seeing that two distinct actions are indicated, first a look round and then more or less groping, wouldn't it be better to say 'if haply my fellow-stumblers and I may discover where we are and whither we are wandering'? Or '. . . discover whither we are wandering and where lies the right path'? Tell me which is the best of the three. . . .

"Do please always tell me when you see something that needs correction. I often correct a passage half a dozen times, and then can't get it right; and a friendly hint is of great service. . . ."

My father's political work and his controversies with H. G. Wells and Bernard Shaw occupied the best part of ten years of his life. All his family deplored the amount of time we felt he was wasting in unprofitable work, especially when it began to tell very severely on his health. But he would listen neither to reason nor persuasion, even from his doctor. Several of his more intimate friends also attempted to dissuade him from continuing his campaigns, but alas!—their efforts did not weigh in the scales against the very much larger number of people who encouraged him and told him he was doing work of national importance.

In the last two years, H. A. J. often acknowledged how wrong he had been to take up propaganda, and to attack Wells and Shaw. He wished that he had finished his nearly completed book, *The Shadow of Henry Irving*. When speaking of it to me he would say, "That's some of the best work I've ever done; it would have been my finest book." The quality of the prose is on a very high level throughout, and there are several passages of great beauty.

Eighteen months before my father died Shaw wrote him the following delightful letter:

"Regina Palace Hotel,
"Stresa.
"27th August, 1926.

"My dear H. A. J.,

"I meant to congratulate you on my seventieth birthday (the 26th July, 1926), but was afraid of sending your temperature up 10 degrees at a critical moment. I am assured now by Max Beerbohm that you are well enough to stand anything; so I insist on affirming that the news of your illness gave me as much concern, and of your safe deliverance as much relief, as if we were still the best of friends. Our quarrel has always been a hopelessly one-sided affair; and I have rejoiced in your vigorous invective far too much to feel any malice at the back of it. Some of it, by the way, was very sound Shavian economics.

"I was particularly delighted with an article of yours on Religion, in a series in—wasn't it the *Daily Express?* Anyhow, it was by far the best of the lot; and I have always since cited it to prove that what you suffer from occasionally is an excess of mental vigour, and by no means a deficiency in essential friendliness for me personally.

"People who obviously pity my dotage have a well-meant but disagreeable habit of reminding me that Sophocles wrote his best plays at 80. I suppose they say the same to you. They know nothing about it; but you seem to me to have more drive and style than ever.   I wish I could say the same for myself; but at present I feel that my bolt will be shot when I have got through the final struggle to finish my book on Socialism, with every word of which you will agree.   The truth is, I am for the moment so completely done up by work on top of illness (the result of an accident) that the writing of this letter would tire me for the rest of the day if the feeling it expresses were not so nourishing.   So you really are doing me good.

"Do not bother to reply—though I warn you I shall put the friendliest interpretation on silence.   This birthday business, involving as many congratulations (on being 70! Good God!!) as your recovery is bringing you, has shown me how easy it is to kill a strong man by a full broadside from the post office.   Just note that I am not to be shaken off, and turn over for another nap with a groan of resignation.

"Ever,
"G. B. S."

My father would not answer this letter, though he showed it to his family and a few very dear friends: Emery Walker, Percy Allen, and H. C. Shelley.   I think he felt that if he answered this letter the old dear friendly relations must inevitably be resumed, and that this would be a betrayal of all his years of work and of the confidence and encouragement given to him by so many of his old friends, and also by enormous numbers of the general public here and in America.

CHAPTER XVII

DURING these years, 1914–1920, in addition to his three books, Henry Arthur wrote a good many "Letters" on current political topics: a letter on "Labour and Lloyd George," just before the General Election in 1918, an Open Letter to the Chancellor of the Exchequer on "How to Raise Money," and several to Mr. Fisher on Education. The state of unrest in Ireland had always interested him. He blamed Gladstone bitterly for many of the troubles which had occurred. In February 1920 the *Evening Standard* published two Letters on Ireland, one of which was headed "Strife, Wreckage, and Ruin over Ireland," and the other "An Open Letter on Ireland."

But during all these years Henry Arthur had not neglected the interests of his beloved Drama. Though he did not write many plays, he wrote to the papers constantly on the subject which always lay closest to his heart; letters on "Shakespeare in England"; two open letters to William Poel; another on "Why English Drama is Crowded Out"; a correspondence with Albert de Courville in the *Morning Post;* an introduction to Mr. Morrison's *Reconstruction of the Theatre;* and several less important letters. His activity was prodigious.

In 1923 my father made a very important addition to his writings on the Drama in the shape of a detailed reply to a questionnaire from Professor Archibald Henderson of the University of North Carolina: "Dramatic Technique as Revealed by Dramatists." [1]

[1] Reproduced in Appendix C.

In May 1919, *The Goal*, originally produced in New York in 1914, was performed at a special matinée at the Palace Theatre, with Leslie Faber as Sir Stephen Famariss. Though H. A. J. always had Irving in his mind in connection with this part, he greatly admired Faber's fine performance.   Faber again played the leading part when the play was produced at the Haymarket Theatre on 12th December, 1923, as a curtain-raiser to *The Importance of Being Earnest*.

When the production of stage plays on the films was still in its infancy, Henry Arthur sold several of his most famous plays outright; among them *Judah, The Middleman, Michael and His Lost Angel*, and *Mrs. Dane's Defence*. He often said, "I'd no idea how the thing would develop, and I thought, well—I've had my money out of the plays, and here are a few extra hundreds."   But it was not long before he realised the great importance of this new dramatic medium.   It is characteristic of his almost complete lack of business acumen that, once the cinema was established as prime favourite among millions of theatre-goers, he again sold outright several valuable properties—*The Silver King, The Lie*, and *Lydia Gilmore*.   When films were established as the favourite amusement of the public, H. A. J. took a deep and increasing interest in their dramatic possibilities and wrote several original scenarios, including a very fine historical film dealing with the early settlement of Virginia.   He greatly hoped this film would be produced, as he was convinced the production would forge another link in the chain of friendship between England and America.

In 1919 my father finished his last play, *The Lifted Veil*. It was never acted, but was afterwards filmed as *Beyond*. In a note which I found after my father's death he says: "I made strenuous but unavailing efforts to work with the producer while it was being done; at least I wished to have five minutes talk with him about it.   But this, I understand, is not professional etiquette. Perhaps this strict rule may one day be relaxed, and I still live in the hope of one day working with the producer, whom I allow to be much more responsible for the actual success of a film play than the author."

He sent me a postcard in December 1919:

"MY DARLING, Just finished the play with my eyes full of tears.—DADDY."

In 1920 Mr. Lasky bought *The Lifted Veil* for £5,000, and he invited my father to go to America to supervise the production. He was so anxious that Henry Arthur should do so that he offered as a minor inducement to pay for his passage. H. A. J. accepted, but, as soon as he got to New York, H. G. Wells's activities "got hold of him," and he stayed there, occupied in writing *My Dear Wells,* to the almost total exclusion of any other business. I do not know if *The Lifted Veil* was ever shown as a film in America, but when Henry Arthur saw the production privately, he said that his play had been altered out of recognition, and, with his usual total disregard of tact, or even common politeness, he paraphrased Horace Walpole's famous remark and said to Mr. Lasky, "You don't know your own damn silly business." He always said, "I never tell lies about art"; and nothing would induce him to praise a play or an actor if he did not admire the play or the acting. How often have I tried on a first night, but always unsuccessfully, to get him to tell a graceful half-truth. He was not a tactless man, but he was not tactful. He made many enemies in the theatrical world by the unabashed bluntness of his criticisms; but he also made many friends who knew that his praise, when he gave it, came straight from the heart. I like to remember, after his devastating and hopelessly incorrect remark to Mr. Lasky, how charmingly he spoke of my father when I met him a few years ago.

During H. A. J.'s stay in New York in 1920 and 1921, he went several times a week, generally with the Herfords, to the private theatre of the Lasky Corporation, where they ran through the newest films for his benefit. He met a great many of the most prominent film stars, and he was especially attracted to Lillian and Dorothy Gish. He renewed his friendship with the latter when she was over here filming Nell Gwynn and other parts under Herbert Wilcox's direction, and he became very attached to her.

He always said that, of all his plays which had been filmed, *The Middleman* was the only one which gave him complete satisfaction, and that for the most part, beyond the fact that his title was used, he would not have recognised his work.

The last production of my father's life, as also one of the most successful, was *The Lie,* which had been played in New York in 1914, but had not been seen in London. It was produced by Lewis Casson at the New Theatre on 13th October, 1923, with Sybil Thorndike in the leading part. Just before and even during rehearsals H. A. J. was suffering from a nervous breakdown, and his family dreaded the strain for him, and the effect on his health, if the play was a failure. We implored him not to make a speech on the first night, as we were a little afraid he might mention Shaw or Wells, or both, and Lady Wyndham sent him a charming, tactful note on the day of production urging him not to take a call. But the reception of the play was tumultuous, the audience would not be denied, and the old man came forward to receive a tremendous outburst of welcoming and affectionate applause, to which he replied with a few grateful words. It was a great moment for him, to come back triumphantly to the hearts and minds of the theatre-going public after many years of defeat and absence. We all went round to congratulate Miss Thorndike on her magnificent performance, and it was more than an hour after the fall of the curtain when my father and I left the theatre. The crowd was so great that a policeman, as well as the fireman, had to be called in to make a passage for Henry Arthur. As he emerged he received another tremendous ovation from his old friends of the pit and gallery, and for about half an hour, surrounded by a laughing, cheery crowd, he was busy signing programmes and autograph-books.

The Lie is the story of two sisters. Eleanor Shale, the elder, a devoted and unselfish woman, shields and protects her younger sister Lucy when she has an illegitimate child. Some time after they both fell in love with Gerald Foster, who has already indicated his preference for Eleanor, but an unhappy mischance puts him in possession of the story that one of the sisters has a child. He questions Lucy, who allows him to think the child belongs to Eleanor. She induces Gerald to marry her before Eleanor discovers her treachery. There is a tremendous scene in the third act when she does so, and also between the two sisters in the last act, but, although Eleanor's life is wrecked, there is a measure of happiness still left to her in her love for Lucy's child, who will live with her, and the devoted love of Gerald's friend, Noll Dibdin.

Many of the notices were highly appreciative, but several of the critics thought that the play was old-fashioned; though all of them spoke of the tremendous reception given to the play and of Miss Thorndike's powerful and beautiful performance.

When *The Lie* was published in England, Henry Arthur wrote a dedication to Sybil Thorndike, in which he said: "I have had many roaring receptions of applause from English first-nighters, but none of them has approached the thundering welcome they gave me when, under the shelter of your wing, myself moved by the inflaming sweep of your action, I stood beside you to acknowledge the prolonged acclamations that greeted us on the 13th October, 1923.

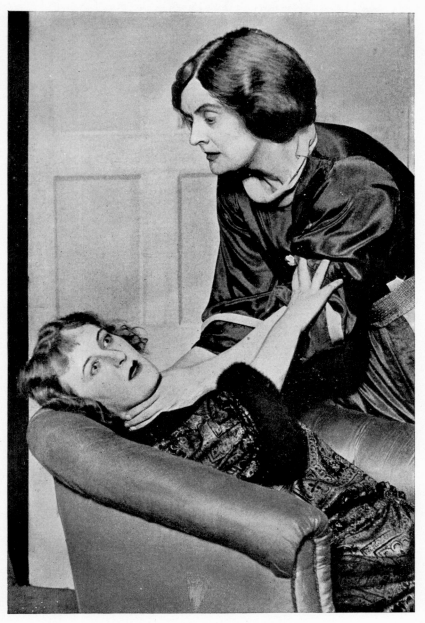

SYBIL THORNDIKE AND MARY MERRALL IN

"THE LIE," THE NEW THEATRE, 1923

"How lucky I was, after six years' absence from the London theatre, to return to it in such company as yours! What words of gratitude will fitly express my debt to you? What words of praise can I choose to describe the patient tenderness of your quiet early scenes, swelling into stronger but still reserved and self-contained emotion, startled at last into the poignant and terrific fury of your great tragic abandonment? Take all the dictionaries, and pick out from them all their superlatives of eulogy, and I will multiply them again and again."

The play was a very great success, and it would have run longer than 187 nights, but it was taken off while still playing to big houses to make way for the production of *Saint Joan*. This was always a sore point with H. A. J., though the Cassons revived *The Lie* successfully at Wyndham's Theatre on 30th May, 1925.

We were always glad to remember that my mother, though she had to be attended by a nurse, was present at the first night of *The Lie,* to rejoice in Henry Arthur's triumph. She died a few months later at Monte Carlo. She had been suffering from heart disease for nearly three years, and during that time she had many very serious seizures, each one of which we dreaded would be fatal. Very early in the morning of her last birthday, in November 1923, she had a very bad attack, in which she remained unconscious for over nine hours. Henry Arthur always gave her a big bunch of carnations and white heather for her birthday and I shall never forget how he kept on coming in and out of the room with the flowers in his hand, his poor distraught face as he leant over her, and the moment when she opened her eyes and gave him a heavenly smile of recognition as he blew her a kiss, made her a funny little bow, and placed the bouquet beside her. I have another unforgettable picture of the two old people together. My father was not particularly absent-minded, but when he was his mistakes were often quite amusing.   Many times at a meal, if we handed him a plate to pass, he would gravely remove a cherry or plum stone from his mouth, put it on the plate, and hand it back to us.   On one occasion when he was staying at Hindhead, he had an engagement for an important business interview in town, and on the way up in the train he noticed to his dismay he had put on his black evening trousers with his new blue coat and waistcoat.   During the last years of his life he was completely absorbed in political work, and on three occasions, when he stood still thinking in the middle of Finchley Road, he was knocked down by motor-cars.   The first time Dr. Stewart Mackintosh was passing in his car and brought him back.   My father was very much shaken, and we put him on his bed; my mother lay down beside the poor bewildered old man, and, stroking his cheek, she said in the most loving, comforting tones, "It's all right, Henry, my dear, I'm here; it's quite all right, I am with you."

My mother's death was the severest blow for all her family.   She was an admirable woman, and always utterly selfless in her devotion to her husband, and to her children. The following incident is illuminating.   Henry Arthur was very fond of a game of piquet or cribbage, which distracted him after his work, and very often he wanted her to play with him when she was feeling ill and distressed. I said to her once, "But, darling, why on earth do you play with him when you don't feel up to it?"   She replied very simply, "Because it is my duty."

Her death was a greater loss to my father than to any other member of her family.   No one gave him such complete and unselfish care and devotion, and he missed her unceasingly.   His sorrow was augmented by his regret for the many occasions when he had not been kind to her.   He was glad to remember that on 31st December, 1923, three weeks before her death, he went up to her bedroom at 12 o'clock to wish her a happy New Year, and, as she turned to him and nodded and smiled her good wishes, he spelt out on his hands in the deaf and dumb alphabet—"The best wife a man ever had." After his death I found one of the printed cards which had been sent to various people in 1924, thanking them for their sympathy. Across it H. A. J. had written, "I will abide by it."

At the time of my mother's death Henry Arthur was in bed with influenza, and, though he disliked the idea of a nurse, we had to get one for him. It was singularly fortunate for my father, and for all of us, that it was Nurse Lilian Shipsey who came to look after him. It is almost impossible to express our gratitude to her for her unceasing and devoted care of my father during the four years she was with him. Very soon after Nurse Shipsey came, she said to him one night when he was in bed, and she had settled him down, "Have you everything you want for the night, Mr. Jones?" and he replied, "Everything, except peace of mind, Nannie." Thereafter the exchange of these words became a nightly ceremony which nothing would have induced either of them to forgo. Although Henry Arthur was very difficult in many ways, and so completely wrapped up in his misery that he never forgot himself for a moment, he did appreciate his nurse's care and devotion.

My father was greatly pleased with the four-volume library edition of his plays, which was edited by his old friend Clayton Hamilton and published in 1925. During the preparation of these volumes Henry Arthur and Clayton Hamilton exchanged many interesting letters. Soon after they first became friends they established a regular correspondence, which continued until my father's death. Henry Arthur was touched and delighted by the immense pains taken by Mr. Hamilton, as also by the penetrating and just criticisms contained in his several introductions.

My father hoped the edition would be published in England, and he wrote the following chaffing letter to Sir Frederick Macmillan:

"28th September, 1925.

"MY DEAR MACMILLAN,

"I hesitate to put before you a scheme that may involve your firm in bankruptcy. You know what a 'worst' seller I am. It is one of the vanities of my old age to have the four-volume library edition of my plays published in England. Can't you come to some arrangement with Little, Brown? There is not the least chance of your making any profit out of the transaction, but I feel sure that God would reward you, either in this world or in the next. Even if he didn't, you would all your life have the satisfaction of knowing that you had done a good turn to the English Drama. And this would also be a consoling thought on your death-bed. With these pious aspirations for your spiritual welfare and a hint how to secure it, believe me,

"Cordially yours,

"HENRY ARTHUR JONES."

The English edition was published by Macmillan.

The year 1925 was to bring my father the intense pleasure of seeing his old friend Brander Matthews, who came over to England for the last time. We saw him several times during his visit, and we went to the theatre with him. One of my happiest memories is that of the two old friends hobnobbing together; but I thought how fragile dear Mr. Matthews seemed in comparison with my father, who was on the crest of his last wave of energy and activity.

During this outburst of work Henry Arthur wrote a fine little article for the twenty-fifth anniversary of the overseas edition of the *Daily Mail*. It appeared on 21st November, 1925. He said: "I try to picture to myself all the millions of Englishmen, born or descended, who are banished from this dear, dear land. They are scattered on every continent, on every lonely isle; in every nation and every tribe of men; in barren wastes and fertile plains; in the icy zones of the poles, and in the burning tropics; in all climates from the furthermost pitch of North-western Canada to the southermost cape of New Zealand. . . . Never has any nation in the past mustered such a company of her sons to span the world with the greatness and worth of her mighty deeds, and to civilise and enlarge the peoples by the benignity of her sway.   Nor in the future will any nation arise that shall pour upon the earth a kindred breed of famous men to claim for their native land so sure and proud a title to enduring admiration and renown, and the praise and honour of mankind. . . ."

He sent a copy of this article to Sir John Martin-Harvey, who, in writing to thank him, said:

"25th November, 1925.

"MY DEAR HENRY ARTHUR JONES,

"You send me a most splendid and inspiring message. I am often asked for 'a talk'—in fact, my tours in Canada are one unending 'talk'—and though there is no great difficulty in interesting those dear Canadians, I couldn't hope to frame a message so eloquent and so stirring as yours.   So I shall jolly well just read it to them whenever I have a chance—as your message, of course!

"Always sincerely yours,

"MARTIN-HARVEY."

From 1921 onwards I lived at Kidderpore Avenue, and after my mother's death my father relied on my companionship more and more as the years went by.   He could not bear me out of his sight, and I could never dine out unless I arranged for someone to take my place.   I often resented the thraldom of hardly ever being able to go out when I wanted to, and we sometimes had "a few words"; but the dear old man was so very pathetic in his dependence on me, so unhappy and distressed when there was even a temporary cloud between us, that I always felt sorry and ashamed that I could not devote myself to him to the complete exclusion of all other interests. During the last three years of his life I gave up all my work and became his secretary. He used to say I was the best secretary he ever had, which was very far from being true; but, as his daughter, I had sufficient authority to spare him small details and all but the most urgent business matters. It was always very difficult to transact any business for him. He rarely said exactly what he wanted done. He was in many ways unreliable and evasive, and often held out hopes he was unable to fulfil. He carried out all his contracts to the letter, but it was not easy to pin him down to exact facts or statements. Perhaps when a particular actor had been engaged for a part in one of his plays, if H. A. J. was at all doubtful of his ability to interpret the part, he would see one or two other people about it, as if no definite arrangement had already been made.

Before my mother died, her health was too bad to permit of her going to the theatre, except very occasionally, and I often went with my father in her place. A first night in which he was greatly interested was that of Conrad's play *The Secret Agent,* produced on 2nd November, 1922. He seldom read a novel, but he liked *Chance* and *Victory* very much. On the day of production H. A. J. sent Conrad a little note wishing him success. He received the following charming acknowledgment:

> "Hotel Curzon,
> "Curzon Street,
> "Mayfair.
> "*3rd November, 1922.*

"Cher Maître—à nous tous,

"Let me thank you with all possible warmth for your kind note of welcome to the 'youngest' dramatist. This kindness so characteristic of you has touched me deeply; it brought vividly to my mind the day when dear Henry

James presented me to you at the Reform Club, the friendliness of your words of appreciation, which I was so proud
to hear, and the grip of your hand.

"If I deserve this word of welcome at all, it is perhaps
by this—that I can assure you that this work, undertaken
of course from impulse, is the product of earnest meditation—even in its defects—and not of airy self-confidence.

"Let me subscribe myself with real gratitude,
                                    "Affectionately yours,
                                            "JOSEPH CONRAD."

"Will you give my affectionate thanks to Mrs. Thorne
for her precious autograph? It is so much like her delightful self."

Henry Arthur was delighted with the way Conrad addressed him, and when we spoke of him, which we did
very often, he would say to me, "How was it Conrad began
his letter?" A few days later, in reply to a letter from
Henry Arthur about the play, which was a great failure,
Conrad wrote to him the following illuminating letter:

                                    "Oswalds,
                                    "Bishopsbourne,
                                        "Kent.
                             "*7th November, 1922.*
"MY VERY DEAR SIR,

"As you see, one of my very few virtues is the virtue of
obedience.

"It was very comforting to read your words of appreciation, where appreciation could be given. Of course I
felt at times the play doomed even before the first night, of
which I had a report from my wife—who now even was
hopeful. But even a play written by an angel could not
have stood up against the weight of a unanimous Press.

The most piously disposed would have been scared off.
There is something awe-inspiring in a hostile cry from
many throats in unison on a single note.   Let this then be
la mort sans phrases.   I ought to have said *condemnatory*
rather than hostile, for of course there was no hostility.
Rather the reverse.   I was very sensible of that while wad-
ing through the Press-cuttings—a thing I have not done
for many years.   What, however, is really painful in this
affair is the thought of loyal work wasted, of men and
women devoted to their art and to whom the success of the
play would have meant so much more than it could have
meant to myself.

"*Voilà*.   One doesn't think till too late—and then
comes remorse, a decent thing, in so far that it is much less
comfortable than callousness, but otherwise of no great
account.   So I am not boasting; I am just telling you in a
spirit of repentance and for the good of my soul.   A sort
of *Confession après la mort*.   That situation, though
fraught with grim irony, could not be presented on any
stage.   It would be misunderstood and would ruin the
play.

"It is most kind of you to ask me to dine.   Just now I
am really not well and, like Mr. Verloc, 'want to be looked
after.'   It has nothing to do with the grimness of the
situation.   I was feeling far from well even before the play
was accepted.   May I write to you when I feel fit to come
up?   And I hope we may have Mrs. Thorne for company.
I am afraid I have shocked and disgusted her on Friday by
my manners and speeches which fell far short of that serene amenity which marks a *vrai homme du monde,* and,
strangely enough, the faces of hairdressers' dummies.
Perhaps because both are strangers to remorse.   My
humble apologies and my repentant love to her.

"I am, dear sir,

"Your ever grateful and affectionate,

"Joseph Conrad."

A CABINET OF "FIRST-CLASS BRAINS" AS SKETCHED BY MATT

In the event of the General Election resulting in a political deadlock, why not call an alternative Government of "first-class brains"? Matt has responded to the suggestion here. The figures are : 1, Mr. Arnold Bennett, Home Secretary ; 2, Mr. H. G. Wells, Minister of Aviation ; 3, Mr. G. K. Chesterton, Local Government Board ; 4, Mr. Bernard Shaw, Prime Minister ; 5, Mr. Rudyard Kipling, Colonies ; 6, Sir Hall Caine, Chancellor of the Exchequer ; 7, Mr. Joseph Conrad, Admiralty ; 8, Mr. Henry Arthur Jones, Board of Trade ; 9, Mr. Thomas Hardy, Minister of Pensions ; 10, Sir J. M. Barrie, Secretary for Scotland ; 11, Mr. Edmund Gosse, Foreign Secretary ; 12, Sir John Lavery ; 13, Mr. Augustus John ; 14, Sir William Orpen—Ministers without portfolio.

FROM "THE GRAPHIC" OF DECEMBER 1ST, 1923

(By courtesy of that journal)

From December 1925 to January 1927 Henry Arthur was to enjoy his last year of work and activity. During that last final spurt of energy we had many pleasant jaunts together, including several first nights. He made a point of seeking out Mr. Malcolm Watson and Mr. S. R. Littlewood, two old friends whose dramatic criticisms in the *Daily Telegraph* and *Morning Post* he never failed to read. He always hoped he would meet his dear old friend Pinero. He spoke of him constantly during the last years, and always with great affection and admiration. He never felt the slightest jealousy of his great contemporary, and he regretted deeply that they saw each other infrequently. He was singularly free from jealousy of other dramatists. I never remember him showing any trace of it in speaking of the work of other men, though, of course, he criticised plays. He had a profound admiration for the work of Mr. W. S. Maugham; and, although he did not know him very well, he had a cordial regard for him. He said to me once, "He's a confoundly good writer, and he's a man who knows there's such a thing as English literature."

He was very fond of Ian Hay, and would speak of him as a "dear fellow." *The First Hundred Thousand* is one of the few books, apart from the old classics, I remember his reading twice. He never spoke of Barrie without saying "He's a charming little genius"; and he never understood why Tree had not realised that *Peter Pan* was a masterpiece when he read it. He did not like most of Shaw's plays; he would say, "Shaw isn't a dramatist; he is a journalist with a sense of the theatre," and he would add, "He doesn't really love his characters." I remember, though, what a delightful evening we both had at the first night of *Androcles and the Lion*. I have never heard my father laugh so much in a theatre. He enjoyed the play enormously. Some years later, writing to me, he said:

". . . I went to the Little Theatre last night and saw *Fanny's First Play* and was hugely delighted—had a thorough good evening—what a brilliant chaos it is— Shaw's world would march all right if there were no children in the world, and only men and women. . . ."

In another letter, written in 1909, he said:

. . . "Going to see *Blanco Posnet* on Sunday night. I like it very much from reading it. . . ."

In a letter to G. B. S., written in 1898, H. A. J. told him very frankly what he thought about his plays:

"5th May, 1898.

"I have read the plays with varied feelings—at times interested, here and there exhilarated, sometimes bored, sometimes, oftentimes provoked, but always with respectful attention. Much of them is not dramatic and would never be interesting in any circumstances to any possible audience, but there is a good deal that is very dramatic and would fail on our English stage because of the defective machinery now in use for conveying the author's meaning and design to our not over-intellectual audiences —by defective machinery, I mean those people from whose mouths our words issue in such a way that sometimes their purport is known, and occasionally a gleam of meaning is seen to be attached to them. And for this we ought to be grateful. There is too much of the journalist and pamphleteer in some of the pieces. Now, I am falsely accused sometimes of being a preacher—there never was a greater mistake—but you really do preach. I've said nothing of the constant jets and spurts of wit that are always dashing against our faces—that goes without saying in any and everything you write. I should like to talk over the plays with you when you have a day or so to spare—perhaps next month."

Many years later he again wrote to Shaw about his plays in the following amusing but naughty letter:

"13th November, 1913.

"MY DEAR SHAW,

"I have a young friend—a very young friend—who hails your recent enlargement of the bounds of morality. He had written a play which seems to me likely to advance your views—if we can only get it produced. Its *dramatis personæ* are five Hottentots, eleven monkeys, and thirteen goats. They are all quite naked, and delightfully unashamed. There is no coherent story, no vestige of a plot, and no discoverable purpose. The characters simply come on, and talk, talk, talk, talk, in the frankest way—I am sure it will please you. The dialogue is not so witty as your own, but it is far more fearless. My own criticism of the piece is that the eleven monkeys seem to me superfluous; our simian gibberings and antics being already sufficiently reproduced in our musical comedies and revues. However, my young friend's monkeys have the advantage of being quite naked, while their congeners in revues and musical comedies are partially dressed.

"And now, how can we get our young friend's play produced? I have sent him on to you, as being the very man to see it through. You may object that if this play is done, you may find it difficult to go one better. Still I take it that we are out to shock people one way or the other, and if this primary object is attained, I hope you will be content with some measure of temporary self-effacement.

"Steadying myself to regain my mental and moral balance,

"I am,

"Always cordially yours,

"HENRY ARTHUR JONES."

He thought a great many modern plays were tawdry and cynical, with cheap, ephemeral themes. One of my sisters said that *Jew Suss* would not make a good play, and H. A. J. replied, "I'd engage to make a play about two flies crawling up a window-pane." But, in spite of this remark, he said to me once, "You must have a big theme if you're going to do a big play. You can't do a big thing on a chorus girl." My father did not like Ibsen, but he hated Tchekov and other Russian dramatists. He went to the first night of *The Cherry Orchard*, and he was almost incoherent about it on his return. He said that the whole play gave him the impression of someone who had visited a lunatic asylum and taken down everything the inmates said. In his Notes he wrote, "I was at the first performance of *The Cherry Orchard*. I noticed that some in the audience pretended to enjoy themselves. I am resolved not to enjoy myself at the performance of a play which bores me." He wrote a very mischievous letter to Nigel Playfair about it, which began, "Oh, my God! Nigel Playfair, oh, my God!" and he went on to say that when he thought of all the happy hours he had spent at the Lyric, Hammersmith, he could almost go down on his knees and embrace Sir Nigel, but when he thought of Sir Nigel taking "several hours of the short life which remains to me to see *The Cherry Orchard*—oh, my God! Nigel Playfair." Unfortunately, my father's opinion of the play was given some publicity; there was a newspaper controversy, and Sir Nigel wrote to H. A. J. about it. He replied at once:

"16th June, 1925.

"My dear Nigel Playfair,

"I did not write to the critic of the *Daily Express*, but in a letter to Basil Macdonald Hastings I told him I agreed with him in his opinion of *The Cherry Orchard*. I did not intend the letter to be published, nor was I asked for

my permission.   However, I don't suppose the controversy will do the piece any harm, and for your sake I am
glad it is a success.

"Always yours,
"HENRY ARTHUR JONES."

"PS.—Please tell Duff and Arnold Bennett."

Henry Arthur wrote again to say how sorry he was,
ending his letter by saying "I hope you will accept my
expression of real regret."   Sir Nigel replied to this letter,
and said:

"20th June, 1925.

"MY DEAR HENRY ARTHUR JONES,

"You must not worry, I quite understand and certainly I
should not dream of letting anything interfere with any
pleasant feelings.

"Yours sincerely,
"NIGEL PLAYFAIR."

He had a very great admiration for Sir Nigel as an actor,
a manager, and a producer, because his work and influence
have been of the greatest benefit to the stage and the cause
of fine drama in England.   H. A. J. always said that, "If
we had a National Theatre, Playfair should be at the head
of it."

Shortly after the production of *The Cherry Orchard*, we
went to the first night of Pirandello's play *And That's the
Truth If You Think It is*.   H. A. J. wrote to Sir Nigel the
next day:

"18th September, 1925.

"I enjoyed myself very much last night, and nobody
shall persuade me that I did not.   But the author has not
remembered the second of Aristotle's two great rules in

playwriting—(1) The plot is the first thing. (2) The end (*dénouement*) is the *chief* thing. I think for the popularity of the play, that Miss Nancy Price's and Claude Rains' parts should be played all through with their tongues in their cheeks. They are both exceedingly fine performances, but they bewilder the average spectator by their tragic significance. I think they should be played with *mock* and not real intensity, with sly but obvious hints to the audience that they are fooling the gossips. . . . Forgive my impertinence. I should like to see the play succeed, as it deserves."

A first night we both enjoyed enormously was that of *The Last of Mrs. Cheyney*. Before the production Henry Arthur wrote the following amusing letter to Miss Gladys Cooper, his application for tickets having been refused:

"*17th September, 1925.*

"DEAR GLADYS COOPER,

"I hoped to see your first performance of *Mrs. Cheyney,* but Mr. Arnold at the box office has returned my cheque for two stalls. I must endure it, but I shall always count it as one of the major misfortunes of my chequered life. I remember that Lord Randolph Churchill was refused admission to the select coterie who assemble in the gambling rooms at Monte Carlo, and according to Byron, George the Third's claims to join a company not less august and purified than a St. James's first night audience were strenuously disputed, and his defunct Majesty only managed to slip into Heaven while Saint Peter's attention was diverted in the scuffle caused by Southey reading his poems. Although my merits are less discernible than were those of George the Third, I hoped that by some favourable misallotment of seats I might have been able to congratulate you on another triumph. I must content myself with sending my heartiest good wishes to you, Ellis

Jeffreys, du Maurier and Lonsdale.   I shall look in on the 500th night.   Meantime let me subscribe myself the humblest of your admirers,

"HENRY ARTHUR JONES."

Needless to say, two stalls were sent to him immediately.

We also went to the first night of John Barrymore's production of *Hamlet* at the Haymarket Theatre. Shortly afterwards Henry Arthur took the chair at a luncheon given in honour of John Barrymore in April 1925. In his speech he said, "If my words should fail to be adequate to the occasion, I offer you an alternative to listening to them which perhaps many of you will gladly accept. You can look at Miss Fay Compton and Miss Gladys Cooper. Many of you have seen Miss Compton's infinitely moving and graceful and lovely Ophelia. It lies too deep for tears. Surely Ophelia has never been more poignantly and sweetly rendered. The other night, when I was watching Miss Gladys Cooper's Iris, I thought of Rossetti's line, 'Beauty like hers is genius.' We will not quote that line to Miss Cooper because when we see her on the stage she makes us think chiefly of her acting. The delightful secret look she throws at her lover in the breakfast scene at Cadenabbia! I've never had a look like that thrown at me. And now that I'm seventy-four, I never shall. Now I must get on to John Barrymore. Before I speak of John Barrymore's Hamlet, I will acknowledge a personal debt to him. I owe him a great deal for having an uncle called John Drew. John Drew has played my Wyndham parts in America with the same success that Wyndham played them in London. . . . On behalf of John Drew I claim that he has inherited much of his nephew's talent and ability for interpreting Shakespeare and Jones. . . . I have seen all the leading Hamlets of the English theatre since Fechter in 1869. Above them all was Henry Irving. Irving's Hamlet at its best—sometimes it was very bad and incoherent—but at its best Henry Irving's Hamlet lifted itself out of all comparison with all other Hamlets of all ages. With that exception, John Barrymore's takes its place in the front rank of great English and American Hamlets of the last two generations. It has great fire and intensity, much tenderness, unity and consistency of conception, freedom from affectation and solemn pretentiousness, straightforward force of simple elocution. It has sovereign merits and no remembered blemishes. . . . One word about John Barrymore the man. He is free from the vanities, affectations, and selfishness that are occasionally to be detected in leading actors. He delights to give every member of his company full scope to score to the utmost. I am very proud to claim him as my friend. . . ."

Of all the plays we saw in 1925, Hardy's *Tess of the D'Urbervilles* interested my father more deeply than any other. He loved the book, which he had read more than once—a thing he very rarely did with a novel. Many years previously Hardy wrote to ask my father's advice about a possible production of the play. He said:

"16th February, 1897.

"DEAR HENRY JONES,

"An American arrangement of *Tess,* based on my draft and suggestions, is to be produced in New York the first week in March, on which production no expense has been spared. Meanwhile my agents over here say I ought to have a copyright performance here on the same day. Now, all this fills me with consternation, for I had secretly hoped that *Tess* was going to fall through altogether, as I have been, and am, more interested in other labours. However, prudence is prudence; and can you tell me how one sets about this sort of thing? Are there people who take it in hand for so much? Some time ago several people well known in London society said they would like to take part in such a performance, and no doubt they would still; 'it would be such fun,' but fancy me getting up a play. My impression is that it is not necessary, but I am not sure.

"Yours sincerely,
"THOMAS HARDY."

We were at the first night at the Barnes Theatre, and, although H. A. J. was seventy-four, he made the long journey to Barnes a few weeks later to see the play a second time, and when the production came to Golders Green he saw it again. My father was deeply moved by the play and the fine acting, and he wrote the following letter to Hardy:

"8th September, 1925.

"DEAR THOMAS HARDY,

"You may like to know what I felt and thought at the first performance of *Tess*. All through, it was an evening of great emotion and deep interest to me. The massive quality of your noble work in the novel stood plainly out in the play like one of the pillars of Stonehenge. There were no grave faults of technique, and there were some excellencies due, I daresay, to the fact that you are not a professional playwright. I challenged the appearance of Alec on the bridal night immediately before the confession. It disturbed the unity of the impression that the scene in the novel had left in my mind. It makes a double distraction in Tess's already too distracted heart, and it divides the volume of interest and movement towards the dreadful moment of the confession. However, Alec had to be thereabouts brought into the play, and I do not pretend to tell you how you ought to have done it. The confession remains one of the most poignant and absorbing scenes in all the range of the drama. It shows what great fame you would have won as a dramatist, if you had given yourself to the theatre—which luckily for English literature you

did not.   The last act was also most deeply moving, and
the end had large solemn tragic beauty and impressiveness.
I found it true to Arnold's favourite word—'Fortifying.'
The play fulfils the purpose of tragedy and purges the
mind by moving us to pity and terror—oh, the deepest,
deepest pity.

"It was beautifully and appropriately played throughout.   Miss Gwen Ffrangcon Davies wrung my heart in the
third and fourth acts.   My daughter and I found ourselves with streaming cheeks.   Miss Davies was so un-
forced, so sincere and restrained.   There was not one
wrong note in her performance.   I cannot remember when
I have been so much touched.   She must not be judged
because she did not render those aspects of the character
which are in the novel and not in the play.   She played
unerringly those scenes which you gave her to play.   I am
sure the play would have lost immensely its beauty
and pathos if Tess had been acted by a robust wench in
a robust way.   That character is not in the play you have
written.

"Ion Swinley, in the measure that his part gave him
the opportunity, is equally deserving of praise.   Angel
Clare is a difficult part to render on the stage in a way that
will send it home to the average spectator.   Ion Swinley's
performance showed careful study and insight, and was of
great value to the play.   His fine voice and presence
helped to make the part attractive.   The most thankless
part of Alec was also capitally played.   The peasants were
credible and veritable rustics.   The Dorset dialect was
well sustained.   Our stage peasants are generally accomplished linguists, and speak a polyglot blend of Yorkshire, Norfolk and Somerset, with marked preference for
'Zummerset.'

"The difficulties of adapting a novel to the stage are
rarely understood and never appreciated.   Aristotle has
illuminated them in the distinction he draws between the

play and the epic. There can be no true or quite satisfactory adaptation of a novel to the stage. To the extent that a play is a consistent organic whole it must differ widely from the novel from which it is quarried, not only in the course of its action, but also in the necessary adjustment of each character to the action. Again, the novelist in writing a play is largely deprived of his chief tool—his style. De Maupassant, whose style is the perfection of delicate jewellery in story-telling, emerged as a crude vulgar melodramatist when he was not at all unskilfully adapted at our favourite St. James's Theatre. . . .

"I offer you my warmest and most sympathetic congratulations on *Tess*. I felt that I must put down these thoughts while they were fresh in my mind. . . . I regret that I have seen nothing of you these last tremendous years. Our last two meetings were in the theatre, when you came with Professor Bradley and me to see *Othello*, and when you had a seat in my box on the first night of *The Case of Rebellious Susan*. If you come to London you will give me a chance to shake hands with you, will you not?

> "Faithfully yours,
> "Henry Arthur Jones."

Hardy's reply was:

> "*13th September, 1925.*

"Dear H. Arthur Jones,

"It was with much pleasure that I received your letter telling me of your visit to the Barnes Theatre for the performance of the *Tess* play. An experienced judgment like your own has a settling effect upon the chaos of opinions I have read in the newspapers as to the general effect of the production, though of course I make allowance for your indulgence towards the manifold defects in the construction of the play. As you probably know, it was written thirty years ago, when both you and I were younger, and our views of the theatre—at any rate mine—were not quite the same as they are now. If I had adapted the novel in those days, I daresay I should have done the job differently; but when, quite by accident, and at the request of the amateur players here, I looked it up, I found I could not get back to the subject closely enough to handle it anew. However, all independent observers agree with you in saying that it did not fail to move the emotions, which is quite as much as one could expect, though one critic, by the way, said that the audience 'all went to be moved, but none were moved'—a puzzling statement which I pass over in the face of the other testimony. I am quite of your opinion in respect to Miss Ffrangcon Davies. She has been down here, and we liked her very much; her great intelligence, too, was striking, while she was free from the vanities one too often finds among the stage people.

"It is a long time since we met. I well remember your *Case of Rebellious Susan,* and, of course, several of your other plays. I sometimes wonder that new plays from your hand do not appear oftener now that the terrible Victorian restrictions are removed, and events can be allowed to develop on the stage as they would in real life.

"I go to London very seldom, finding that, though I am quite well while here, the least thing upsets me when I am away, which is, I suppose, not unnatural at my age.

"I gather from your presence at Barnes that you keep fairly well. My wife can remember meeting you, and sends her kind regards. She went up to the Thursday matinée, but was not there at the first night.

"How many have disappeared for another stage since we first sat in a theatre!

"Yours sincerely,

"THOMAS HARDY."

Henry Arthur wrote again:

"16th September, 1925.

"DEAR THOMAS HARDY,

"I was much gratified by your kind and intimate letter. I did not understand some of the notices, neither their tone, nor their point of view, nor the account they gave of the play. But there has been much freakishness in dramatic criticisms during the last twenty years. . . .

"During and since the War I have been drawn away from the theatre. We seem to be tending towards a social and political catastrophe. I have been busy in controversy and propagandism—a dreadful destiny in one's old age. But I am coming back to the theatre as soon as I can get my hands and brain free. I had a great success with *The Lie* at the New Theatre fifteen months ago.

"I envy you your serenity. I remember, when I visited you at Dorchester in 1895, thinking that I could not live so much in seclusion. But how wise you have been.

"I think you may like to see a paper of mine on 'Religion,' which, with some deletions, will be published in the *Daily Express* on next Thursday. I find my heart has softened towards all creeds in these last few years. I would like to think that your own outlook is less stern and bleak as you draw near to the nobility of death.

"With my kindest thoughts,
"Faithfully yours,
"HENRY ARTHUR JONES."

Hardy told my father that he had never put an incident or a character in one of his books that he had not warranty for in real life.

The last play we went to see, only a month or two before his death, was *Many Waters*. My father took a deep interest in Monckton Hoffe's career, and for many years he had predicted a great future for him. When the play was produced, Henry Arthur wrote to congratulate Mr. Hoffe, from whom he received the following delightful letter:

"21st July, 1928.

"DEAR MR. HENRY ARTHUR JONES,

"I cannot tell you how much I appreciate the very kind motives that prompted you to write to me as you did. I feel quite convinced that your transcending purpose and vitality creep somehow into the ink and paper of a letter from you, for to have it even in one's pocket is indeed a most stimulating sensation. I hope you will be sure and let me know when you are coming to see my play.

"I may mention that there was a young man once who went up into the gallery of Wyndham's Theatre for six nights in succession to see a play called *Mrs. Dane's Defence,* and that some years later its author promised that young man, then grown older, that he would send him a signed copy of that well-remembered inspiration.

"Very, very sincerely yours,

"MONCKTON HOFFE."

Of course H. A. J. sent Mr. Hoffe a copy of *Mrs. Dane's Defence.*

When we went to see *Many Waters,* Henry Arthur was feeling very ill before we left for the theatre, and during the first act he showed evident signs of an approaching heart-attack, so that I had to take him home immediately the act was over. His great courage during these heart-attacks was beyond all praise. It is well known that the pain of angina pectoris is more unbearable than any other pain, and that a prominent symptom is an appalling feeling of impending death. In one attack, as soon as he could speak, he said, "I do hope I haven't disturbed Dorinda"—her room was above his. In his second attack, just as he was getting easier, when Dr. Mackintosh warned him he must not exert himself in any way, he replied with a wistful smile, "No, the only thing to do at seventy-five, is as Mistress Quickly said to Falstaff, 'When are you going to patch up your old body for Heaven?'"   My father often said he thought there must be something the matter with his heart, but I always replied very scornfully, "How you can imagine you've got anything wrong with your heart when you remember what Mummy looked like in her attacks, I don't know—it's only that wretched catarrh on your chest," while Nurse and Dr. Mackintosh would say much the same thing, and I believe we almost succeeded in dispelling all his fears.

In spite of a highly strung disposition, he was remarkably free from morbid ideas as to the state of his health. He never fancied he had a pain, and his doctors and nurses knew that when he mentioned any particular symptom it was not an imaginary one.   At this time, when he was suffering, not only from angina pectoris, but also from chronic catarrh, a double rupture, the after-effects of three severe operations, and cataract, he said in complacent tones one day, "I may say I've never had a sore throat or a headache."

CHAPTER XVIII

DURING the whole of 1925, although my father was working, he did so with increasing difficulty; as he said himself, "I have to flog the old machine to keep it going." He relied more and more on the effects of alcohol. None of us ever saw him drink between meals, and I should be surprised if anyone told me he had ever taken a cocktail, but he was very fond of wine. He was so exhausted after his morning's work that he would drink a tumbler or more of sherry at lunch, and again at dinner. In vain Dr. Mackintosh warned him of the increasing damage he was doing to his kidneys. He could not believe that a stimulant to which he had been accustomed for so many years could be harmful. He wrote one or two letters to the papers.on Prohibition, and was vastly pleased when he was quoted very generally in the Press as having said that he had drunk a bottle of wine every day for forty years and that he was none the worse for it.

When Nurse and I, acting under Dr. Mackintosh's orders, tried to cut down his allowance of alcohol, he was just like a fractious baby crying for its bottle. We watered the decanter of whisky, and that was successful for a short time, but when he found out the unfortunate maid came in for a totally unmerited scolding. Sometimes he became quite furious with us when we remonstrated with him; he got so cross that we were afraid it might bring on a heart-attack. But he was not a bad-tempered man, in spite of his many quarrels; nor was he noticeably quick-tempered.

His kidney trouble became so serious that Nurse Shipsey returned early in January 1926, to remain with us until he died.   Various palliative measures were tried, but they were unsuccessful, and for the most part only increased the poor old man's sufferings and discomfort.   Mr. Kidd performed supra-pubic cystotomy in July 1926, and he came through the operation magnificently.

Just before my father's operation he received the following beautiful, tender letter from "Max":

> "Villino Chiaro,
> "Rapallo.
> *"14th May, 1926.*

"My dear Henry Arthur,

"I have been thinking of you much during the past horrible week or so[1]—and now I write to say how glad I am with you that England has done well.   I suppose there may be difficulties yet; but they won't matter so much: the long-impending big fight has been fought and won. England has all sorts of faults—dullnesses, stupidities, heavy frivolities, constantly pointed out by you.   But in politics somehow she always is—somehow slowly, dully, but splendidly—all right.   I have often thought, in reading your brilliant and violent rebukes of her, that you hadn't quite as much faith in her as she deserves.   You didn't overstate her dangers; but I felt that you believed not quite enough in her power to meet these and deal with these successfully in her own fumbling and muzzy way, by her own dim (damnably dim, you would say) lights. You are a die-hard, and she is a die-soft.   She says mildly, 'No violence, pray!   I quite see your points of view, dear gentlemen all!   I'm full of faults.   Really I rather doubt whether I deserve to survive.   Yet I hope, I even intend, to do so' . . . and she *does*—the dear old thing!   *Brava, bravissima,* dear silly old thing!

"Dear Henry Arthur, I know how happy you are feeling

---

[1] The reference is to the General Strike.

—and I write to add my happiness to yours. The past week has made for my wife and me 'a goblin of the sun,' and the big roses in our small garden looked horrible. In writing to me at about Christmas-time, you said I did well to be out here, because of all the trouble brewing in England. But really out here, in this alien golden clime, one feels more acutely any dangers to England. What a relief it was to us both, my wife and me, when, early in 1915, we settled down in England! And Civil War is of course much more distressing to the heart and to the imagination than war with any number of more or less natural enemies. And oh, what pæans our hearts sing that the wretched affair is, to all intents and purposes, over—and that the right side has won.

"I think King George's Message to the people very finely composed. I read it with emotion. Had you been he, the message would have been still finer, and I should have read it with still greater emotion. But it wouldn't have been so exactly right for the occasion. For the purpose of interpreting the deepest feelings of the British People, I back Hanover against Bucks every time!— though I sometimes wish Hanover had a little of Bucks's sparkle, all the same.

"Your affectionate,
"MAX BEERBOHM."

"PS.—I never can remember the Christian or surname of anybody I haven't met constantly. Thus I forget those of the charming and gifted young man who was my fellow-guest when I dined with you last May at the Athenæum. Otherwise I would ask you to give him my kindest regards. The name of DORIS does not escape me. And to her I send my love.

"PPS.—Old friendship—there's nothing very much better than that. I am reminded of this truism by my PS. about dining with you last May at the Athenæum. I have my faults (like England), but am sensitive to impressions and retentive of these. I do so well remember being ushered in by a waiter to that Writing-Room to the right of the hall. Up from a table rises H. A., and quickly advances, with that forward thrust of the head (that I have so often caricatured), and looking not a day older, though it was long since I had met him; and with just the same kind eager look in his eyes. And, as we shook hands, he placed his left hand over my right hand—and then I placed *my* left hand over *his*, in glad response.

"Whatever happens to the world, things of this kind will go on. Life will always have dear good moments.

"M. B."

H. A. J. replied to this letter during his convalescence. Max answered:

"Villino Chiaro,
"Rapallo,
"8th August, 1926.

"My dear Henry Arthur,

"You had no business to write to me. I resented your letter very much. It seemed to me an impudent defiance of all the laws of convalescence. However, you have always been pugnacious, and have now reached an age when you are past all hope of reformation: doctors and daughters and nurses can but bow their heads beneath your indomitable will and place the inkpot beside the cup of chicken-broth. And of course—in spite of all my disapproval—I was immensely glad to behold the Henrico-Arthurian caligraphy, and very grateful, and much touched —touched by your kindness in thanking me for that little sketch of Irving. Doris (whom, please, thank from me for her delightful accompanying letter) said that you would like to use the sketch as an illustration in the course of your study of Irving. And of course it doesn't need saying that I should be very proud of seeing that sketch in such a setting. I am so glad it appealed to you. I think it *has* caught something of the subject—the Cabotin-turned-Cardinal as it were. Forgive this cheap alliteration! But you are not to tell me that you forgive it. At most, you are to dip a clean pen in the chicken-broth and write 'I forgive you' in the air. Sympathetic aerial rays will waft the message to this address. As to G. B. S., I entirely understand your feelings about his vagaries. It is very queer that a man should be so gifted as he is (in his own particular line nobody has been so gifted, I think, since Voltaire) and so liable to make a fool of himself. I never read anything of his without wishing that he had never been born *and* hoping that he will live to a very ripe old age! One of the reasons is that he, like you, is entirely free from any kind of malice. That is one of his great points. And that is why you would, I am sure, be very willing to shake hands with the demon!

"Love to Doris and to all your house,

"From your affectionate,

"MAX BEERBOHM."

This operation was a fresh martyrdom for my father, and the misery of his existence, a mass of complicated dressings and tubes, became quite impossible, even for a man of his lion-hearted courage and endurance. In spite of the great risk, Mr. Kidd advised a further operation for the removal of the prostate, and early in December he went into a nursing-home in Dorset Square. He made a splendid, uncomplicated recovery, and I believe he created a record by leaving the nursing-home a week earlier than is usually permitted after so grave an operation. In the first few days he was never left alone for a single moment. He complained that he could not sleep at night, and when Dr. Mackintosh said, "How is that?" he replied in bitter tones, "It's a great many years since I've slept with a light or a female in my room at night, and I don't like it."

Whilst he was at the home, two of his oldest friends, Ellen Terry and Sir James Crichton-Browne, came to see him. Their visits delighted him, but he was just a little resentful at the well-being and activity of these two octogenarians. In a letter to Brander Matthews in 1924 he said:

"*9th July, 1924.*

"MY DEAR BRANDER,

". . . Yesterday we motored down to have tea with Ellen Terry, who is living in a wonderfully preserved old cottage at Smallhythe near Rye. She bought 4 old cottages and built in pairs, with a garden between them. . . . At 76, with bad eyesight, bad hearing, fitful memory, and general infirmity, she is splendidly young and vivacious, with inexhaustible gaiety of heart and her abiding charm. We had a lot of talk of old times, and made comparison of Irving's different characters. I came away much cheered, and also rebuked—for I am still in peevish rebellion against old age, the condition of the Drama, the impending dangers to the British Empire, the clumsy structure of the prostate gland, and other evils that magnify themselves by reason of my enforced leisure. However I hope I am gradually pulling round. All my life I have alternated between extravagant good spirits and these black months with giant despair. I would give much to have a Sunday evening with you. I am sending you by Leider a copy of the original privately printed Chiswick Press edition of *The Liars*.

"Always yours, dear old friend,

"HENRY ARTHUR JONES."

Only those who knew my father intimately and who saw him frequently could realise the misery and despair of the last few years of his life. The mainsprings of his character were courage, industry, and perseverance, and the enforced inactivity caused by ill-health and nervous depression left him like an old machine with only his courage as a working lever.   He never forgot himself for a single moment, and, except when people came to see him, he rarely opened his mouth without speaking about himself; he would complain bitterly of the despair he felt, the uselessness of being alive and unable to work, the horror of sleeplessness.

Although he was completely wrapped up in his own troubles, his natural and unfailing kindness of heart often asserted itself.   His most frequent question to me was, "Is there anything I can do for you, my darling?   Are you sure there is nothing I can do?"   He would ask all his children this question, and sometimes he would sit and puzzle his brains, and then say, "Can't I do something for so and so?"   He was always a loyal and devoted friend, and it was during these years that he realised to the full the sweetness and support of many of his oldest and closest friendships.   He was uneasy unless he saw Sir Emery Walker regularly; I love to remember their welcome to each other and how, when Sir Emery was going to dine with us, as soon as the door-bell rang, H. A. J. would struggle out of his armchair to meet his friend with outstretched hand.

During the last months of his life he went to the Garden Party at Buckingham Palace, to Miss Eva Moore's garden party, and to an "at home" at Lady Alexander's, but these efforts were almost beyond his strength.   In November he insisted, against his doctor's orders, upon going to the private view of Max Beerbohm's caricatures.   He was delighted when his old friends came to see him.   Mr. William Stone, Mr. Malcolm Watson, and Sir Sidney Low were always greatly welcome whilst Mr. Littlewood, Mr. Shelley, and Mr. and Mrs. Percy Allen dined with us almost weekly.   He valued their companionship, which cheered and distracted him without making any demands on his failing powers. Though he was not a witty man, he was always a very interesting and often a brilliant conversationalist, and it was amazing how often he would throw off all signs of depression and weakness, to become an arresting centre of interest, when he had visitors. In spite of the fact that he often dropped out words, or even left a sentence unfinished, he was a very fine *raconteur* and we never tired of hearing him repeat various stories, especially those about Henry Irving, whom he mimicked very well, while he made many penetrating and illuminating comments on his acting. He said once, "The difference between Irving and Tree as actors, if I had to put it in two lines, was that Irving always made a character come to him—Tree went to the character." And on another occasion, "If I could call up from the dead any performance from the past, I shouldn't know whether to choose Edmund Kean's Othello or Irving's Iago"; and he went on to say, "When acting, in long speeches never put down sixpence unless you can put down eightpence or a shilling after it." He made interesting comparisons between Fechter, Irving, and Forbes-Robertson as Hamlet. He said, "Fechter was very fine as Hamlet—a Victor-Hugo Hamlet—robust compared with Irving's. Forbes-Robertson's Hamlet was a young lady's Hamlet compared with Irving's."

Mr. Percy Allen, in an article on my father entitled "A Recollection," published in the *Daily Telegraph* on the 10th January, 1929, told the following story:

"Many an evening, each in his armchair, we talked together of the art that he loved, and unforgettable were these scenes from and comments upon the theatre-world of the past fifty years, presented with a shrewdness of insight and humour and with a vivid power of phrase that made them live while you listened. One after another, out the memories and the criticisms would come—of Tree, 'the man I should choose first for company, of all the actors I have met'; of Irving, 'by far the greatest actor and personality of the men of the theatre of my day'—a statement followed one evening at dinner, by a dash from his seat across the room, in thrilling imitation of 'the chief' in the play-scene from *Hamlet;* after which, back in his seat again, came—with that delightfully characteristic twinkle —the whisper, 'This is hardly good for the digestion.' The speaker, remember, was then 74 years old!

"My friend's memories of Irving were often tinged with a shade of regret. 'My life,' he said to me more than once, 'has been one of intense work; I have enjoyed it, and have won great success in it, and I am not grumbling; but only about three times, when writing my hundred plays, have I written what I wanted to write and not what circumstances have compelled. Had Irving accepted *Michael and His Lost Angel*, which I wrote for him, he would have landed me at the top of my profession.' "

My father said to me once, "Irving made a failure as Malvolio, yet to-day if you were to see him you'd say, 'We don't get such acting nowadays.' " He told me he heard Irving read Becket for Dean Farrar at Canterbury, in the Chapter House. My parents went down with Lady Dorothy Nevill and her daughter, Miss Meresia Nevill. H. A. J. said, "He was very beautiful, but he wasn't a good elocutionist." On another occasion he said to me, "Irving's great point in Shylock was his exit of contempt at the end. Kean's great point was the outburst beginning 'Hath not a Jew.' " To digress for a moment—I think it worth recording that I never once heard my father make any kind of derogatory remark about Jews, or speak of them as a people without admiration. Many of his dearest friends, Charles Frohman, M. H. Spielmann, Sir Beerbohm Tree, and Sir Sidney Low were Jews, and he greatly admired Sir Herbert Samuel, whom he knew less intimately.

My father read *The Liars* to Irving and Ellen Terry.

MR. BANCROFT   MR. HENRY IRVING   MR. CARL HENTSCHEL   MR. H. A. JONES
(*President*)

The Annual Dinner of the Playgoers' Club, 1893: Henry Irving replying
to the toast of "The Drama"

(*By courtesy of "The Sphere"*)

He told them beforehand that it would not suit them, but he had promised to read them his next play. H. A. J. also told Irving the plot of *The Physician*, and later H. D. Traill, the author of *The Medicine Man*, told my father that Irving had given him the idea for his play. Irving and Henry Arthur often dined together. The last time Irving dined at Townshend House he parted from H. A. J. at 5.30 on a summer morning. On another occasion in Grafton Street, when Mr. Bram Stoker was the only other guest, the three men had nine bottles of wine between them. In speaking of Mr. Bram Stoker to me, my father said, "Bram was a good, a faithful friend, but his book was a slop of eulogy." My father told me that for a short period there was a break in the long friendship between Bram Stoker and his great chief. One evening Irving was at the Garrick Club when Mr. Stoker's name was mentioned. He said dryly, "Bram—Bram Stoker—*Mr.* Bram Stoker." H. A. J., in recounting this story, said, "It was deadly—said with that carbolic utterance——" and he added, "Irving wasn't verbally witty, he never said anything witty, but what he said was so corrosive." Henry Arthur delighted to tell the following story about Richard Mansfield and our greatest English actor. Mansfield came over to London and rented the Lyceum Theatre, where he played *Richard III*, one of Irving's greatest successes. My father said that he omitted to pay the rental of the theatre. He was at the Garrick Club one night, descanting to Irving upon the heroic efforts needed to play this very trying part; he said that it took every ounce of his strength, and he spoke of the prodigious vitality required from anyone who undertook the part. Irving leant over, and, tapping him on the knee, said very dryly, "I wouldn't do it, my dear boy, I wouldn't do it."

After some first night at the Lyceum which was a great failure, having been preceded by other failures, over which Irving had lost a great deal of money, my father, who had been round to see him, stayed talking so long that he and Irving were the last people to leave the theatre. H. A. J. told me, "He was very depressed, so I asked him if he knew who had the biggest debts of any body in the world. He said he didn't know, but he seemed quite cheerful when I told him Julius Cæsar."

My father would often recall Ellen Terry's many delightful performances; though he said, "Ellen Terry was a charming Juliet," he added, "but she didn't freeze your marrow in the potion scene. What I do like in a big scene is to feel it all down your back." The day she died he said to me, "They are saying Ellen Terry was the greatest actress we had; she wasn't, Mrs. Kendal was, but she hadn't Ellen Terry's charm."

Speaking to me one day of the old schools of acting compared with the modern, H. A. J. said, "There was all the difference between a rich draught of rare old fruity port and a good *vin ordinaire*," but he also said, "Every English actor I've known was an amateur as regards technique compared with Coquelin." I believe if I had said, "What about Mrs. Kendal?" he would have agreed to my exception. Speaking about acting one day, he said, "You never know with a part—how much of this have I given—how much is the actor's?"

My father took Sir Michael Foster, the great physician, to see Sarah Bernhardt in *Adrienne Lecouvreur*. After the death scene, which my father said "was a terrific affair," Sir Michael turned to him and said, "I wish, Jones, you'd take me round to see some of these actors and actresses, so that I can tell them how people really do die."

It was natural that Henry Arthur often talked about Shakespeare to us and with his friends. His favourite Shakespearian play, as also the first he ever saw, was *Macbeth*. When Miss Thorndike staged the play in 1927, he said: "I should like to see *Macbeth*, it is the play of Shakespeare's I love above all others." But he said more than once, "I think that *Lear* is on the whole the greatest thing that has ever come out of the human intellect. It is bigger than *Macbeth*—but I don't like it so much." The Bacon controversy was mentioned one day, and H. A. J. said immediately: "Shakespeare was a man of the theatre, Bacon wasn't. There are so many things which indicate to me that Shakespeare wrote the plays. I was born in the Midlands, where life hadn't changed much in three hundred years. The sheep-shearing scene in *The Winter's Tale* for instance—I've been at similar scenes. Bacon could not have written the opening of *Macbeth*, *Othello, Hamlet*—only a man of the theatre." He spoke with regret and indignation of the conditions which prevailed in the theatre nowadays compared with the seventies and eighties, when Shakespearian companies appeared regularly in a great many provincial towns. He insisted that the acting in those days was on a much higher level, and in his Notes he said, "Lord forgive all humbugs; Lord forgive all those who are making a reputation out of Shakespeare without understanding anything about him."

He said to me one day, "I don't hope that Shakespeare will hold his own against musical comedy, but I do want him to have a little niche of his own somewhere." When sending a subscription to the Sadler's Wells Fund, Henry Arthur wrote to Miss Baylis as follows:

"3rd November, 1925.
"DEAR MISS BAYLIS,

"Now that the spirit of Shakespeare has departed from Stratford-on-Avon, and that he has been driven out of the West End Theatres, you are almost the sole depository of Shakespearean stage traditions, and the lonely brave adventuress in Shakespearean enterprise.

"So I send to you my small cheque for the restoration of Sadler's Wells. I am confident that under your administration, it will kindle the enthusiasm and draw the atten-dance of lovers of Shakespeare in North London. You know how heartily I wish you success. 'The glorious gods sit in hourly synod about thy particular prosperity.'

"But how the little cherub who sits up aloft to watch over human absurdities chuckles with irony to note that, with London's thirty or forty fashionable theatres, Shake-speare is shooed away to find a refuge in the Waterloo Road and Pentonville!

"Faithfully yours,
"HENRY ARTHUR JONES."

We were discussing the merits of some book one day, as to whether it contained lasting qualities, and Henry Ar-thur said, "The only two things which last in literature are common sense and imagination—Boswell's *Johnson,* Bun-yan's *Pilgrim's Progress.* Molière was the incarnation of common sense, Shakespeare was the incarnation of com-mon sense and imagination." On another occasion he said, "The plays which have lasted deal with the perma-nent human emotions of mankind. *Macbeth* has lasted hundreds of years because it deals with ambition—it tells a story. *Othello* has lasted because it deals with jeal-ousy." A few weeks later he declared, "Including Shake-speare's, there aren't thirty plays with nourishment in them."

He was fond of talking about the Restoration Drama-tists, whose works he knew as well as he did those of Shakespeare. He declared that "Congreve at his best was altogether finer and more subtle than Sheridan."

He always insisted that play-writing was a very difficult form of art, and to emphasise his contention he said one day, "For every classical play in the English language, bar Shakespeare, there are twenty immortal poems. A novel-ist's task is easier, but a great novel is as great as a great play. It all depends upon the best way of saying it."

He always contended that good nonsense was the most difficult form of literature, and that *Alice in Wonderland* is about the best nonsense there is. He also placed hymn-writing very highly.

As has already been stated, Henry Arthur was never at any time a reader of novels. He exclaimed one day, "Do you know—I say it with the greatest shame—I've never read Jane Austen." Among the few modern novels I remember his reading were two of Conrad's and *The Octopus,* by Frank Norris; of this book he said, "It is a great book. I read it some years ago—a very fine work—an epic novel." Another book he read about this time was Henry James's *The Turn of the Screw.* It appalled him, and he agreed with me that it is an evil, though a very powerful, piece of work. H. A. J. said to me, "I used to see Henry James in the Reform Club, and it would take him twenty minutes to say 'Good morning,' and then he wouldn't say it without qualification. He couldn't say two and two make four, he could only go into the whole question of the multiplication-table."

The last few years of his life he read very few books; his nervous depression made concentration impossible. His reading consisted almost entirely of, as he would phrase it, "pecking at the papers." On Tuesdays he would say, "Is there half a laugh in *Punch* this week?" and he always looked for the Belcher drawing first. He would tick off on his fingers as follows: "*Punch* on Tuesday, Dean Inge's article in the *Evening Standard* on Wednesday, the *Times Literary Supplement* and the *Patriot* on Thursday, on Friday the *Spectator,* and Saturday the *Saturday Review*"; whilst every day he "pecked" at copies of *The Times,* the *Morning Post,* the *Daily Express,* the *Daily Mail,* the *Daily Chronicle,* the *Evening Standard,* and the *Evening News.*

In 1912 he rearranged his library, and whilst so engaged he sent me the following letter:

"17th October, 1912.

" . . . I'm gradually getting my library straight after immense pains to sort them out.   There are some very grim results too, owing to the exigencies of space, size, binding, and class and quality of literature.   I gave Thomas à Kempis as a spiritual guide to Voltaire, but I thought Thomas might perhaps get worsted, so I put him to bed with Rabelais, as being more in accordance with the eternal fitness of things.   Sophocles, too, is not quite of the same order of mind as Vanbrugh, the Restoration dramatist, but they are just of the same stature of body, so they have got to hobnob.   What will be the result of their collaboration I cannot foretell, nor what accommodation Brieux will find alongside Scribe.   Shaw was sure to make a disturbance wherever I put him, so I shoved him next to T. W. Robertson.   All the smaller fry are in a chorus of confusion, but the shabby style of some of them and the shabby bindings of others entitle them to very little respect."

My father was very fond of Samuel Butler's works.   He was never tired of quoting with great relish the following saying from Butler's *Note Book:* "It is all very well for mischievous writers to maintain that we cannot serve God and Mammon.   Granted that it is not easy, but nothing that is worth doing ever is easy"; and also from *Erewhon:* "And as luck would have it Providence was on my side." Speaking to me about Emerson's *Essays,* Henry Arthur said, "They are like a string of jewels, but somehow you don't remember them; they don't bite in like Carlyle, they aren't co-ordinated.   They told me at Harvard he'd write down a thought or a sentence and it might come in for anything."   He went on to ask me, "Of what man or of what thing does he give you a concrete vision?" and he continued, "There's one very fine thing he said—the advice that he gave—I ought to have taken and didn't—Emerson said, 'There are people making a stir in the town and everyone acclaims them, and you know what humbugs they are, and you feel you ought to go after them; leave them alone—they are exposing themselves.'" H. A. J. added, "Who said, 'No man is written down except by himself?'"

He made many illuminating comments on his own work; in particular I remember his saying, "I've never started to write a line of a play until I have beaten out the plot. Character and play should spring into the author's brain as a complete concept." On another occasion, speaking of the illusion of the theatre, he referred to a cat walking across the stage, and said, "Any intrusion of reality convicts the whole thing of being an imposture."

Writing to Mr. M. H. Spielmann in 1918, he made the following interesting observation on the material he had stored away for writing his plays:

"20th February, 1918.

" . . . I have never photographed a single character or taken one from mere observation. But all my life I have listened to people talking, and being an inveterate eavesdropper, nothing is sacred to me in private conversation. A character cannot walk out of real life into a play. He would not fit into the scheme. He has to be put into the right relations with the other characters and harmonised with them and with the story. People in real life are damnably unreal when they get on the stage—or so real that you want to kick them back into the street or into their Pentonville omnibuses. After all these years, my lumber room of consciousness is stored with *disjecta membra* of humanity. When I want a character I imagine him—from memory. And the moment he begins to talk I know whether I have fished up a real live human being from the chaos. . . ."

Even when he was feeling miserable and depressed, I could generally get him to discuss any subject which interested me. He was a good conversationalist because he had a very vivid and retentive memory, and in speaking of long-past events he would recall some small incident which made his stories live. He had in addition what I can only describe as a trick of memory. Over and over again, and sometimes apropos of nothing, he would startle us by making statements such as the following: "Fifty-three years ago to-day I was having my first *table d'hôte* meal with your dear mother. Sixty-three years ago to-morrow my uncle, after great imploring, gave me a day's holiday, and I went by steamer from Ramsgate to Dover. Thirty years ago to-day was the first night of *The Tempter*." He had a remarkable memory for dates and anniversaries, and, although I myself could never remember, he would tell me the exact date when I left to go to Morocco, to Cyprus, to Egypt, and the equally memorable dates when I came home.

When we talked of literature my father nearly always spoke of Dickens, whose work he loved greatly all his life. He told us, "The best adaptation of Dickens was *David Copperfield,* when I was a young man in the City. Winifred Emery's father was in it, and oh! how good he was." Speaking of Dickens's characters, he said, "I don't know that Pecksniff isn't the most gorgeous of the lot—there's Micawber and Pecksniff; but Pecksniff is the best." One day when we were talking of George Eliot my father said, "A lot of people boomed her up as being superior to Dickens. She's different, but she hasn't got the magic and the imagination. She's a good deal more like real life than Dickens."

The last entry I made in my little book, "H. A. J.'s Table Talk," was on 2nd December, 1928, when he said: "The more I read Dickens the more I place him as the second figure in English literature."

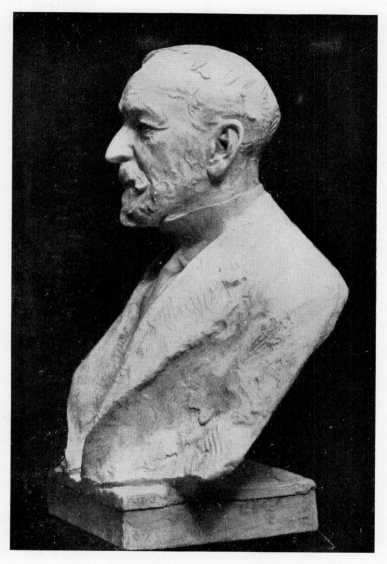

THE AITKEN BUST OF HENRY ARTHUR JONES

CHAPTER XIX

THE sorrows and failures of the last ten years of my father's life were greatly alleviated by the companionship of his five grandchildren. He was a delightful, adoring, and indulgent grandfather. Whatever the state of his health or nerves, he always welcomed their company and he was glad when my daughter Dorinda came to live with us in 1926, on leaving school to go on the stage. He took a great interest in her career, and there was nothing he would not do to help her in every possible way. He gave her a volume for her Press cuttings, in which he wrote:

"MY DARLING DORINDA,

"I hope this book will soon be filled with discriminating criticisms of your acting, and I am sure that so far as your efforts are concerned, the praise will be deserved.

                    "Your loving grandfather,
                         "HENRY ARTHUR JONES.
    "11th April, 1927."

He was delighted that she loved many of the same books as himself, and at her request he gave her, for her birthday in 1925, a copy of *The Pilgrim's Progress*, with this inscription:

"MY DEAR DORINDA,

"Here is a great piece of English prose from a man who had as little schooling as I had. He might have been also a great writer of English comedy, but he was a Puritan, and the Puritans hated the theatre. But as a matter of

337

fact he did write comedy.   The trial scene in *Vanity Fair* is one of the finest bits of comedy in the English language—if I know anything about English comedy.

"Your loving Grandy,
"HENRY ARTHUR JONES.

"10th February, 1915."

The following is one of the letters he used to send her when she was abroad; it was written when she was at Athens during the War:

"12th December, 1917.

". . . Has it occurred to you that I have not sent you any chocolates for a long while?   I hope you won't think me unkind, but I thought it would not be right while so many little children in England cannot get enough sugar. Still, Christmas coming round, just to remind us that there were times when we used to be merry, I thought I would stretch a point.   But then Sir Eyre Crowe told me they could not take parcels in the Foreign Office bag.   However, I thought I would risk a little one, so I sent you a little parcel.   I daresay when it got to the Foreign Office Sir Eyre Crowe took it to Mr. Balfour and said, 'Look here! What are we to do with this?'   Which I am sure made Mr. Balfour look very grave, and say with a frown, 'Doesn't Miss Thorne's grandfather know that we are short of shipping room?   What kind of a man is this grandfather?' To which Sir Eyre Crowe answered, 'Oh, he's a poor, silly man who has spent his life in trying to reform the English Drama.'

" 'What a waste of time!'   Mr. Balfour exclaimed. 'What sort of a man is this Judge Thorne?'

" 'He's an upright judge who feareth not God, neither regardeth man,' Sir Eyre Crowe replied, being addicted to the bad habit of misquoting Scripture; though you wouldn't think it, to look at him.

" 'But what is he a judge of?' Mr. Balfour continued, being determined to get at the truth of the matter.

" 'So far as opportunity offers, he is an excellent judge of cigars,' Sir Eyre Crowe replied, being anxious to say a good word for Billie and justify his present appointment.

" 'All this seems to be an evasion of the point at issue,' Mr. Balfour sternly declared.

" 'What sort of a woman is Mrs. Thorne?'

" 'There's no need to say anything for her,' Sir Eyre Crowe answered. 'She says quite enough for herself.'

" 'And this Miss Dorinda Thorne? What kind of a person is she?' Mr. Balfour questioned.

" 'Oh, she's the dearest, sweetest, lovingest, cleverest, best-behaved little angel that ever visited this sad earth,' Sir Eyre Crowe responded with a warmth of conviction that would have been unbecoming in a high Foreign Office official if he hadn't felt sure he was speaking the exact truth. Though, as he was evidently anxious you should get the chocolates, he may have yielded to a little exaggeration. Mr. Balfour scrutinised him keenly and then said in a cold, stern tone, 'No gush!'

" 'Well, you ask Billie Thorne, or her Mummy, or anybody who knows her,' Sir Eyre pursued. 'And she's not only well-behaved, but what is almost as important, she's not at all bad-looking. Send for her old Grandy and ask him.'

" 'There doesn't seem to be any immediate necessity for that,' Mr. Balfour deliberated, pacing up and down the room.

" 'And she's a splendid judge of chocolates,' Sir Eyre put in, being now determined as much for the sake of getting his point as of your getting the chocolates.

"Mr. Balfour continued to pace up and down in an agony of indecision, the question of the shortage of shipping being very serious.

" 'Oh, very well,' he said at length.   'Let Dorinda have the chocolates this once.'

"Sir Eyre Crowe wrung his chief's hand in gratitude and said he should never have cause to repent his decision.

"And so I hope you got the chocolates all right.   But I'm afraid you will think that the Foreign Office needn't have made such a great fuss about such a small packet of chocolates.   It shows how careful they are about the shipping just now.   And as I couldn't send you as many chocolates as I should have liked, will you ask Mummy to spend ten shillings more in buying you something in Athens, if anything is left in the shops there; or will you tell me what you would like and I will send it over for you, and try to make you happy in the New Year?   And now, with as many kisses as your heart and face have got room for,

"I am,

"Your loving old Grandy,

"HENRY ARTHUR JONES.

He loved very dearly his granddaughter Jean, Winifred's daughter, who always came twice a week with her mother to visit him.   When my sister Winifred went on the stage, he took the keenest interest and delight in her career, and, after she was grown up and married, he turned to her constantly for companionship and sympathy.   In his nervous breakdowns she cheered and comforted him as much as or more than my mother could because of her deafness.   After my mother's death he relied even more on his eldest daughter, and her constant visits to Hampstead with Jean were the greatest joy to him—a necessity to his well-being.   He called Jean his Songster or his Warbler, and he never tired of hearing her sing to him.   The last two years, just before she went home, she always sang "Abide with Me"; he would say it cheered and comforted him throughout the long and generally wakeful nights. His pet name for Jessica, Gertrude's daughter, was "My adored one." Her boys he saw more rarely, as they were at school, but he talked of them constantly. He would say "Michael has one of the best brains I've ever known. He'll be a fine man." And he had many a happy chuckle when Gertie told him the latest funny remark Peter had made.

He wrote a charming article, "Chats with My Grandchildren," which appeared in the Christmas number of *Fellowship* in 1921. In this article he told the children all about his own childhood. He said:

" . . . One of my grandfathers was a farmer and lived in a large old farmhouse that was built in the days of Charles the Second. They knew how to build houses in those days. But then they had no Minister of Education to keep young carpenters and bricklayers at school till they were eighteen. . . .

"My grandfather's labourers could have about as much new milk as they wanted for their families. Farm labourers then had about twelve shillings a week, and ought to have been very miserable upon it. But such was their ignorance and their stupidity, that as a rule they were quite happy, and some of them lived very jolly lives. . . . While attending to his farm, and his bake-house, and keeping 'The Three Pigeons,' my grandfather gave a good deal of his spare time to carpentering. And what a splendid carpenter he was! After he was dead, my father and I would sometimes walk along the path through the fields he had farmed. We used to come to a sturdy thick-set stile, with posts like a giant's legs, and a broadish top beam, where you might sit and rest if you were tired. 'Your grandfather made this stile,' my father would say. That stile still straddles firmly across your great-great-grandfather's fields, though it's near a hundred years ago since he built it in his spare time from farming, baking, and inn-keeping. . . .

"I was born in another farmhouse, in another little

Buckinghamshire village. That was in 1851. . . . People in 1851 didn't dress in the same way as they did when Shakespeare was born. But they thought in very much the same way, and they used many of the old English words that Shakespeare used when he was a boy. We always had tallow candles to light us, and we used to say 'dout' the candle, just as Shakespeare did. There are many words in Shakespeare's plays that were in the common talk of our farm labourers. They just spoke them without any showing off, and hadn't the least idea they were talking poetry. I've heard my father say things off his own tongue that might have come out of the Bible or Shakespeare. . . .

"I've such lots of things to tell you about what England was like in my boy days, but it's time for you to go to bed. Kiss me all of you and say 'Good night.' What's that, Jessica? As I was born in the county next but one to Shakespeare, why don't I write better plays? You dare to ask me that? You ought to be put in the stocks for putting a question like that to your grandfather. It isn't kind of you. I shall not answer you, miss. Now that just shows what children are like in these days."

On his seventieth birthday he gave a special luncheon-party for all his grandchildren, for which he composed the following menu:

LUNCHEON

to be given by

HENRY ARTHUR JONES

TO HIS GRANDCHILDREN

on his 70th Birthday, 20th Sept., 1921.

HENRY ARTHUR JONES AT 69

Pickled Trunnions
Filets of Poucher Bonne Femme
Baked Banbury Mush
Squibbles on Toast
Truffled Guffins
Boogoose Bordelause
Varicose Beans
Danderchits in Aspic
Wombles
Stuffed Spanish Crippets
Churdle Pie
Mulligatawny Fritters
Nostrum Roes à la Diable
Piblets
Trundleberry Gin.

His last two birthdays were marked by great celebrations. All his children and grandchildren spent the day with him, and there was a constant procession of visitors as well as a stream of letters and telegrams of congratulation. He was so pleased with them all, in particular the following letters from Mr. T. P. O'Connor and Sir James Barrie. "Tay Pay" wrote:

"20th September, 1926.
"MY DEAR HENRY ARTHUR,
"Allow me to join your myriads of friends in congratulating you on having reached your seventy-fifth birthday. As I will be seventy-eight on 5th October, I regard you, as they say in Ireland, as only a 'gossoon.'
"When you told me at a dinner where I had the pleasure of sitting beside you of the tremendous handicap you were under by your previous operation, and when I looked at your smiling and good-humoured face, I said to my friends I thought you were the bravest man I know. I did not know that you were to prove yourself even braver

by your splendid courage during your recent trial.   Long may you live!   But in heaven's name drop politics; you belong to a higher profession.

"Yours affectionately,

"T. P. O'CONNOR."

Barrie said:

"*21st September, 1927.*

"MY DEAR H. A. J.,

"Though I am a day late, none the less sincere are my congratulations on your birthday, and I hope it was a very happy one.   Your letter and still more the momentary appearance you made at my little birthday lunch was, or rather were, a very delightful thing to me, for you have long had my admiration and esteem, and I trust all is well with you.

"Yours affectionately,

"J. M. BARRIE."

On these occasions I was able to persuade him to grant interviews, though he was generally very reluctant to do so.   He would say, "I will not be boosted," and more than once, after a long and interesting interview with a reporter, he would expressly forbid that any part of the conversation should appear in print.   It was in vain that I pointed out that an interview, or a mention in the Press, was useful in keeping his name before the public; the reply was always, "I hate being boosted."   In spite of this, when his Press cuttings came, he would occasionally read them over more than once.   Sometimes, when he thought we were not looking, Nurse and I would see the old man's hand stealing out to the little table by his big chair to pick up and re-read a criticism or comment which had given him pleasure.

During the last few years my father's thoughts turned towards hopes of a future life. As I have already stated, except as a child and in very early manhood, H. A. J. was not a practising Christian, and during the plenitude of his powers he rarely, if ever, dwelt on such matters. For many years he was a pronounced agnostic, and, when we were living in Portland Place, my sister and I met with great opposition from him when we wanted to be baptised and confirmed. I do not know exactly when his attitude changed, but as long ago as 1919 when he and I were both suffering from sleeplessness, he constantly urged me to pray. I was not a professing Christian at that time, and his entreaties annoyed and worried me, and finally I begged him to leave me alone. While I was away for the week-end, he sent me the following beautiful little letter:

"1st November, 1919.
"MY DARLING,

"I'm sorry you misunderstood my last little bit of advice. Perhaps I should have said that you should pray for strength to bear it all with fortitude. Take this line every night, and in praying for sleep throw all your troubles on the Great Power that made us—use your own words such as 'Drive away all troubled thoughts. Smooth them and take them from me—Let me feel beneath the Everlasting Arms.—Take me under the Shadow of Thy wings.—With Thy own hands close my eyes.' Encourage yourself to use words like this and to believe that they will be heard and answered. Spend five or ten minutes repeating them every night, and you will find that the longer you use them the more easily you will be able to throw off your troubles at night, and get some sleep. . . .

"YOUR LOVING DADDY."

I know that from this time onwards my father prayed regularly every night, and once during the day-time I opened his study door and found him on his knees. Shortly before he died he said to me in pathetic tones, "The curious thing is" (this was a favourite expression of his), "I believe if I go to Heaven I shall be too tired to play my harp." My mother's death shook him profoundly, and he could not bear the thought that they were separated for ever. He was always saying to Nurse, "Nannie, you must get your priest to come and see me"; but Nurse felt as I did, that it was impossible for my father to believe in any kind of dogma. In his Notes he said, "I have thrown away all dogma and all theology. Now I can understand and enjoy my Bible." In another Note a few pages further on he said, "He maketh His sun to rise on the evil and on the good, and sendeth rain on the just and on the unjust. But what a pity it is He doesn't smite the evil with sunstroke, and send enough rain on the unjust to drown them. He did in the time of Noah, but in the last few years He hasn't exercised the same discrimination."

I am glad that two friends of mine, the Rev. Joseph Johnston and Dr. Carnegie Simpson, an ex-Moderator of the Presbyterian Church of England, came to see Henry Arthur from time to time. I would leave him alone with them to talk about his doubts and fears, and I know he was always comforted and reassured after their visits. H. A. J. said to me a few months before he died, "I feel more acutely the unkind things I've done than the wrong things, and I've done enough of both. I remember a thrush I had as a boy; it used to call out for food, and I didn't answer it often, and I often think of it now." Another clerical friend who came to see him was the Rev. B. C. Jackson, the Vicar of St. Luke's Church in Kidderpore Avenue. One morning in the summer before his death my father was sitting in the garden when Mr. Jackson passed by and stopped for a chat. After H. A. J.'s death Mr. Jackson wrote to me that he would always remember this particular occasion, as my father said to him, "You know, Mr. Jackson, I'm not a church-goer and I couldn't go now, but Jesus said, 'Blessed is he that hungereth and thirsteth after righteousness,' and then he added with great emphasis, 'and I *do* do *that.*'" The last thing at night I would go in to say good-night. He would always say, "Come and give me a sweet kiss, my darling," and very often, just as I had got to the door, he would call out, "Come and give me another sweet kiss"; and then he would add, "Now I am going to find something comforting in the Bible." One of the loveliest little pieces of prose he ever wrote is an inscription in a Bible he gave to our dearly loved friend Dr. Thompson, and which now belongs to me. Here it is:

"19th November, 1922.

"MY DEAR DOCTOR MAN,

"Here is a curious collection of old books. They contain much queer theology; some grotesque science; a good deal of doubtful history; many funny tales and fables, and occasional passages of shocking immorality. But they also contain golden precepts of conduct, bursts of the highest spiritual aspiration, and utterances of the noblest poetry. They show the way of life to those who are wise enough to look for it in their pages. The more I read them, the more I love them and the more good I get from them. But then I read them just as I would read any other book, knowing that their authors were fallible, mortal men, like

"Yours affectionately,

"HENRY ARTHUR JONES.

"(Except that they wrote much better literature than I do)."

I place this passage on a level with one of his most remarkable essays, that on "My Religion," which appeared in the *Daily Express* series of that name in 1925. It is a noble expression of faith, great in conception, fine in feeling, and strikingly beautiful in execution.   It is supreme among his minor works.   A few days after his death, on 7th January, 1929, the *Daily Express* republished the following passage:

"I believe that all this vast universe is living, intelligent Spirit in its very tiniest atom.   I believe that we can rest in its faithfulness and punctuality.   It is not a lying Spirit. It is a truthful and honest Spirit.   Facing and accepting all the angriest convulsions and hurricanes of that universal Spirit; facing and accepting all the woes and disasters and diseases and brutalities and blinding sorrows that it visits upon us; facing and accepting all the torments of the flesh and agonies of the mind that man endures—I believe there is yet a great balance of sentient happiness and joy and beauty; and interpenetrating the Cosmos to its utmost limit, I discern an infrangible law compelling all its atoms in one long march of unity and order of purpose to secure that balance of happiness and joy and beauty.

" . . . My creed is a narrow plank, but I find it sure under my feet.   I tread onwards with no misgiving. . . .

"I am not distressed about immortality. I cannot clearly enough picture to myself any future state of being that will be so different from this present state that I feel obliged to make special preparation and do extra packing for it. My ordinary every-day spiritual luggage will suffice me to carry me through the journey, however long it may be. I am not building upon immortality, but I will joyfully receive it if it is conferred upon me. . . ."

But the passage I love best begins:

"Whatever call to wander in strangely haunted spheres of ether, or fields of asphodel, in new modes of being, amid new duties and new pleasures, whatever call to prolong and fulfil its existence my spirit may obey when it has earned its release from the flesh, it is to this earth that it passionately turns and returns and clings to-day: this

earth that is the mother of all that I know and feel: this
earth where I have lived and sinned and suffered and loved
and fought and stumbled and triumphed and despaired,
and eaten my fill and drunk deep draughts of pleasure and
success and bitter cups of misery and defeat and shame;
this earth whose dawns and sunsets and variegated pagean-
tries are nicely suited to my eyes, and her harmonies and
discords exactly tuned to my ears; this earth whose winds
and angry storms have buffeted me, but whose blue skies
and halcyon days have restored me—this very earth, the
only place where my foot finds firm standing, and where my
spirit feels herself at home."

After his death Bernard Shaw spoke to me about this
article; he praised it very highly, saying that it was fifty
per cent. finer than any other article in the series.

Among the many letters of congratulation he received, he
was particularly delighted with those from Rudyard Kipling and the Bishop of Liverpool.   Kipling said:

> "Bateman's,
> "Burwash,
> "Sussex.
> "*2nd September, 1925.*

"Dear Arthur Jones,

"Thank you very much for your note and the enclosure,
which naturally interested me keenly.   I expect that every
man has to work out his creed according to his own wave-
length, and the hope is that the Great Receiving Station
is tuned to take *all* wave-lengths.

"As to the general unrest of things, it looks as if the
harvest was nearly ripe to the reaping and the sickle would
be put in soon.   No one will be more pathetically surprised
than the gentlemen who did the sowing.

> "Most sincerely,
> "Rudyard Kipling."

Dr. David wrote:

"Bishop's Lodge,
"Park Avenue,
"Liverpool.
"*23rd September, 1925.*

"MY DEAR HENRY ARTHUR JONES,

"I am very grateful indeed for your article. I have read most of them so far, but have learnt much more from yours than from any of the others. And the spirit behind it is, if I may say so, most attractive—anyhow, it moves me strongly towards you. The paragraph beginning 'I believe that all this vast universe——' puts a side of my own faith for me far better than I could have expressed it for myself.

"Of course what keeps us apart is just those troublesome things, words. I can't help thinking that most of us overrate their capacity to contain truth, and that if we had a subtler medium of communication we should often agree where now we differ. It seems to me that the foundation must be facts. Therefore if vast numbers of people are to have convictions, there must be statements of these facts and their relations, but the result must be to some extent Babelic till we get a sounder idea of what words can do and what they can't. . . .

"Yours very gratefully,
"ALBERT LIVERPOOL."

In the following passage in "My Religion" Henry Arthur referred to his dear old friend Conan Doyle: "Still I will snatch as much as I can from annihilation, and I shall find no Paradise intolerable if Arthur Conan Doyle is there on its threshold to welcome me." Sir Arthur expressed his pleasure at my father's words in this letter:

"My dear Friend,

"I am not emotional—anyhow, on the surface—but you really brought tears very near my eyes when you spoke of our meeting at the gate of Paradise. That you will be there I am very sure, and I can only hope that I won't miss the rendezvous.   Pray read my own little effusion that you may realise the sanity of my position.   I read Bennett to-day—but we can't live on negatives, I being a positive.

"With all affection,
"Arthur Conan Doyle."

My father had always been greatly interested in Spiritualism and occult phenomena, and all his life long he read a great deal of literature dealing with these subjects.   He would often chuckle when he read stories about poltergeists, and he said to me once, "There's a tremendous play to be made out of it.   Can't you see the fun there would be?"   But, in spite of Conan Doyle's eloquent persuasiveness, Henry Arthur was never won over to a belief in Spiritualism.   Sir Arthur wrote to him:

"Sussex.
"*14th April, 1928.*

"Thank you for your kind letter.   At our age we can hope to learn the truth of these things very soon—though the world is the better the longer you stay here.

"Queer that you should feel a want of that bodily warmth and homely comfort in the prospect and not realise that this is exactly what we offer.   I have a hundred descriptions if I have one from those who have gone before, and they all talk of their homes, their comforts, their libraries, their pursuits—the joy of using every human faculty to the utmost in an extended field of action.   You will write there as here—and I will probably continue to bore my friends with my views—the only excuse in this instance being that I know it is true, and I know also what consolation it always brings when man needs consolation. Fenimore Cooper's last words were 'I thank the Fox girls for the peace I feel now.'

"I must get you into my shop. I have objects of interest there."

In answer to this letter we went down to visit the shop, and spent a most interesting morning there with Sir Arthur.

These articles on Religion were published in book form, and in a copy my father gave to Dr. Carnegie Simpson he wrote, "I am a believer."

CHAPTER XX

For the last few months of his life my father was failing rapidly. In October 1928 he said to me, "I'm so tired, I'm getting near home, Doris, and I don't mind how soon I get there." Until the day of his death, when Dr. Risien Russell saw him and told us that he could not possibly live many hours longer, we did not know he was suffering from an incurable and very rare disease, myasthenia gravis, a gradual paralysis which affects all the muscular powers. He used to say to his nurse, "Nannie, you must get me a new pair of knees," and for a long time he was very unsteady when he walked. Just at the last he could not always articulate clearly or sign his name properly.

His spirit was so valiant that he did occasionally conquer and throw off these physical disabilities, notably when Max Beerbohm came to see him on 5th December. For two hours Henry Arthur was his old self, so greatly delighted was he to be with "Max" again. Nothing in the last year of his life gave him greater pleasure than this visit. Cunninghame Graham came to see him a week or two before Christmas; Captain Allan Pollock, whom he loved and saw too rarely, came up on Christmas Eve; Malcolm Watson had tea with him eight days before he died; and again he rallied at the call of old and valued friendships. It was a great spirit that could so conquer and overcome the body.

Eleven days before he died he went to the Stoll studios to see my daughter make her début in the film version of *The Silver King*. He was too feeble to walk any distance, so they carried him on to the set. He was greatly interested, and the visit distracted him. Nor was he unduly fatigued, but came back to have a sound half-hour's nap by the fire. He was very pleased with the many Press notices which appeared about this visit, as much for my child's sake as for his own, and he re-read several of them.

The end came on 7th January, 1929. On Saturday, 5th January, he complained of feeling ill and stayed in bed. In the evening his temperature was over 100, but we attributed this to a return of kidney trouble. On Sunday he was no better, but not apparently in any danger until the evening, when his temperature rose to over 103. We immediately telephoned for a night-nurse. He said to Nurse on Sunday, "I mean to get well, Nannie." When he was very ill, he was as sweet and manageable as could be imagined. Almost his first words to the night-nurse were to ask if he could do anything for her. Nannie and I did not leave him till nearly one o'clock. The next morning, 7th January, the night-nurse reported that he had taken quite a fair amount of nourishment, and for a moment I felt he was going to get over it. During the last three days of his illness, which was acute pneumonia, Nannie asked him constantly, "Are you in any pain, Mr. Jones?" And he replied each time, "No, Nannie, thank you; I'm quite comfortable, I've no pain." The first thing on Monday morning he asked for Ju, and the cat remained on his bed all day and would not come down for lunch; we had to take him down at six o'clock. I told him several times during the day that Oliver would be down about buying machinery for his job, and that Gertie would be back, and each time he said, though he was pitifully indistinct, "I'm so glad." They were the last words we heard him say.

Before lunch he became unconscious, and only rallied momentarily after that. Nannie had her hand in his to-

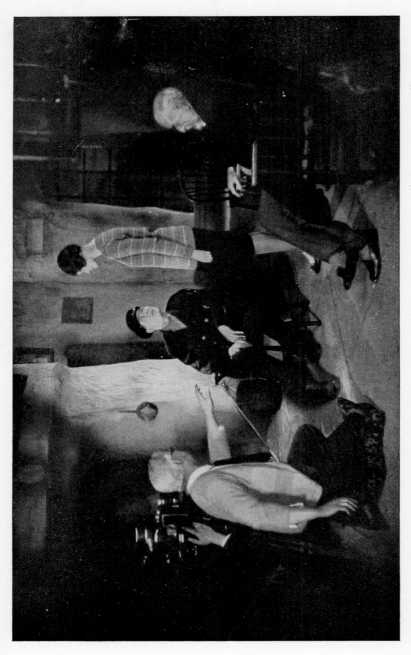

THE LAST PHOTOGRAPH OF HENRY ARTHUR JONES—THE FILMING OF "THE SILVER KING"

Welsh-Pearson-Elder Studios, Cricklewood, December 28, 1928

wards the end, and she said, "If you know me, Mr. Jones, just press my hand"; he could not, and she then said, "Can you turn your eyes towards me?" and he did so at once. He knew Peg and her daughter Jean just before dinner, and Dorinda when she went off to the theatre, and he made an effort to say "Good-bye, my darling," as usual.

I was telephoning to Dr. Mackintosh, when the end came with great suddenness and perfect ease at a quarter to ten. Just a little sigh and it was over. As I came into the room, my sister Peg said, "Oh! Dorry, he's gone," but when I leant over him there was a faint breath on my cheek, and for a moment we wondered desperately if we would use oxygen to try to revive him, but it was obviously useless to make any effort to bring him back from peace.

*   *   *   *   *   *   *   *   *

When he lay dead he did not look very much younger. The beautiful shape of his head was striking, and, though the mouth was stern, there was a shadow of his dear familiar smile round the eyes. He was so emaciated that the general impression was that of a figure which was scarcely life-size.

I shall always remember that the first message of sympathy we received, before 9.30 the next morning, was a card from Mr. Gordon Selfridge, and that the first flowers which arrived a little while afterwards were from his old friend, Professor George Baker.

The funeral service, conducted by the Rev. Joseph Johnston, was held at St. Andrew's Presbyterian Church at Frognal on Thursday, 10th January, and he is buried at the Hampstead Cemetery, Fortune Green Road. We chose his favourite hymns, "Abide with Me" and "Lead, Kindly Light," and the beautiful Psalm beginning, "The Lord is my Shepherd, I shall not want."

The pall-bearers were his son Oliver, his grandson

Michael Albery, Emery Walker, Cunninghame Graham, Ian Hay, and Ralph Wotherspoon. My deepest sympathies were with dear Sir Emery Walker, who in acting as a pall-bearer paid a last tribute of love and admiration to a close and unbroken sixty years' friendship. We also asked Sir James Barrie, Rudyard Kipling, and Sir Arthur Pinero to be pall-bearers, but they were all prevented by illness from attending the funeral.

His old friends Malcolm Watson, H. C. Shelley, George Bishop, Sir Sidney Low, Percy Hutchinson, and Gordon Selfridge were at the funeral service. Among the many messages of sympathy sent with the flowers I shall always remember Sir James Barrie's card, "In deep affection"; Mr. Shelley's message, "Henry Arthur Jones—Great Englishman—Master Craftsman—Beloved Friend—*Vale*"; and the touchingly appropriate lines from Matthew Arnold that Oliver chose, "Let the victors when they come, when the forts of folly fall, Find thy body at the wall." A memorial service was held at St. Martin's-in-the-Fields on 14th January.

I value highly every letter of sympathy I received after my father's death, and I was deeply touched because nearly all his friends said what a "lovable" man he was. It is difficult to choose from hundreds of letters, but those I received from Sir James Barrie, Sir Sidney Low, and Bernard Shaw have, I believe, a particular interest, as also Harold Terry's tribute in a letter to my sister Peg. Sir James Barrie wrote:

"11th January, 1929.

"DEAR MRS. THORNE,

"It was very sad to me not to be able to pay that last honour to your father, but I have been in bed for a month with bronchitis and so it could not be done. Now I'm getting away into some sunshine I hope.

"I felt deeply gratified by your feeling that he would

have chosen me. I shall always hold him in affection and high honour.

"Yours sincerely,

"J. M. BARRIE."

Sir Sidney Low wrote:

"*8th January, 1929.*

"DEAR MRS. THORNE,

"I am deeply grieved to know that dear Henry Arthur has passed away.

"In the last few years, owing to my less robust health and the general stress of things, I had not seen him often. But I have known him long and well, and had a very high regard and affection for him. I admired his fine intellect, and his honourable, kindly, and sincere character.

". . . He was a great dramatist and writer, greater I think than is yet generally recognised. I am convinced that some of his comedies will hold their place among the classics of our stage, and will be seen and read long after the works of many of our contemporary playwrights have been forgotten. He was a brilliant master of English prose also; and though I regretted that he spent too much time on ephemeral controversy, his books are models of distinguished writing, full of eloquence and wit.

"I think his industry, perseverance, and undaunted energy were amazing. So was his courage. Few men could have borne up so bravely, and so cheerfully, against the physical disabilities from which he had suffered so long.

"Withal he was one of the best of men—genial, kindly, humorous, and affectionate. I hold it a great privilege and honour to have been numbered among his more intimate friends.

"I know how you must feel his loss. You have at least the consolation of remembering that he lived longer than most of us expected, and retained a large measure of vigour, and I hope of happiness, because of the constant devotion and care by which he was surrounded.

"My most earnest sympathy, and my wife's, are with you and your sisters.

"With all kindest regards and remembrances,

"I am,

"Always sincerely yours,

"SIDNEY LOW."

When my father died, I wrote to G. B. S. and said that I thought he would like to know my father died very peacefully and that he did not suffer at all in his last short illness; and that he never mentioned Mr. Shaw's name during the last years without saying, "I've no personal malice against Shaw," while he often spoke with gratitude of the praise G. B. S. gave his work. In reply he wrote:

"11th January, 1929.

"MY DEAR MRS. THORNE,

"Thank you for your very kind letter. I never had the slightest doubt that the real old friendly relations between your father and myself were there all the time underneath the top dressing of denunciatory rhetoric which amused us both. After the War, which doesn't count, as everyone was mad then, it was a queer sort of play which perhaps only a fellow-playwright would have understood.

"What distressed me was the quarrel with the public which he entered on with *The Princess's Nose* and *The Triumph of the Philistines,* in which, having to give Alexander an amiable part, he accounted for it by representing him as having been brought up in France! His biographer will have to account for that embitterment. It certainly had nothing to do with any failure of his powers, in which I could detect no falling-off whatever up to the end. But it was there. Wells and I were only part of a world that was too foolish and cruel for him to suffer gladly. Without you there would have been no refuge for his wounded affections.

"Now you are free; and your freedom is a loss. That is what happens; but it will all heal up; and you will be able to rejoice in his memory without the anxiety of his illnesses. You were his favourite child; and that, I think, gives you a special property in him.

"So away with melancholy; and buy a perfectly gorgeous spring dress. I am sure he would have liked that. Long faces should not be pulled on the death of a hero.

"Ever,
"G. B. S."

The following is a passage from Mr. Harold Terry's letter:

"13th January, 1929.

"Obituary notices have laid stress upon his naturalness, his courage, his perennial youthfulness, but, of those that I have read, none has placed emphasis upon what was to me, and to many other young dramatists, an outstandingly rare feature of his character—his abiding and sympathetic interest in the work of younger men, and his keen desire to assist them, even to his own disadvantage, in framing a constitution that would protect them from the tyranny and sharp practice of a commercial theatre. In this he stood alone amongst his contemporaries and for this—had he possessed no other title to our love and esteem—his name will be for ever held in honour amongst us."

My father would have been pleased that there were a great many obituary notices in the French Press, as well as in several Spanish and German papers. Mr. Galsworthy wrote to me that he had seen a very fine tribute in a leading Brazilian daily. Most of the English obituaries, and nearly all the American notices—there were over five hundred—would have pleased him, but he would have been amazed and wounded at the very general misunderstanding of the message to the public which he left in his will. The newspaper headings "Disappointed Dramatist," "Henry Arthur Jones in his Will Scolds the Public" would have horrified him. There were notable exceptions, such as the leading article in the *Daily Express,* which showed a fine interpretation and appreciation of the motive which prompted him to write the message, and another in the French paper *Comœdia.*

In his will, dated 3rd August, 1927, he left gifts to his old friends Emery Walker and M. H. Spielmann, and to all his children. He left me all his papers, autograph letters, and unbound manuscripts; and his bound manuscripts were to be divided among his four daughters and his son Oliver.

He said, "Lastly I wish to be buried in the plainest and simplest manner, and that a simple stone shall be erected over my remains and on it inscribed:

HENRY ARTHUR JONES
Born 20th September, 1851
Died

'Then I said I have laboured in vain, yet surely my judgment is with the Lord and my work with my God.' "

In August 1928, he said to me, "Have I told you what I mean when I say on my epitaph, 'I have laboured in vain' ? I mean I have tried all my life to make people understand that the Drama is the highest and most difficult part of English literature." He said much the same thing to me on very many occasions. His choice of this epitaph was not the choice of an embittered man. He was disheartened often, but never bitter, nor would it be correct to say he was a disappointed man. He said constantly,

"No one has received greater praise than I have. I am
sure I should never have given my work half as much
praise as the critics have." But he was a very modest man,
and, in spite of the many tributes he received praising his
contributions to English literature—from H. D. Traill,
William Archer, Sir Sidney Low, Augustin Filon, Professor
Lyon Phelps, W. D. Howells, Brander Matthews, Professor
Paul Shorey, Montrose J. Moses, and many other distinguished English and American critics, and, above all, from
such pre-eminent judges as Matthew Arnold, Bernard
Shaw, and Max Beerbohm—I do not think he was ever
whole-heartedly convinced that any of his work would live.

And here is his last message to the English people on
his efforts for the art he loved passionately, enriched with
his work, and served faithfully and devotedly for over fifty
years:

"I have attained great and continued success on the
English stage, and my efforts have been abundantly recognised and rewarded. I acknowledge this with deep and
hearty gratitude, but, on several occasions when I have
felt encouraged to offer to the Public my best work, regardless of popular success, I have been so unfortunate as to
meet with the condemnation alike of the Press and the
Public. I say this in no spirit of bitterness or disappointment, but as an excuse for sometimes offering to the Public
plays that have been below the level of my aspirations,
and of their expectations. I have done this in the hope
of capturing that wide and popular approbation without
which no dramatist can hope for influence and authority.
I am convinced that England cannot have a modern Drama
worthy of her place among the nations, a modern Drama
in which she can take a just and lasting pride, and for
which she can claim the esteem of other nations, until our
Theatre is brought into relation with our literature and
until the great body of English men of letters take a dili-

gent and understanding interest in the Theatre. In this conviction I have endeavoured, through the greater part of my life, to draw English men of letters to the Theatre. I have also tried to persuade English playgoers to read and study modern plays, that they may take a more intelligent interest in what is set before them in the Theatre, and may get a more refined and enduring pleasure from plays when they see them acted. I am conscious that I have largely failed in both these aims. It is with some hope that the causes I have advocated may yet succeed that I ask English men of letters and English playgoers to accept from me, in a spirit of forbearance and friendliness, this legacy of a last few words."

APPENDIX A

THE PLAYS OF HENRY ARTHUR JONES

DATE	TITLE	FIRST PERFORMANCE	SUBSEQUENT PRODUCTIONS
1869	THE GOLDEN CALF.*	—	—
1878	IT's ONLY ROUND THE CORNER. Play in 1 act. Published by Samuel French & Co. in Lacy's Acting Edition of Plays, vol. cxix, 1883. Privately printed at Ilfracombe by John Tait.	Theatre Royal, Exeter, 11th Dec., 1879 (Wybert Rousby).	Performed under the title HARMONY RESTORED, Grand Theatre, Leeds, 13th Aug., 1879. Strand Theatre, London, 1884. Performed under the title THE ORGANIST, Lyceum Theatre, New York, May 1892. Royalty Theatre, London, 1895.
1878	CHERRY RIPE.* Comedietta. Believed to have been privately printed at Ilfracombe by John Tait.	—	—
1879	HEARTS OF OAK. Domestic drama in 2 acts. Privately printed at Ilfracombe by John Tait.	Theatre Royal, Exeter, 29th May, 1879 (G. W. Harris, Miss Agnes Birchenough).	Town Hall, Yeovil, 1879.
1879	HONOUR BRIGHT. HEARTS OF OAK re-written with fuller dialogue. Privately printed at Ilfracombe by John Tait.	—	—
1879	ELOPEMENT. Comedy in 2 acts. Privately printed at Ilfracombe by John Tait.	Theatre Royal, Oxford, 19th Aug., 1879 (F. Merer, Miss Agnes Birchenough).	Theatre Royal, Belfast, 1880.

* Never produced.

DATE.	TITLE	FIRST PERFORMANCE	SUBSEQUENT PRODUCTIONS
1879	A DRIVE IN JUNE.* Privately printed at Ilfracombe by John Tait.	—	—
1879	A CLERICAL ERROR. Comedietta. Published by Samuel French & Co. in Lacy's Acting Edition of Plays, vol. clii., 1904. Privately printed at Ilfracombe by John Tait.	Court Theatre, 16th Oct., 1879 (Wilson Barrett, Miss Winifred Emery).	Princess's Theatre, 1883. Charles Wyndham Celebration. Lyceum Theatre, 1st May, 1896.
1879–80	HUMBUG.* Play in 3 acts. Privately printed at Ilfracombe by John Tait.	—	—
1879–80	A GARDEN PARTY.* Play in 3 acts. Privately printed at Ilfracombe by John Tait.	—	—
1880	AN OLD MASTER. Comedy in 1 act. Published by Samuel French & Co. in Lacy's Acting Edition of Plays, vol. cxix, 1883. Privately printed at Ilfracombe by John Tait.	Princess's Theatre, 6th Nov., 1880 (C. W. Carthorne, Miss Maud Milton).	—
1880	LADY CAPRICE.* Comedy in 3 acts. Privately printed at Ilfracombe by John Tait.	—	—
1881	HIS WIFE.	Sadler's Wells, 16th April, 1881 (E. H. Brooke, Miss Bateman).	—
1881	HOME AGAIN.	Theatre Royal, Oxford, 7th Sept., 1881.	—

* Never produced.

DATE	TITLE	FIRST PERFORMANCE	SUBSEQUENT PRODUCTIONS
1882	A BED OF ROSES. Play in 1 act. Published by Samuel French & Co. in Lacy's Acting Edition of Plays, vol. cxix, 1863. Privately printed at Ilfracombe by John Tait.	Globe Theatre, 26th Jan., 1882 (Arthur Dacre, Miss Goldney).	—
1882	THE SILVER KING. Drama in 4 acts. (In collaboration with H. A. Herman.) Published in the Four Volume Edition of Representative Plays by Henry Arthur Jones, by Macmillan & Co., and Little, Brown & Co., New York. Printed by Samuel French & Co., London and New York.	Princess's Theatre, 16th Nov., 1882 (Wilson Barrett, E. S. Willard, Miss Eastlake).	Wallack's Theatre, New York, 27th Jan., 1883 (Osmund Tearle, Rosa Coghlan, Herbert Kelcey). Princess's Theatre, 1885 and 1889. Olympic Theatre, 1891. Lyceum Theatre, 1899. Adelphi Theatre, 1903. Strand Theatre, 1914. Command Performance, His Majesty's Theatre, 22nd May, 1914.
1882-3	THE WEDDING GUEST.* Play in 1 act. Privately printed at Ilfracombe by John Tait.	—	—
1883-4	REX.* Drama in 5 acts.	—	—
1883-4	VLADIMIR.* Play in 4 acts.	—	—
1883-4	THE JOLLY WATERMAN.* Comedietta in 3 acts.	—	—
1884	BREAKING A BUTTERFLY. Play in 3 acts. (In collaboration with H. A. Herman.) Privately printed.	Prince's Theatre, 3rd March, 1884 (Beerbohm Tree, Kyrle Bellew, Miss Lingard).	—

365

* Never produced. The only trace of *Vladimir* and *The Jolly Waterman* is an entry, in a ledger belonging to Henry Arthur Jones, that the MSS. and typed copies were in his strong-room.

DATE	TITLE	FIRST PERFORMANCE	SUBSEQUENT PRODUCTIONS
1884	CHATTERTON. Play in 1 act. (In collaboration with Henry Herman.)	Princess's Theatre, 22nd May, 1884 (Wilson Barrett, Miss Mary Dickens).	—
1884	SAINTS AND SINNERS. Play in 5 acts. Published by Macmillan & Co., 1891, by Samuel French & Co., London and New York, and in the Four Volume Library Edition of *Representative Plays by Henry Arthur Jones*, by Macmillan & Co., and Little, Brown & Co., New York, 1925.	Vaudeville Theatre, 25th Sept., 1884 (Thomas Thorne, Miss Cissy Graham).	Madison Square Theatre, New York, 7th Nov., 1885 (J. H. Stoddart, Marie Burroughs). Vaudeville Theatre. 27th Jan., 1892.
1885	HOODMAN BLIND. Play in 4 acts. (In collaboration with Wilson Barrett.)	Princess's Theatre, 18th Aug., 1885 (Wilson Barrett, E. S. Willard, Miss Eastlake).	Princess's Theatre, 26th Nov., 1892.
1885–90	WELCOME LITTLE STRANGER.	—	—
1886	THE LORD HARRY. Romantic play in 5 acts. (In collaboration with Wilson Barrett.)	Princess's Theatre, 18th Feb., 1886 (Wilson Barrett, E. S. Willard, Miss Eastlake).	—
1886	A NOBLE VAGABOND. Drama in 4 acts.	Princess's Theatre, 22nd Dec., 1886 (Charles Warner, Miss Dorothy Dene).	—
1887	HARD HIT. Play in 4 acts.	Haymarket Theatre, 17th Jan., 1887 (E. S. Willard, Beerbohm Tree, Miss Marion Terry).	—

366

DATE	TITLE	FIRST PERFORMANCE	SUBSEQUENT PRODUCTIONS
1887	HEART OF HEARTS. Play in 3 acts.	Vaudeville Theatre, 3rd Nov., 1887 (Special matinée). (Leonard Boyne, Miss Kate Rorke).	—
1887	SWEET WILL. Comedy in 1 act. Published by Samuel French & Co., London and New York, in Lacy's Acting Edition of Plays, vol. cxxxi, 1893.	New Club, Covent Garden, 1887 (Lewis Waller, Miss Norreys).	Shaftesbury Theatre, 25th July, 1890.
1888	BAB.*	—	—
1889	WEALTH. Play in 4 acts.	Haymarket Theatre, 27th April, 1889 (Beerbohm Tree, Mrs. Beerbohm Tree).	Palmer's Theatre, New York, 9th March, 1891 (E. S. Willard, Marie Burroughs).
1889	THE MIDDLEMAN. Play in 4 acts. Published by Samuel French & Co., London and New York, and in the Four Volume Edition of *Representative Plays by Henry Arthur Jones,* by Macmillan & Co., and Little, Brown & Co., New York, 1925.	Shaftesbury Theatre, 27th Aug., 1889 (E. S. Willard, Miss Maud Millett).	Municipal Theatre, Amsterdam, Jan., 1890 Palmer's Theatre, New York, 10th Nov., 1890. (E. S. Willard, Alice Burroughs, Maxine Elliot). Avenue Theatre, 1891. Comedy Theatre, 1894. Knickerbocker Theatre, New York, 13th Feb., 1905.
1890	JUDAH. Play in 3 acts. Published by Macmillan & Co. (Preface by Joseph Knight), by Samuel French & Co., and in the Four Volume Library Edition of *Representative Plays by Henry Arthur Jones,* by Macmillan & Co., and Little, Brown & Co., New York, 1925.	Shaftesbury Theatre, 21st May, 1890 (E.S. Willard, Miss Olga Brandon).	Palmer's Theatre, New York, 29th Dec., 1890 (E. S. Willard, Marie Burroughs). Avenue Theatre, 30th Jan., 1892.

* Never produced. The only trace of *Bab* is an entry, in a ledger belonging to Henry Arthur Jones, that the MS. and typed copies were in his strong-room.

DATE	TITLE	FIRST PERFORMANCE	SUBSEQUENT PRODUCTIONS
1890	THE DEACON. Comedy sketch in 2 acts. Published by Samuel French & Co., London and New York, in Lacy's Acting Edition of Plays, vol. cxxxiii., 1893.	Shaftesbury Theatre, 27th Aug., 1890 (E. S. Willard, Miss Annie Hill).	—
1891	THE DANCING GIRL. Drama in 4 acts. Published by Samuel French & Co., London and New York, and in the Four Volume Library Edition of *Representative Plays by Henry Arthur Jones*, by Macmillan & Co., and Little, Brown & Co., New York, 1925.	Haymarket Theatre, 15th Jan., 1891 (Beerbohm Tree, Miss Julia Neilson).	Lyceum Theatre, New York, 31st Aug., 1891. (E. H. Sothern, Virginia Harned). His Majesty's Theatre, 16th Feb., 1909.
1891	THE CRUSADERS. Comedy of modern life in 3 acts, 1891. Published by Macmillan & Co., 1893 (Preface by William Archer), and in the Four Volume Library Edition of *Representative Plays by Henry Arthur Jones*, by Macmillan & Co., and Little, Brown & Co., New York, 1925.	Avenue Theatre, 2nd Nov., 1891 (Lewis Waller, Miss Winifred Emery, Miss Olga Brandon). Draperies and furniture made by William Morris.	—
1891	THE MAD COOK. Scenario for farce.	—	
1893	THE BAUBLE SHOP. Play in 4 acts. Published by Samuel French & Co., London and New York.	Criterion Theatre, 26th Jan., 1893 (Charles Wyndham, Miss Ellis Jeffreys, Miss Mary Moore).	Melbourne, Australia, Aug., 1894. Empire Theatre, New York, 11th Sept., 1894 (John Drew, Maud Adams).
1893	THE TEMPTER. Tragedy in verse in 4 acts. Published by Macmillan & Co., 1898 (Preface dedicated to William Archer), by Samuel French & Co., London and New York, and in the Four Volume Library Edition of *Representative Plays by Henry Arthur Jones*, by Macmillan & Co., and Little, Brown & Co., New York, 1925. Privately printed by the Chiswick Press.	Haymarket Theatre, 20th Sept., 1893 (Beerbohm Tree, Fred Terry, Miss Julia Neilson, Miss Irene Vanbrugh).	—

DATE	TITLE	FIRST PERFORMANCE	SUBSEQUENT PRODUCTIONS
1894	THE MASQUERADERS. Play in 4 acts. Published by Macmillan & Co., 1899, by Samuel French & Co., London and New York, and in the Four Volume Library Edition of *Representative Plays by Henry Arthur Jones*, by Macmillan & Co., and Little, Brown & Co., New York, 1925. Privately printed by the Chiswick Press.	St. James's Theatre, 28th April, 1894 (George Alexander, Herbert Waring, Mrs. Patrick Campbell, Miss Irene Vanbrugh).	Run resumed St. James's Theatre, 11th Nov., 1894, with Evelyn Millard as "Dulcie Larondie." Empire Theatre, New York, 3rd Dec., 1894 (Henry Miller, William Faversham, Viola Allen). Sydney, Australia, March, 1895.
1894	THE CASE OF REBELLIOUS SUSAN. Comedy in 3 acts. Published by Macmillan & Co., 1897 (Preface dedicated to Mrs. Grundy), by Samuel French & Co., London and New York, and in the Four Volume Library Edition of *Representative Plays by Henry Arthur Jones*, by Macmillan & Co., and Little, Brown & Co., New York, 1925. Privately printed by the Chiswick Press.	Criterion Theatre, 3rd Oct., 1894 (Charles Wyndham, Miss Mary Moore).	Lyceum Theatre, New York, 29th Dec., 1894 (Herbert Kelcey, Isabel Irving). Wyndham's Theatre, 16th May, 1901. Criterion Theatre, 1st June, 1910. Criterion Theatre, 19th Sept., 1910.
1895	GRACE MARY.* Tragedy in 1 act, in the Cornish dialect. Published in the Four Volume Library Edition of *Representative Plays by Henry Arthur Jones*, by Macmillan & Co., and Little, Brown & Co., New York, 1925, and in *The Theatre of Ideas*, Chapman & Hall, 1915. Privately printed by the Chiswick Press.	—	—
1895	THE TRIUMPH OF THE PHILISTINES. Comedy in 3 acts. Published by Macmillan & Co., 1899, and by Samuel French & Co., London and New York. Privately printed by the Chiswick Press.	St. James's Theatre, 11th May, 1895 (George Alexander, Miss Elliott Page, Miss Juliette Nesville).	—

* Never produced.

369

DATE	TITLE	FIRST PERFORMANCE	SUBSEQUENT PRODUCTIONS
1896	MICHAEL AND HIS LOST ANGEL. Play in 5 acts. Published by Macmillan & Co., 1896, by Samuel French & Co., London and New York, and in the Four Volume Library Edition of *Representative Plays by Henry Arthur Jones*, by Macmillan & Co., and Little, Brown & Co., New York, 1925. Privately printed by the Chiswick Press.	Lyceum Theatre, 15th Jan., 1896 (J. Forbes-Robertson, Miss Marion Terry).	Empire Theatre, New York, 13th Jan., 1896 (Henry Miller, Viola Allen).
1896	THE ROGUE'S COMEDY. Play in 3 acts. Published by Macmillan & Co., 1898, and by Samuel French & Co., London and New York. Privately printed by the Chiswick Press.	Garrick Theatre, 21st April, 1896 (E. S. Willard, Miss Olliffe).	Wallack's Theatre, New York, 14th Dec, 1896 (E. S. Willard, Olga Brandon).
1897	THE PHYSICIAN. Play in 4 acts. Published by Samuel French & Co., London and New York. Privately printed by the Chiswick Press.	Criterion Theatre, 25th March, 1897 (Charles Wyndham, Miss Mary Moore).	—
1897	THE LIARS. Comedy in 4 acts. Published by Macmillan & Co., 1904, by Samuel French & Co., London and New York, and in the Four Volume Library Edition of *Representative Plays by Henry Arthur Jones*, by Macmillan & Co., and Little, Brown & Co., New York, 1925. Privately printed by the Chiswick Press.	Criterion Theatre, 6th Oct., 1897 (Charles Wyndham, Miss Mary Moore).	Empire Theatre, New York, 26th Sept., 1898 (John Drew, Isabel Irving). Bijou Theatre, Melbourne, Australia, 29th Oct., 1898. Wyndham's Theatre, 1900. New Theatre, 1904. Criterion Theatre, 1907. Criterion Theatre, 1910. Playhouse, New York, 1915. St. James's Theatre, 1917.
1898	THE MANŒUVRES OF JANE. Comedy in 4 acts. Published by Macmillan & Co., 1904, and by Samuel French & Co., London and New York. Privately printed by the Chiswick Press.	Haymarket Theatre, 29th Oct., 1898 (Cyril Maude, Miss Winifred Emery).	Daly's Theatre, New York, 27th Nov., 1899 (Ferdinand Gottschalk, Mary Mannering).

DATE	TITLE	FIRST PERFORMANCE	SUBSEQUENT PRODUCTIONS
1899	CARNAC SAHIB. Play in 4 acts. Published by Macmillan & Co., 1899. Privately printed by the Chiswick Press.	Her Majesty's Theatre, 12th April, 1899 (Beerbohm Tree, Lewis Waller, Mrs. Brown-Potter).	—
1900	THE LACKEY'S CARNIVAL. Play in 4 acts. Privately printed by the Chiswick Press.	Duke of York's Theatre, 26th Sept., 1900 (Allan Aynesworth, Miss E. Wynne Matthison).	—
1900	MRS. DANE'S DEFENCE. Play in 4 acts. Published by Macmillan & Co, 1905, by Samuel French & Co., London and New York, and in the Four Volume Library Edition of *Representative Plays by Henry Arthur Jones*, by Macmillan & Co., and Little, Brown & Co., New York, 1925. Privately printed by the Chiswick Press.	Wyndham's Theatre, 9th Oct., 1900 (Charles Wyndham, Miss Lena Ashwell, Miss Mary Moore).	Empire Theatre, New York, 31st Dec., 1900 (James Richman, Jessie Millward, Margaret Anglin). Wyndham's Theatre, 5th June, 1902. Special Matinée performances, Lyric Theatre, New York, 15th and 17th Nov., 1906. New Theatre, 16th May, 1912.
1902	JAMES THE FOGEY.* Play in 4 acts. Privately printed by the Chiswick Press.	—	—
1902	THE PRINCESS'S NOSE. Comedy in 4 acts. Privately printed by the Chiswick Press.	Duke of York's Theatre, 11th March, 1902 (H. B. Irving, Miss Irene Vanbrugh).	—
1902	CHANCE THE IDOL. Play in 4 acts. Privately printed by the Chiswick Press.	Wyndham's Theatre, 9th Sept., 1902 (H. V. Esmond, W. Graham Browne, Miss Lena Ashwell).	—

* Never produced.

DATE	TITLE	FIRST PERFORMANCE	SUBSEQUENT PRODUCTIONS
1903	WHITEWASHING JULIA. Comedy in 3 acts. Published by Macmillan & Co., 1905, and by Samuel French & Co., London and New York. Privately printed by the Chiswick Press.	Garrick Theatre, 2nd March, 1903 (Arthur Bourchier, Miss Violet Vanburgh).	Garrick Theatre, New York, 2nd Dec., 1903 (Guy Standing, Fay Davis).
1904	CHRYSOLD.* Play in 5 acts. Privately printed by the Chiswick Press.	—	—
1904	JOSEPH ENTANGLED. Comedy in 3 acts. Published by Samuel French & Co., London and New York. Privately printed by the Chiswick Press.	Haymarket Theatre, 19th Jan., 1904 (Cyril Maude, Miss Ellis Jeffreys).	Garrick Theatre, New York, 4th Oct., 1904 (Henry Miller, Hilda Spong).
1904	THE CHEVALEER. Comedy in 3 acts. Published by Samuel French & Co., London and New York. Privately printed by the Chiswick Press.	Garrick Theatre, 27th Aug., 1904 (Arthur Bourchier, Miss Violet Vanbrugh).	—
1904	FELISA.* Spanish play in 6 scenes.	—	—
1905	THE SWORD OF GIDEON.* Play in 4 acts. Privately printed by the Chiswick Press.	—	—
1906	THE HEROIC STUBBS. Comedy in 4 acts. Privately printed by the Chiswick Press.	Terry's Theatre, 24th Jan., 1906 (James Welch, Miss Gertrude Kingston).	—

* Never produced.

DATE	TITLE	FIRST PERFORMANCE	SUBSEQUENT PRODUCTIONS
1906	THE HYPOCRITES. Play in 4 acts. Published by Samuel French & Co, London and New York. Privately printed by the Chiswick Press.	Hudson Theatre, New York, 30th Aug, 1906 (Richard Bennett, Leslie Faber, Miss Jessie Millward, Miss Doris Keane). First London performance, Hicks's Theatre, 27th Aug, 1907 (Leslie Faber, Vernon Steel, Miss Marion Terry, Miss Doris Keane).	—
1907	THE EVANGELIST. Tragi-comedy in 2 acts. Privately printed by the Chiswick Press under the title THE GALILEAN'S VICTORY.	Knickerbocker Theatre, New York, 30th Sept., 1907 (Howard Kyle, Miss Dorothy Thomas).	—
1908	DOLLY REFORMING HERSELF. Comedy in 4 acts. Published by Samuel French & Co., London and New York, and in the Four Volume Library Edition of *Representative Plays by Henry Arthur Jones*, by Macmillan & Co., and Little, Brown & Co., New York, 1925. Privately printed by the Chiswick Press. One Act Version, published by Samuel French & Co., New York, under the title DOLLY'S LITTLE BILLS.	Haymarket Theatre, 3rd Nov., 1908 (Robert Loraine, Miss Ethel Irving).	Fine Arts Theatre, Boston, 21st Sept, 1922.
1908	DICK.* Farce in 3 acts.	—	—
1909	THE KNIFE. Play in 1 act. Published by Samuel French & Co, New York.	Palace Theatre, 20th Dec, 1909 (Arthur Bourchier, Miss Violet Vanbrugh).	—
1909	LOO VALLANCE.* Play in 3 scenes.	—	—

* Never produced.

DATE	TITLE	FIRST PERFORMANCE	SUBSEQUENT PRODUCTIONS
1910	FALL IN ROOKIES. Play in 2 scenes. Privately printed by the Chiswick Press.	Alhambra Theatre, 24th Oct., 1910 (Farren Soutar, Mrs. Leslie Faber).	—
1910	WE CAN'T BE AS BAD AS ALL THAT. Play in 3 acts. Privately printed in New York, 1910.	Nazimova's 39th Street Theatre, New York, 30th Dec, 1910 (Nye Chart, Miss Katherine Kaelred). First English performance, Croydon Hippodrome, 4th Sept., 1916 (Frank Esmond, Miss Violet Vanbrugh).	—
1911	THE OGRE. Play in 3 acts.	St. James's Theatre, 11th Sept., 1911 (George Alexander, Miss Kate Cutler).	—
1912	LYDIA GILMORE. Play in 4 acts.	Lyceum Theatre, New York, 1st Feb., 1912 (Lee Baker, Miss Margaret Anglin).	—
1912	THE DIVINE GIFT.* Play in 3 acts. Published by Duckworth & Co., 1913 (Preface dedicated to Professor Gilbert Murray, LL.D.), and in the Four Volume Library Edition of *Representative Plays by Henry Arthur Jones*, by Macmillan & Co., and Little, Brown & Co., New York, 1925.	—	
1912	HER TONGUE.* Play in 1 act. Published in *The Theatre of Ideas*, by Chapman & Hall, 1915.	—	

* Never produced.

374

DATE	TITLE	FIRST PERFORMANCE	SUBSEQUENT PRODUCTIONS
1913	MARY GOES FIRST. Comedy in 3 acts and an epilogue. Published by Samuel French & Co., London and New York, and in the Four Volume Library Edition of *Representative Plays by Henry Arthur Jones*, with a dedication to Miss Marie Tempest, by Macmillan & Co., and Little, Brown & Co., New York, 1925. Printed by the Chiswick Press for G. Bell & Sons (Preface dedicated by Miss Marie Tempest).	The Playhouse, 18th Sept., 1913 (C. V. France, Miss Marie Tempest).	Comedy Theatre, New York, 2nd Nov., 1914 (Franklin Dyall, Marie Tempest).
1914	THE GOAL. Play in 1 act. Published in the Four Volume Library Edition of *Representative Plays by Henry Arthur Jones*, by Macmillan & Co., and Little, Brown & Co., New York, 1925, and in *The Theatre of Ideas*, by Chapman & Hall, 1915. Privately printed by the Chiswick Press.	Princess's Theatre, New York, 26th Oct., 1914 (Holbrook Blinn). First London performance, Palace Theatre (matinée), 20th May, 1919 (Leslie Faber, Miss Lilian Braithwaite).	Haymarket Theatre, 12th Dec., 1923.
1914	THE LIE. Play of English Life in 4 acts. Published by George H. Doran Company, New York, 1915 (Preface dedicated to Miss Margaret Illington), by Samuel French & Co., London and New York, and by F. E. Morrell, London, 1923 (Preface dedicated to Miss Sybil Thorndike).	Harris Theatre, New York, 24th Dec., 1914 (C. Aubrey Smith, Miss Margaret Illington, Miss Violet Heming). First London performance, New Theatre, 13th Oct., 1923 (Robert Horton, Miss Sybil Thorndike, Miss Mary Merrall).	Wyndham's Theatre, 30th May, 1925.
1915	COCK O' THE WALK. Comedy in 4 acts.	Cohan Theatre, New York, 27th Dec., 1915 (Otis Skinner, Vernon Steel).	—
1916	THE RIGHT MAN FOR SOPHIE.* Play in 4 acts.	—	—

* Never produced.

375

DATE	TITLE	FIRST PERFORMANCE	SUBSEQUENT PRODUCTIONS
1917	THE PACIFISTS. Parable in farce in 3 acts. Privately printed by the Chiswick Press.	St. James's Theatre, 4th Sept., 1917 (J. Sebastian Smith, Miss Ellis Jeffreys).	—
1917	FINDING THEMSELVES.* Play in 3 acts.	—	—
1919	THE LIFTED VEIL.* Play in 8 scenes.	—	—
1922	THE WOMAN I LOVED.* Unfinished play.	—	—

FILM SCENARIOS

DATE	TITLE	FIRST PERFORMANCE	SUBSEQUENT PRODUCTIONS
1920	VENETIA SUPERBA.*	—	—
1920	TOM TOBIN, POLICEMAN.*	—	—
1920	VENTURESOME NAOMI.*	—	—
1920	Film dealing with EARLY HISTORY OF VIRGINIA.*	—	—

* Never produced.

APPENDIX B

THE WRITINGS AND SPEECHES OF HENRY ARTHUR JONES

BOOKS

1875. Novel entitled *The Devil and I.**
Unnamed three volume novel.

1895. *The Renascence of the English Drama.* Published by Macmillan
& Co.

1911. *A Volume of Personal Record* by Dr. James Frederick Furnivall,
containing Memories by Henry Arthur Jones, Stopford Brooke,
Sidney Lee, and Others.

1913. *The Foundations of a National Drama.* Published by Chapman
& Hall. Published in the United States by George H. Doran.

1915. *The Theatre of Ideas.* Published by Chapman & Hall.
Playwrights Texts, The Times Literary Supplement, Oct. 25th.
A Letter from Henry Arthur Jones to "S".

1919. *Patriotism and Popular Education.* Published by Chapman &
Hall; 1st edition, 1919; 2nd edition, 1919.

1921. *My Dear Wells.* Published by Eveleigh Nash & Grayson; 1st
edition, November 1921; 2nd edition, March 1922. Published in
the United States by Dutton & Co., November 1921; two editions.

1924. *What is the State?* *

1925. *What is Capital?* Published by Eveleigh Nash & Grayson. 1st
edition, February 1925; 2nd edition, May 1925.
Mr. Mayor of Shakespeare's Town.*
The Shadow of Henry Irving.*

ARTICLES, PAMPHLETS, LECTURES, LETTERS TO THE PAPERS, SPEECHES, ETC.

1874. Letter to *Exeter and Plymouth Gazette. Daily Telegrams,* 2nd Dec.,
"The Dean's Hospital Sermon."

1878. Short Story, *An Idyll of Devon.**

1880. Letter to *Era,* 29th Aug., on *A Perfect Woman.*

(?)1882–90. Article, "How I wrote *The School for Scandal.*" * Exact
date uncertain.

* Unpublished.

377

1883. Letter to *Daily News,* 24th March, a reply to Mr. Merivale.

Article in *Nineteenth Century,* September, "The Theatre and the Mob."

Article in *Musical World,* "Dramatic Renaissance."

1884. Letter to *Daily News,* 29th Sept., on *Saints and Sinners.*

Speech delivered at opening of Playgoers' Club, 7th Oct., "The Dramatic Outlook." †

Article in *Pall Mall Gazette,* 8th Oct., "How Plays Are Written."

Letter to *Truth,* 16th Oct., on *Saints and Sinners.*

Article in *To-Day,* December, "A Playwright's Grumble."

1885. Article in *Nineteenth Century,* January, "Religion and the Stage."

Letter to *Era,* 2nd Sept., on *Hoodman Blind.*

Original Recitation, "The Last Scene of All."

1887. Lecture at Temperance Hall, Bradford, on "Being Rightly Amused at the Theatre." †

Letter to *Era,* 12th Nov., on *Heart of Hearts.*

1889. Lecture at New Islington Public Hall, 24th Feb., "White and Blue." †

Letter to *Globe,* 26th Feb., "The Modern English Stage."

Letter to *Manchester Examiner,* 5th March, "The Decay of the Manchester Stage."

Article in *Nineteenth Century,* July, "The First Night Judgment of Plays."

Letter to *Daily Telegraph,* 16th Nov., Theatres and Music Halls."

1890. Letter to *New York Dramatic Mirror,* 14th April, "Realism and Truth."

Article in *Fortnightly Review,* 1st July. "The Actor-Manager."

Lecture at Toynbee Hall, 1st Nov., on "Being Rightly Amused at the Theatre." †

Lecture at Newcastle, 16th Nov., "The Renaissance of the Drama." †

Speech at Royal Theatrical Fund dinner, in response to toast of the Drama.†

1891. Lecture to National Sunday League, 19th Feb., "Playmaking." †
Article in *New Review,* July, "The Science of the Drama."

Letter to *Pall Mall Gazette,* 21st Aug., "The Actor-Manager Controversy."

Letter to *Times,* 23rd Nov., on "Programmes of the Avenue Theatre."

1892. Article in *New Review,* January, "The Literary Drama" (A reply to H. D. Traill).

† Reported in leading daily papers and some weeklies.

Lecture at Playgoers' Club, November, "Our Modern Drama: Is it an Art or an Amusement." †

1893. Article in *Young Man*, March, "Can We Have an Ideal Theatre?"

Article in *New Review*, June, "Middleman and Parasites."

Article in *New Review*, July, "The Bible on the Stage."

Article in *New Review*, August, "The Future of the English Drama."

Article in *St. James's Budget*, September, "How They Write Their Plays."

Article in *Nineteenth Century*, October, "Dr. Pearson on the Modern Drama."

Lecture at City of London College, 12th Oct., "Has the Drama any Relations to Education?" †

Letter to *Christian World*, 16th Nov., "Puritans going to the Theatre."

Letter to Society of British Dramatic Art.*

1894. Speech proposing the health of Medical Staff of Great Ormond Street Hospital for Children, May. Reported in the Press.

Essay in *Vox Clamantium*, "A Lay Sermon to Preachers."

1895. Speech at Actors' Benevolent Fund annual dinner, 18th Dec.†

(?)1895–1905. Article, "Plays with a Purpose." Exact date uncertain. No record of publication.

1897. Lecture at Toynbee Hall, 13th Nov., "The Drama and Real Life." †

1898. Speech at dinner in honour of Coquelin aîné, Reform Club, 15th May. A few reports in the Press.

Letter to *Daily News*, 28th June, "Should the Drama be Endowed?"

1899. Speech as Chairman of the Authors' Club, 30th Jan. A few reports in the Press.

1900. Speech at annual dinner of Playgoers' Club, 28th Jan.†

1901. Article in *Nineteenth Century*, March, "The Drama in the English Provinces."

Speech at a dinner in honour of Henry Arthur Jones at New Vagabond Club. Reported in the Press.

1902. Article in *The Author*, 1st May, "The Censorship of Plays."

Article, "Founding a National Theatre." Privately printed by Chiswick Press.

1903. Letter to Arthur Bourchier, published in *Times*, 26th Feb.

Letter to *Times*, 5th March, "A Plain English Answer."

* Unpublished. † Reported in leading daily papers and some weeklies.

Article in *Nineteenth Century*, April, "Literary Critics and the Drama."

1904. Article in *Nineteenth Century*, March, "The Recognition of the Drama by the State."

Lecture at Royal Institution, 18th March, "The Foundations of a National Drama." †

Article in *Neues Wiener Tagblatt*, September, on the occasion of the International Press Congress at Vienna, "The Need for a National English Theatre."

Two letters to Beerbohm Tree, 29th Nov. and 7th Dec., on "Finding Fault with Actors." Published in daily Press.

Letter to *Times*, 7th Dec., "The State of the Drama."

Speech at annual dinner of Press Club, Sheffield, "The English Drama." Reported in the Press.

1905. Open letter to Miss Keith, 21st Oct., "The Best Method of Presenting Shakespeare's Plays." No record of publication.

1906. Article in *Daily Mail*, 29th Sept., "The Reading of Modern Plays."

Lecture at Harvard University, 31st Oct., "The Corner Stones of Modern Drama." Also translated into French. Reported in United States Press.

Lecture at Yale University, 5th Nov., "Literature and the Modern Drama." Reported in United States Press.

Speech at dinner given by Charles Klein at Delmonico's in honour of Henry Arthur Jones. Reported in United States Press.

1908. Speech in response to toast of the Drama, Maccabeans' dinner, 21st June. Reported in daily Press.

Address to British Empire Shakespeare Society, 17th July. Reported in daily Press.

Two speeches at dinners of American dramatists. Reported in United States Press.

1909. Letter to the Right Hon. Herbert Samuel, M.P., September, "The Censorship Muddle and a Way Out of It." Privately printed by Chiswick Press—extracts quoted in leading newspapers.

Letter to *Times*, 6th Nov., "The Censorship Committee."

Speech delivered to the Society of Women Journalists, 27th Nov. Reported in daily Press.

1910. Lecture to the O. P. Club, 6th Feb., "The Standardising of the Drama." Reported in daily Press.

Letter to *Times*, 7th Feb., "The Drama and Theatre Licenses."

Lecture at Alhambra Music Hall, 27th Feb., "The Licensing Chaos in Theatres and Music Halls." Reported in daily Press.

Lecture to Shakespeare Society, King's College, April. Reported in daily Press.

† Reported in leading daily papers and some weeklies.

Lecture to the Ethnological Society, 4th May, "The Delineation of Character in Drama." Reported in daily Press.

Speech at Oxford Union Society debate, 2nd June, "The Establishment of a National Theatre." Reported in daily Press.

Speech in response to toast of the Drama at the Corporation Library Committee dinner, Guildhall, 20th June. Reported in daily Press.

Letter to *Daily Express,* 21st Sept., "Theatres and Halls."

Letter to *Daily Express,* 26th Sept., "Laughter on the Stage."

Letter to *Times,* 1st Oct., "Housman and the Censor."

Letter to the Right Hon. Winston Churchill, M.P., 7th Nov., "The Censorship Muddle." Reported in daily Press.

Letter to *Daily Telegraph,* 26th Dec., "Music-Hall Sketches."

1911. Lecture at Columbia University, 26th Jan., "The Aims and Duties of a National Theatre." Reported in United States Press.

1912. Article in *Daily Telegraph,* 20th April, "Arrival Scenes on New York Pier."

Article, August, "The English National Theatre." Known to have been published, but reference not traced.

1913. Letter to *Referee,* 11th May, "Dissenters and the Drama."

Speech at annual dinner of Stage Society, 18th May. Reported in daily Press.

Letter to *Times,* 23rd June, "The Licensing of Plays."

Speech after judging annual elocution competition of British Empire Shakespeare Society, 8th July. Reported in daily Press.

Letter to *Times,* 7th Sept., "Shakespeare in England."

Lecture to Sheffield Playgoers' Club, 29th Sept., "Municipal and Repertory Theatres." Reported in local and some London papers.

Letter to *Times,* 1st Nov., "The Lord Chamberlain and Music Halls."

Circular letter to incoming Mayors, 11th Nov., "Municipal and Repertory Theatres." Privately printed.

1914. Letter to *Daily Mail,* 15th Jan., "Much Plainer Words to an 'Englishman.'"

Letter to *Daily Mail,* 26th Jan., "More Plain Words to an 'Englishman.'"

Letter to *Times,* 23rd May, "Children on the Stage."

Letter to Times, 14th April, "The Appeal of Domestic Melodrama."

Letter to *Times,* 29th Aug., "To English Girls."

1916. Pamphlet, "Shakespeare and Germany," written during the Battle of Verdun. Privately printed by Chiswick Press.

Letter to *Times,* 29th Oct., "The League of Peace."

1917. Letter to *Times*, 27th Jan., "A Plea for Publicity."

Letter to *Times*, 14th June, "Shakespeare and the Stage."

Letter to *Times*, 6th Nov., "Reconstructing Society."

1918. Letter to *Times*, 3rd Oct., on Marshal Foch.

Open letter to Mr. Lloyd George on "Labour and Lloyd George at the Election." Privately printed by Chiswick Press.

1919. Letter to *Morning Post*, 4th March, "The Speculator and Popular Apathy."

Letter to *Morning Post*, 8th March, "The Science of Wise Living."

Letter to *Morning Post*, 14th March, "Pure Commercial Gain."

Letter to *Morning Post*, 26th March, "Æschylus and Sophocles."

Letter to *Morning Post*, 12th April, "The Nature of Revues."

Letter to *Evening News*, 2nd May, "The Commercialism of the Theatre."

Article in *Evening News*, 3rd May, "Why English Drama is Crowded Out."

Article in *National News*, 4th May, "Our Puerile Stage Plays."

Letter to the Rev. J. Morgan Gibbon, published in *Daily News*, 17th May, "The Stage and Dissent."

Letter to *Land and Water*, 31st May. A reply to a criticism of the Preface to Morrison's *Reconstruction of the Theatre*.

Article in *Dramatic Times*, 14th June, "A Few Hints to Young Playwrights."

Letter to *Evening Standard*, 4th Dec., "Teachers' Pay."

Pamphlet, *Last Words on the Drama*. Privately printed by Chiswick Press.

1920. Article in *Evening Standard*, 25th March, "Kathleen, sister Kathleen."

Article in *Referee*, 25th April, "Emotional English Actresses and other Matters."

Article in *Daily Telegraph*, 29th April, "The Drama and the Film."

Article in *Daily Graphic*, 25th May, "My Unacted Plays."

Letter to Mr. J. H. Thomas, published in *Evening Standard*, 21st June, "An Open Letter on Ireland."

Speech after judging annual elocution competition of British Empire Shakespeare Society, 16th July. Reported in daily Press.

Article in *Sunday Express*, 25th July, "The Triumphant Film." Also published in *Photoplay*, May, 1921.

Article in *Sunday Express*, 8th Aug., "Twenty-three Questions about the British Drama."

Open letter to the Chancellor of the Exchequer, published in *Evening Standard*, 12th Aug., "How to Raise Money."

Letter to *Times*, 6th Sept., "The Birmingham Repertory Theatre."

Six letters to Mr. H. G. Wells, published in *Evening Standard:* 16th Sept., "Mr. Wells will take a trip to Russia"; 17th Sept., "Mr. Wells packs up and starts"; 26th Oct., "Mr. Wells finds order in Petrograd"; 3rd Nov., "Strange things get into Mr. Wells's head"; 28th Nov., "Mr. Wells invents a new kind of honesty"; 5th Dec., "Mr. Wells gets further entangled."

Article in *Yorkshire Post,* 4th Oct., "The Forbidden Word."

Open letter to the Right Hon. H. A. L. Fisher, M.P., published in *Evening Standard,* 12th Oct., "That's the Way the Money Goes."

Article in *Evening Standard,* 14th Oct., "Education and Life."

Letter to *Globe,* 16th Oct., "Prohibition."

1921. Article in *World's Work,* January, "The Tax-Wise Men of Aristopia."

Article, 2nd Feb., "Why I am not Writing for the English Theatre." Reference not traced.

Article in *Photoplay,* May, "Motion Pictures and the Speaking Stage."

1921. Four letters to Mr. H. G. Wells, published in *Morning Post:* 4th Aug., 11th Aug., 16th Aug., 21st Sept., "My Dear Wells."

Letter to *Pall Mall Gazette,* 27th Aug., "Civil Service."

Two articles in *Times,* 29th and 30th Aug., "The Heroines of the Film." Also published in *New York Times,* 28th and 29th Aug.

Two letters to *Morning Post,* 13th and 21st Sept., "Bernard Shaw as a Mischief-Maker." Also published in *New York Times,* 28th Aug.

Open letter to Sir Squire Bancroft, 17th Sept., on H. A. J.'s withdrawal from committee of J. H. Barnes testimonial matinée. Privately printed.

Article written specially for Library of Queen's Dolls' House, 24th Dec., "English Dukes and American Millionaires."

Article in *Fellowship,* December, "A Chat with my Grandchildren."

1922. Letter to Anatole France, published in *Journal des Débats,* 5th Jan.

Speech at Authors' Club dinner, 9th Jan. Reported in daily Press.

Speech at Twenty Club dinner, 31st Jan. Reported in daily Press.

Article in *Times,* 21st Feb., "The Film Play."

Letter to the Right Hon. H. A. L. Fisher, M.P., published in *Morning Post,* 4th March, "The Education Fetish."

Speech read by Denis Eadie at Fellowship League meeting, 4th May. Reported in a few papers.

Letter to *Times,* 10th July, "Shelley's *Cenci.*"

Article in *Daily Telegraph,* 27th July, "The Repertory System."

Letter to *Morning Post,* 21st Aug., "France, Be Patient with England!"

Appreciation of George R. Sims, published in *Referee,* 10th Sept.

Letter to *Morning Post*, 15th Sept., "America and the Great War.*"

Speech at British Empire Society's dinner, 30th Sept. Reported in daily Press.

Presidential speech at After Dinner Club dinner, 18th Oct. Reported in daily Press.

1923. Letter to *Morning Post*, 8th Jan., "Lenin and His Doctors."

Series of articles in *English Review*, June, July, August, and November 1923, and March 1924, "Bernard Shaw as a Thinker."

Article in *Daily Telegraph*, 29th Oct., "The Drama and the Film."

Article in *Daily Telegraph*, 8th Nov., "Plays with a Purpose."

Article in *T. P.'s and Cassell's Weekly*, 17th Nov., "In the Days of my Youth."

1924. Article in *English Review*, December, "Christmas Meditation on Alcohol."

1925. Open letter to Editor of *Fortnightly Review*, 17th Dec., on Mr. Shaw and Professor Henderson.*

Speech at English Speaking Union luncheon to John Barrymore, 7th April.†

Letter to *Times*, 29th April, "Socialism and the Banks."

Article in *Morning Post*, 4th July, "Aristopia."

Letter to Gladys Cooper, published in *Sunday Express*, 20th Sept., "Playwright Shut Out."

Article in *Daily Express*, 24th Sept., "My Religion."

Letter to *Times*, 26th Sept., "Light in Milton."

Letter to *Times*, 20th Oct., "Lost Art Treasures."

1925. "Henry Arthur Jones: Self-Revealed"—*Virginia Quarterly Review*, 1925; *Nation*, 5th Dec., 12th Dec., 1925. Reply to Professor Henderson's questionnaire (see Appendix C).

Extract from *Mr. Mayor of Shakespeare's Town*, published in *Daily Mail*, 20th Oct.

Letter to *Daily Express*, 14th Nov., "Henry Arthur Dissects Bernard Shaw."

Quotation from Emerson, published in *Daily Express*, 21st Nov.

Article in *Overseas Daily Mail*, 21st Nov., "This Dear Dear England."

Two letters to the Mayor of Stratford-on-Avon, published in *Stratford-on-Avon Herald*, 20th Nov. and 4th Dec.

1928. Quotation from Matthew Arnold, published in *Daily Express*, 12th March.

(?) Article on "The Need for a National Theatre." Probably about 1904. Known to have been published, but date uncertain and reference not traced.

* Unpublished. † Reported in leading daily papers and some weeklies.

APPENDIX C

DRAMATIC TECHNIQUE REVEALED BY DRAMATISTS

REPLY TO PROFESSOR ARCHIBALD HENDERSON'S QUESTIONNAIRE *

(1) *What mental process occurs when you write a play?*

It is very difficult to give a succinct answer to this question. With me, the primary mental process is spontaneous and automatic, like dreaming awake. And this process often goes on while I am busy with other things—in a separate compartment of consciousness. Of course I keep a measure of control and selection over the waking dream, and, as it takes a more definite shape, this power of control and selection increases, and other mental processes are brought into play—the construction of a concrete piece of action gradually unfolding itself; attempts to realise each of the personages as a living man or woman I know, and who speaks and acts throughout the play with his own voice and purpose, and not with mine; the gathering together of all the threads of interest and action and weaving the various characters into them, as weft into warp, until they form a continuous correlative whole.

(2) *Do you always first draw up a scenario?*

When the nucleus of the play has formed itself, and the characters have taken on flesh and blood, I begin to make notes of whatever may serve as a reminder or direction to me in writing the play. I jot down the various incidents in various sequences till I get the right and final one. I mark the keynotes of character, the necessity of emphasising this point or that. I write out scraps of dialogue on which the action depends, or which denote the relations of one character to another—anything that may serve to illuminate the story and make it easy for the spectator to follow on the stage. I throw into this heap of memoranda all the shifting and variable raw material of the play as it comes into my head. I do not make out a straight, clear scenario, for the reason that the main scheme of the play, as it evolves, is always vividly in my mind, and I do not need to put it on paper. At the end, my scenario consists of hundreds and hundreds of disconnected notes, signposts, and suggestions, the greater part of them jotted down after I have divided the play into acts, but with no order or plan that would be intelligible to a reader who had not first seen or read the play. I take great care always to be thoroughly acquainted with all my chief characters, and to study the *milieu* they have lived in, so that if I am challenged I could credibly sketch their entire history.

(3) *Does a specific incident constitute the starting-point of a drama?*

Sometimes a single striking incident or situation may start the train of a play and gather to it an auxiliary series of incidents and situations. Sometimes a succession of incidents may *dart simultaneously* into the brain. The whole of the third act of *The Liars,* with its numerous developments, came to me, not as a sequence of situations, but at one

* See Chapter XVII., p. 292.

glance, as one sees a landscape, foreground and middle distance and background all at once. As I have said, this part of playmaking is as automatic as dreaming. But after the original conception has taken root there is much conscious effort and shaping in compelling the scheme to go on all fours.

(4) *Or, do you begin with a group of clearly defined characters, and let the situation develop from the conflict of the characters?*

Character and action in a play should jump together and be inseparable. I should find it impossible to start a play with a group of well-defined characters, unless I had imagined their actions at the same time, and also their reactions upon each other. It is, however, a common thing to start a play with one leading character and build a scheme of action round him, drawing in other important characters as the scheme takes shape. But, on the stage, character is in a vacuum until it is revealed by action. Until you have some sort of a story, however meagre, you have no play. Again, it is possible to imagine a *milieu* containing certain types of character, but, until you realise them and set them doing things, you have no play.

(5) *Will you take one of your own plays—and indicate, very fully, how you built up the drama?*

From my answers to the other questions, you will gather that my plays have generally grown round a nucleus. A dramatist cannot build up a play until he has some rough scheme of action in his mind. I found the nucleus of *Mrs. Dane's Defence* in a newspaper account of an action that was brought by a Mrs. Osborne for defamation of character. Mrs. Osborne had been staying with a friend, who afterwards spread a report that Mrs. Osborne had stolen her jewellery. The matter gained some publicity, and, to defend her character, Mrs. Osborne was obliged at length to bring an action. Lord Chief Justice Russell—then Sir Charles Russell, K.C.—defended her, and believed in her innocence. Everything seemed to be going well for his client, until a firm of jewellers intervened with some damaging evidence against her. Although the matter looked very suspicious, Mrs. Osborne triumphantly exclaimed in court: "Ah! now my innocence will be proved!" Upon this, Sir Charles Russell, much puzzled by her manner, went with her to her home, and subjected her to a searching cross-examination, which came to its climax in his indignant exclamation: "Woman, you are lying!"

I used this sentence as the climax of my cross-examination scene in *Mrs. Dane.* I laid by this scene in my mind for future use. The stealing of a piece of jewellery did not offer a plan for a strong emotional play. I therefore changed it for the stronger motive of a woman fighting desperately to uphold her reputation and retain her lover. This was a very gradual and complicated process, and it was many months before I had evolved the complete scheme as I finally wrote it. I can't give any precise details of how I evolved the scheme in my own mind. It took many different shapes before it assumed the final one, but from the beginning I always had in view the cross-examination scene, with its prolonged agony of the tortured woman, as the great scene of the play. This is, of course, only a particular instance—other plays have grown in other ways. For instance:

Early in the eighties, I saw a paragraph in the paper commenting severely on the practices of "The Middleman." I thought that would be a good title for a play. A year or two afterwards, I saw Willard play an inventor in a play of the late Tom Taylor. I thought that character would be a very effective one in a good scheme, and I linked it with the title *The Middleman*. But, although I had the leading character in my mind, I had no play. I fitted the story of *The Middleman* to the character of the inventor and to the title. The scheme and the title lay dormant in my mind, until, by constant dwelling upon them, and turning them over, the main story came into my mind, and I worked at it, and filled in the various characters to fit the action.

In this connection, the points that are worth dwelling upon are these: That whatever may be the force and insight of your character drawing; whatever may be the loftiness of your ideas and opinions, until you have smelted them into a story, you have got no play that will hold a general audience; and I would particularly impress these points upon a young dramatist. Of course, there is nearly always a temporary reputation and a momentary success to be gained by anyone who is clever enough to discover some new way of boring people in the theatre.

(6) *Do you think it possible to teach or train anyone to become a dramatist?*

I think it possible to impart the main rules of writing plays, but I do not think it possible to teach or train anyone to become a dramatist. The technique of playwriting can only be learned by constant study, observation, and practice in the theatre itself; books and verbal instruction are of comparatively little help or value.

(7) *In writing a play, do you begin from one central or dominant or controlling idea?*

With myself, a play often springs suddenly from a certain character in a certain situation. I do not start from "ideas" or "opinions." I take the keenest interest in social matters, and I think I may claim to have studied them. But the dramatist's main business, and his great delight, is to paint men and women faithfully as he sees them—not to air his "ideas" and "opinions," but, by their actions, the dramatist must frame his characters in a story. So far as he uses the stage to exploit his "ideas" and "opinions," he is not a dramatist, but a propagandist. This is not to say that the dramatist may not deal with the great issues of life, and even with the passing problems of the day, if he can exhibit them in an interesting story. But the true vocation of the dramatist is to hide himself behind his characters, and to let them have the whole stage. But in trying to conceal himself behind his personages he often reveals himself most conspicuously. In any case, he can scarcely avoid throwing sidelights and reflections of his "ideas" and "opinions," and incidentally offering some criticism of life.

(8) *What principal factors must be borne in mind in the writing of a play?*

(*a*) That it is to be presented to an *audience,* a crowd of listeners, the most of whom have only a limited energy of attention to bestow upon the piece, and whose interest needs to be unflaggingly sustained from moment to moment. Therefore the play must be compact within the time that the audience of the day are able or willing to concentrate their attention.

(*b*) That, being addressed to general average audiences, it should try to meet them on the common ground of the permanent passions, emotions, follies, vices, and humours of humanity. It should not be written for a clique, or for a coterie of superior persons. Repertory theatres have failed in England because their promoters have mainly produced freakish and eccentric pieces, and have tried to elevate the drama by offering plays that keep the general public out of the theatre.

(9) *Do you visualise your characters?*

In most cases, not very clearly. The outside of Hamlet may be different in a dozen different impersonations, and not one of them can claim to be the Hamlet that Shakespeare *visualised*. But every one of them may claim to be the Hamlet that Shakespeare *conceived*. When I set out to draw a character, I have some general idea of his appearance, dress, cast of features, etc. But it is clear that many characters can be played with equal truth and effect in various guises and make-ups, and sometimes with widely differing personalities. I try very hard to *conceive* and *realise* every character, before I bring him on the scene; to know exactly his spiritual make-up, his mental habits, and ways of expressing himself, so that, if I were compelled, I could give reasons for his acting and speaking as he does at any moment of the play. I take great pains with my dialogue, and, so far as the necessary conventions of the theatre will allow, I try to make it the exact utterance of the character in that situation. When I write a scene, I hear every word of it spoken. Here, again, the best work is automatic, and the best and truest dialogue is not that which is taken from real life, but that which registers itself upon the inner ear as the veritable utterance of that particular character.

(10) *Do you draw your dramatic characters from real life?*

A character in real life may give hints and suggestions to a dramatist. But I have never photographed any individual and put him into a play. The mass of human life in all its infinite variety lies round about a dramatist, like a rich quarry of disordered strata—precious stones and metals and rocks, all inextricably mixed and distorted. It is for him to choose from the amorphous heap just that which he needs for his purpose of fashioning his group of figures, all of them related to each other, every character related to every other character, and none of them becoming a definite credible human being except he is hewn out of and taken away from real life, and re-fashioned and re-vitalised by the author in a world of his own, which is but a microcosm of real life.

(11) *Do you create characters who are composite of several individuals?*

Every character is a multiple character. We differ from each other, not so much in possessing opposite qualities, as in possessing varying blends and proportions of the same basic human qualities. In the limits of a play the dramatist can exhaustively portray only a few leading personages. The great majority of his personages can only expose those minor aspects of their characters which are relative and necessary to the development of his scheme. All the remaining aspects of their characters are purposely left in partial obscurity. Doubtless, a dramatist often composes a character from subconscious memories of several individuals. That is the true "creation" of character. If I were asked to describe the process whereby I have summoned my personages on to the stage, I should say: "I have imagined them from memory." I have kept a close watch on all the men and women I have met. I have listened to every conversation that has fallen within my earshot. I have thrown all my observations and experiences into a common melting-pot, and have drawn from it fresh specimens and types of humanity that are new and consistent individuals compounded out of the massed material.

(12) *Do you ever begin a play at the end or in the middle, writing the last act, say, before you write the first?*

I never begin to write a play until the whole scheme of it has taken a definite shape in my mind, and until I can get a rough view of all its leading scenes and characters. But I make a great number of notes as the play grows, and sometimes I jot down a few sentences of any scene that vividly impresses itself upon me. Sometimes I have to take my plan to pieces after I have constructed it, and always there are minor alterations to be made. But I always begin to write with the first act clearly mapped out, and the remaining acts roughly mapped out in their sequence. I dwell upon the play for a considerable time before I start to write it, trying to know my characters intimately, so that the story may grow by its own impulse, rather than by my forcing.

(13) *To what trade, science, art, is the writing of dramas most analogous?*

The drama in itself has no connection with trade. But the author should always bear in mind that theatre management is a business which must put up its shutters, if it continues to lose money. Goethe has said: "Shakespeare and Molière wanted, above all things, to make money by their plays." The drama, again, is not analogous to science, though a sense of scientific exactitude and some knowledge of science are often valuable aids to a dramatist. The drama is very closely allied to the art of fiction, as I have shown in my essay on Brunetière's *Law of the Drama*, where I dispute his contention that they are opposing arts. The drama, as Professor Brander Matthews has pointed out, has a great affinity to oratory, in that it makes an instant popular appeal to an audience no larger than can be reached by the voice. The drama has a close analogy to the art of sculpture, in that its highest forms are ruled by large, lofty conventions, and far removed from the small actualities of real life.

(14) *Do you know anywhere, in any literature, the confessions of a dramatist, as to how he wrote a play?—on how a play* SHOULD *be written?*

I do not know of any detailed confession or explanation of any dramatist as to how he wrote a play. But, in recent years, several dramatists have spoken and written about their art, and have given hints and glimpses of how they write their plays.

(15) *Have you, at any period of your career, altered your dramatic technique? Explain fully why.*

The technique of writing plays has changed so much during the nearly fifty years that I have been writing for the English theatre, I dare say I have changed with it. To get a footing on the English stage, I had to write melodrama. The technique of melodrama is different to some extent from the technique of comedy. But, though the technique of playwriting changes, the main principles of dramatic construction remain the same. Perhaps it would be more correct to say that the conventions, rather than the technique of playwriting, change from time to time. I have not deliberately changed my technique, but, as I studied and practised playwriting, my technique became firmer and more assured. After the great popular success of *The Silver King* (in which I owed much to Henry Herman and Wilson Barrett), it took me eleven years incessant study in the English theatre, watching and directing almost every new play, before I could take a play to a manager, printed and ready for rehearsal, so that he could put it on the stage without the alteration of a single line. *The Masqueraders, The Case of Rebellious Susan, The Liars,* and my other plays since 1894, have been rehearsed from printed books, and in most of them not a line has been changed since they left my study.

(16) *Do you take your plots from real life? Specify in particular plays.*

I have indicated in my former answers how my plots grow. Any incident in real life, any paragraph in a paper, any scene of history, or even some small scrap of talk, may be the starting-point of a plot. I have never been without a good supply of plots. God sends them without my asking. I have a large drawer full of incomplete plots, jottings, suggestions, characters, and themes waiting for stories to be fitted to them.

(17) *Do you ever build your play around a single individual, making that character the focus or central point of the play?*

Nearly all the great plays of the world are built round a single leading character—*Macbeth, Hamlet, Lear, Œdipus,* etc. Historic plays are generally built round a single character. I have often started with a single leading character, letting the other characters and the story grow round him, as in *The Middleman, Mrs. Dane, The Hypocrites,* etc. When the first idea of *The Liars* came to me, Falkner, and not Sir Christopher, was the chief part, and I could have built the story round Falkner. But in that case the play would have developed into a drama rather than a comedy. But as the piece grew in my mind it irresistibly shaped itself into a comedy. The fact that the great majority of plays of all kinds are mainly the story of one or two leading characters is an explanation, and a justification, of the star system. When we go to see *Hamlet,* we go, not so much to see the play, as to see some notable actor in the leading part.

INDEX